Provincetown Artists:
An Oral History

Charles Giuliano

Berkshire Fine Arts, LLC
North Adams, Massachusetts

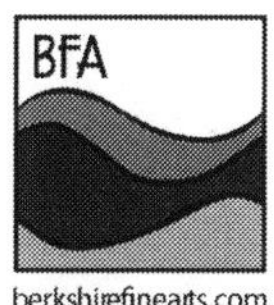

Published by Berkshire Fine Arts, LLC
Book Design by Studio Two, Heather Rose and Amanda Hill

Berkshire Fine Arts, 243 Union Street, Unit 208, North Adams MA 01247
ISBN 978-0-9961715-9-5
Library of Congress Control Number: 2025907564

For my wife Astrid Hiemer for her constant enthusiasm and support.

Also by Charles Giuliano

Annisquam: Pip and Me Coming of Age (with Pippy Giuliano)

Museum of Fine Arts Boston: 1870 to 2020, An Oral History

Counterculture in Boston: 1968–1980s

Topsy Turvy

Gloucester Poems: Nugents of Rockport

Ultra Cosmic Gonzology

Total Gonzo Poems

Shards of a Life

Love Made Visible: Scenes from a Mostly Happy Marriage, by Jean Gibran (Introduction)

100 Boston Painters, by Chawky Frenn (Essay)

Selected Exhibition Catalogs

Pioneers from Provincetown: The Roots of Figurative Expressionism, by Adam Zucker (Essay: "Sun Gallery and a Return to the Figure in the 1950s")

Lester Johnson: In Memoriam (Essay)

Randall Deihl: An American Realist (Essay)

James Aponovich Recent Paintings (Essay)

Harriet Casdin Silver: The Art of Holography (Essay)

Lester Johnson (Essay)

Contents

Provincetown Introduction

Surrounded by ocean and dunes, artists have been drawn to Provincetown since Charles W. Hawthorne founded his Cape Cod School of Art in 1899. The seminal generations of artists were lured by spectacular nature, clear light, and cheap rent in a working Portuguese-American fishing village.

There was an influx of artists returning from Europe during WWI and a second wave fueled by the GI Bill after WWII. Many came to study with Henry Hensche, who continued the plein air teaching of Hawthorne, and abstraction, taught by Hans Hofmann.

The Provincetown Art Association, which was founded in 1914, was staunchly conservative, dominated by artists who adhered to the mantra *truth to nature.* Momentum shifted dramatically when a critical mass of progressive artists and intellectuals initiated the summer-long exhibitions and symposia of *Forum '49.* In 1950, a number of the participating artists signed the petition protesting the conservative jury of the Metropolitan Museum's contemporary exhibition. In a group photo for *Life Magazine,* they were captioned as "The Irascibles."

These progressive artists came to be known as abstract expressionists, action painters, or simply The New York School. Jackson Pollock visited Provincetown, and according to Reggie Cabral, drank at his A House. Though he was not present, two of his works were included in a *Forum '49* exhibition at the pop-up, summer-long Gallery 200.

As the matrix of advanced art shifted from Paris to New York, Pollock became as renowned and influential as Pablo Picasso. Provincetown spawned exhibitions and dialogues that spun off in the downtown galleries of New York's Tenth Street with debates at the Cedar Bar and Artists' Club. Gradually the flow of artists largely shifted to the Hamptons, which represented an easier commute than to Cape Cod.

During visits in the 1960s, I crashed in the dunes. At first light the routine entailed a fresh loaf of Portuguese bread and breakfast on Macmillan Pier. From my second one-man-show at Swetzoff Gallery in Cambridge, I sold enough work to buy an Alpha Romeo. It was soon put to use.

In the summer of 1966, a friend, Paul Haldeman, the national artistic director for the United Church of Christ, conceived a portfolio of lithographs of biblical subjects to be distributed to the member churches. I was taken on as a consultant which entailed finding leading artists willing to create representational images. It was my job to visit and sign them for the project.

One of the artists was Karl Knaths. We met briefly in his Provincetown home and studio. While we talked, his wife, Helen, looked on, but did not participate. A lithograph stone was shipped to him and the print was included in the portfolio.

Based on a work *Lilacs* in the Museum of Fine Arts, I knew and admired him, as did many at that time. He had been one of the founding generation of the Provincetown Art Association and developed as one of its progressive artists. Never having been to Europe, he was theoretically influenced by his sister-in-law, Agnes Weinrich, who had studied cubism in Paris. She and Helen settled in Provincetown because of WWI. Knaths was in love with Agnes but married Helen. It's complicated. Until her death in 1946, Agnes lived with Karl and Helen.

As a Boston University graduate student, I proposed Karl Knaths and Provincetown as a dissertation project. It was supported and approved by Dr. Margaret Smith, who soon left for Wake Forest University. My thesis advisor became Dr. Patricia Hills, whose primary focus is leftist feminism. Having completed a master's degree under Hills, I proceeded with Provincetown research.

The summer of 1986 was productive. When I arrived unannounced, initially, Ellen O'Donnell, then director of Art Association was blunt. "I'm in the middle of the season and can't help you," she said. That soon changed, and she has been a friend and ally ever since.

While she was too busy to meet with me, that happened later, Ellen set me up with Dr. Nathan "Nat" Halper who, she said, "Knows everything and everybody." That first of many Provincetown interviews started on a bench in the Hawthorne Gallery of Provincetown Art Association and Museum (PAAM). It continued at his home where he showed me works including early monotypes by Knaths.

In turn, Halper introduced me to his "partner" Mervin Jules, an artist and collector. He was, at the time, board chair for PAAM. Jules proved to be one of many who were enormously generous during my research, I was later a guest in his home with other participants of a panel presented at PAAM. My roommates included gallerist Stefan Stux, realist author and curator, John Artist, then MFA curator Amy Lighthill, Boston artist Doug Anderson then in the Whitney Biennial, and Ted Spagna of the Mass Council for the Arts and Humanities. During another weekend hosted by Rhoda Rossmore, I met and became close to the artist Benny Andrews, who was then visual arts coordinator for the National Endowment for the Arts and Humanities.

Provincetown became a connecting point, creating many resources and vectors for ever-widening research. Initiated with a focus on Knaths, the interviews and topics widened to a larger embrace of a community that spawned major movements. During hectic summer seasons, Provincetown was a brain trust and epicenter for advanced American culture.

Its clearest manifestation at that time was the legendary Long Point Gallery. I interviewed several members of that cooperative: Leo Manso, Judith Rothschild, Fritz Bultman, Budd Hopkins, Tony Vevers, Sideo Fromboluti, and Nora Speyer. During an installation I photographed Robert Motherwell and Vevers plotting the hanging. Those images are included in this book, and in 2024, I presented a portfolio of them to Jim Zimmerman, the archivist for PAAM. He has been helpful in providing vintage images for the book.

The mid-1980s proved to be a bodacious time for Provincetown. Nobody was funding my research, but it was still relatively affordable to visit. In my archive is a receipt from a guest house at $35 a night. Frank D. Schaefer's White Horse Inn was cozy and filled with work of local artists. Filmmaker John Waters was an annual tenant.

On Shank Painter Road there was a luncheonette with wonderful Portuguese kale soup. There was much to enjoy regarding food and hospitality. Openings led to after-parties. There was usually a place to crash, with hair of the dog for breakfast. One notable occasion was a bunch of us crowded into the new condo of the magnificent Dee Kennedy. Another time, Peter Plamondon let me bunk in. Mary Armstrong and Stony Conley hosted my sister Pip and me when he was a fellow at Fine Arts Work Center.

At that time there was a delicate social/political balance of artists, the indigenous Portuguese fishing community, and gays. Provincetown was a party town but with a mix of families and tourists.

Once-quaint fishing shacks and working-class homes have since been gussied up and gentrified. That's the thesis of an intriguing but controversial book *Provincetown: Art, Sex and Money on the Outer Cape* (2002) by Peter Manso, the son of Long Point artist, Leo Manso.

Now young artists and writers come to the Fine Arts Work Center, but can't afford to stay after that. There are cheaper off-season rentals, but that means vacating when rents spike. In general, other than established artists who own or have inherited property, artists have been gentrified out of Provincetown.

Over the years, I have returned many times, in more recent years, with my wife, Astrid Hiemer. Significantly, these have been off-season visits, including attending the Tennessee Williams Festival in the fall. Theater has been an important aspect of Provincetown from the early years of Eugene O'Neill and the Provincetown Players to Tennessee Williams, who rented a shack from Knaths.

Visits always combine work and pleasure. There are shows to see and interviews to conduct. During a week of research in October 2024, we enjoyed magnificent weather. Astrid walked the dunes at Race Point where we went each day at sundown.

As a guest curator, I have worked with PAAM on two major exhibitions. The first was *Kind of Blue: Benny Andrews, Emilio Cruz, Earle Pilgrim and Bob Thompson*, 1986. My curatorial essay was published by *Provincetown Arts Magazine*. In 2013, I provided a catalog essay for Adam Zucker's exhibition, *Pioneers from Provincetown: The Roots of Figurative Expressionism*.

As abstract expressionism came to dominate American art, younger artists were influenced, but pulling away. There was much discussion of a potential "return to the figure" which was anathema to the influential Clement Greenberg who advocated formalism. From 1955 to 1959, indications of a paradigm shift to figurative expressionism were on display in the small but crucial Sun Gallery. I interviewed Yvonne Andersen, an artist who, with her poet husband Dominic Falcone, ran Sun Gallery. They took over the jewelry shop and gallery of Earle Montrose Pilgrim. This book includes a critical study of Pilgrim and his work.

One of the artists who Pilgrim introduced and subsequently showed at Sun Gallery was Lester Johnson. Through Karl Hecker of David Anderson Gallery (the son of Martha Jackson) I worked with Lester and wrote the catalog essay for his traveling exhibition organized by Westmorland Museum of Art.

A key to survival in Provincetown was buying real estate when it was still affordable. No visit to P'town is complete without a visit with conceptual artist Jay Critchley. Back in the day, he and his partner, since deceased, bought a funky home and generous backyard for $38,000. *Provincetown Magazine* publisher and writer, Chris Busa, son of the artist Peter Busa, bought in long ago. There were always lively dialogues with Chris who published a number of my essays. He died a few years ago.

Recently, we encountered gallerist Berta Walker, now in her 80s, and on top of her game. The 2024 season marked her 35th year. Wisely, early on, she acquired a home for the gallery. In a raucous interview we shared anecdotes, including ones about her famous father, Hudson Walker, a collector and philanthropist.

Walker was a nice guy compared to Walter P. Chrysler who founded a Provincetown museum that later transferred to Norfolk Museum with 10,000 works in 1971. The Virginia museum was renamed Chrysler Museum of Art. Vevers recounts how the mega-rich collector tried to wear down artists to bottom-feeding prices. Walker quit the board of the museum when it was revealed to have many fakes. Chrysler, who brought Andy Warhol to Provincetown, left town leaving behind unpaid bills and ill will.

In recent years, the Provincetown Art Association and Museum has thrived and expanded under Christine McCarthy as director. The physical plant was doubled and upgraded with the permanent collection now three times more extensive than before her tenure. We discussed that challenge in detail. A 2015 exhibition and catalog, *A Century of Inspiration,* provides a check list of works in the permanent collection.

This book compiles primary source material but does not aspire to create a comprehensive history. Hopefully, the reader will devour many tasty morsels of the feast that comprises the remarkable story of art in America's most renowned creative community.

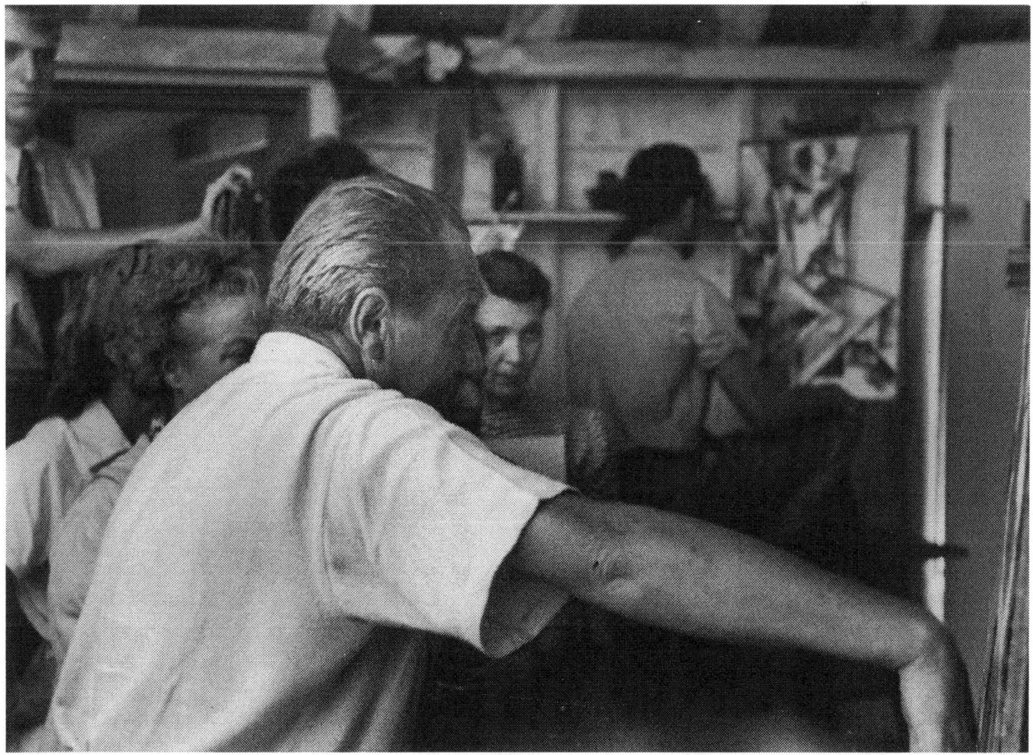

Artists came to study with Hans Hofmann on the GI Bill. Bill Witt photo. Courtesy of PAAM.

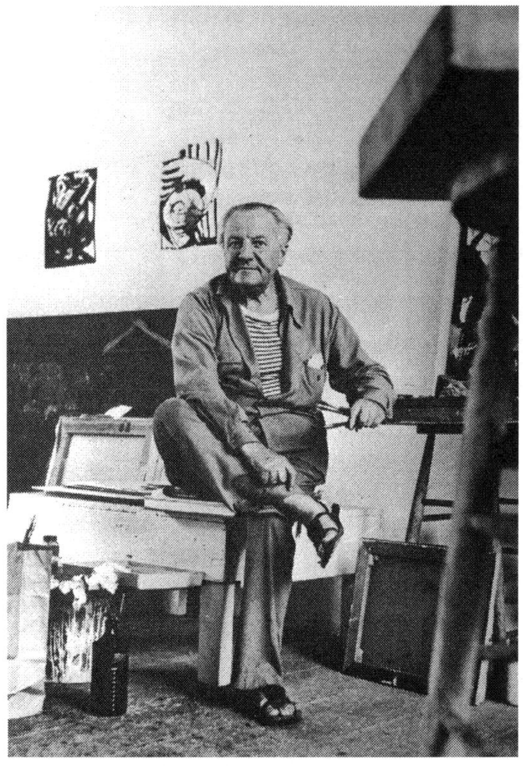

Hofmann in his studio. Courtesy of PAAM.

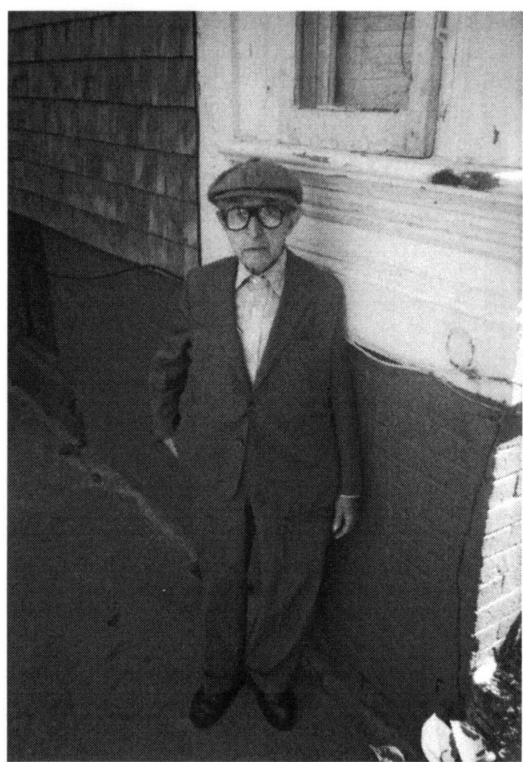

Diminutive Raphael Soyer and his brothers summered in Provincetown. Giuliano photo.

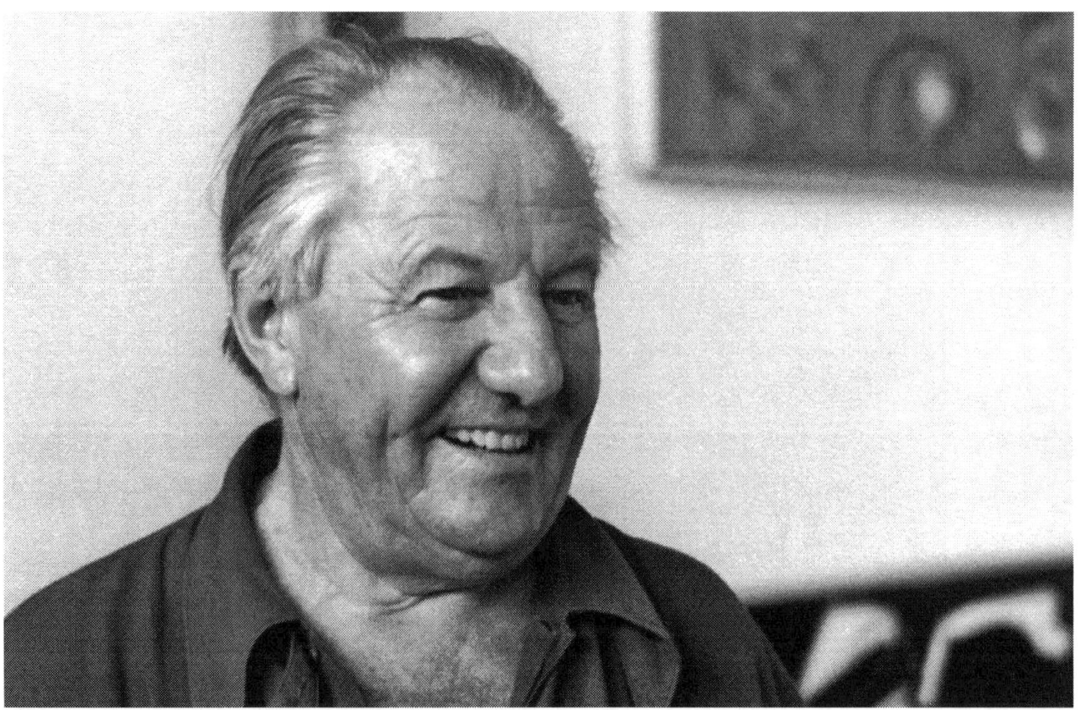

Hans Hofmann. Courtesy of PAAM.

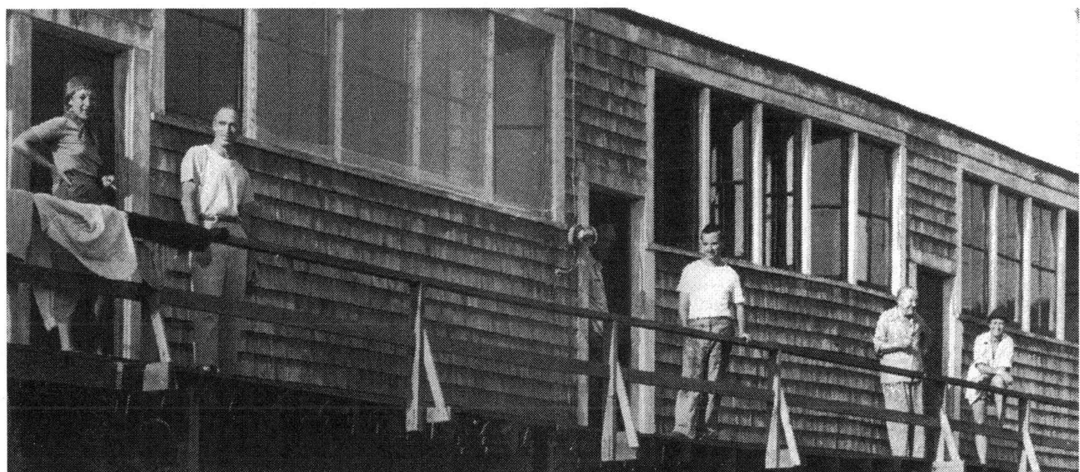

There were artist studios in Day's Lumber Yard, now Fine Arts Work Center. Left to right: Peter and Florence Grippe, Fritz Bultman, Hans Hofmann, and unknown. Courtesy of PAAM.

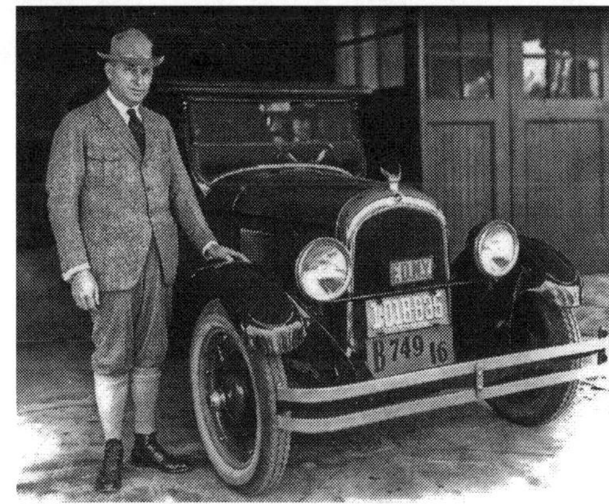

Carmaker Walter Chrysler founded a museum in Provincetown which later moved to Norfolk, Virginia. Courtesy of PAAM.

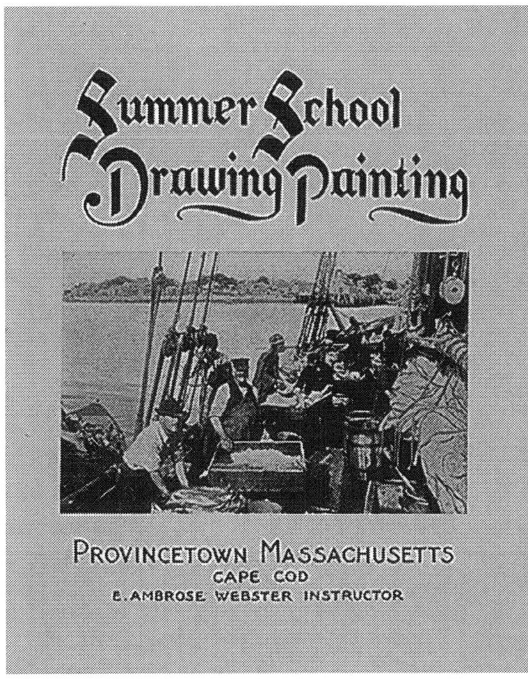

Flyer for E. Ambrose Webster summer art school. Courtesy of PAAM.

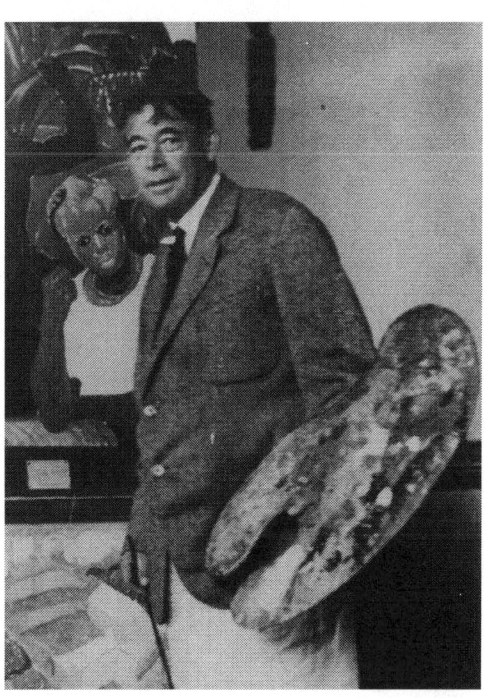

E. Ambrose Webster an early artist and teacher, courtesy of PAAM.

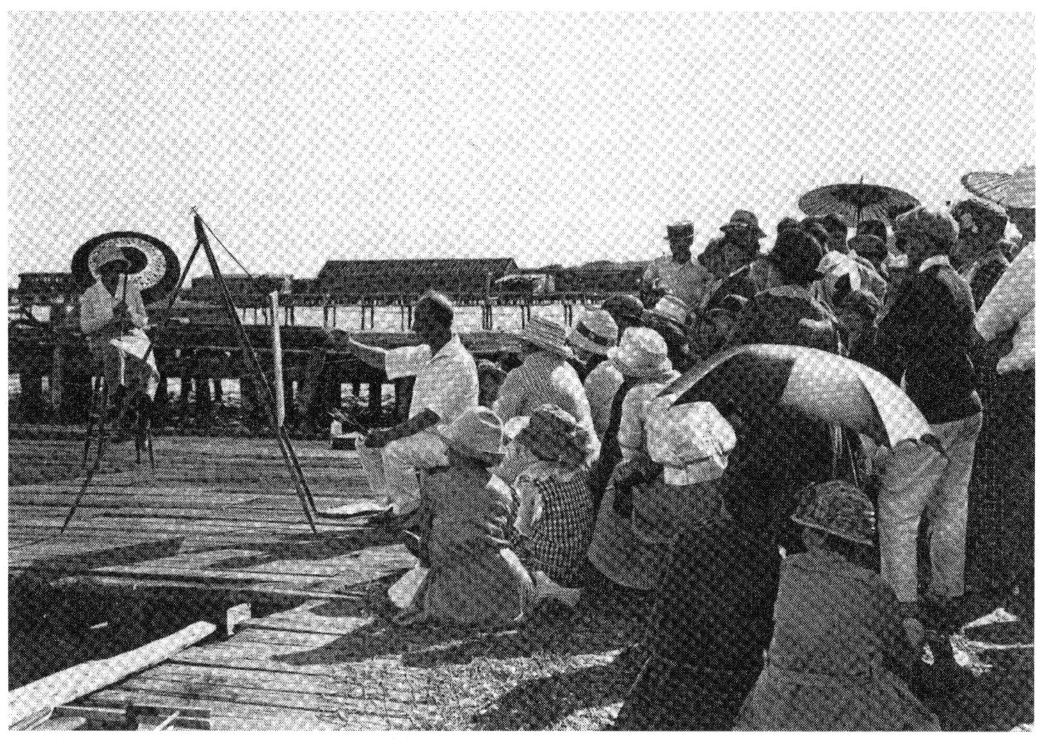

Charles Hawthorne class. Courtesy of PAAM.

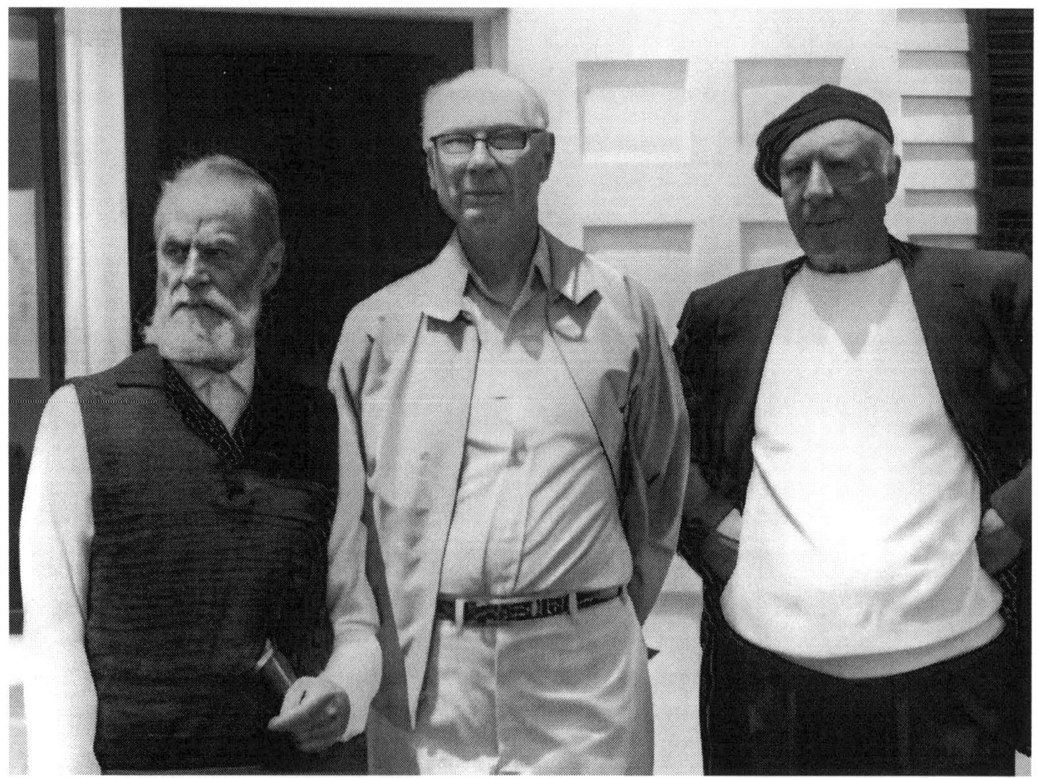

Edwin Dickinson, Ross Moffett, and Karl Knaths. George Yater photo. Courtesy of PAAM.

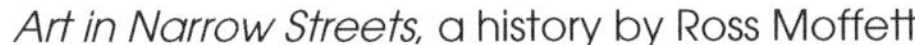

Art In Narrow Streets

BY ROSS MOFFETT

THE FIRST THIRTY-THREE YEARS
OF THE
PROVINCETOWN ART ASSOCIATION
1914 - 1947

Art in Narrow Streets, a history by Ross Moffett.

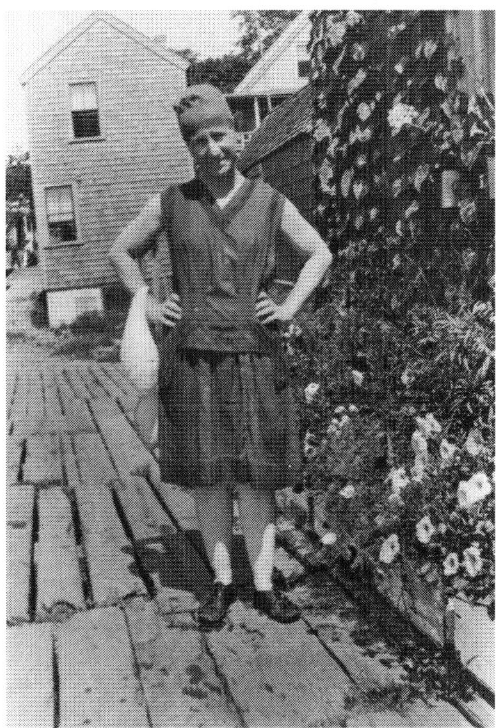

Artist Blanche Lazzell was an early modernist. Courtesy of PAAM.

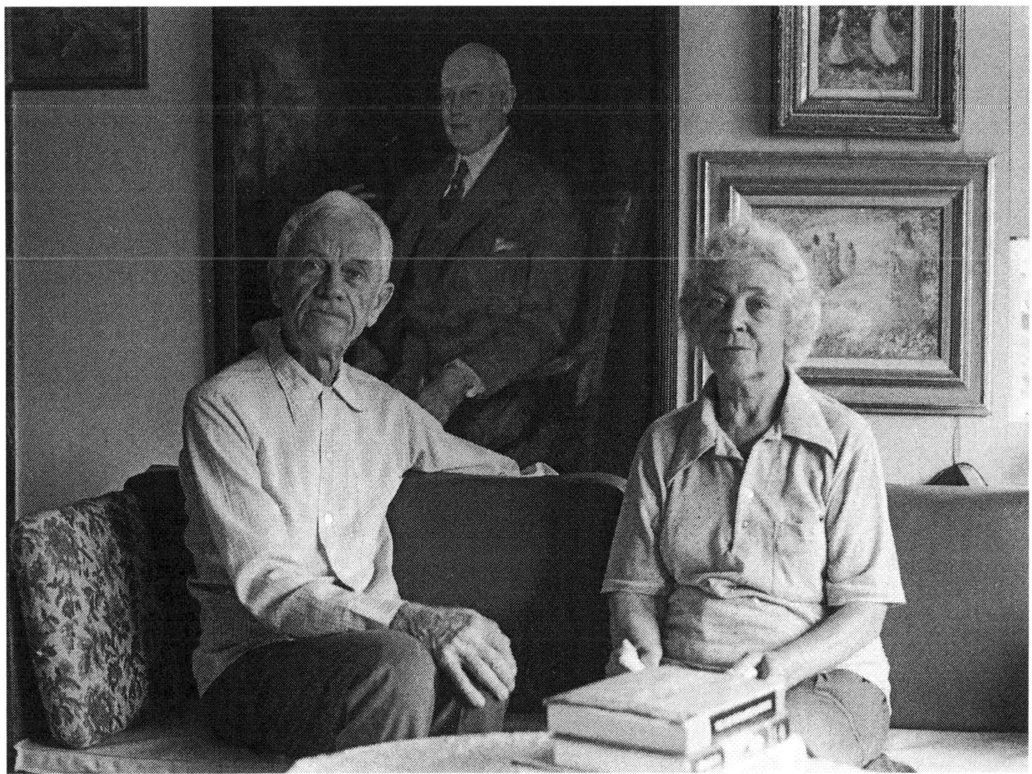

Artsit and teacher, Henry Hensche and Ada Rayner. Norma Holt photo. Courtesy of PAAM.

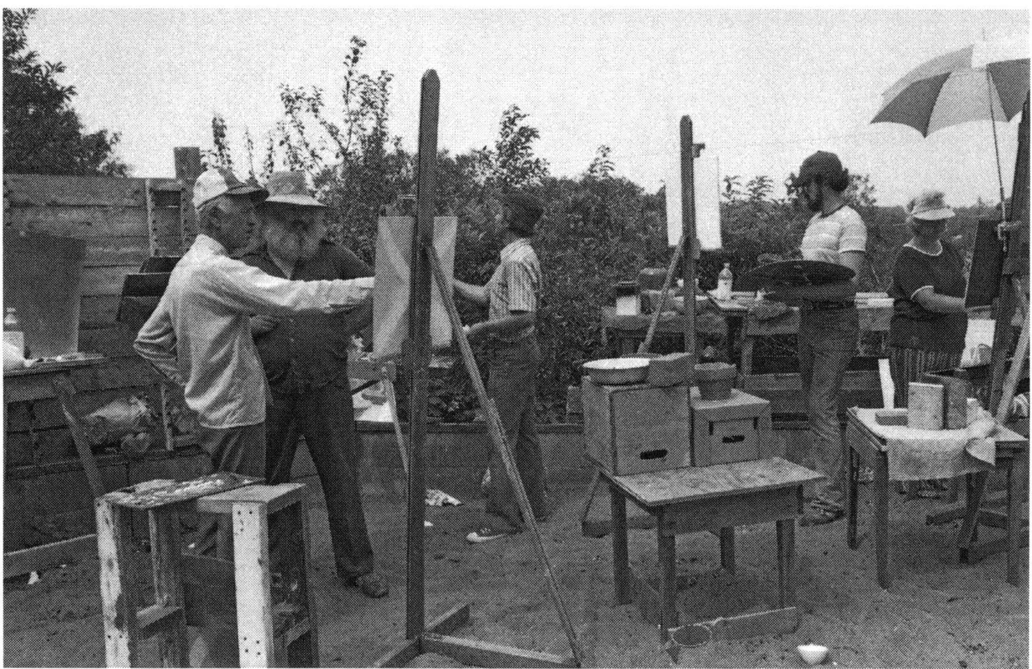

Henry Hensche teaching. Courtesy of PAAM.

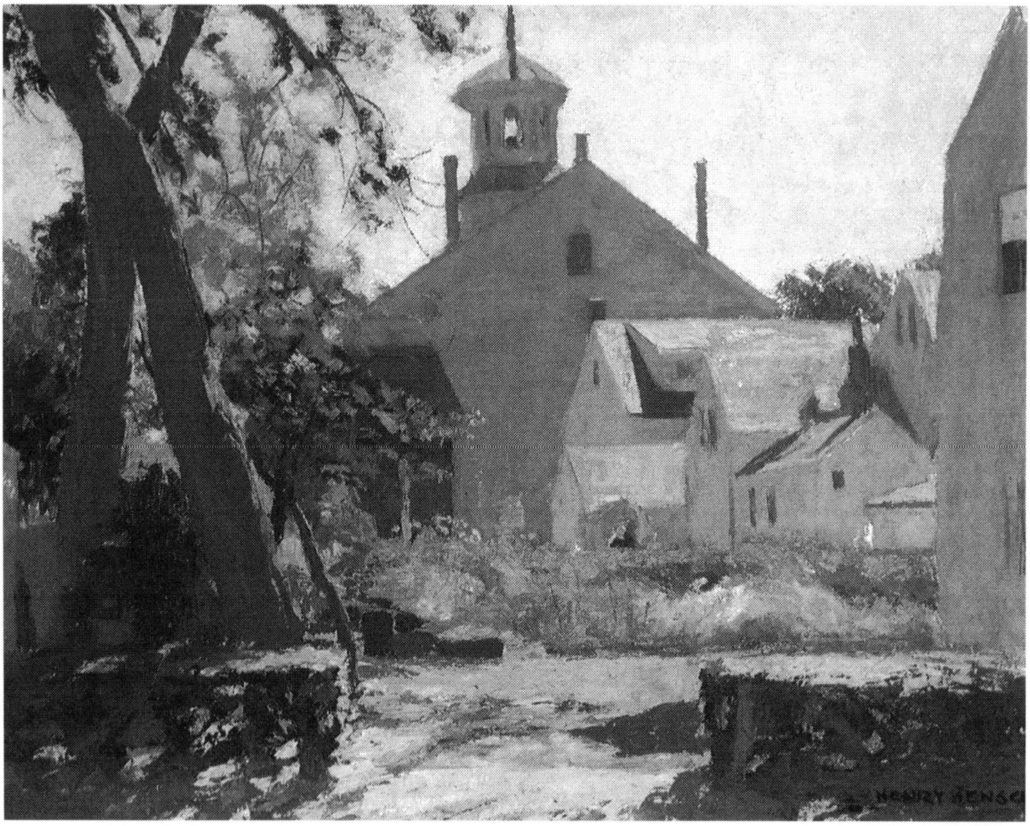

Hensche painting. Courtesy of PAAM.

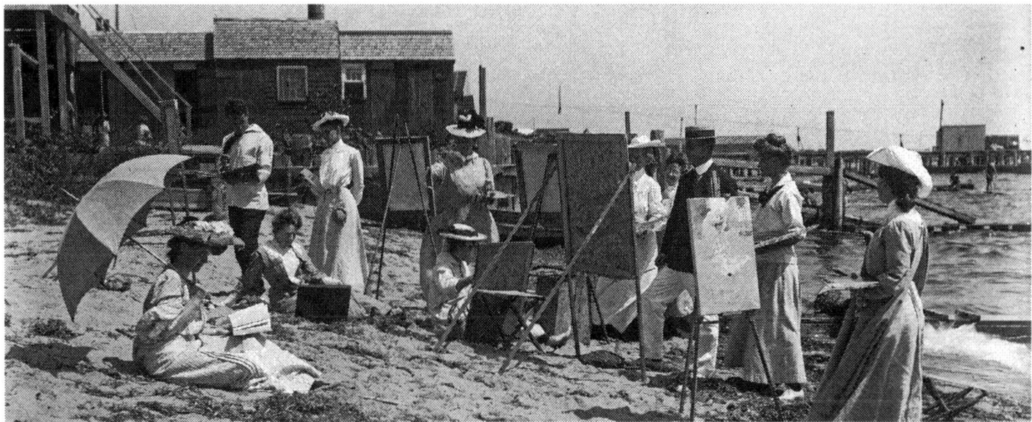

Charles Hawthorne class painting. Courtesy of PAAM.

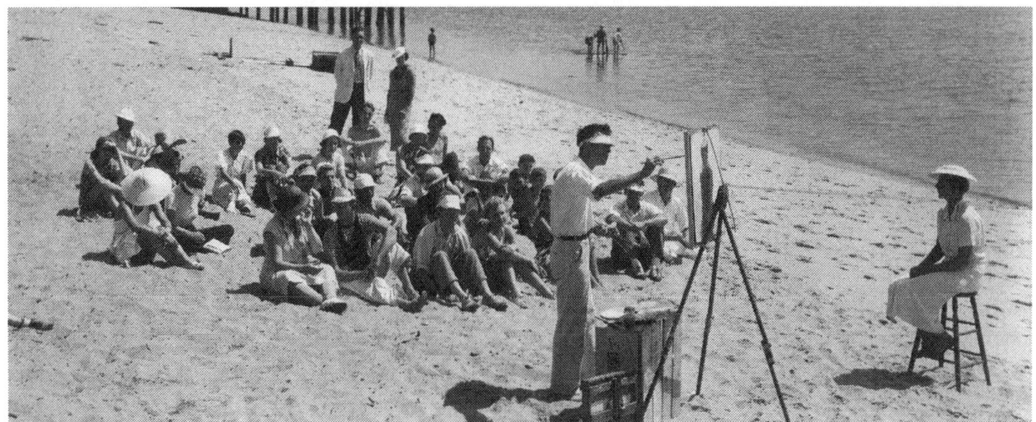

Hensche painting on beach. Courtesy of PAAM.

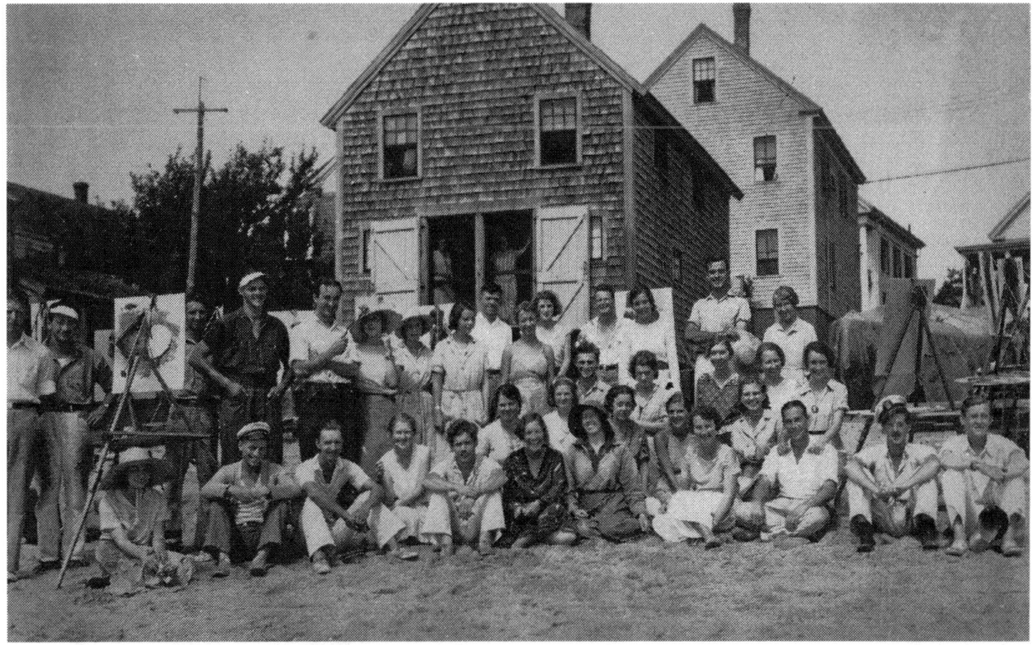

Students of Hensche, 1930s. Courtesy of PAAM.

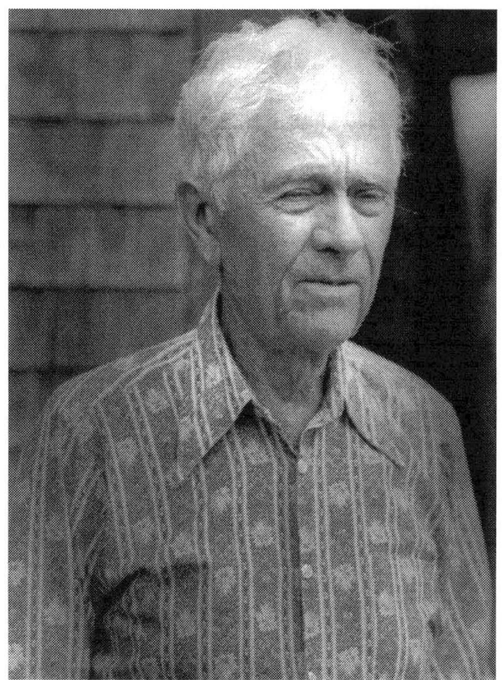

Henry Hensche. Marian Roth photo. Courtesy of PAAM.

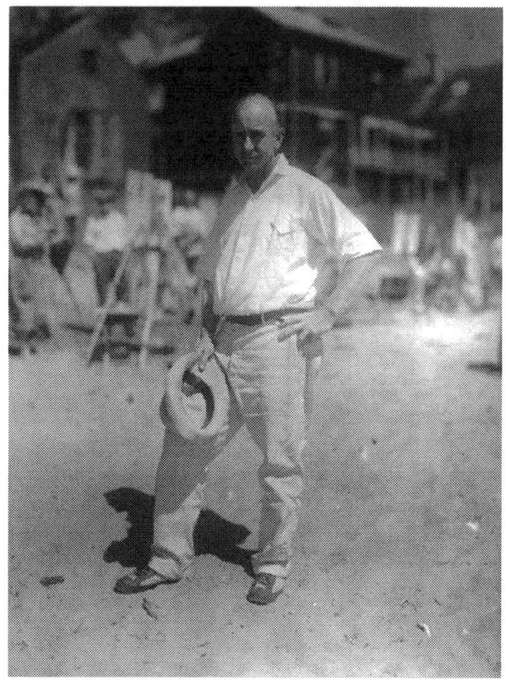

Charles Hawthorne. Courtesy of PAAM.

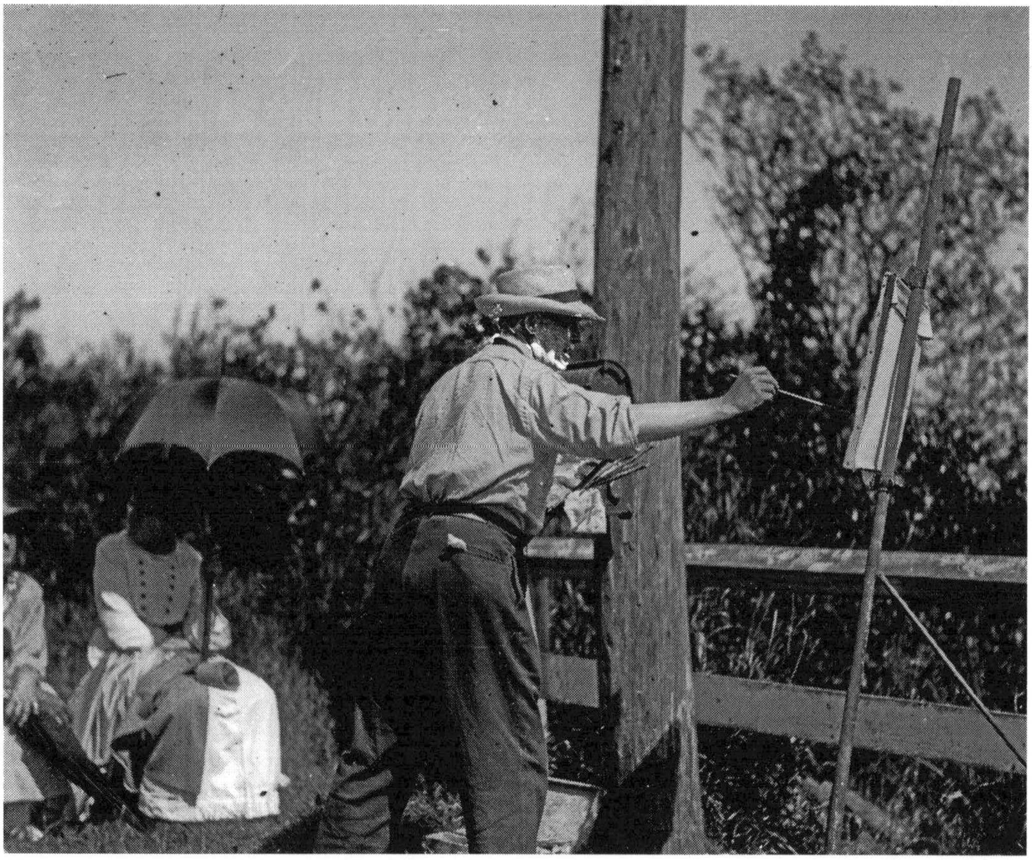

Webster teaching 1916. Courtesy of PAAM.

Underappreciated Artist Karl Knaths

In 1919, after a two-year stint in the army and a brief stay in New York, Karl Knaths (1891–1971) settled in Provincetown where he remained for the rest of his life. Initially he rented a shack, formerly occupied by Eugene O'Neill, for $30 a year

Having won awards and been featured in numerous museum exhibitions, he had an established national reputation. His work is in major museum collections: The Phillips Collection, Albright Knox Museum, Metropolitan Museum of Art, Art Institute of Chicago, Museum of Modern Art, Whitney Museum of American Art, Museum of Fine Arts, Boston, Los Angeles County Museum of Art, Peabody Essex Museum, and the Philadelphia Museum of Art.

The work is best represented by the Phillips Collection in Washington, D.C. It includes thirty-five oils, four watercolors, four woodcuts, three collages, and one lithograph.

In 1922 Knaths painted *Geranium in Night Window* which Duncan Phillips acquired in 1926. It was included in his exhibition *Eleven American Painters*. The artist had his first one-man show in 1924 at Daniel Gallery in New York. His second was at Phillips Memorial Gallery, as it was then known, in 1926. Phillips proved to be his most ardent and consistent patron.

Between 1938 and 1950 Knaths and his wife, Helen, visited Washington, D.C., where he lectured each winter at the museum. He also taught at Bennington College in Verrmont, as well as lectured at Black Mountain College in Ashville, North Carolina and

Maine's Skowhegan School of Art.

With the rise of abstract expressionism, his style of lyrical figurative cubism declined in favor. He continued to make regular sales at the prestigious Paul Rosenberg Gallery, which, after his death, for several years managed the estate. There were causes for the decline of critical evaluation and monetary value of the remaining work. Some 100-plus canvases and numerous works on paper were taken back by Ken Dermaris, a bank officer and executor of the estate. This flooded the market with discounted work. The bank approached a number of galleries, but as a business decision, finally decided to get out of the art market. That meant having nobody to look after the promotion and reputation of the artist.

The exhibition *Karl Knaths: Five Decades of Paintings*, 1973–1974, with an introduction and numerous poems by Charles Edward Eaton and catalogue by Isabel Patterson Eaton received brutal reviews. It traveled to six venues: The William Hayes Ackland Memorial Art Center at the University of North Carolina; Fort Lauderdale Museum, Florida; Witte Memorial Museum, San Antonio, Texas; Phoenix Art Museum, Arizona; The Phillips Collection, Washington, D.C.; and the Provincetown Art Association.

In the 1950s there was little modern and contemporary art on view at the Museum of Fine Arts Boston. One of the few works which I much admired at the MFA was *Lilacs* by Knaths. It was a work notable for its abstraction and refined color. It was deaccessioned in 2004 and sold at Christie's for $13,145. In 2007 it was resold at Sotheby's for $32,000, the current auction record for the artist.

Knaths was born in Eau Clair, Wisconsin into a German-American family of bakers. The family soon moved to Potage, Wisconsin, where he was raised. He was a teenager when his father died, and he was apprenticed to an uncle, George Dietrich, also a baker. German was spoken at home. In later years he would read and translate philosophy and art-related texts as a part of a study group. He and Hans Hofmann would converse awkwardly, each critical of the other's command of the language. Knaths had a deep love of music, but Joan Wye, an artist bilingual in German who was a close associate of the Knaths and collaborated with him on translations of art historical texts, told me that he found Hofmann bombastic and "Wagnerian," a composer of which Knaths was not particularly fond.

In high school he met Zona Gale, who won the Pulitzer Prize for drama in 1921. Upon his graduation from high school in 1910, she convinced his uncle to release him from apprenticeship. The following year he studied at the Milwaukee Art Institute. Gale introduced him to Laura Sherry, the director of the Wisconsin Players. He became caretaker of the playhouse and one of its set designers. In 1911, on advice from Gale, Knaths began studies at the School of the Art Institute of Chicago.

In 1913, the *Armory Show* caused a sensation when it introduced European modernism to America. It was a culture shock to a provincial art world then represented by the Ashcan School of Realism. The show traveled from New York to Chicago, ending in Boston, where it caused hardly a murmur. Knaths got a job as a guard for the exhibition in Chicago. Overall, it had no immediate impact on his work, but he was most interested in the work of Cezanne.

In 1917, Knaths rejoined the Wisconsin Players as the group's scenery painter during a tour of East Coast theaters. In Provincetown the Players performed Gale's *Mr. Pitt*. He returned as a resident two years later.

Young artists came to Provincetown to study painting with Charles Webster Hawthorne (1872–1930), who founded the Cape Cod School of Art in 1899, and E. Ambrose Webster (1869–1935). Hawthorne sustained the techniques of his teacher William Merritt Chase (1849–1916). There were subsequent generations of art schools and private instructors. The Provincetown Art Association and Museum continues that tradition.

With the outbreak of WWI, 1914 proved to be a watershed year marked by the founding of the Provincetown Art Association. Artists returned from study in Europe or came to Provincetown as a default ambiance. It was then a sparsely settled Portuguese fishing village notable for its Cape Cod light. There was the compelling combination of spectacular views to paint and cheap rent.

The critical mass of artists underscored the need to show their work. Oliver Newberry Chaffee Jr. (1881–1944), who had shown in the *Armory Show*, was one of the founders of the Provincetown Art Association. Other founding artists included Gerrit Beneker, Edwin Dickinson, Oscar Gieberich, Frank H. Desch, Charles Demuth, Marsden Hartley, Kenneth Stubbs, Mary Bacon Jones, Catharine Carter Critcher, Sarah Sewell Munroe, and Margery Ryerson. For the first two years, the Association met monthly at members' homes or at the home of its first president, William H. Young, who was president of the local Seamen's Savings Bank. As lectures were included, the meetings moved to the Church of the Pilgrims near Town Hall. There were two juried exhibitions in the summer of 1915 at the Provincetown Town Hall.

In 1919, the Association purchased the former home of fishing captain Solomon Bangs at Bangs Street and Commercial Street. In 1921, the Association added an adjacent property at 460 Commercial Street, which was renovated for use as a gallery.

Reflecting his academic training, the early work of Knaths was a form of regionalist realism. That changed immediately in Provincetown. From 1919–1920 he created a suite of monotypes that, in their radical abstraction, compare to the artists shown by the most progressive New York dealer, Alfred Stieglitz (1864–1946). They were purchased from the estate by Nathaniel Halper and his business associate Mervin Jules, as well as by collectors Jim and Jean Young. I have not viewed these important works since the 1980s. They were signed Otto as well as Karl. At that time, he abandoned Otto, which was the name of his father.

His personal and professional life changed soon after taking up residence, when he met the sisters Weinrich. They had visited Europe to study, Helen at a conservatory and Agnes as an artist. She was exposed to modernism in Berlin and Paris where she derived cubism from Albert Gleizes (1881–1953).

Agnes Weinrich (1873–1946) was Knaths lifeline to modernism. Through her he soon adapted a form of lyrical cubism. With time and research there were other theoretical developments in his work. Agnes, however, provided his career with a jump start. As one of Provincetown's seminal modernists and white line printers, her work is well regarded, with prints selling for as much as $5,000.

In May 1898, Agnes and her sister Helen, then called Lena, had traveled to Germany with their aunt, a German-born music teacher named Rose Werthmueller. When Werthmueller returned home, they stayed on, living in Berlin with German relatives. Their father died while they were abroad and left them an inheritance that allowed them to live modestly for the rest of their lives.

While Knaths respected Agnes as a colleague, she was not interested in marriage. The alternative was Helen who had time to be a wife. In 1922, Knaths married Helen and moved into the house that the sisters had rented. He was then 30, Helen 45, and Agnes 46. As the house was cold and drafty, they spent winters in a New York studio. Knaths preferred rural life, but to advance his career, spent time in New York and Boston as well as with Phillips in Washington, D.C.

In 1921, he exhibited paintings at New York's Society of Independent Artists for the first of many occasions. Knaths showed two and Agnes Weinrich three paintings in this large non-juried show without prizes. In 1926, Knaths' work appeared in another show, Katherine Sophie Dreier's *Société Anonyme* exhibition, held in Brooklyn.

In 1924, Helen and Agnes bought land on which Knaths constructed a house and studio using materials from a razed rectory. It was a modest house with a small studio on the second floor. He constructed several small structures that served as studios and rental properties. Tennessee Williams lived in one while writing *The Glass Menagerie.*

Agnes was the primary housekeeper. After her death Helen was incapable of assuming that role. She was reclusive and sedentary. She would play piano only when alone. Joan Wye recalled hearing her through the window. Knaths insisted that she play for him on Sundays.

They employed a housekeeper who resided on the property. In later years, there were students like Tim Bright and Bernie Beckman who swapped instruction for chores. Knaths was skilled at handyman work, and according to Wye, had some 18 caps and outfits for these various jobs from roofing to plumbing. His clothes, and that of his helpers, came by mail from Sears & Roebuck. Self-conscious about premature balding, he generally wore a beret.

While not inclined to socializing, he got along well with the fishermen who dried their nets near his house, which was initially open property. When attending openings, he went early and left before the arrival of other guests. During the winter he hosted a literary circle, but nobody was invited to dinner. Wye recalled annual viewings of new work before it was sent to Rosenberg. He spoke briefly about each painting. Notably, no refreshments were served to the twenty or so guests.

During the Great Depression he joined the WPA Mural Project. He painted a number of murals, including the *History of Science* and *History of Music* for Falmouth High School. This work is discussed in the dissertation on the WPA in Massachusetts by Dr. Edith Tonelli. He also created *Frontier Mail* in the post office at Rehoboth Beach, Delaware.

His work was being shown in New York. In 1931, he left Daniel Gallery for Edith Halpert's Downtown Gallery, then the J.B. Neumann Gallery. At the recommendation of dealer and collector Hudson Walker, he joined the prestigious Paul Rosenberg Gallery in 1945. Known for Picasso and modernism, as a patriotic gesture during the war years, the gallery showed Knaths, Milton Avery, and American painters. His first show with Rosenberg was a critical success. It was short listed as one of the best gallery shows of 1947. For modest, but decent prices, the gallery sold some 15 to 20 works each year until his death. Knaths was convinced that he needed to produce to maintain his and Helen's humble lifestyle.

Taking over his finances and estate planning, Demaris convinced him that he was a man of means. Helen, who survived him by seven years, was well provided for, including at-home hospice care.

The lifestyle of Knaths was modest and methodical. He rose at 5 a.m. and was in the studio from 7 a.m. to noon. Then he would read, do chores, and take walks. After supper he would read and be in bed by 8 p.m. There was no work on Sundays, which were spent with Helen. Though raised Catholic, he was not a church-going man. He was, however, intensely interested in philosophy and mysticism.

From his estate, Wye coveted the copy of *Oahspe,* which he promised to her.

(*Oahspe: A New Bible* is a book published in 1882, purporting to contain "new revelations" from "...the Embassadors of the angel hosts of heaven prepared and revealed unto man in the name of Jehovih..." It was produced by an American dentist, John Ballou Newbrough (1828–1891), who reported it to have been written by automatic writing.

"Karl was very interested in the book," Wye told me. "He scribbled in it throughout. When some time after Karl's death I asked Helen, she knew nothing about the book. I found it on his bedstand."

He was also interested in the writing of Emanuel Swedenborg (1688–1772) the Swedish Christian theologian, scientist, philosopher, and mystic. He became best known for his book on the afterlife, *Heaven and Hell.* Knaths aspired to channel divine inspiration into the creation of his work.

The study group that met weekly, primarily during the winter season, included Wye, her then husband, Jim Forsberg, the artists Myron Stout and Judith Rothchild, as well as her husband, the author Anton Myrer. Stout was impatient when Knaths veered off art to discuss religion and philosophy.

During the 1920s, Knaths had studied, and sometimes translated from German, theoretical publications of theorists and artists, including Carl Einstein, Wilhelm Ostwald, Piet Mondrian, Wassily Kandinsky, and Jay Hambidge. He was also influenced by Gino Severini's *Du cubisme au classicisme; esthétique du compas et du nombre.*

The group worked on translations of art texts not available in English, including the writing of Juan Gris and Mondrian. He read *Siddhartha* by Herman Hesse in English. Wye loaned him a copy in German and says that he read it in two days.

From theoretical sources Knaths developed a system for composition and color. Like other artists of his generation, he relied on the diagrams of Jay Hambidge (1867–1924) in his influential book *The Elements of Dynamic Symmetry.* During a visit to the Fogg Art Museum, the artist Jack Levine showed me Hambidge-based drawings that Knaths produced as a student of Paul Sachs.

Knaths, like Kandinsky, related the arrangement and selection of color as equivalent to intervals in music. His students, Ferol Sibley Warthen and Judith Rothschild, explained to me how they applied them.

They used the *Color Harmony Manual* published by the Container Corporation of America. It is based on Wilhelm Ostwald's (1853–1932) classification system with 37 colors and 28 hues each. There are some 1,000 removable plastic clips. Knaths mixed color in clam shells numbered corresponding to the clip.

As Eaton explains in the 1973–1974 catalog, "Believing that there are definite measurable correspondences between musical intervals and spatial proportions, he had worked out a graph which he showed us on his studio wall. Spatially numbered from 1 through 30 on the vertical and octaves of musical intervals on the horizontal, colored lines radiate from the common center. Each of these colored lines represent a musical note in that C, for example, is red. C# is red orange… E is yellow…F# is green…B is purple… to C is red. Thus, from one red line to the next is an octave. He would use this chart to get his different proportions for the canvas by means of placing one leg of the caliper at the base and the other at a selected point on the spatial scale. For the intervals thus obtained he had corresponding cutouts, which he called his 'piano,' and which he used to mark off the intervals on the canvas. The use of exactly measured intervals from the Ostwald color charts, and space proportions based on musical intervals is the basic element of the Knaths 'Method.'"

There were meaningful artists that Knaths interacted with from around 1914 when the Provincetown Art Association was founded. In the early years Edwin Walter Dickinson (1891–1978) and Ross Embrose Moffett (1888–1971) were friends and colleagues. They are often linked. Both artists studied with Hawthorne and continued with a conservative tradition. Moffett is best known as the author of *Art in Narrow Streets: The First Thirty-Three Years of The Provincetown Art Association,* 1914–1947, a slim volume that was published in 1964. Particularly for psychologically charged self portraits, Dickinson is regarded by art historians as one of the great, under-appreciated artists of his generation.

For decades there was a rift in the art association between traditional and modern artists. Knaths and Weinrich were early jurors of progressive exhibitions. That changed with the organization of exhibitions and programming comprising *Forum '49*. Significantly it was organized outside the Art Association. Knaths exhibited and participated as a panelist for the program which underscored issues and radical change in advanced American art.

Representing what may be regarded as the apogee of his career; in 1950, he was accorded first prize, for *Basket Bouquet* in the controversial Metropolitan Museum exhibition *American Painting Today.* In the late 1940s, his work was featured in articles in *Art News* and the *New York Times.* In 1949, he was featured in an article by Elaine de Kooning, "Knaths Paints a Picture," in *Art News.*

Famously, a letter of protest for not including their work in *American Painting Today* was sent to the Museum with a copy to the *NY Times.* Those who signed the letter were Jimmy Ernst, Adolph Gottlieb, Robert Motherwell, William Baziotes, Hans Hofmann,

Barnett Newman, Clyfford Still, Richard Pousette-Dart, Theodoros Stamos, Ad Reinhardt, Jackson Pollock, Mark Rothko, Bradley Walker Tomlin, Willem de Kooning, Hedda Sterne, James Brooks, Weldon Kees, and Fritz Bultman. The supporting sculptors were Herbert Ferber, David Smith, Ibram Lassaw, Mary Callery, Day Schnabel, Seymour Lipton, Peter Grippe, Theodore Roszak, David Hare, and Louise Bourgeois.

Life Magazine dubbed them "The Irascibles." Significantly, among those that signed the letter were organizers and participants in *Forum '49*. Knaths, as prize winner for the Met show, was on the wrong side of the controversy. With the subsequent rise to global prominence of abstract expressionism and the New York School, the work of Knaths gradually fell out of favor. There continued to be honors and awards, like the 1961 Brandeis University Creative Arts Award for Painting, and prizes (1962, 1963, 1965) from the National Academy of Design.

After his death there were memorial exhibitions at the Phillips Collection (1971) and Rosenberg Gallery (1972). There were mixed responses to Charles Eaton's traveling exhibition.

In the *Washington Post* Paul Richard wrote that "Karl Knaths (1891–1971) was not a master-at anything save choosing colors—and his pictures have begun to date...Knaths will be remembered as a masterful colorist but minor artist."

For *Art International* Carter Ratcliff was more positive. "He never abandoned cubism but he did avoid its internationalist excesses. Of the American Cubists he was one of the few who is both genuinely American and genuinely a cubist."

In a 1974 *Art in America* review Donald Kuspit wrote, "The autopsy of Knaths' career has yet to be performed. Knaths is an example of a contemporary provincial artist—a role epitomized by his refusal to visit Europe. Persisting in his provinciality he made a virtue of it, but his art failed because of it... Knaths' art suffers from a poverty of purpose, a dirth (sic) of problems, and it is ultimately meaningless humanly—for the natives it is meant to enlighten as well as artistically." The catalogue was dismissed as "...an excellent example of retardataire criticism—sentimental, roundabout, pretentious-but one appropriate to Knaths's mild-mannered modernism... At best Knaths is quaint, at worst boring. His art is an object lesson in the limited integrity and shallowness of style that comes of compromising with reality and art."

In *AiA* Eaton responded that the Kuspit review "...is an example of the necrophiliac school of art criticism." He cited numerous awards and prestigious collections. Kuspit replied, "That an artist is collected does not mean that he is understood. Honorific talk about his person is not an analytic approach to his art. I am not opposed to sentiment per se, but I am opposed to it when it is used to apotheosize an artist so as to obscure understanding of him. I would like to point out the fact that Eaton owns four out of the 50 works which were in the Knaths exhibition, and many more that were not, puts him in an ambiguous critical position."

It takes a generation to recover from an ill-conceived and poorly curated exhibition. The Provincetown Art Association and Museum opted for another look at Knaths. In *The Boston Globe,* Cate McQuaid wrote in 2014, "The Art Association and Museum, which has been celebrating its birthday all year, has a sparkling show of works by a longtime Provincetown resident and an accomplished modernist painter, *Karl Knaths: Between Form and Freedom*.... He entered into a cool, methodical lifetime investigation of form, color, and space. Always a cubist, he broke scenes down into lines and planes; he shuffled foreground and background; he folded realism into his abstracted worlds.

"A few terrific paintings here wholeheartedly embrace representation. Knaths made the delightfully strange *Composition* in 1936, when he had a gig with the Works Progress Administration. It verges toward the social realism typical of WPA paintings, but with a screwy cubist edge. Two men sit at a table; a woman stands behind them with a broom, a cat on the floor scratches its ear.

"The figures are peculiarly flat, and one chair's back tilts oddly to the left. The wall behind looks like a stage set. The scene is dusky, save for the clamor of lemon and lime colors in the furniture and the blue of the woman's apron. *Composition* is full of odd tensions.

"Most of the paintings here, though, lean toward harmony. *Net Mender* and *Clam Diggers* from the late 1950s turn fishing village genre pictures into prisms of color, rhythms of light. Knaths depicts the net mender in sharp and sweeping black contours: The tilted square of his shoulders, the arc of the net. His body gathers greens and blues from the water behind him; the triangle of a sail in the distance echoes his angularity."

In a 1966 speech at PAAM Knaths stated, "I feel very serious about painting and about the art of painting. I think people can get not only the pleasure of seeing pictures but can develop themselves, can be made to see things that they wouldn't see otherwise that will enrich them. I think that the exhibitions are a good thing for people to see and hope that with it, they can develop other appreciation and reach whatever potential they have. The same with the artists that they do the same thing—that they work and develop and reach their own potential."

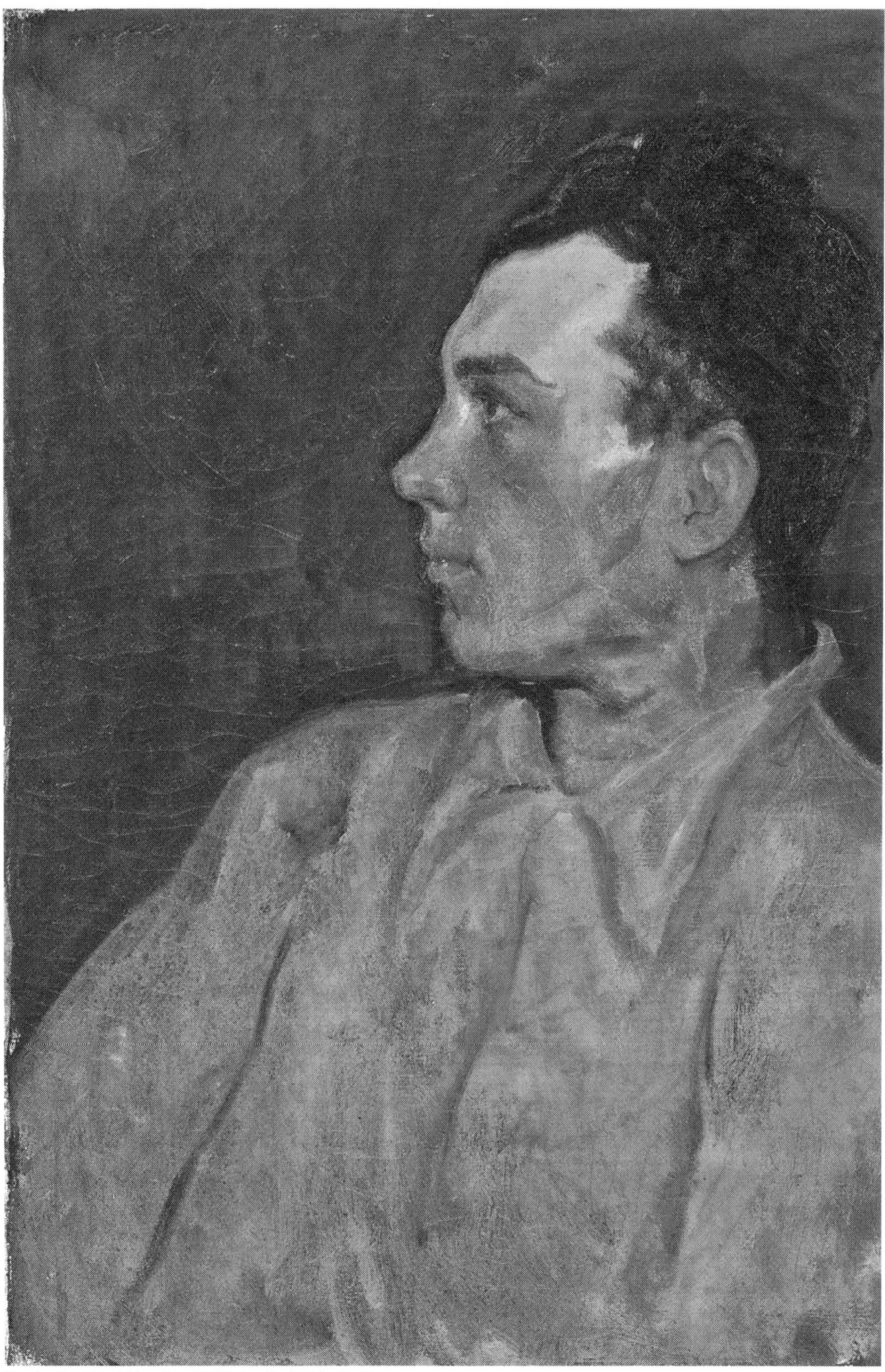

Portrait of Karl Knaths, 1925, by Ross Moffett.

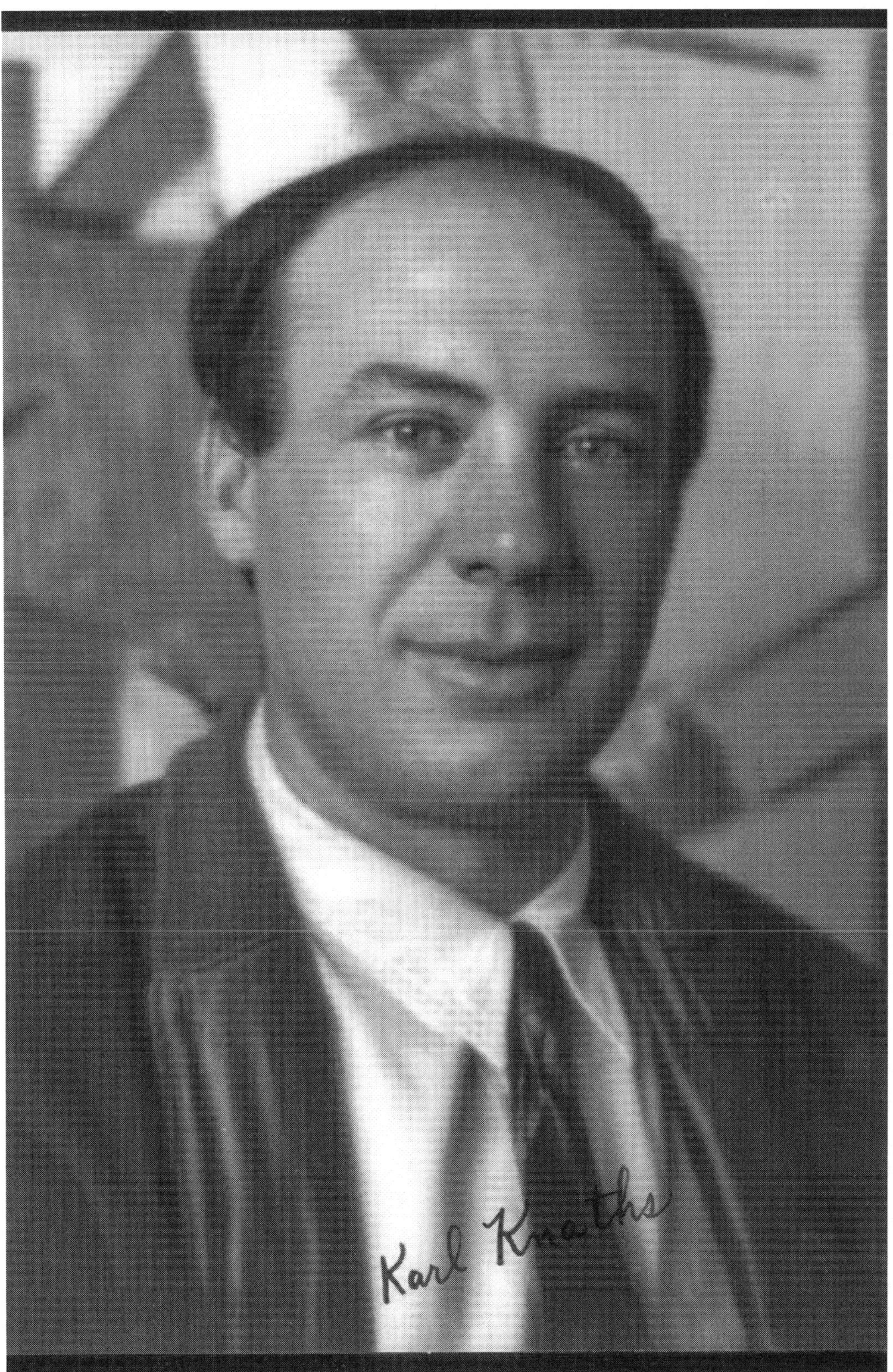

Karl Knaths. Courtesy of PAAM.

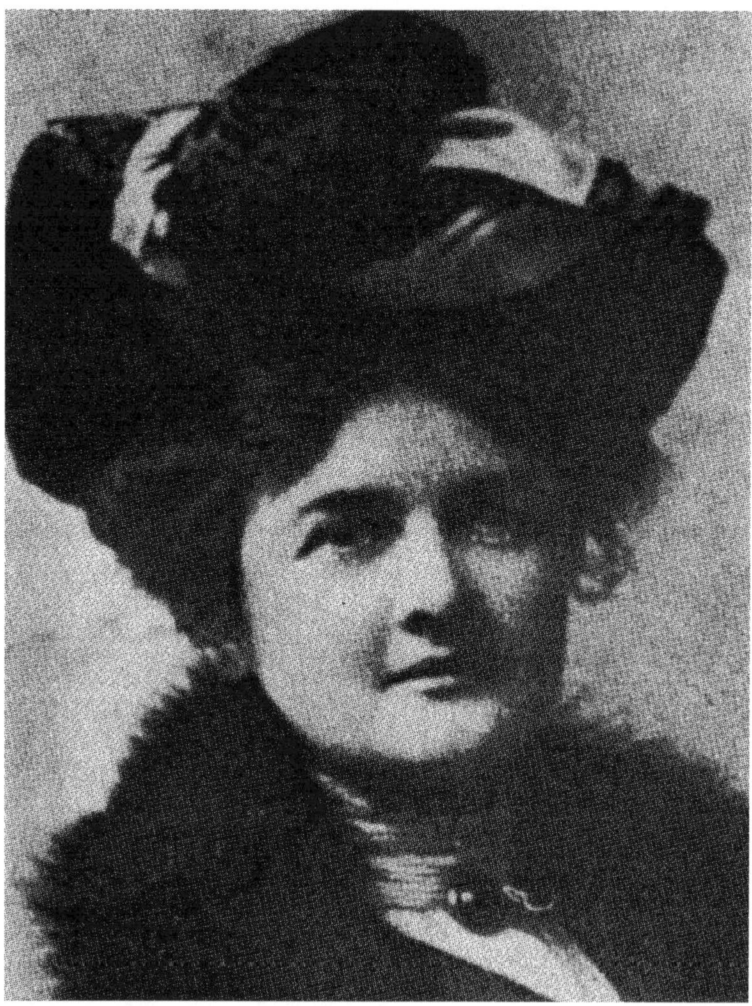

Agnes Weinrich was the sister-in-law of Knaths. Courtesy of PAAM.

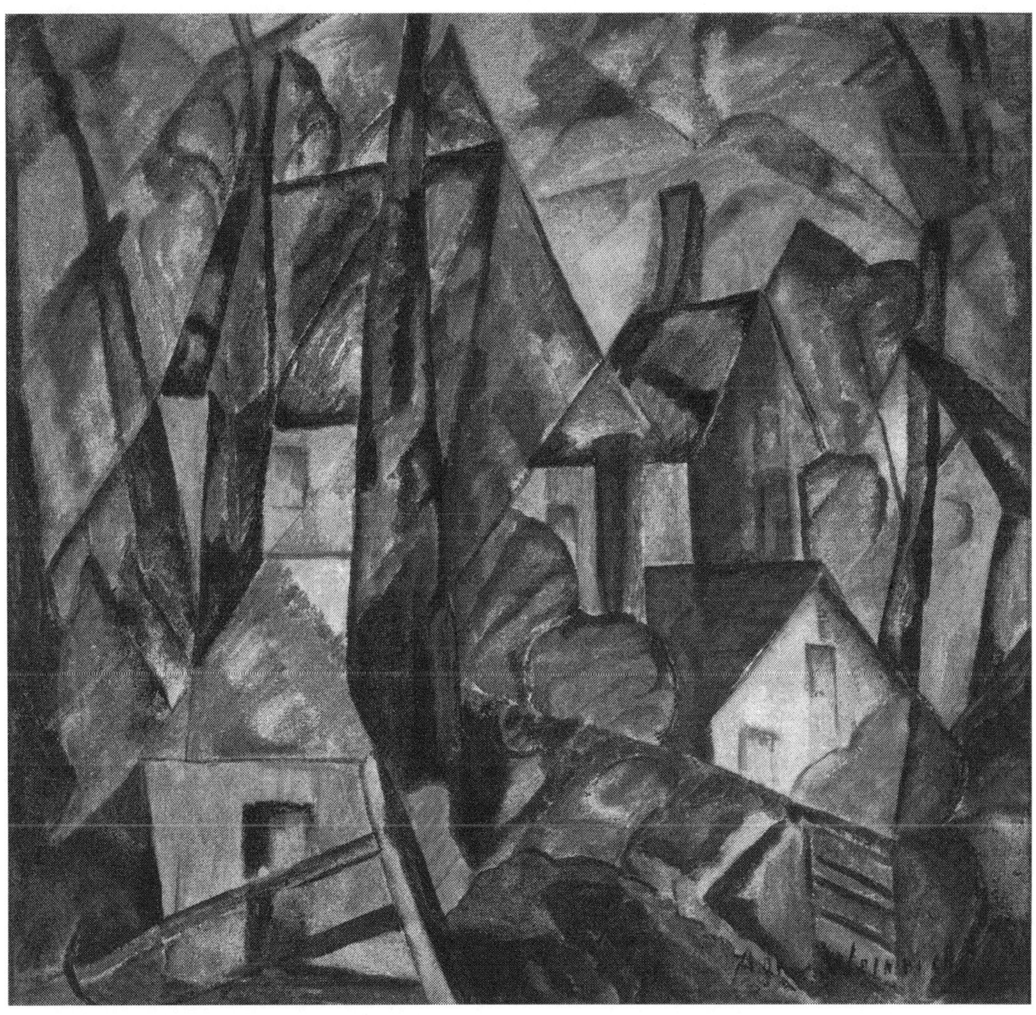

Painting by Weinrich, who worked in a cubist style.

Banker Ken Demaris, Executor of the Knaths' Estate

The estate of Karl Knaths was managed by Ken Demaris. Initially, he worked with Alexander Rosenberg, the son of Paul Rosenberg, the dealer for Knaths from the 1940s. During his lifetime, the norm for Knaths was to sell 15 to 20 paintings a year through the gallery. In the five years after his death in 1971, the gallery made 30 to 40 or so sales. The bank decided to end the relationship and call back the paintings. The focus was to sell off the paintings to create assets for two trusts: one for the widow, Helen, and the other for their heirs. Demaris made efforts to sell in bulk to galleries. That never happened. The bank sold to a number of individuals, then sold 120 or so works to the private dealer Ed Shein. A number of those works were then donated to the Danforth Museum and to Brockton Art Museum. The latter is now Fuller Craft Museum, which no longer exhibits the fine arts.

Interview with Ken Demaris By Phone: August 16, 1983 Trust Officer, Shawmut Bank, Orleans, Massachusetts

Charles Giuliano I would like to obtain whatever materials you have regarding the estate of Karl Knaths.

Ken Demaris We have given all of the data to Bob Brown of the Archives of American Art (a research center within the Smithsonian Institution). We have settled the estate and that information would now be in our own archives. Our materials have been transferred in trust three to four years ago. All of the paintings are gone. The last were sold to Ed Shein. Knaths was handled for many years by Rosenberg, and we had been working with Alexander Rosenberg.

The will was probated in the Barnstable County Court House. The death certificate is on file at Provincetown Town Hall. What you would be looking for is the Federal tax return which would include all assets, including paintings.

CG Other than Knaths, who bought from the estate? What did Reggie Cabral buy?

KD Cabral bought one or two paintings and some scraps (in trunks), works on paper. When Knaths worked, it was usual for him to make a number of tracings of a drawing before it was transferred to a painting. He called them pencil or pen prints. He produced these items a number of times before making an actual painting. In his studio was a drawer with a hundred or so of these items. Cabral bought them for $1,000.

CG It's said that he has notebooks and drawings.

KD No, just drawings. The notebooks were given to the Archives of American Art, about 50 of them or perhaps less. They contained his philosophical writings, as well as notations, which he kept in sketchbooks.

CG So no pages were taken from them?

KD No, they were kept intact.

CG Cabral has none of that material?

KD No, just scraps. Talk to Shein about this, and he'll tell you that Cabral has nothing of importance. There was nothing worth buying from Cabral.

CG What did Nat Halper buy from the estate?

KD He bought five or six watercolors and one or two paintings. He was a shrewd man.

CG He bought the self portrait.

KD That's not a very good painting.

CG Halper also bought monotypes, are you confusing them with watercolors?

KD Negative. No, wait a minute, they may have been monotypes. Why do you ask these questions when you already know so much about it?

CG In Halper's case, he showed me what he had and referred to some work on consignment in New York. Because he passed away a couple of months ago, I have no way to confirm what he owned. I am trying to be accurate about what was in the estate and where it has gone. That's ever more difficult as work gets further dispersed. A number of works, through Shein, have been donated to the Brockton Art Museum (now Fuller Craft Museum) and Danforth Museum. It is important to establish their provenance. Did Jim and Jean Young buy from the estate?

KD They bought a couple of paintings and some ink drawings. They knew him and even bought some of the furniture. They bought work directly from him.

(Shein sold 40 paintings to the Youngs.)

CG Who got the painting *Moby Dick*?

KD That was purchased by an individual from New York who leased it to the Sullivan Brothers. They have it in their office in a stainless-steel frame. The individual bought five paintings, but I don't recall his name as that was about ten years ago, when we first got the estate. I would like to know what all this has to do with art history? You should catalog the paintings, but why are you bothering to find out who bought drawings? They were not important to Knaths. The paintings were. The drawings were mostly done when Agnes Weinrich was around. He never thought much of them. Tirca Karlis, who knew Knaths, asked him for drawings to sell in her gallery. He liked her and let her have them, but he wasn't proud of them. There were 181 pieces in the estate, of which 90 per cent were paintings. The Rosenberg Gallery sold 30 or so paintings when they managed the estate. About 50–60 paintings went to other individuals.

CG Isn't it normal for a gallery to handle an artist's estate? What was behind the decision to terminate the relationship with Rosenberg Gallery?

KD It was a business decision rather than an aesthetic one. During his lifetime,

Knaths sold 15–20 paintings each year. In the five years after his death, Rosenberg just sold 20 odd paintings. The decision was made to liquidate the holdings and make income producing assets. His widow (Helen) survived him by seven years.

CG Had he provided for her, and was she comfortable in those years?

KD Yes, he had provided for her.

CG What happened to the assets when she died?

KD That's a private matter and I will not discuss the trust. It went to individuals in Iowa.

CG Knaths was from Wisconsin.

KD Her family was from Iowa, his were bakers from Wisconsin. I knew Knaths for about five years before he died. He was a very private man. Sorry, but I have to get back to work.

Interview August 18, 1983
At the bank

CG How did Knaths bring his affairs to the bank?

KD In 1969, I was going through various accounts with the bank manager in Provincetown. At that time, Karl had a lot of money in a checking account which was not interest bearing. On that basis, I went to talk about it. I discussed that he had many assets that had been sold to him that didn't parallel what his objectives were. He had mutual funds that a stockbroker sold to him. He was accruing capital gains and paying taxes on them. His cash flow was poor. He felt he had to sell so many paintings a year to cover that, which was ridiculous. He could have taken that money, which he did, and invested it in stocks and bonds which were income producing.

CG So he had poor investment advice, and the gallery was not assisting in that.

KD Precisely.

CD If that's 1969, Karl would have been in his 70s.

KD He died in 1971 at 77.

CG What was his financial status at that time

KD Karl didn't feel that he was a wealthy man, but I proved to him that he was. At that time, he may have had $500,000, but didn't realize it. That included their home in Provincetown, as well as 200 acres of farmland in Des Moines, Iowa. He had $70,000 in a checking account, and $100,000 in mutual funds. If you add to that the value of his paintings, we are managing close to $1 million for his accounts.

CG He always conveyed the impression of being humble and poor.

KD When we signed the trust agreement, I offered to take Karl and his wife out to dinner. He came but his wife couldn't. He was proud because his wife had gotten him a new jacket for Christmas. He ordered the cheapest meal on the menu. He ordered a beer, which he liked. He drank it during the meal. At that point Karl felt that I had advised him properly. He was comfortable to have established two trusts, one for his wife, and the other for their family.

CG Did he have surviving relatives?

KD He had a cousin and heir Francis Dunn who lives in Washington, D.C. She (Helen) had relatives in Iowa.

There was a change of policy on the part of management of the gallery. It was the practice of Paul Rosenberg to seek talent and invite representation. Karl said that he was invited. When his (Rosenberg's) son Alexander took over, the emphasis was on Picasso and the Europeans. He may have sold ten paintings a year by Knaths and got $7,000 each for them. He made a third commission and may have made $20,000. For the sale of a single Picasso, he could make $100,000. The son deviated from the practice of his father, but honored relationships his father had established. I had several meetings with Alexander Rosenberg.

CG Did you meet Paul?

KD He was out of the picture, and I only dealt with Alexander. He was kind and receptive and articulate about Karl's work. When Helen died in 1978, the position changed from her being the primary beneficiary to others. The paintings, being a substantial part of the trust, we had to change it to income producing. We made the decision to sell all of the works. We tried to get Alexander and other individuals to buy them.

CG Did Karl get a stipend from the gallery?

KD Negative, he just got commission from sales.

CG The gallery sold about 15 paintings a year. He also sold out of the studio, work that had been rejected by the gallery.

KD I wouldn't say he made a lot of private sales. He would not consign the work to local galleries because of his contract with Rosenberg. He did consign a few to Tirca Karlis, but primarily drawings. There was also consignment to a dealer in Wellfleet, whose name I have forgotten. He had a few works.

CG You say that 181 paintings were returned by Rosenberg.

KD (shuffling through papers)

CG Forty-four paintings in Massachusetts. What does that mean?

KD And 194 in New York. We had to contend with two states for tax purposes. In Massachusetts that includes those in his home and on consignment to Wellfleet Art Gallery: two oils, four ink drawings, and one watercolor, *Tom Gaglione*. In his home, he had 38 works including oils, watercolors, and drawings. Then he had 194 works in New York. The earliest was *Johnny Appleseed* from 1941 through works from 1970.

CG Was there an attempt to determine how many works he created in his lifetime?

KD I attempted to do that based on 20 sales a year for 25 years. In addition to that were roughly 200 in the estate. You mentioned 181, but I think that was for the oil paintings. In total he had 238 paintings in the estate. That includes ink drawings and watercolors as well as oil paintings. All that material has been liquidated.

CG How did the bank feel about getting into the art business?

KD I found it very interesting. I made the decision at the time. Looking at sales of the work, based on costs for the estate, and whether we should get into the business of holding them, just as we had gotten into holding the Iowa real estate. The reason being that we looked at these as growth-potential assets. In Helen's estate, the real estate was valued at $250,000. It's now worth $650,000. It has appreciated $400,000 since 1978. That's just in five years. With the works of art, we didn't do as well, but we did well. We don't have a composite figure for what the paintings were sold for on average. We sold many of them for $3,500 each and the bulk of them the last time for $1,800 each.

CG Ed Shein told me that he bought 125 paintings from you at $1,800 each. He sold them for $2,400 each over a period of three years.

KD That's probably true. We tried to sell the best works through Rosenberg from 1971 to 1979 or 1980. In that period, he (Alexander) sold 30 paintings at good prices. The most he got was $7,500 for *Clam Diggers* in 1972. In 1971, he sold one for $3,500; 1972, $4,000; 1975, $6,500. The highest I got for an individual sale was $6,000. Initially, we sold 35 paintings to Shein for $3,500 each.

Simons was the guy who bought *Moby Dick* and five or six other paintings. Then we went into committee to decide whether or not to stay in the art business. Rosenberg wasn't promoting the artist, so the issue was whether we would spend money on marketing. The decision was made not to and to get out of the art business. At the time, we researched every major art gallery in Massachusetts.

At that point we looked at the economics. Let's assume that we had a request to go international with the artist. Assume that there were left some hundred paintings that we could get $3,000 for. Over ten years we could make $300,000. It's going to cost some $100,000 for promotion and the value of that money. When you discount the cost of promotion, the price per painting is more like $1,500 each. For us to sell paintings for $1,800 each seemed like a coup.

CG So you were making $300 each over your best estimate? On that basis it was a shrewd move.

KD In my opinion, yes.

CG On the back of paintings that Shein was selling were Rosenberg labels with prices in the range from $5,000 to $10,000.

KD Exactly. That's pure pie in the sky. When you have a hundred paintings on a wholesale basis, then obviously you are not going to sell for retail prices. If you are willing to wait, then fine. We waited for ten years and still weren't successful in selling half of our holdings through the gallery that had been predominant in his career. We were reluctant to toss over that relationship. We approached other galleries but were not interested in consignment and they were not interested in purchase.

CG How did Shein become involved?

KD He contacted me and looked at slides of all the paintings. He negotiated to buy 35 paintings. They were some of the best available works just a year or two after the death of the artist. I think we got $100,000 from him at that point. In the last deal with Ed, he bought all the remaining paintings.

CG What were you asking for works on paper?

KD From $1,000 to $1,500 for a watercolor and $500 for ink drawings. I made 42 sales with $3,630 the average price for an oil painting and $658 for a watercolor with the average ink drawing for $327. We started out with 194 of 238. 194 were in New York, and 44 in Massachusetts. We made 10 bequests, and I sold 42, making $102,000 on those sales. When Helen died in 1978, I had 173 oils and three watercolors.

CG Other than their families, were there other beneficiaries of the estate?

KD Upon the death of Helen's cousins, the Chicago Art Institute and the Phillips Museum are the remainder beneficiaries of the trust. He is giving back what they gave to him.

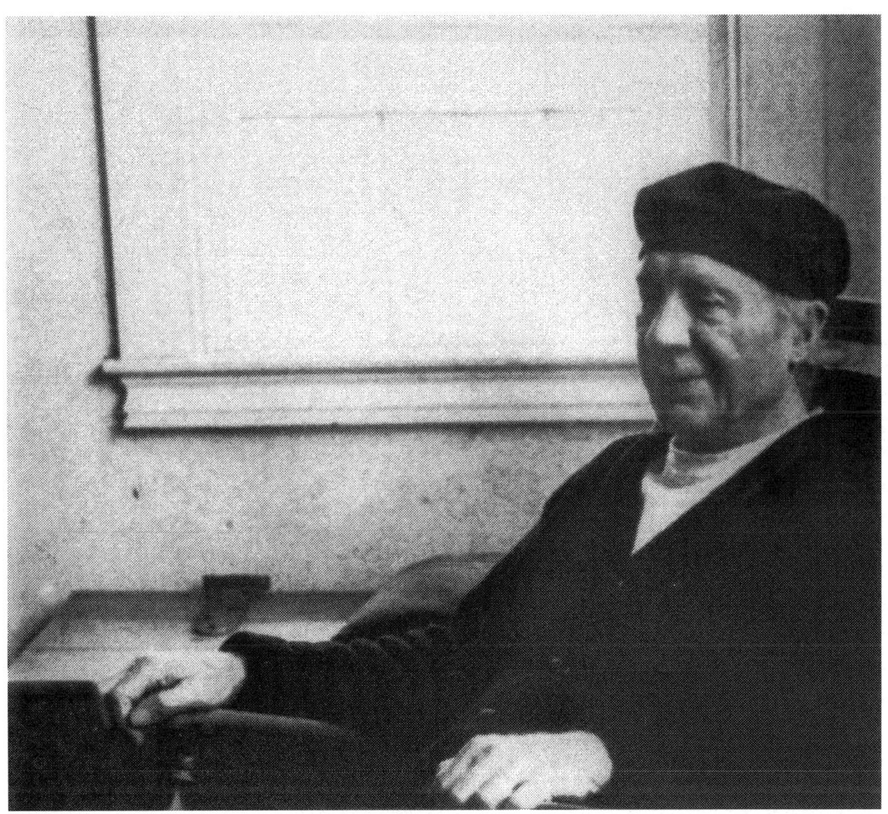

The bank managed the estate of Knaths. Courtesy of PAAM.

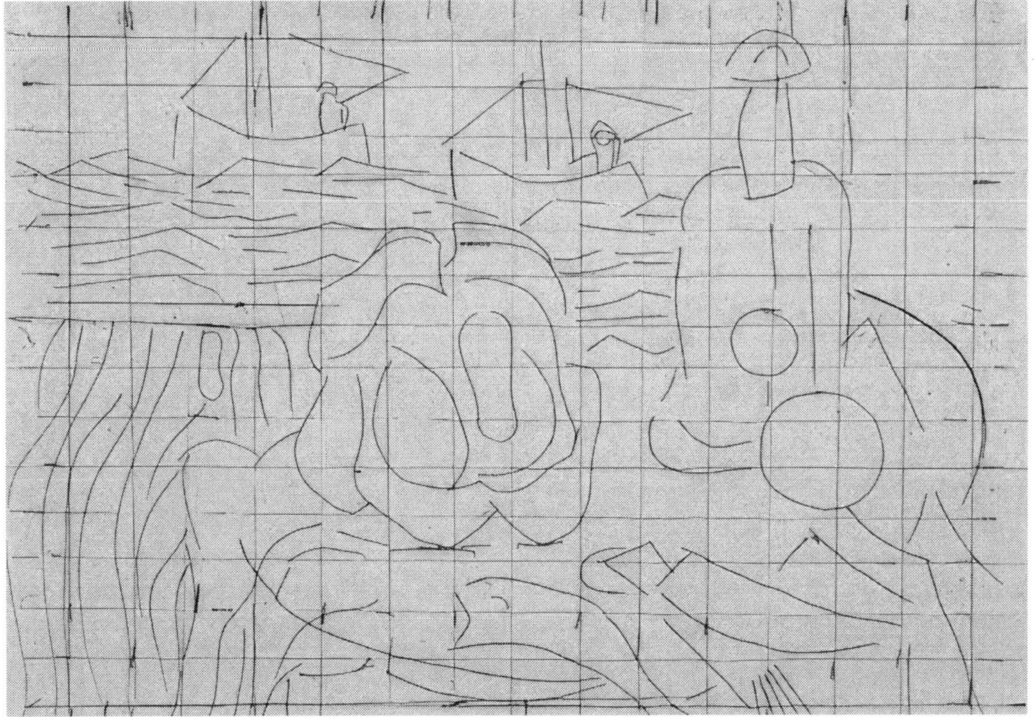

A grid drawing by Knaths was included in the estate.

White Line Printmaker Ferol Sibley Warthen

Ferol Katherine Sibley Warthen (1890–1986), also known as Mrs. Lee R. Warthen, was an American painter and printmaker. Warthen was born Ferol Sibley in Aberdeen, South Dakota. She received a full scholarship to the Columbia Art School in Ohio, which she attended from 1908 until 1910. From 1911 until 1913, she was a student of William Merritt Chase and Kenneth Hayes Miller at the Art Students League of New York, and she received her bachelor's degree in education from Ohio State University.

She studied with Karl Knaths during his annual, six-week courses at the Phillips Museum in Washington, D.C. With a neighbor, Angie Myrer, who also studied with Knaths, she occasionally interacted with the reclusive artist in Provincetown. When she spoke with me in 1982 at the age of 92, she explained the complex color system that she learned from Knaths. Her works, particularly the white line Provincetown Prints, are admired and collected.

Interview with Ferol Sibley Warthen August 1, 1982 In her studio in Provincetown

Charles Giuliano What can you tell me about Karl Knaths?

Ferol Sibley Warthen I studied with him. He was our best artist. Off and on I saw him in Provincetown, but I studied with him in D.C. at the Phillips Museum. He came, I think in 1938, (1938 to 1950) and taught six weeks at a time. Prior to that, I knew of him by coming to Provincetown. Angie Myrer and I had been friends, and she came to Washington to study with Karl. In Provincetown, she and I visited him from time-to-time. He didn't teach here.

(Angie Myrer was the mother of the novelist Anton Myrer, who was married to the artist Judith Rothschild. The three were involved in plans to publish Knaths' treatise *Ornament and Glory.* They approached Ken Demaris, executor of the Knaths estate, for funding, which was denied. Nothing came of the plans.)

I have been coming to this spot on Commercial Street since 1950.

CG May I ask how old you are?

FSW Ninety-two. I've had good health. I'm still active, and here are some of my prints. These are the woodblocks. In 1930, I studied woodblock printing with Blanche Lazzell.

CG Did you do monotypes?

FSW No, but I wanted to.

CG What was Knath's teaching method?

FSW He introduced you to the color wheel. From that he taught us to make color chords, as in music, with intervals. To make a color chord you had one key color and then take a third as an interval or you might take fifths.

(She went to find a chart) You see these are the three colors (demonstrating dial and wheel). Analogous colors relate. While this and this (pointing across the wheel) are the opposite. This and this, they all have their opposites.

CG I see that the first number is a large triangle with yellow. The next large triangle, five, is orange, the next, nine, is violet. Thirteen is blue and 17, turquoise, 21, green. Within these major triangles are minor ones.

FSW That's the Ostwald color system, but I didn't bring the color charts from Washington. I have the whole set of color tiles (This entails individual swatches of specific colors, such as you would find researching colors in a hardware store. This allows the artist to mix and match colors precisely.)

CG (referring to work in the studio) Are these studies that you made with Knaths?

FSW These are just studies. Here's the idea. Select a key color and use this wheel. You can change and have another key color. Take a yellow and the opposite of that is blue. But it wasn't always considered to be the most harmonious. So, you would go to the adjacent color. These were triadic intervals, which were useful, and you could use all the colors all the way around.

CG In his notebooks we see numbers.

FSW They were all numbered. He knew the colors by numbers. If you knew the numbers, you knew what colors he used. This is a chart I made, and these were the chips.

CG It says 6 PELE. What does that mean?

FSW It would be the 6th color on the triangle of depths of color. Sorry, I don't have the Ostwald chart which explains it. It would be a dark color, which could be dark or light. Here would be your intervals.

CG Can you explain them to me?

FSW I'm not very good at remembering and explaining all of this.

The bright, intense color is on the edge of the wheel. That P & G would be taken down to dark with white on the top and all the colors in between. That's the range. This is the same thing, only a different-sized wheel.

CG Can you explain what we're looking at. It's dated March 1943.

FSW This is a triadic interval, apparently, and this is the yellow and the opposite. He built this connection with the yellow, and with this connection here to show the light—the dark red and the interval of yellow-orange. Then he used the numbers on the wheel.

CG So this is how he worked out the colors in his paintings. Bob Brown (Archives of American Art) told me that he had a large chart in the studio.

FSW It could have been the wheel, or anything based on it. The intervals were important to him.

CG I am looking at a drawing marked *Ferol, project 3, 1943, Violin Study.* I notice two superimposed triangles. How did you derive the colors you put on here? Do they match the Ostwald chart? Is that how you did it?

FSW It would be based on the wheel. Shall we say that's 2, 6, 7, 8, 10, 11 and two over here it's 16. Then you skipped all of these. You didn't need those.

CG This color 16 looks different from that 16.

FSW You might say we used them as symbols. That's a very dark blue. On this chart PL was almost black.

CG The numbers then are 1 to 24 on the chart.

FSW That's right. The letters are the intermediate colors.

CG In other words, between the numbers and the letters, you could go to the chart and figure out the colors in a painting.

FSW Yes, you only need the number and the letter.

CG In the notebooks, you see page after page of numbers and letters. Until now, they completely confused me. According to what you say, they are color schemes for paintings.

FSW Yes, I think so. Was there anything else on the page?

CG Sometimes a crude sketch as well as numbers and letters.

FSW That was enough for him. Then he mixed the color in clam shells according to his number.

CG Did he discuss the aesthetics of certain combinations? How do you choose the dominant color?

FSW You have enough ingenuity to make your choice.

CG Sometimes the combinations are strange and have nothing to do with local color or the landscape.

FSW They didn't need to.

CG You could have a purple sky or green moon.

FSW Sure, that's painting. He wasn't matching nature.

CG In other words it was combinations of color that interested him. Did he ever discuss Swedenborg and philosophies?

FSW He asked us to read it, but I didn't do more than dip into it. He was spiritual in his thinking. I don't remember much. My mind doesn't work that way.

CG Did he teach you to grid the paintings?

FSW No.

CG You see the structure and underlying lines over and over in the work.

FSW It's mathematical, proportional areas. It's up to you to study them out.

CG Did he teach anything about that?

FSW No, not much. You might say, it was our own choice. I got into that later, when I was in Washington. I got into cubism and studied Juan Gris.

CG What was Knaths like as a teacher and a man?

FSW We thought he was good. You know there was a lot of criticism about him. I always thought he was the best American painter. They thought he was too free in his paintings. He was a free painter, but to him it was logical.

CG Did the work seem logical to you?

FSW Yes, I think so. I would have liked to paint like Knaths, but you know, you don't paint like somebody. What I mainly got from him was color and some compositions which I worked out, but mainly it was color.

CG Did you find his system useful?

FSW It was for me.

CG They were short, six-week semesters.

FSW I lived in Washington and he had been there a year when I went to the Phillips. I had seen his painting of a rooster in a box. I liked it so much I thought I might study with him. Which I did, fortunately. In 1949, when my husband died, I came here. 1950 was the year when I studied with Blanche Lazzell.

CG Do you have family?

FSW One daughter and three grandchildren.

CG Did you socialize with him?

FSW Oh yes, we knew him. My friend Angie lived over there, and he would come in. He came to see Angie more than he ever came to see me. He was a longtime member of the Art Association and knew other artists and was part of the community. He knew what he wanted to do and progressed into it.

CG Did you know Hans Hofmann?

FSW I went to some of his Friday or Saturday lectures.

CG Was Knaths more of an influence than Hofmann?

FSW I was more logical. I was thinking.

CG So Knaths was more logical?

FSW As you are with music, with composition, he was in painting. It's a way of thinking. He was unique. I think he had more or less of a struggle. At that time, people didn't want to do anything with rules and regulations. Such as, I would say, Hofmann. His method and teaching were different. He was more free.

CG Did you know Milton Avery?

FSW Knaths liked him a lot. I only met Milton once.

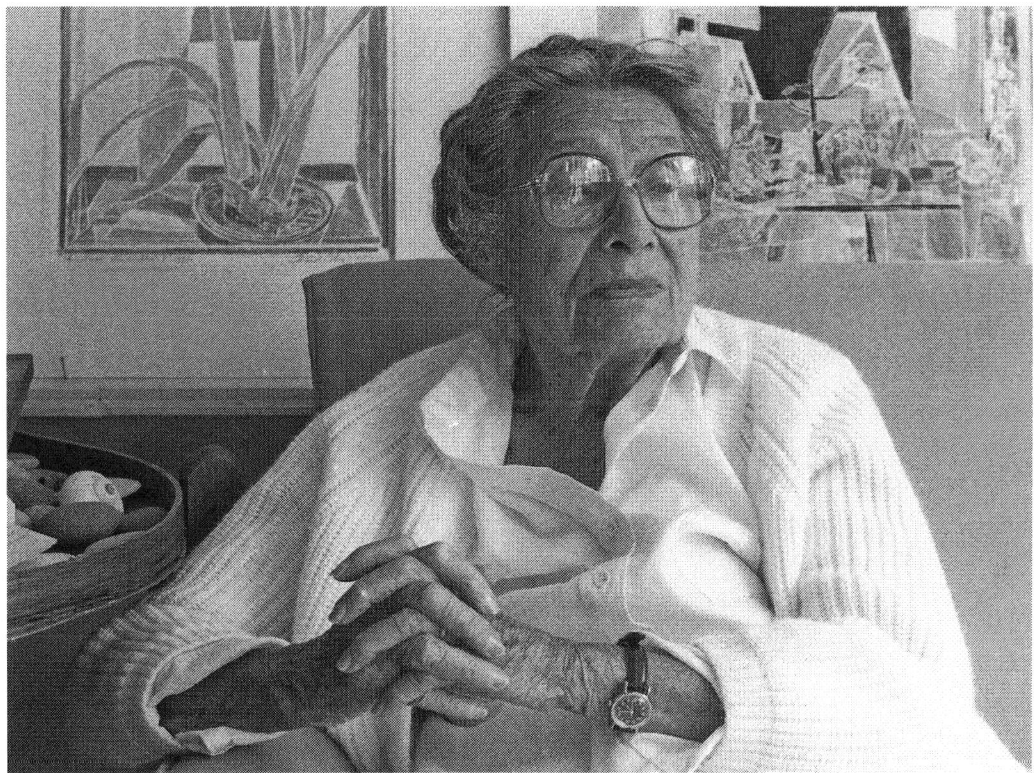

Ferol K. Sibley Warthen (1890–1986). Giuliano photo.

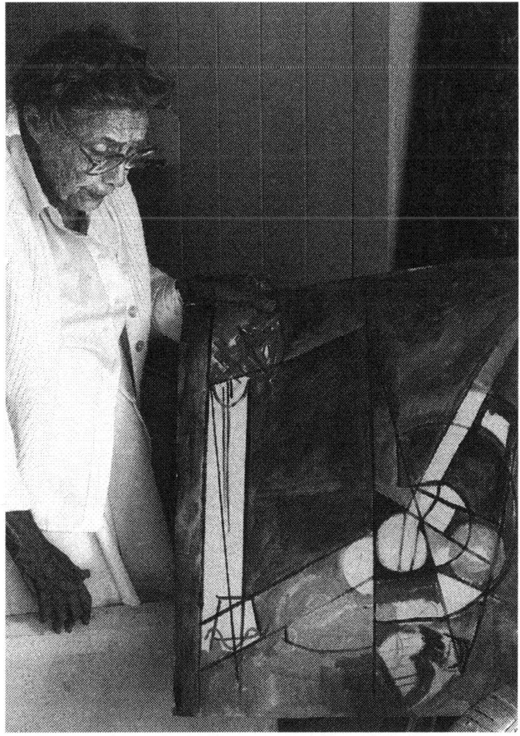

Ferol showing one of her paintings.

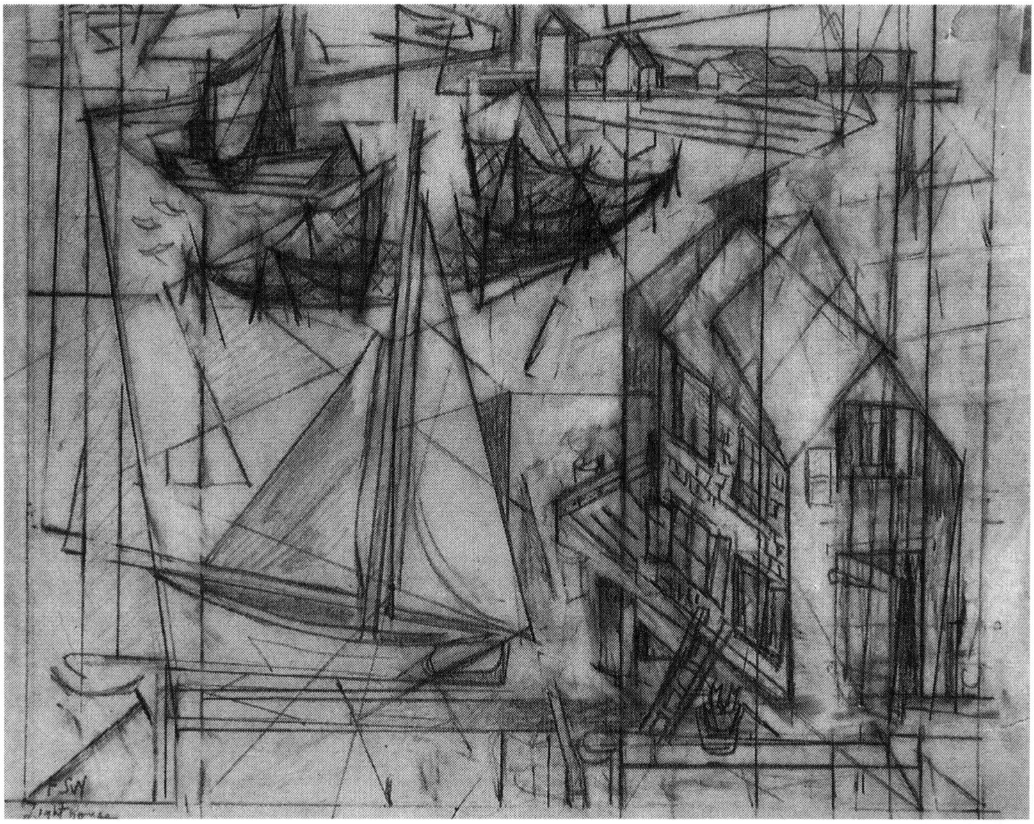

Sketch for *Light House.*

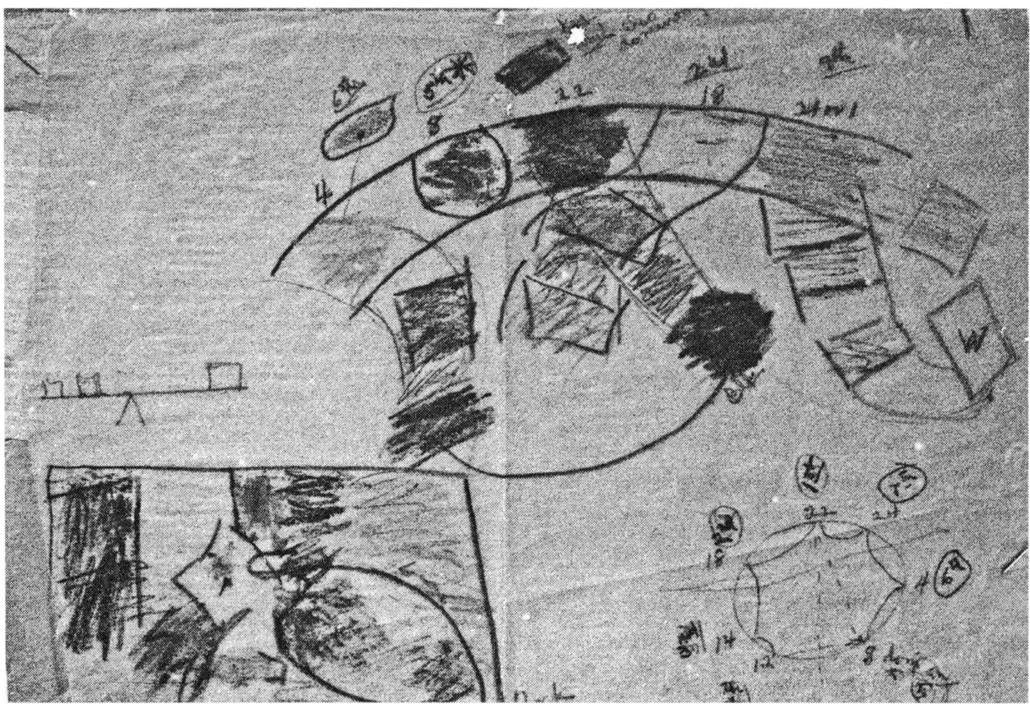

Color chart for *Duck Decoys.*

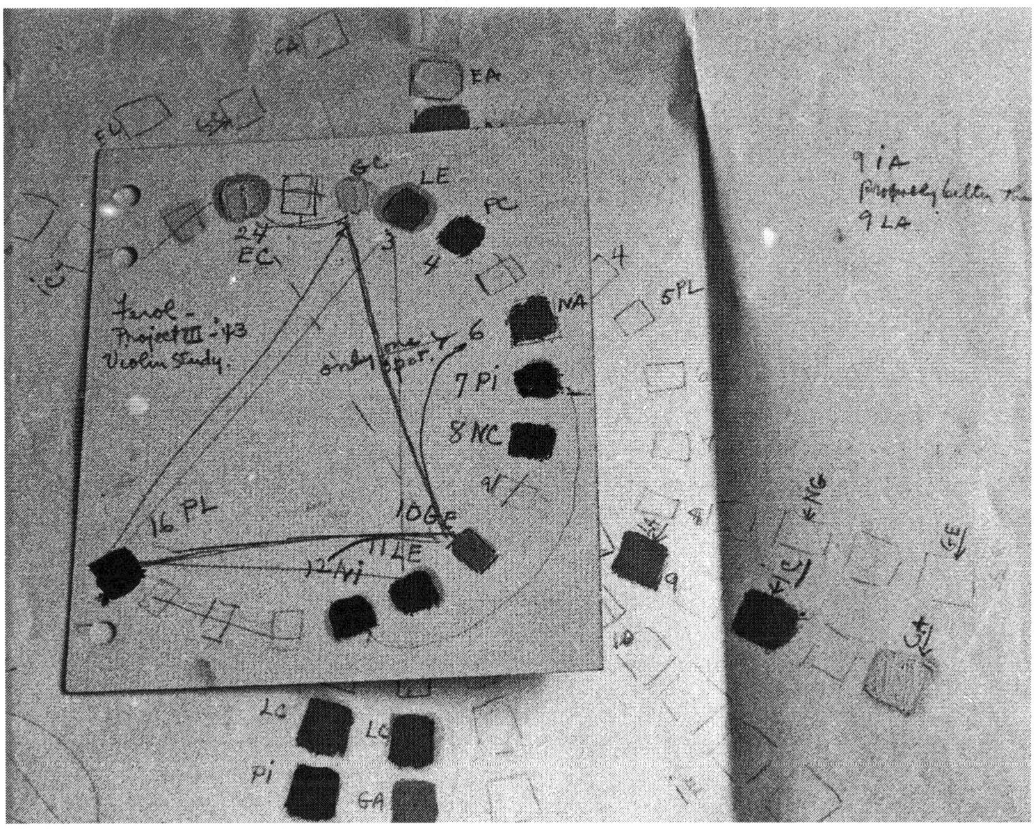

Color chart for *Violiin*, 1943.

Nathan Halper, a Joyce Scholar, Collector, Curator, and Director of Historic HCE Gallery

Ellen O'Donnell, then director of the Provincetown Art Association, was in high season when I arrived for interviews. She was too busy to talk at that time, but introduced me to Nat Halper who proved to be my first contact. We met at PAAM in the main gallery and sat on a bench.

What follows is an excerpt from the *New York Times* obituary.

"Dr. Nathan Halper, a writer and authority on James Joyce, died June 26, (1983)... He was 75 years old and lived in Provincetown, Massachusetts and Manhattan.

"Dr. Halper wrote for many publications that specialized in Joyce and was a contributor and advisory editor of *The James Joyce Quarterly,* published by the University of Oklahoma. He also contributed to such magazines as *Partisan Review, Commentary* and *The Nation*. His most recent work, *Studies in Joyce,* is scheduled to be published this fall by University Microfilms International of Ann Arbor, Michigan.

Dr. Halper was co-chairman of the Second Provincetown James Joyce Symposium, held last month under the sponsorship of the Provincetown Art Association and Museum and several Joyce organizations.

"He was born in Manhattan and graduated from Columbia University, where he also received his doctoral degree."

Interview with Nathan Halper
August 1982
Provincetown, Massachusetts

Nathan Halper I'm one of the trustees here. I'm the one who has known the affairs of PAAM and this town longer than anyone. I'm the antiquarian and have had my finger in the pie. I still do to some degree. I used to have a gallery here (HCE) for 15 years.

Charles Giuliano What can you tell me about Karl Knaths (1891–1971)?

NH There is an artist, Ross Moffett, who painted a portrait of Knaths when he first came here somewhere between 1915 and 1919. Ross Moffett was more or less his age. The picture depicted him as an apple-cheeked boy from Wisconsin. The painting may be owned by Moffett's daughter who lives on The Cape. We've been trying to get her to give it to us.

There was a small Knaths show of mostly drawings and monotypes at Barbara Fiedler Gallery which is opposite the Phillips Museum. I sent a small self-portrait that I own and asked her to loan her portrait. So both were shown.

CG What do you own of Knaths?

NH I have a late 1967 self-portrait. It's much wilder than his usual work. Although you can see the grid, the color is much more fauvist and the drawing is expressionist. It's wild.

CG What do you know about the grid? Usually there is a center point then radiating lines.

NH I'm not an artist, so what I have heard is second hand. I've seen paintings he's done in different forms. At some point he got a theory of design and color based on the Golden Section. He mixed color in clam shells. You can see the clam shells in the self-portrait I have. He mixed small quantities of paint and put one at each intersection, just a little drop. He then determined the color scheme. There would be some form of progression or design. They didn't usually go far from each other, which is why the paintings often look soft and pastel like.

CG The late paintings are different. There's less detail and they're flatter. When did you meet him?

NH When I first came, there were the Weinrich sisters. The older one, Agnes, was a very good painter. As an artist, at the time, she was more advanced than Knaths. They had been to Europe and of the artists here at the time, they knew more about the outside world. Karl was learning things from her. Everyone speculated that he would marry her, but he ended up with Helen, a pianist.

Agnes was strong minded where Helen was a bit of an invalid. She lived to be more than a hundred and was, at the time, Provincetown's oldest citizen.

In those early years Knaths was a rebel. He teamed with Ross Moffett and Edwin Dickenson. In the 1920s they were the town's leading rebels. Earlier, the town was full of academicians. Charles Hawthorne (1872–1930) was considered to be a rebel within the academicians. The National Arts Club (Gramercy Park, New York, of which I am a long-standing member) considered him to be as wild as you can get. He had the concept of painting in color. When Hans Hofmann (1880–1966) arrived, he very much admired Hawthorne's paintings. There are writings that document that. So, when new artists painted in a manner inspired by the Armory Show (Knaths) locally, they were considered to be terrible. There were enough of them that there were big fights in the Art Association, and it evolved into having two juries for exhibitions. Sometimes that resulted in having two different shows. That meant a modern show and traditional one. The modern show would have artists like Knaths and Dickenson.

CG Weren't some of the early modern shows organized by Knaths and Weinrich?

NH If you look through the early catalogs you will see one or the other of them on the jury.

CG So they were part of the new art scene.

NH That makes it sound more earth shattering than it was. It was just a tempest in a tea pot. They were chosen as jurors so often that they became the old guard. That changed in the 1940s when, as a group, the abstract expressionists came here. Some came during the war.

CG When did Hans Hofmann come?

NH He was here in the 1930s. He had a studio in Day's Lumber Yard (now the Fine Arts Work Center). His school was where Hawthorne's originally was. He and his students were regarded as lunatics by the locals. An artist told me that when he first came, he didn't have the courage to say that he studied with Hofmann because people would think that he was nuts. Hofmann didn't come into his own until after the war. The GI Bill sent students to him from all over the country. His winter school was on 8th Street. He bought the large house of Frederick Waugh. He lived there and used the studio for teaching. He himself painted where the Fine Arts Work Center now is. I don't know if Knaths approved of him. The colors were so violent.

CG In the Knaths files of Archives of American Art there are transcripts of several Hofmann lectures.

NH There are lots of things floating about. Reggie Cabral bought things from the Knaths estate. That included a trunk full of things. I saw a couple of notebooks where he listed what he considered to be the good painters.

Reggie Cabral owns the A House. He became interested in art when he married a painter. Of native Portuguese heritage, he became interested in the history of this art and acquired whatever documentation he could. You never know what kind of a mood he's in. He may show you the Knaths material.

(Cabral played cat and mouse then blew off an appointment to see his collection. Arguing that he knew more about art than I did he said, "Jackson Pollock drank at my bar.")

CG Does he still have the Knaths material?

NH I know he does, but probably hasn't looked at all of it. Much of the material included unframed drawings (Torn from notebooks by bank executor Ken Demaris.) He showed me a notebook of great artists with Knaths' name attached. It may have been an afterthought by Knaths who considered himself in their tradition. John Marin was one, but none of the abstract expressionists were included.

CG What did the abstract expressionists think of him?

NH Take someone like Adolph Gottlieb. He started as a traditional painter and respected technique. He knew his business like you might say about a carpenter. They considered Knaths to be old fashioned. More recently I heard Motherwell sniff about "those grids." They felt that they had freedom that guys like Knaths did not, that he was too confined by theory. One of the older artists who they all respected was Milton Avery. They felt that he was the best of two worlds. He worked their way although there were scenes with one mass of color against another mass of color. The abstract expressionists didn't want anyone else in their galleries. But they would tell the gallerists to "Get Milton Avery, we'll show with him."

One night Motherwell, Helen Frankenthaler, David Smith, and Kenneth Noland came into my gallery and said, "We want to see the Avery pictures." Frankenthaler said, "Tell Mrs. Avery that she can have any picture of mine for this painting." She was full of arrogance, but Sally Avery responded, "nothing doing." The wives are generally more arrogant than the artists, particularly the widows.

CG What do you know about the Knaths estate?

NH When he died Helen was still alive and I don't know if he had organized his estate. Several years before he died, he was asking me what had been done with the Milton Avery estate. There had been all kinds of problems with the Avery estate. Helen was not an active person, and he couldn't leave it in her charge. I got the impression that he anticipated dying fairly soon. So, he made an arrangement with the bank that they would take the estate when he died. The First National Bank, later Shawmut, became the trustees under the vice president, Ken Demaris. They wanted to get rid of the paintings, which they regarded as a damn nuisance and something they knew nothing about.

CG How many works were there?

NH They had some works from the studio and more things came back from the Rosenberg Gallery. Bob Brown from the Boston branch of Archives of American Art came to me to make tapes. At one point he was late and apologized saying, "I was in Orleans looking into the Karl Knaths estate." I asked if they had anything left. He said, "Yes, some monotypes." Mervin Jules, the retired head of the art department of City College, and I went to see what they had. We bought one painting, *Self-Portrait.* as well as all the monotypes, one watercolor, and 13 or 14 drawings. We became partners, though I hadn't been in the art business for years.

CG Do you still have that material?

NH A lot, although we sold a couple of monotypes. There were other paintings, and a man from Providence (Ed Shein) bought a number. He was a dealer without a gallery. He had clients and knew or advised on what they were looking for. He bought about 45 paintings, sold them, and then went back for more. He bought what was left, so perhaps a hundred paintings. Jean Young had come and gotten a bit of everything. I think there were Weinrichs in the estate which they inherited from Agnes.

Right now, we're looking for Weinrichs because the Smithsonian is going to have a show of Provincetown woodblock White Line prints in August 1983. It will open here then travel with a catalog. So, we're looking for Weinrichs.

(Bror Julius Olsson Nordfeldt (1878–1955) developed a technique for creating multi-colored prints entailing a single block. The designs were hand inked leaving a white line. This approach was adapted by a number of Provincetown artists.)

CG Are they hard to find?

NH Yes, compared to Blanche Lazzell who was one of many women artists here. I think we can find six to ten prints by Weinrich. Jim Young acquired a wonderful Weinrich painting which hung in Knaths' home. The Youngs had a show at Everson Museum.

(*Karl Knaths 1891–1971: Works on Paper 1919–1930,* Forward by Ronald Kuchta, catalog and text by Jean Young and Jim Young, illustrated, unpaginated, Everson Museum of Art, Woodstock Publishers, 1982.

(That exhibition of some 150 works on paper was offered to Bard College. It was expanded with 22 paintings, 86 works on paper, and six of the artist charts. The Bard curator, Linda Weintraub included illustrations of manuscripts and transcribed texts for his theoretical treatise *Ornament and Glory.*

(*Ornament and Glory, Theme and Theory* in the work of Karl Knaths curated by Jean Young and Jim Young, Edith C Blum Art Institute, Milton and Sally Avery Center for the Arts, Bard College Center, Allendale on Hudson, New York. October 9 to November 21, 1982, 72 pages, illustrated, published by Bard College, 1982)

Ron Kuchta (1935–2020) had been curator for the Chrysler Museum here so he showed Provincetown artists at Everson.

(He curated a major show and catalog for Everson. *Provincetown Painters: 1890s to*

1970s Everson Museum of Art, April 1 to June 26, 1977. He stated in part "...This exhibition pays tribute to Provincetown on its 250th anniversary as a town [it was incorporated in 1777 before which it was a part of Truro, its immediate neighbor to the south, today a much smaller community]. *Provincetown Painters* consists of the works of many artists; some nationally known: Charles Hawthorne, Milton Avery, Marsden Hartley, Charles Demuth, Stuart Davis, Childe Hassam, Ernest Lawson, Ben Shahn, Raphael Soyer, Niles Spencer, William Zorach , Frederick Waugh, Chaim Gross, Karl Knaths, Edwin Dickenson, Hans Hofmann, Robert Motherwell, Adolph Gottlieb, Franz Kline, Red Grooms, etc.)

"Others best known locally, who may deserve to be better known: Ambrose Webster, Mary Cecil Allen , Gerrit Beneker, Oliver Chaffee, Reeves Euler, Henry Hensche, Charles Heinz, Bruce McKain , Phil Malicoat, Blanche Lazzell, Gerrit Hondius, William Freed, Lillian Orlowsky, Nanno De Groot , Arthur Cohen, etc.; and a few anonymous ship painters, completely unknown. Some of these artists have spent only a few summers in Provincetown: Childe Hassam, Marsden Hartley, Jackson Pollock, Lee Krasner, etc.

"Others have spent their entire mature lives, summer and winter in Provincetown: Henry Hensche, Karl Knaths, Bruce McKain, Phil Malicoat, Reeves Euler, Jim Forsberg , Sal Del Deo, Myron Stout, etc.

"Some spent practically all their summers for many years in the Provincetown area: Charles Hawthorne, Edward Hopper, Frederick Waugh , Hans Hofmann, Robert Motherwell, Jack Tworkov, William Freed , Lila Katzen, Alvin Ross, Fritz Bultman, etc.

"And artists came and settled from all over America, Europe, and Japan: Hans Hofmann from Germany, Reeves Euler from Nevada, Edward Corbett from California, Bruce McKain from Indiana, Fritz Bultman from Louisiana, Nanno de Groot from Holland, Xavier Gonzalez from Spain, Taro Yamamoto from Japan, Peter Hutchinson from England, and Nassos Daphnis from Greece."

We thought everything was cleaned out except for a few watercolors and seven or eight paintings. There were a couple of trunks filled with stuff. We should have taken a shot at them. Reggie Cabral came and bought three oils as well as the trunks, which he hasn't gone through yet. We had a Dickenson show and Shein bought a painting for the biggest price of anything we have sold.

CG There seems to be a lot of work around. Was Knaths prolific?

NH He painted for 50 years. The works were returned by his gallery.

CG Would they have been better off with Rosenberg?

NH Not really. Knaths was in decline and the gallery was making few, if any, sales. The estate was selling paintings for a couple thousand dollars. Judging from what they sold to Shein, nothing went for more than $5,000. I'm sure that Shein asked for higher prices.

There were periods when he sold well for good prices, in the late '20s and early '30s. He won a major prize in a show at the Metropolitan Museum for a painting of Lilacs. He had a period of being hot and again in the 1950s. But in those days, prices were low. I sold an Avery for $3,500, and today it would sell for $350,000. Any Avery which I had back then would sell today for 20 to 100 times what we had asked. Even the small print in the PAAM show, which is $2,000, I originally sold for $25. I remember a small Motherwell for $90 that nobody bought.

CG Do you have any of that work?

NH It was on consignment. I did buy, and have, a few Averys.

CG How important was Knaths in the overall scene?

NH He was regarded as one of the Old Masters. He read a lot of mystical stuff (Swedenborg) and would write it out in his notebooks. He was interested in James Joyce.

He would see in it the infinite and sublime.

When I first came here in the 1930s, I got on the WPA Writer's Project. Provincetown was probably the only place in the country that had a joint union of artists and writers. Almost out of necessity they got together. I was secretary and Knaths was one of the members, so we met that way.

We were on social terms and a couple of times he came to the house with his wife. We wanted to reciprocate and 5 p.m. seemed like the right time but it was embarrassing as we caught them in the middle of their supper. Apparently, that was the usual thing for them. He got up early and would paint then take a walk. He wore a white sweatshirt and hat. A lot of the drawings and some of the paintings depict a walking figure.

CG Did you have conversations?

NH Yes, but I kept away from that as my conversation was realistic with practical concerns. His would always be about some damned principle or other. His talk tended to be theoretical, although like many painters, he had practical skills. He built their house for instance.

CG Did he have students?

NH Near where he lived was an old lady, Ferol Warthen, now in her 90s. She and her friend Angie Mira, who is now dead, studied with him. Ferol had some of his watercolors. They were with him a lot. There were several young artists, but they have drifted off. Jim Forsberg, who ran the art store, spent a lot of time with him.

In any artists' organization you have discussions about quantity vs. quality. They are all in the same boat, but somebody is bound to say, "I'm only interested in good painting." The question always is, who is going to decide that? So, there are always going to be fights and arguments and that hasn't changed. Knaths resigned from PAAM at least a half dozen times. A couple of years later he would say, "we're all painters" and come back. It went back and forth all the time.

CG Did you hear him lecture?

NH In 1949 there was Weldon Kees, a poet and jack-of-all-trades. He was a painter, poet, musician, who was into everything. He was an advisor to New Directions, the publishing house. He wrote for the *Partisan Review.* He was associated with the abstract expressionists. He, Adolph Gottlieb, and Gottlieb's cousin, the poet Cecil Hemley, organized something called *Forum '49*. Hemley's father-in law, an art dealer, bought a garage (that became Gallery 200). They organized panels and lectures every Thursday evening and a number of important people participated. Francis Biddle, the Solicitor General, spoke. Gottlieb and Motherwell spoke, as did Knaths. There are no transcripts of the talks, but posters exist that list the events and participants.

CG Do you recall what he said?

NH In my terms I have always found Knaths to be vague. His paintings had grids, but if you asked him about them, he would give you a lot of vague stuff about the Golden Section.

(Knaths used geometry to compose his paintings. They were derived from diagrams in The Elements of Dynamic Symmetry, by Jay Hambidge. His The Diagonal was copyrighted in 1919 and published by Yale University Press in 1920. The system was widely influential. The artist and Harvard professor Denman Ross taught it to his protégées, Hyman Bloom and Jack Levine. It had no lasting influence on Levine, who told me, "It was just something he taught us." There are examples of those exercises in the collection of the Fogg Art Museum.)

CG His responses then were poetic?

NH Yes, but with what I would call pseudo precision, like a lot of mystics will give you.

CG It was well worked out in this mind.

NH Or stuff like the pyramids of Egypt. How they could tell you all kinds of things about the world. They have it all worked out mathematically. If you don't see it that way, it seems like a dream world.

(No doubt Halper is referring to the 19th century work of Charles Piazzi Smyth who with John Taylor theorized in 1859 that the Great Pyramid of Giza was built by the biblical Noah. Smyth went on an expedition to Egypt in order accurately to measure every surface, dimension, and aspect of the Great Pyramid. He measured the dimensions of the stones, the precise angle of sections, such as the descending passage, and photographed both the interior and exterior of the pyramid. He made astronomical calculations and determined the pyramid's accurate latitude and longitude.

Smyth claimed that the measurements from the Great Pyramid indicated a unit of length, the pyramid inch, equivalent to 1.001 British inches that could have been the standard of measurement by the pyramid's architects.

He found the number of inches in the perimeter of the base equaled one hundred times the number of days in a year and found a numeric relationship between the height of the pyramid in inches to the distance from Earth to the Sun, measured in statute miles. He also advanced the theory that the Great Pyramid was a repository of prophecies which could be revealed by detailed measurements of the structure. He conjectured that the Hyksos were the Hebrew people, and that they built the Great Pyramid under the leadership of

Melchizedek. While his theories were debunked, Egyptologists do not dispute the accuracy of his measurements.)

CG In his manuscripts and writings there are a number of signs, figures, and symbols. Is there someone who might explain them to me?

NH You will find people but no doubt they will be talking in the same way that he did. If Reggie Cabral lets you look at the notebooks, you will find things. In his notebooks, for instance, he listed the great paintings, five from antiquity and five from the contemporary scene. That would give you a sense of what he valued in a painting and work from there.

CG He led a simple life. Did he have money and was it a factor?

NH Back then you didn't need to have a lot of money. He built his own home. Back then you could live quite well on $2,000 a year. You could dig for clams and the fishermen often gave artists fresh fish. In the summer he had a vegetable garden. I don't know about his medical expenses or what he spent for paint. I don't know how successful he was in selling work, but prices were low. If he got $1,500 or $600 that was pretty good.

CG Which he had to split with Rosenberg.

NH In those days galleries just took a third. Not like 50 percent and up that's common today. He was in the WPA in the 1930s.

(In her dissertation for Boston University, Edith Tonelli, on the WPA in Massachusetts, discussed murals by Knaths on Cape Cod.)

CG He painted murals for the WPA.

NH I didn't know that as I was involved with the writers and not the artists. You might talk about artists and the WPA with Bruce McKain who is still around from those days.

CG Do you live here year-round?

NH Six months here and six in New York. From 1936–1940 I lived here year-round. Since then, I've spent two more years here year-round.

CG Did you have a gallery in New York?

NH Not after the one I had here (HCE) for two reasons. The kind of space I had here, in New York even in those days, would cost six figures a year. The access to people I had who came here I wouldn't have had in the city. Look at the people I represented here, Milton Avery, Robert Motherwell. One year I had David Smith, and another year Franz Kline, Louise Nevelson. I even had connections to the Marsden Hartley estate.

Let's walk through this show (PAAM) and I'll show you some of the people I represented. (We strolled as he pointed to prints and drawings on display.) Budd Hopkins, George McNeil, Avery, Motherwell, Varujan Boghosian, Nanno de Groot, Wolf Kahn, Jack Tworkov for three years, Hans Hofmann, Nassos Daphnis. I had Adolph Gottlieb for three or four years, Myron Stout, Jim Forsberg, Seong Moy, Lester Johnson, and Leo Manso. Those are some of the people I had.

CG Did you sell work?

NH When I started, the older dealers told me it would take five years to become established. In my fifth year, I finally made about $100. For the next five years I made pretty good money considering that I was only open for ten weeks.

CG Did you make a living from the gallery?

NH Not really but I had other sources of income. For those five good years I made enough money to go to Europe and buy pictures for the gallery, as well as put together a fine collection for myself. I have Knaths, a few Averys, a Frankenthaler, a David Smith drawing. A couple of Dickinson drawings are worth a lot more than I paid for them. In fact, out of the gallery I could make a lot more than I ever did then. I could sell my Avery and do quite well.

CG Are you lending Avery to the upcoming Whitney show?

NH No, but they did a long interview with me. I bought a charcoal by Myron Stout. The Whitney borrowed it for their show. They insured it for $8,000 but I actually paid $66.

CG Things have gone up.

NH Haven't they. If I had spent $25,000 or $2,500 a year over ten years, the value of that collection would be more than $1 million. If you chose well, it was the best investment in the world. I bought a Jan Müller, everyone said he was a good painter. You could get a Müller for $50. I bought one painted on a shingle for $25. I also bought a cheap Lester Johnson.

CG Did you know Bob Thompson?

NH He was around every now and then. I have a few Thompsons. There were all kinds of artists floating around and you could get their work for next to nothing.

CG What did you pay for the Knaths' self-portrait?

NH I know but better not tell you because we have it up for sale at $6000. So, it couldn't have been for much.

CG What's his price range today?

NH That's up in the air because no gallery represents the work. Knaths sells for what traffic will bear. It's scattered around and I don't know what (Ed) Shein gets for a painting. Mervin Jules and I bought the Knaths' self-portraits together. We're ready to keep it indefinitely. Mervin offered to buy my share. It's just a good piece and I have it hanging in my house.

CG Can I take a look at it?

NH Sure. (Walking on Commercial Street toward his house.) It's a period of decline for Knaths because there are cycles. With time people are in complete decline, then they can be hot again and vice versa. I can remember when nobody gave a damn about the Ashcan School. Next year there will be a show of Provincetown's colored woodblock prints. (Multi-colored prints from a single block called White Line Prints.) One of the artists, Blanche Lazzell, a damned good artist, needed money, and I couldn't sell a single print for $100. I had to organize a raffle with people putting in $10 each. Now that same print I can sell to a dealer, a dealer, mind you, for $1,200.

That interest has risen in the past few years, not just for her, but the whole woodblock school who were considered to be nothing. It takes a change in fashion over 25 to 50 years and that hasn't happened for Knaths yet. Or for artists like him who adapted aspects of cubism.

CG Would you agree that the earlier works of Knaths are stronger than the late ones?

NH I agree. The monotypes from 1919–1920, when he first arrived here, are as a group stronger than his later paintings.

(I saw a number of these works in the collection of Jim and Jean Young with some signed Otto Knaths. With fresh originality, they were on a par with the best of American modernists.)

At the time, he, Edwin Dickinson, and Ross Moffett were the rebels. What they were doing was unique. That's why Mervin and I are so interested in the late Knaths' self-portrait because it seems like a creative burst. Whether it is good art or not, there is a burst of vigor. There is a bit of savagery which had been missing.

It was painted around 1967, which is when he was thinking about what to do with his estate. That he was a very sick man did things to him.

CG The manner in which he planned for the estate was problematic. Why didn't he use Rosenberg Gallery for estate planning?

NH The gallery had other fish to fry. Dealers were not making money on artists of his generation. They were selling Eakins and the Hudson River School but making nothing on contemporary art.

CG What did the monotypes sell for?

NH The AAA Gallery, Jules is a friend of their's, and the Metropolitan Museum were organizing a show of monotypes. They were interested, so we matted and framed some and sent them to the gallery. We put prices on them, but they didn't sell any. They were sent back with a note that our prices were too high. For that little (Young curated) show in Washington, D.C. at Fiedler Gallery, sold just one. It was consigned for $980, but I have no idea what they got for it. Then I sold one to a New York dealer and art historian. He told me it was for his collection and not for resale. I think he paid $1,200. In each case, we looked at the AAA consignment value then adjusted accordingly. We got anything from $800 to $2000. Shein would know because he had a lot of Knaths that he bought from the bank that wanted to get rid of them.

CG Did Duncan Phillips come to Provincetown?

NH Not to my knowledge but Knaths would see him when he taught each year at the Phillips. He would buy paintings from Rosenberg, who represented Karl and a couple of other Americans. They represented them, but didn't make money from them. Avery was with Rosenberg for a time and told me this story. Rosenberg had just sold a Renoir at a huge profit as he bought it for next to nothing in Paris. A few days later Avery was in the gallery. Rosenberg was tearing his hair out as nothing had sold for three days. He heard him call a guy and say, "Joe you remember that print you wanted that I was asking $150 for? I can let you have it for $100." They had to have action.

An older dealer told me that they went crazy on rainy days. They had the Americans because they would come in and talk to them. In the 1950s Babcock told me, "This is the first year that I have broken even on my contemporaries." Rosenberg never made anything on Knaths.

CG Did Avery make money?

NH He finally did in the 1950s around 1958.
(Enter Halper's house and view the Knaths' self-portrait.)

CG Wow.

NH Have you ever seen anything like that before? Now you see why we bought it over several other painting that were offered to us. You can see why we are not anxious to sell it, and if we do, for a good price. It has everything you want in a Knaths. It has the grid and he's mixing paint in clam shells.

CG Do you ever see a Knaths without the grid?

NH Here's a monotype, but I have a better one upstairs. It's like his paintings, but because of the medium the colors are stronger. We have work by a lot of the artists we represented some of whom gave us things.

CG Did Knaths know Avery?

NH They knew each other and had similarities, but weren't together much. Who was together with Avery and visa versa was (Marsden) Hartley. They knew each other and some of their sea things were similar. When Knaths came to the gallery to see Avery, he wasn't impressed as Hans Hofmann was. I saw Hofmann stare at an Avery for 15 minutes then say, "Dat is uh masterpiece." Knaths was snooty because Avery didn't have grids. Avery was the least grid-like man you would see. He probably had his theories, but not like Knaths.

CG You were fortunate to find so many monotypes.

NH A guy said to me that he had just been to see what's left of the Knaths estate. We also have some unframed ones which are in D.C., but this is the peak.

CG I agree with you that the monotypes are excellent.

NH I haven't seen it, but I've been told that someone in Woodstock (Jim and Jean Young) have one that's just as good.

CG Do they have titles?

NH Some do, but there is no way of knowing if they are his titles or ones given by the estate. All of the monotypes were done in 1919–1920.

CG Why did he stop?

NH He was doing other things. When we sent them to Washington (Fiedler Gallery) they called us in a tizzy, "Who the hell is Otto Knaths?" At that point, he wasn't sure and was vacillating between Karl and Otto. Often, he would create something then do it again in another medium.

In New York, I have a drawing of a rooster. Reggie Cabral said, "It's a print." No, I insisted, it's a drawing because it has ink spots, but he did it after a print. We found a watercolor of the same subject, and he may have also done a painting. Avery was also apt to do that. Any one of these (pointing to drawings) he may have done over and over. But after 1919–1920, he quit making monotypes. Overall, I don't know how many he did. and he may have done one later.

CG (Pointing to a monotype) What would you say that is?

NH An abstraction.

CG It's very advanced for its time.

NH It's very different from his later abstraction, as they were less structured. Though you can see a structure and possibly it may even have been abstracted from a figure. It's hard to say what's the source and subject. At the same time that he was working this abstractly, some of the others are more realistic.

CG How many monotypes did you acquire?

NH All that was available, about 13. The fellow in Woodstock (Youngs) got a couple of them.

After Avery had his first heart attack he said, "God, I'm not through yet." His paintings were always high key and even more so after that. Of his absolutely last ones, I have a picture of his wife which he actually called *Green Hat*. Except for the composition, you would never know that it's an Avery. The strokes agitated him, and I guess that's what happened to Knaths as well. There is something savage in the self-portrait. I showed it to Motherwell with the comment that it's the gutsiest painting that Knaths did. Bob replied "It sure is. He was always so damned delicate with his greens." He got a glimpse of death, and it was a kick in the ass.

(Showing me) Here is a monotype called *Horizontal Composition* with a white form in the center.

CG Why did Knaths change his name from Otto to Karl? (This simple explanation that signing work OK was too close to Oskar Kokoschka.)

NH It might have been the war. (Karl was less Germanic that Otto.) He was the kind of guy who might have gotten involved with numerology. There was a painter here, Edwin Euler, who changed his name to Reeves Euler. He told me it was better for his PR or it might have been the better vibrations of numbers. I wouldn't be surprised as Knaths got involved in all kinds of things: numerology, astrology, alchemy. I think he was Jungian rather than Freudian.

CG Didn't Knaths know Euler? I tried to reach him, but he had passed away.

NH He passed away in March. I don't know how they got along because they were quite different. Euler was very conservative. He was from Idaho (1896–1982).

CG Who were Knaths's allies?

NH Jim Fosberg and maybe Myron Stout. There were people who chatted with him, the women (Ferol Sibley Warthen) but he was a loner. Not that he wasn't friendly, which he was. The fact that he was mystical, and its precision, there were very few people he could talk to about his theories and beliefs.

There's a professor emeritus from Columbia, Otto Luning. Another Otto who was also from Wisconsin. I was at his house when I said, "I know another Otto from Wisconsin, Otto Knaths." He said, "Oh, I know him quite well." They had rapport as two men of German heritage from Wisconsin.

CG How did Knaths get along with townspeople?

NH Very well because he was well behaved and good with his hands, which was always admired. He built his house and may also have done the cottages on the property. He minded his own business and didn't cause a rumpus.

He was interested in very vague things on a very precise level or very precise things on a vague level. But he was never precise about precise things or vague about vague things. In the early days of WGBH FM and educational television, he would listen in his spare time to "content that was very instructional." He was like a lot of guys with a scholarly bent who had never been to college. They just like to have information.

We have the drawing for the Ahab painting. Demaris can tell you who has the painting. It's got this dramatic stuff of a guy throwing his hands all over.

He could tell you if he wants to. You never know with guys on Cape Cod. Sometimes they'll tell you everything and other times just dry up.

(Looking through his address book) David Tunic, 21 East 81st Street has some monotypes on consignment. There were three works lost at a framer's where there was a robbery.

CG What do drawings sell for?

NH There is no regular market. There was a show at a gallery near the Phillips and they sold for $200 to $600. People bought from the estate and there were drawings here and there going for $400 to $500. The market was flooded a couple of years ago, perhaps people thought it was an opportune time to pick up a Knaths. We didn't try to sell our Knaths because everyone else was. So, the hell with it. Just wasn't worth the hassle, though I didn't see much out there this year. You see them in small galleries or auctions.

Reggie Cabral has a trunk load of them. He could flood the market but doesn't need the money. He's more apt to give them to a museum. He doesn't want the IRS to get an idea of how much he has. I think he paid $200 for the contents of a trunk because it was just rubbish to the bank. They were the last things left and unframed. The IRS doesn't believe you when you say I just paid $200. They say stop giving us that shit.

There was a guy from Canada who came and bought Avery and Hofmann for under $5000. Later he had a show, and the papers reported the worth of the collection as over $2 million. The Canadian IRS looked into it and said, "We've looked at your taxes and where the heck did you get $2 million to buy the collection?" He probably invested $25,000 at $2,500 annually over ten years, but he had to settle with them. Guys like him want to keep a low profile when they're honest and they're not always honest. The IRS doesn't know a good goddam about art evaluations. They investigated me several times, but I never paid them a penny because I kept accurate records.

After 15 minutes the IRS guy said, "Ok, you're all clear, but can we have a cup of coffee while you tell me what the hell the art business is all about?" Two or three times I had to deliver impromptu lectures on the art business.

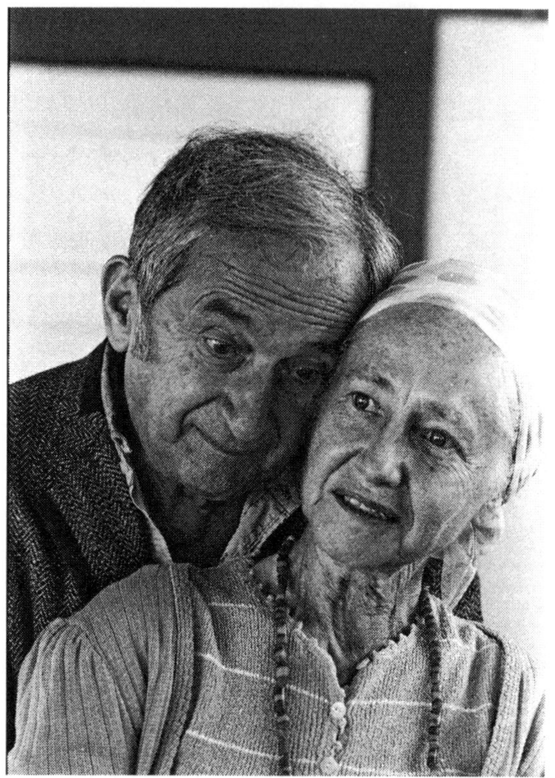

Nat Halper and Helen Marjorie Windust. Norma Holt photo. Courtesy of PAAM.

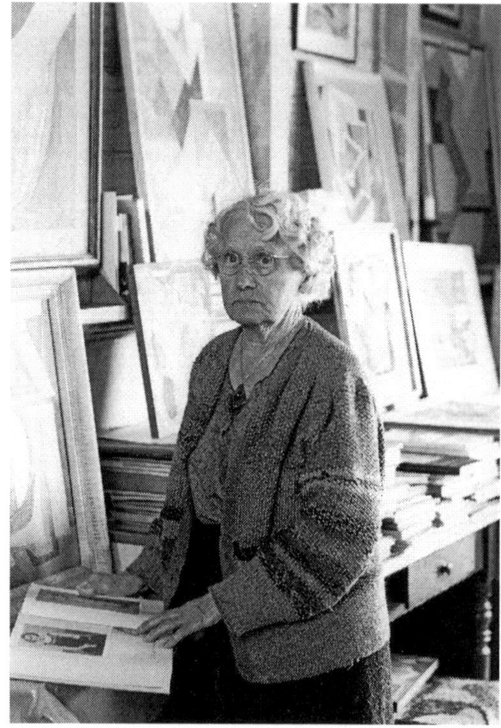

Halper and Jules acquired prints by Blanche Lazzell. Courtesy of PAAM.

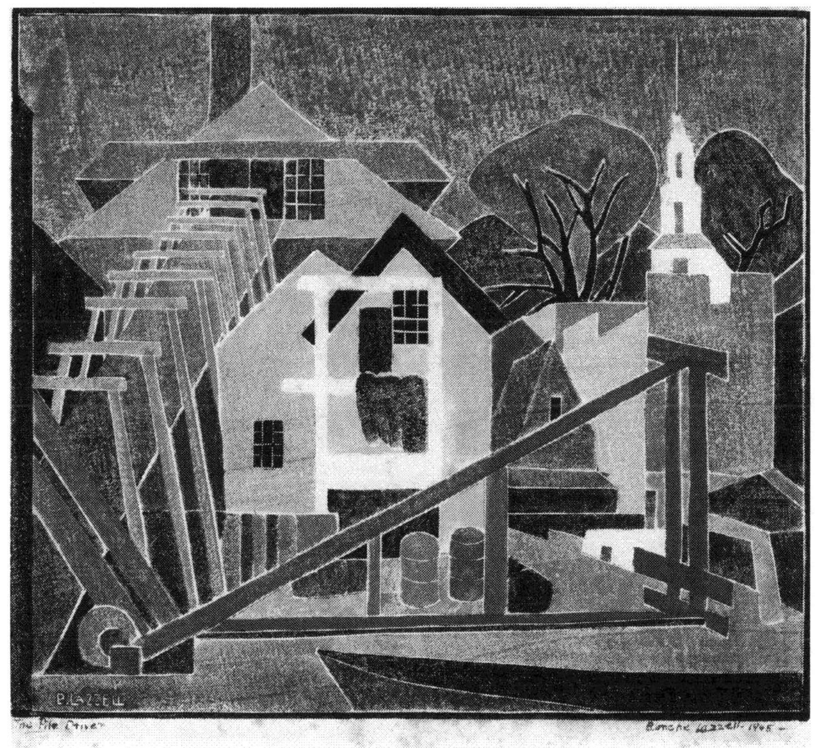

Pile Driver, 1945, white line print by Lazzell. Courtesy of PAAM.

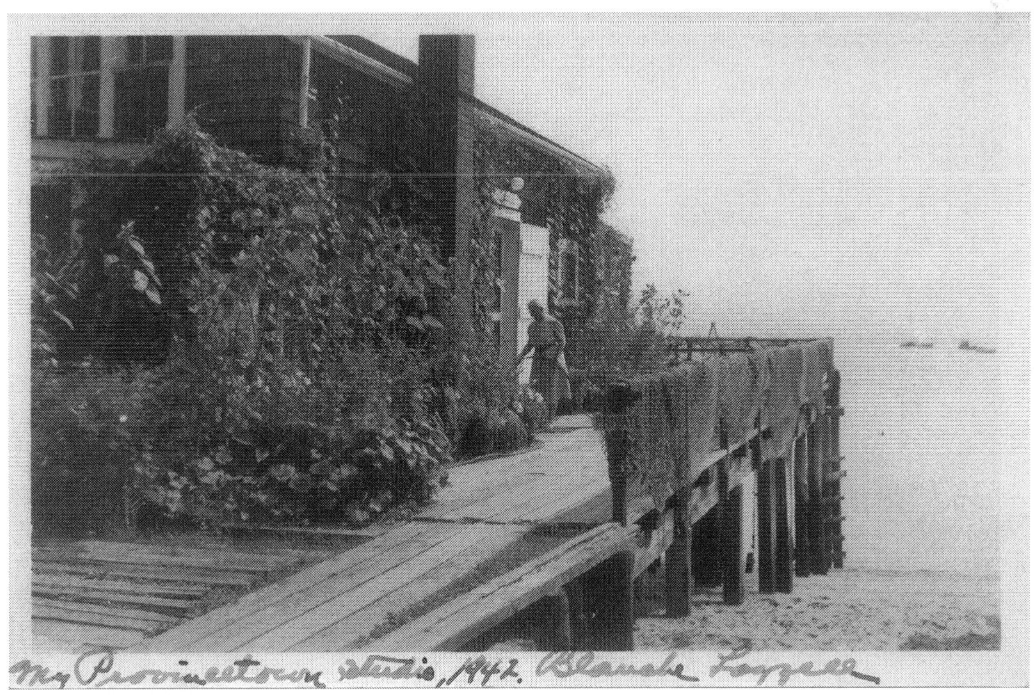

Lazzell studio. Courtesy of PAAM.

Mervin Jules, an Artist, Collector, and President of Provincetown Art Association and Museum

Mervin Jules (1912–1994) was known for his silk-screen prints. He contracted polio as a child which damaged his legs. He used crutches to walk. When we met, he had been president of the Provincetown Art Association and Museum for a year. He was close friends with Joyce scholar and gallerist, Dr. Nathan Halper. As an artist he pursued representational figuration with subjects, often motivated by social justice. He was friends with abstract expressionists including Jackson Pollock, who he knew when they studied with Thomas Hart Benton at Art Students League. He occasionally acquired work by winning at poker. He and Halper acquired works from the estate of Karl Knaths, who was a long-time friend. When there was a panel discussion at the Art Association, he generously offered his home for a few of us to stay.

Mervin Jules Interview
July 24, 1984
Provincetown Art Association and Museum

Charles Giuliano What is your relationship with the Art Association?

Mervin Jules Currently, I am president of the Art Association, but have been a member since I first came here in 1945. That was a brief visit. I started coming regularly in 1948. In '45 we came for our honeymoon. My wife had a roommate,

Ione Walker, who came with her father long before as an organist/composer. From time-to-time Rita was invited to visit Ione. Before that, I wasn't aware of the Cape as a summer place. There was a boat from Boston, but friends drove us down. We stayed on the strip, which didn't have as many motels as it does now.

In 1945, I was appointed to Smith College and this seemed like the nearest summer place. We stayed each summer, depending on what we could afford. We rented, but there was a time about 30 years ago when an influx of analysts from Boston and New York were buying up everything in sight. Places that we had rented were no longer available and rents went up. Our last rental was what is now Ann Packard's house, which cost $1,600 for the season. For that kind of money, we could buy our own place.

CG What did you pay (a house on Commercial Street with water view)?

MJ That was 29 years ago, and we paid $12,600. It was the smartest move of my life. It's waterfront property, but not winterized.

CG What do you do?

MJ I'm a printmaker. I'm a graduate of Maryland Art Institute and a native of Baltimore. After four years at MAI, I spent a year at the Art Students League (in New York). Then I returned to Baltimore and had an exhibition there. Nothing sold, and I announced to my father that I was moving to New York. My father said, and I remember it distinctly, why not stay here where you will be a big fish in a small pond? I replied that it was OK to be a big fish but that there wasn't any pond.

CG That's what the Cone Sisters said about Baltimore and why they gave their collection to the Baltimore Museum of Art.

MJ I saw the collection when it was in their home. They made it available to visitors. You just had to call, say you were sincerely interested, and they let you in. It was my first encounter with modern art.

CG Did you meet them?

MJ Oh yes, but I don't have a clear memory as they were elderly. They were cousins of Gertrude Stein. The Cone family had the patent on blue denim. The Cone sisters were among the earliest physicians. They graduated from Johns Hopkins.

(Claribel Cone and Etta Cone, collectively known as the Cone sisters, were active as American art collectors, world travelers, and socialites during the first part of the 20th century. Claribel trained as a physician and Etta as a pianist. Their social circle included Henri Matisse, Pablo Picasso and Gertrude Stein. Gertrude Stein also studied medicine in Baltimore but immigrated to Paris. Later the Cone Sisters also moved to Paris where they collected with a focus on Matisse.)

Later I visited the Phillips Museum, which is where I met Karl Knaths who taught there.

CG Recently I saw your work in a Boston University exhibition of socially concerned artists. Were you in the WPA?

MJ No. I had my first show in New York at the Hudson Walker Gallery in 1937 when I was 25. I made just enough to get by, so I didn't qualify for relief. When I lived in Baltimore I had many jobs. I was a union organizer and worked in a haberdashery store. Even when in school I worked. I didn't make much but you didn't need much.

I was president of the Artists' Union in Baltimore. I joined the Artists' Union in New York when I was there as a student, and subsequently, a year later when I returned. I shared a studio with Axel Horn who was active in the Union. I was friends with Chet Moore who went to New York and helped me get into the Union. He became a painter and collector of African art. I was having shows in Detroit and would visit him there. We collaborated on a series of silk screens for children. It was a portfolio of eleven prints. We were friends with Victor D'Amico who was head of the Education Department at MoMA. Because of our portfolio, they decided to have a competition of works of art for children. We submitted and won awards, which is how we got into the Artists' Union.

CG Were you involved in anti-war activities?

MJ I was a member of the League Against War and Fascism. I was on their board. I was also involved with Artists Equity.

CG Did you maintain your political activities or become disillusioned and drop out?

MJ I can't pinpoint the exact time.

CG Was it when Hitler and Stalin signed a non-aggression pact?

MJ No, I accepted the rationale for that. I still believe it was a stall to give Stalin time to prepare. My disillusionment came after that.

CG Your painting in the Boston University show depicted a hand smashing the window of a bakery to steal a loaf of bread. Was that inspired by Victor Hugo?

MJ I can't define the genesis of ideas. At the time, most of my work was regarded as symbolic rather than being didactic and documentary. I did paintings of the dispossessed living on sidewalks. I did paintings of people sleeping in Union Square which were thought of as being symptomatic of the nature of society.

CG Did you make studies which were used for paintings?

MJ No, I did it all from memory. I did a set of illustrations for *PM*, a tabloid that was started in New York. The writer, who became the editor, had an assignment to cover the unemployed. It was a tabloid with a liberal slant. I was asked to illustrate it. I spent a couple of nights at the Salvation Army on the Bowery.

It was a horrible experience. Prior to that, because of union activity, I had been in a coal mining region. It was bootleg mining as the mines were shut down. Axel and I lived among the miners. I rarely did actual sketches. I absorbed. Early on, I found that when I made sketches, I accumulated a lot of material which I came to regard as superficial. I would just study and rely on a photographic memory. I've done portraits from memory. Just from seeing him in the gallery, I did a portrait of Hudson Walker. A small part of that was thinking that I would become a medical artist. I was accepted into the program at Johns Hopkins. I stayed there for a while, but found that it was a rigid, non-creative approach. We were trained to observe something very accurately for a brief period of time, then recapitulate that, be it an operation, or what have you. I attribute my observational ability to that experience. By that time, a process of elimination had begun. If you remember what's essential, you are not confused by a lot of superficial detail which doesn't contribute to what you are trying to express about the thing.

The subject matter evolved. Change is a word that always expressed a very different kind of thing. I never felt it was very different. Instead of making paintings that were involved with individual expression, I began to make paintings that were a response to man-to-man and man to society. The work took on a more humanist direction. I felt that was a development to a more meaningful approach.

CG What were you doing in the '40s and '50s?

MJ I was making pictures of people, children and families. It was more personal and involved more emotion than previously.

CG How did you respond to abstract expressionism?

MJ I knew many of the artists before they were known as abstract expressionists. Mark Rothko was a friend. We showed at ACA Gallery in the 1930s when Herman Baron and ACA Gallery was on 8th Street.

CG What did ACA stand for?

MJ American Contemporary Artists. This is before Rothko became involved with abstract art. He attempted to buy and destroy his early work, but I had seen them. I knew others, including Robert Motherwell when he was in the Hamptons.

Before we moved to Northampton, we used to summer at a place called South Sea which was opposite to South Hampton. It was on the Sound and close to the Hamptons. I got to know and was very friendly with Jackson Pollock. I saw him there as well as in New York. James Brooks was another artist I knew back then.

I've reported on Pollock in taped interviews many times. There have been so many books on Pollock that by now every square inch has been covered. Axel Horn was also in Benton's class. We had a studio at 92 Fifth Avenue. Benton's studio was on 17th Street. 92 was between 14th and 15th Streets. We hung around together even after we were no longer Benton's students. He was interested in hillbilly music and some of us played. Axel played guitar and I also played an instrument. Rita, Benton's wife, generously fed us spaghetti. Pollock was around and I knew him from that period. Benton has a summer place on Martha's Vineyard and Pollock stayed with them. That lasted for about seven or eight years. At the time, he was painting Bentonesque pictures. I owned a couple of them. When I got married and moved out of the studio, I gave them to Axel. Later, when he married and moved out of the studio, he left them behind

Frankly, I was more interested in the work of Siqueiros.

(David Alfaro Siqueiros, born José de Jesús Alfaro Siqueiros, 1896–1974, was a Mexican social realist painter, best known for his large public murals using the latest in equipment, materials, and technique. Along with Diego Rivera and José Clemente Orozco, he was one of the most famous of the "Mexican muralists.")

Occasionally, he would work in our studio when he was doing easel paintings. We were good friends with him, and he would stay with us when he was traveling from Mexico to Spain during the Spanish Civil War. It was a loft studio with a room above where Axel lived with his wife. There was also a room with no windows. It had been used by the photographer Saul Liebchen. When Siqueiros was with us, he had an idea to make something that could be shown during demonstrations. He made a model of it in that room. It was painted with Duco and spray guns which was a technique he developed. It was a half cylinder to be carried on sticks. As it passed you would view the sides, so it served as a means of propaganda. He painted it in our loft, but it never got out of that room. There was no way to get it out the door. Things back then did not have the monetary value that they do today.

CG Pollock worked with Siqueiros.

MJ That's true, but I never actually saw him working with Siqueiros.

CG Did you know Pollock in Provincetown?

MJ Yes, but it was very casual. He was here in the 1940s, but I don't know the exact date.

CG Did you see the photo in the Long Point show which was a group photo from *Forum '49*?

MJ Nobody seemed to recognize the woman in the middle, who I identified as Ruth Cobb, the wife of Lawrence Kupferman.

CG The wall behind them shows works by Karl Knaths, Fritz Bultman, Jackson Pollock, Weldon Kees, and Judith Rothschild.

MJ Perhaps Ellen (O'Donnell director of PAAM) has mentioned it, but next year we are having a show based on *Forum '49*.

CG Were you here then?

MJ Yes, it was a very exciting time. I was not involved with the abstract movement but had friends who were. In 1945, Knaths gave up his job at Bennington to turn full time to painting. He recommended me for the position. We had been friends since D.C. I interviewed for the Bennington job. They offered me a job about the same time that I got an offer from Smith College. I was drawn to Bennington after a great interview, but chose Smith.

CG Can we discuss *Forum '49*?

MJ It was an exhibition and program organized by artists with a progressive, avant-garde orientation. They showed artists who were here at the time. I was friendly with Kupferman and went to a couple of the lectures. They had a jazz evening, but I didn't attend that.

CG Weldon Kees organized the jazz evening. Did you know him?

MJ No.

CG You knew Knaths. What can you say about him?

MJ I met him in Washington.

CG In the 1940s?

MJ No, earlier than that. I went to New York in 1937, so it was earlier than then. When we started to come here, I knew him well. I was often at the Phillips Museum, but I didn't know Duncan Phillips. There was an exhibition area with bedrooms incorporated into that. Frequently there were paintings on the floor. I was there looking at a Braque as well as Matisse's *Black Mirror*. A tall, thin, red-haired gentleman came in and sat beside me and asked me what I thought of the pictures. He said, "I'm considering swapping one of my Daumier's for one of these pictures." It was the greatest concentration of Daumier's on the East Coast. By then I knew who he was, but became very indignant that he would give one away.

He had a very strange attitude and budgeted what he could afford to spend in a year. I later learned this from Hudson Walker. When he continued to spend past the limit, he continued buying with the idea that it would come out of the next year's budget. Occasionally he swapped. After that first exchange, I would see him there from time-to-time. About that time a conservator at the Walters Art Gallery in Baltimore questioned the authenticity of his Daumier, *The Revolt.* I knew the conservator and he queried me as to my knowing that picture. I absolutely assured him that it was authentic. I had studied all the Daumier's I could, and had a gut feeling, not a scholarly one, that the painting was authentic.

CG Did Phillips acquire your work?

MJ Yes, he has a number of them. I know two or three for sure. I was in a group show in Baltimore and he bought a picture of a box in a burlesque house. That was my first painting to be acquired by a museum. Subsequently, he bought some others. The only time they were shown was during the war. For some reason Phillips decided not to show Europeans, so a lot of Americans went up. He bought a lot of Knaths, about one a year.

The first Knaths he bought was *Geranium in a Night Window.* I owned a print of it which I sold to the National Collection (Smithsonian) before the Provincetown Printmakers exhibition. Nat Halper and I bought from the Knaths estate as did Jim and Jean Young.

CG The Youngs bought from Ed Shein, who bought the bulk of the estate.

MJ I went to see the paintings. I saw several prints, plus blocks, and photographed them. I showed them to (Nat) Halper and said we have to show these artists, they're early and have been forgotten.

CG Was it your idea for the Provincetown Printmakers show?

MJ It was a joint thing because I worked very closely with Nat (Halper). Once we had done some digging, we asked Janet Flint to do the catalog. She was familiar with some of the artists because she had acquired their work for the collection. In 1982, we visited Washington to discuss progress with her. She suggested that if we were willing to postpone for a year, the Smithsonian would jointly sponsor the exhibition and produce the catalog. The Art Association never had enough money for catalogs, particularly ones in color, which was essential for this show. I knew her previously from the sale of a Karl Knaths.

CG What did it sell for?

MJ I think $800.

CG Did you own any work by Blanche Lazzell?

MJ I had three Lazzells, one of which was a monotype which Halper showed in 1955. Another was a woodcut of her studio, and the print showed that she had mastered the (white line) technique. The third work was a landscape oil painting influenced by Ambrose Webster. It was done in the late period, when she had simplified forms. I loaned the print to the show.

CG What show was that?

MJ At Mary Ryan Gallery in New York of Provincetown prints. It ended yesterday and I can show you the review. I located a lot of examples for her show. Getting back to the Provincetown Printmakers show (Smithsonian and PAAM) by then we had gathered some 200 examples. When we came to the decision to work with them, we sent everything we had, including the 200 prints. She was to curate the final selection. The show had about 76 prints, which she selected from 200. We found a selection owned by a woman named Smith who was the daughter of one of the artists. Her mother had acquired 50 prints by her colleagues.

CG Who was her mother?

MJ I've forgotten, sorry but I'm terrible with names. She lives in the West End and is friends with Angie Myrer. (That may well be Ferol Sibley Warthen who did White Line prints.)

CG A result of that show is increased value and a market for the prints. (Online we saw prices from $11,000 to $85,000 for Lazzell prints.) In Ross Moffett's history, *Art in Narrow Streets*, there is a brief mention of the mostly women printmakers.

MJ This history is yet to be explored. A number of them were women returning from Paris because of the war. Gertrude Stein mentioned Ethel Mars and Maude Hunt Squire. I have the original list of artists which I drew up when we were working on the project. Nat knew Blanche Lazzell; he had that kind of mind. We were good friends for a long time. His wife, Marge. was a classmate of mine at the Art Students League. When we moved here, I joined Beachcombers and met Nat. We were interested in art and chess.

CG Did you share his interest in James Joyce?

MJ No. Once a week we played poker. We both wanted to own a Knaths painting. I only had a print. We tried to find out who had the estate. I've always liked his work. Hudson Walker put on a small exhibition.

He was a New York dealer who gave me my first show in 1937. He came here early on because his wife's parents coming here when she was quite young. When he married Ione, she encouraged him to come here. From 1937 to 1940, he had a gallery on 57Th Street. He studied art at Harvard and ran a small gallery in Cambridge. It didn't last long, then he came to New York and married.

They honeymooned in Europe where he acquired art to start a collection and gallery. He came to New York in 1937 and established the Walker Gallery. He had the first decent show of Käthe Kollwitz based on work that he acquired in Europe. Alfred Stieglitz used to represent Marsden Hartley. There was a fight between Georgia O'Keeffe (wife of Stieglitz) and Hartley. So, Hartley was looking for a gallery and Walker picked him up. When Hudson was here, he owned some Knaths, so we went to see them. Knaths was friendly, so we went there as well. Hudson arranged to have Rosenberg represent Knaths.

Hudson was one of the movers. When he closed the gallery, he took it upon himself to place all of his artists. That's something that, to my knowledge, no other dealer has done. He arranged for Knaths and Marsden Hartley (1877–1943) to go to Rosenberg. He died not long after, but from 1940 on, he was with Rosenberg. I bought my first Hartley from him in 1937.

CG Do you still have it?

MJ Yes, I have six Hartley's. I paid good money for them. The first one I bought was a crab with a sea shell. He did a series of seven, all the same size.

CG Did you know him here?

MJ No, but I knew him in New York when he was represented by Hudson. The second one I bought from Rosenberg. I bought one at the Forestall estate auction. He was the Secretary of the Navy. I won two Hartley drawings in a poker game. Nat (Halper) used to handle Hartley things that Hudson owned. He had some drawings and a gouache of a crab. When we played poker, I turned my winnings over to Nat. At the end of the year, I looked through his inventory and bought things with my winnings. I bought a lot of things from Nat over the years.

CG So Nat was a lousy poker player.

MJ No, he was pretty good, but not the other guys. I was playing for money, not for paintings. But when you have cash winnings they disappear. Nat and I have been friends for years and we had this arrangement. We both wanted a Knaths and heard that the bank had the estate. We made an appointment to see what they had, which turned out to be about a dozen monotypes. I was into them and had acquired a number of monotypes. I had never seen his monotypes (1919–1920). I acquired a number of monotypes and some drawings. They were not the one that you see with an estate stamp. They were ink drawings signed by Karl Knaths. The monotypes are signed Otto Knaths.

CG I saw them at Nat's.

MJ Those are ours.

CG He said that some of them were on consignment in New York. For when they were done, they were as abstract as anything being created by the Stieglitz group at that time.

MJ No question about it. When he went with Rosenberg the gallery was attempting to build his reputation. When he died, Helen was unhappy with what they were doing and pulled the work out of the gallery.

(This is not accurate. It is unlikely that the widow was involved with estate decisions. It was the bank representative, Ken Demaris, who asked that the work be returned. Rosenberg continued to show Knaths with catalogs but generated few sales. By then it is likely that the best works had been sold.)

Helen's sister, Agnes Weinrich, was an artist. The Youngs (Jim and Jean) have a lot. I don't know how many but they have a large painting of two figures and a piano. It hung in the dining room. You can see ideas that he borrowed.

CG He respected her work.

MJ Nat and I visited the bank. There were a number of paintings that I didn't care for, as well as two or three gouaches, very early paintings. There was a price list with evaluations from 1971, when he died. By now it was already 1980. I was absolutely excited about the monotypes. So, I said to Nat, let's make an offer for all of them, some drawings, a watercolor, and the *Self-Portrait.* They accepted our offer.

CG The monotypes are not on the estate list, which just has paintings.

MJ There are two estate lists; one for his and another for Helen's. A lot of work was sold from his estate and her list was much smaller. There were not more than 35 items left.

CG Can we get back to how Knaths was taken on by Rosenberg?

MJ Because of the war, the gallery decided to take on American artists. So, they represented Milton Avery, Marsden Hartley, and Karl Knaths. That's all they wanted. They had no interest in them other than that they were American artists.

CG They dumped Avery but kept Knaths.

MJ They couldn't deal with Avery. Very little happened with Avery (sales) until near the end of his life.

CG They represented Knaths from 1949 through his death in 1971, as well as the estate for some time. During his lifetime, Paul Rosenberg was careful in handling Knaths. When the estate was taken back, the bank sold a lot of it to Ed Shein. The result was a market flooded with a lot of uneven work. That damaged the artist's posthumous reputation.

(Shein states, "I signed paperwork with First National Bank to sell each painting for $2400 of which I got $600. The Youngs (Jim and Jean) bought 40. There were 125 total that I picked up at Rosenberg's.")

MJ In a similar way, Rosenberg handled Hartley very well. He built up their prices and got their work into important museums. They got recognition. Knaths, for example, won a prize in the Carnegie International. That helped to establish their value.

CG Jean Young studied with Knaths at the same time as Judith Rothschild.

MJ We made the offer and left a deposit. Nat didn't have a check to cover his half. But, because he was known, and had an account with them, they let us take the work back to his house. I told Nat that I had no place for them here. We went through them and I took two monotypes and the watercolor. He took two monotypes and two drawings. We formed a partnership and decided that we would only sell to galleries or collectors. We weren't planning on exhibitions. We got in touch with Barbara Fiedler, who had a gallery opposite to the Phillips Museum. We decided to only consign to her work related to the museum's collection. That entailed drawings and studies but not the self-portrait which didn't relate to anything. We sold quite a bit.

CG Between the two of you, how many monotypes were there?

MJ I think there were eleven, but I'm not certain.

CG What's your opinion of them?

MJ I love them. The one that Nat got is the best I've ever seen. We took turns selecting.

CG Is it the one with a mountain and a rider in front?

MJ Yes. It's one of the greatest. The others I didn't particularly care for. I now only have one. The other I sold to Felice Dewitt. It had an image on each side. We priced the monotypes at $800. The Youngs have a number of them. Most of what they have is a number of small sketches with the estate stamp. I don't know what happened to the few which we didn't buy.

We made a lump sum offer to the bank. We then tried to prorate it in terms of the cost to us. The self-portrait we acquired for $2,500.

CG That's consistent with the $2,400 which Shein was asking for paintings.

MJ Yes, but that was later. This was in 1980.

CG I asked Shein about the self-portrait and he thought it was a terrible painting. What about it attracted you?

MJ As a theme, I'm fascinated by self-portraits. I paint a lot of self-portraits. Last year I curated an exhibition for the Century Association. I'm a member, as is Nat. I'm now chair of the exhibition committee and we have 16 shows a year. There are eight large shows and eight small ones. I organized a show of self-portraits by Centurians who were also members of the National Academy. To become a member of the National Academy you have to give them a self-portrait that must pass a committee for acceptance. They have a self-portrait of practically every member. If you don't do self-portraits, a member would paint a portrait of you. In the space we can show 35 or so works. We selected 15 past members and twenty living members. When the show was hung, I spent a lot of time looking at them. Self-portraits are very revealing, as they have been through the history of art.

(The Century Association is a private social, arts, and dining club in New York City, founded in 1847. Its clubhouse is located at 7 West 43rd Street near Fifth Avenue in Midtown Manhattan.)

CG What were your feeling about the Knaths painting?

MJ It embodied his theory of color. He had an elaborate theory written on the firebricks of his studio. The color orchestration in the painting embodied all of that. I related to a double self-portrait lithograph, which I already owned. It was commissioned by the Association of American Artists (AAA). They own the edition of which very few sold.

CG The painting shows his clam shells (with premixed paint) and it has a wild expression which was untypical of his work.

MJ Normally he took the work further but this is thinly painted with washes of color. You can still see the preliminary grid. It was a gift to his wife in 1968. I'm trying to recall how I learned that. It was not in his estate as he had already given it to her.

CG Did you know Helen?

MJ Very superficially. Hudson and I visited Knaths once a year, usually in August. We would look at new work and talk about it. If he thought we had forgotten, he would call us.

CG A great show for the Art Association would include Knaths, Weinrich, Moffett, Lazzell, and Dickinson, the early work until 1940.

MJ A show that I have in the back of my mind would be about all of the schools. It would begin with Charles Hawthorne, Ambrose Webster, and Elmer Browne. Davidson had a school here as well as Hans Hofmann, William L'Engle, Leo

Manso, and Victor Kendell. The schools are essential to what made Provincetown an artist's colony. They attracted students, many of whom became professionals. The Art Association has started a school and that tradition should be maintained. It creates an awareness for making Provincetown the arts center which it is.

I found a watercolorist from Truro who taught at Columbia in its Department of Education. He convinced the university to offer academic credit for a course he taught which mostly attracted teachers. Sabina Teichen was in that class which ran for 12 to 13 years. Lisa Farnsworth had a school in Wellfleet, as did Xavier Gonzalez. I want to have a show of all of those Lower Cape schools.

CG And, of course, Henry Hensche. Do you know him?

MJ Yes, but we don't have polemical discussions. As long as I'm president of the Art Association I don't show my work because I don't want to be accused of using my influence. I became president a year ago.

CG Who was president before you?

MJ Ciro Cossi, and before that Larry Richmond. I have been a member of the Art Association for a long time but not on its board.

CG What's different about the Art Association?

MJ When I came on board, I realized that there was a schism between abstraction and representation. That resulted in two juries. I tried to get rid of that and have one jury. There are all kinds of rumors including that Hofmann wanted to donate a number of his paintings and that it was rejected. It's not an established fact. but I have heard this from multiple sources. There is no documentation.

CG Ellen (O'Donnell Rankin, then director) told me that only recently they acquired their first Hofmann. What a tragedy.

MJ It's a tragedy if you consider that they could have gotten anything. Not just from Hofmann but many other artists, if we had involved them. To address that, we started the young artists exhibitions within the past five or six years. That's very positive. We have one or two young artists on the nominating committee. Since I've become director, we have appointed five native Provincetown individuals to the board, including (collector and A House owner) Reggie Cabral and John Snow,

Sumner Robinson. These are people who have been interested and supportive, but not involved.

CG Is there a future for the arts in Provincetown?

MJ My boss at Smith College called me a person who was nostalgic for the future. I have never for a moment entertained the notion that it will not be. There are ups and downs with problems that are difficult to solve. But it's too important to let it die. I refuse to recognize that possibility. We have a wonderful person in Ellen O'Donnell and there are all kinds of little things that add up; lot of different elements that we can start to connect.

Until recently we didn't have a heating system. The Art Association was dead in the winter. A board member paid for that. Now in the winter, we have a resident theater group. We have exhibitions and 200 people showing up for openings. We have aerobic dancing, sketching classes, French lessons, and other activities.

CG Ellen said that people come from all over the Cape for winter theater performances. You have to acknowledge that there were years of decline.

MJ There were economic reasons for that. Housing got priced out for artists and young people. When young artists came to study with Hofmann there were affordable places to stay.

CG What is the role of Provincetown as a place for gay people.

MJ During WWI, when artists came here returning from Europe, a number of them were lesbians. They came because they were welcomed by the Portuguese fishing community. They were staunchly Catholic and comprised the year round and winter residents. They were conservative, but accepted radicals like Jack Reed and Louise Bryant or Eugene O'Neill and the Provincetown Players. There was no attempt to reject them. They contributed to the economy and that seemingly was recognized. The attitude was live and let live and this was understood by the artists.

CG Has rising real estate cost and increase of the gay community changed Provincetown as a locus for artists?

MJ In the 1960s and 1970s there were as many was 23 galleries. They were supported by housing that attracted potential collectors. They bought property and settled here. That gradually disappeared, which is when Nat's HCE Gallery closed.

CG Do you have trouble getting around on crutches?

MJ Nat had a car which he kept here. Wherever he wanted to go, we would drive. We went to Philadelphia and Washington. I drive everywhere I go, not in that little electric thing.

CG Is it a golf car?

MJ No, it's a real car. I thought this was the ideal place to have an electric car. It's small so I can park and go anywhere. It's non-polluting, inexpensive. A friend called and thought I might be interested. It was a demonstration model which I got cheap and have had it for the past six years. It has a charger and all you have to do is plug it in. A charge lasts for about 35 miles. I can get as far as Wellfleet, but it's perfect for around town.

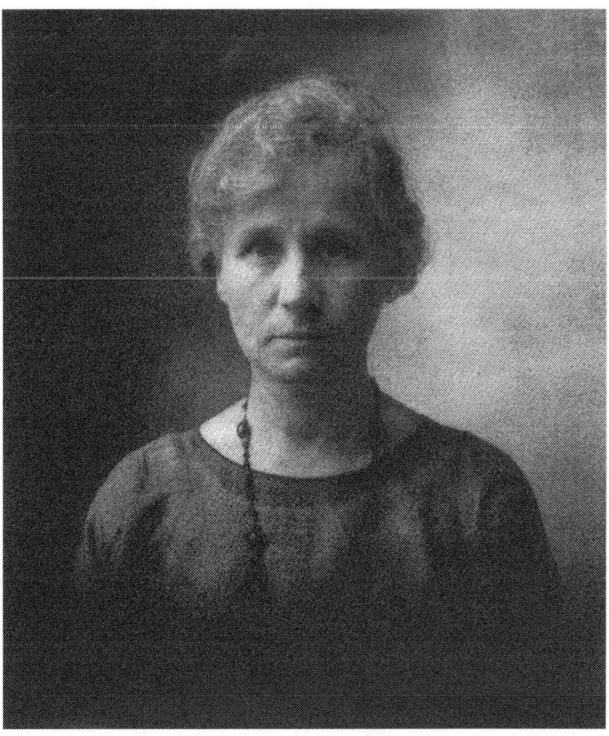

Jules and Halper sold works by Blanche Lazzell. Courtesy of PAAM.

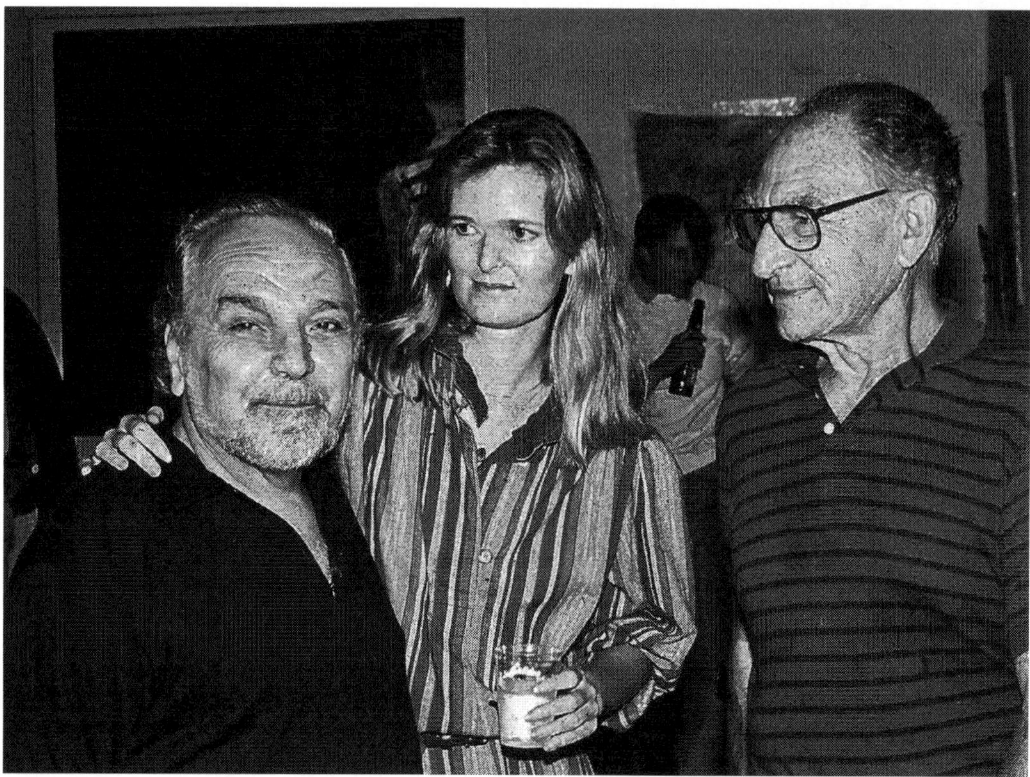

Left to right. Collector and trustee, Reggie Cabral, PAAM director Ellen O'Donnell, and Mervin Jules. Giuliano photo.

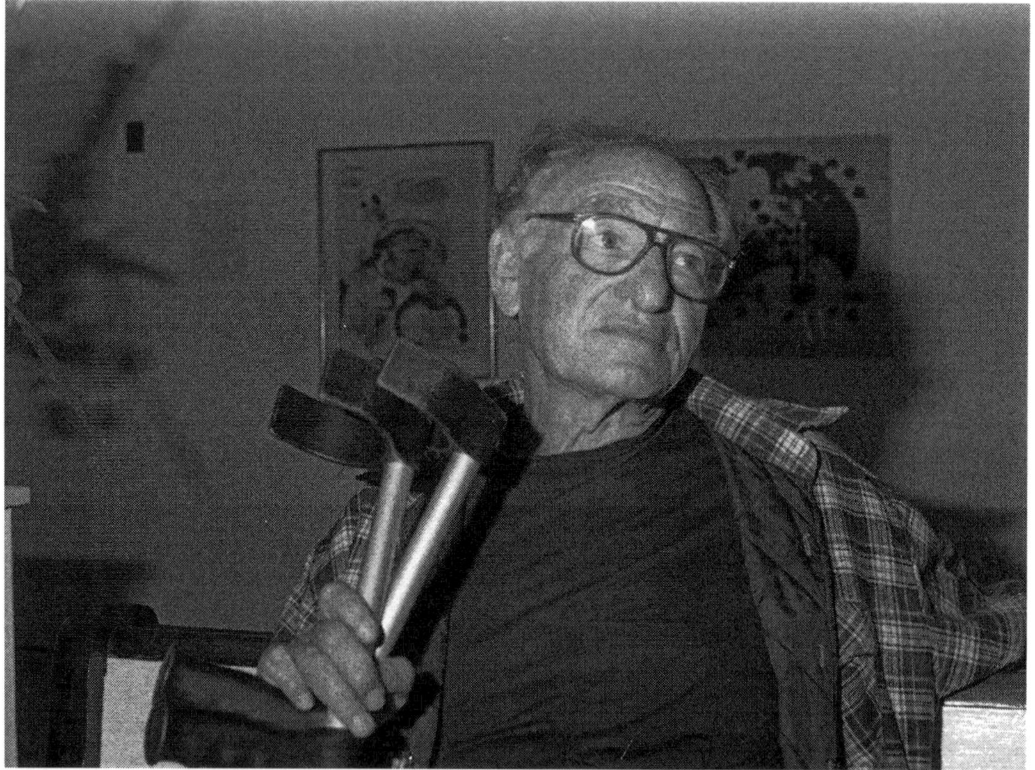

Mervin Jules got around Provincetown with an electric car. Giuliano photo.

Tony Vevers, Long Point Artist and Art History Teacher

Tony Vevers (1926–2008) was born in England. Evacuated to the U.S. in 1940, he served in the army as a staff sergeant during WWII. He attended Yale on the GI Bill. He taught at Purdue University from 1964 to 1988, with summers in Provincetown. There he showed with Sun Gallery, which included emerging figurative expressionists. Later he was a founding member of the cooperative Long Point Gallery.

Interview with Tony Vevers
Date: August 1986
Long Point Gallery, Provincetown

Charles Giuliano We are sitting in Long Point Gallery. You were one of its founders.

Tony Vevers It started in 1977. Leo Manso had a school here. He rented, as now do we from the American Legion. His partner, Victor Candell, died the year before. Leo felt it was time to close the school, but he didn't want to give up the space. At that time there were very few galleries in Provincetown. The art scene was on the down swing. Our thought was to have a good gallery which showed local artists and somehow upgrade the art scene. We were trying to establish a level that was missing. After a great deal of organization in New York, the group was formed.

Everyone wintered in New York except for me and (Varujan) Boghosian, who taught at Dartmouth. (Robert) Motherwell winters in Connecticut, and I teach at Purdue in Indiana. I've summered here for 20 years.

Mostly I teach art history. Before that I did carpentry.

CG Do you have degrees in art history?

TV No. I got into it because I had always been interested. I teach 19th and 20th century, as well as art since 1945.

Prior to Long Point, I organized a couple of shows in 1974 and 1976 for HCE Gallery with Nat Halper. I rented the old HCE Gallery and also put on a show at the Tennis Club.

(It was the first exhibition in the space which later housed Group Gallery, directed by the late Grace Consoli, then the renowned DNA Gallery. Tony was a member and avid tennis player.)

These were one-man shows, but they gave the idea that there was room for a gallery. There was no gallery showing contemporary work. If you look back at 1960–62 there were 20 or more galleries. There was tremendous vitality, but the art world got bigger. With a bit more money, what was going on here was small stuff. Martha Jackson and Virginia Zabriski had galleries here. The Sun Gallery closed in 1962 (with two more years under artist Bill Barrell) and HCE in 1966. The scene withered away. Everyone in Long Point Gallery was here, but with no place to show.

CG What about the Provincetown Art Association and Museum?

TV It was in doldrums then, but has picked up the past five or six years. It is now more interesting and vital. I think Long Point had a lot to do with their revitalization. After we started, the Group Gallery was formed at the Tennis Club. Every year there seem to be more new galleries. Two new galleries opened this year, Massimo and West End Gallery moved to the East End. There is a gallery across the way from us (Commercial Street) which has just opened. It's where West End Gallery had an annex last season. There is a lot of vitality and the impetus has to be credited to Long Point.

CG Can you describe the first season. Were egos an issue? Did everyone agree on the need for the gallery?

TV We had an overall plan and created a schedule. There were to be so many group and one-person shows. We had a director who had been involved with New York galleries, but we had no idea what was going to happen. I think we are surprised to be going strong eight years later. The sense of camaraderie has really grown. I hadn't known all the artists. Carmen (Cicero) and I had met, but I didn't know him well. Fritz (Bultman) I had known since 1951, and I've known Bob Motherwell since 1957. Boghosian, I have known for some time, as well as Budd Hopkins.

CG Was there a common aesthetic and generational factor?

TV Perhaps it was an age thing, as we were in our 60s. Budd is the youngest and Leo is 72.

CG So the spread was 50s through 70s.

TV Boghosian, Ed Giobbi, myself. and a couple of others were within a year or two. We are all in our late 50s, give or take a year. We are all quite different. Nora (Speyer, who died at 101 in 2024) paints quite realistically, as does her husband, Sideo (Fromboluti). We shared a sense of self confidence. One person, Rick Klauber, dropped out. He was the youngest. He and his wife moved outside of the area, so quite rightly he left the gallery. The only rule was that artists had to be residents of this area.

CG Are you open to new members?

TV We have invested so much effort and commonality that it would be a mistake to admit one artist and not another.

Since the first year, we have published three sets of posters. This is another thing we have in common. It's unique to a gallery such as this as we make a poster to sell that helps to finance our operation. It came out of our first meetings. As a cooperative, we have annual dues which are now $400. In the beginning, we put money in as it was needed. We had to remodel the space and put in lighting. In the first year we each put in $500.

CG There was no assurance that it wasn't money down the drain.

TV Halfway through the first season we realized that there would be a lot of expenses. That's when the director Rick Librizzi came up with the idea of a poster. We made 14 different originals and sold each one for $300. They weren't prints but rather originals including drawings and paintings from each member. So, each poster was unique. They sold quite quickly. We made a print of the original and sold that. The prints sold for $100 to $125. The edition wasn't very large. They quickly sold out.

The next year we were more organized. We created a silk screen print with four colors. They sold for more. The edition was 75 and they sold for $500.

CG How many members are there in Long Point.

TV Right now thirteen.

(1977–1998. The founding members were Varujan Boghosian, Fritz Bultman, Carmen Cicero, Sideo Fromboluti, Edward Giobbi, Budd Hopkins, Rick Klauber, Leo Manso, Robert Motherwell, Paul Resika, Judith Rothschild, Sidney Simon, Nora Speyer, and Tony Vevers. Later in the gallery's history, Robert Beauchamp, Paul Bowen, Gilbert Franklin, Dimitri Hadzi, Renate Ponsold, and Michael Mazur also became members. Some notable friends of the gallery were Nassos Daphnis, Jack Tworkov, and Myron Stout.)

The last poster was *A Grey Day,* which was named for a show that we had. It was our most popular poster. We have sold 50 of them at $150 each from an edition of 125. Sales of the prints have paid most of our bills. We have a regular assessment just to assure that we have money in our account. This year we opted to pay dues in addition to print sales to have a steady cash flow. The gallery takes 25% of sales. The artist gets 75%, the director 10% and 15% for the gallery. Last year was our most successful (1983) and we had $40,000 in sales.

CG What are the annual operating expenses?

TV Last year it was estimated to be $12,500. This year, give or take, it should be about that. The season runs from July 4th through Labor Day. There is a deficit which we cover with dues.

CG Do some of the artists sell while others do not?

TV That's hard to say. Over the years we have sold about equally. Of course, Motherwell's paintings sell for a lot more than the rest of us.

CG I understand that he has an agreement with Marlborough Gallery that he can sell one painting a year but there is no limit on selling prints.

TV He can sell prints. I believe that's the agreement. He enjoys the friendship of the group. He was a founding member of the Artist's Club in New York. He has always liked a sense of community. Motherwell commented that he likes the meetings that we have every two weeks. They are held in the afternoon and we have wine and cheese. We discuss business and then stay and chat for an hour or so. It's a lot of fun and we enjoy getting together. Every now and then we go to a restaurant or have a party. We have festivities every summer. Sometimes the gallery picks up the tab or we pay for it ourselves. It's why we are loathe to take on new members because we have this shared history.

CG Of course that creates an incentive for artists to found other galleries.

TV Group Gallery at the Tennis Club was very much modeled on us. Co-ops are not new. There was Tanager Gallery in New York in the 1950s, which showed young artists. The difference is that we are older and not just in it to show. We are in it because we enjoy each other.

CG There is an analogy of out-of-work-musicians banding together to open a nightclub.

TV In the 1950s Tanager and Hansa galleries were important for showing young artists. There were 10th Street galleries that generated a lot of activity. A complaint about Long Point is that some of the shows have been similar. For a long time, we just had group shows, though lately they have themes. We found that by having themes the shows became more vital and they are more fun to do.

CG How and why did you first come to Provincetown?

TV We first came in 1955. My wife (the artist Elspeth Halvorsen) had just had our daughter Stephanie, who draws well but is more interested in performance. Tabitha, our second, is an artist. We had been living in New York and wanted to move to the country. We had the offer of a free place on the water. That was the winter of 1955-'56 and we accepted the offer, which came through Milton Avery's daughter. I had known Milton for some time and he knew that we wanted a place. Somehow, they heard of this free place and passed along the word. Within a day or two, we loved it and felt very much at home. There were very few artists around in the winter. We came in the fall.

CG Who was around?

TV Myron Stout had just moved here. I knew him from the city. Jim Forsberg was running the Studio Shop, so we met him. Ciro and Sal had opened a restaurant. (Ciriaco Cozzi and Salvatore Del Deo met in Provincetown in 1947 as students of Henry Hensche.) Taro Yamamoto was around. Karl Knaths was from the older generation.

CG Edwin Dickinson?

TV He was more of a Wellfleet artist. I didn't meet him until some time later. Of course there was Karl, Phil Malicoat (a student of Charles Hawthorne who settled in 1931), Bruce McCain (1900–1990, a Hawthorne student) and Eddie Euler (Edwin Reeves Euler, 1913–1980). That was the winter group.

It's different now (at Fine Arts Work Center) with a lot of young artists and people interested in theater. There are probably several hundred people in the winter. I was here two winters ago and it seemed to be very active. Of course, a lot of people come for weekends, but the whole thing appears to be different.

CG What were your circumstances in 1955?

TV We managed to save about $500. With a free place and living frugally, we were able to scrape through until spring. Then I got a construction job, but it was tough going. I had been selling quite well showing in several galleries, particularly the City Center Gallery, which showed young artists. I had a one-man show at Tanager Gallery. Showing in New York, I was doing pretty well and lost ground when I moved here, but at the time I thought it was worth it. More or less on my own, I started painting as a teenager. I had a lot of support from my school (Hotchkiss). When I graduated, I won a prize, which helped me. I was in the service in Europe for two years, then went to Yale when I got home. I majored in painting and drawing. It was a Beaux Arts program, but very thorough. It was just before Josef Albers (1888–1976) and very 19th century.

CG Who was there?

TV Dean Keller was an instructor. His teaching was modeled after Bridgeman, who was a draftsman. He also taught life painting. They had a terrific art history program with Vincent Scully and George Heard Hamilton. So, I had a very good art history background that came in handy later. I went to Europe for a couple of years and studied at the academy in Florence. When I returned to New York I studied with Hans Hofmann. That brought me back into the 20th century. I didn't study with him in Provincetown.

More than anything else what I learned from him was how noble it is to be an artist. I think I understood what he was teaching in terms of space. I liked that he always talked about Titian and Rembrandt.

CG Did you see his work? He didn't show for a long time.

TV He was just beginning to show. I remember seeing his work at Kootz. It was very different from what he did in class. He was a very inspiring teacher. When he walked into the room, you could hear a pin drop. I studied drawing, and we worked with the model in charcoal. Push/Pull entailed color, so he didn't talk about that. I think the Push/Pull thing has been overworked. I run into faculty in the Midwest who teach Push/Pull and they don't know what they're talking about. It was a very logical approach to color, but I didn't study painting with him. One thing that Hofmann emphasized was the space around the model. You had a total sense of the picture plane.

CG Do you teach studio classes?

TV Yes, life drawing.

CG Let's go back to that first "free" winter. Did you have to move out in the summer?

TV In the spring, all of our friends from New York came looking for places. Angelo Ippolito (1922–2001, an abstract expressionist) was a friend. Now he lives and teaches in Binghamton, New York. Then Miles Forst (1923–2006) and Steve Pace (1918–2010), who was one of my best New York friends. All of these people were coming and it felt like being back in New York again.

CG Were Jan Müller and Bob Thompson around at that time?

TV Bob didn't come until after Jan Müller's death in 1958.

CG I thought they were friends.

TV They may have met through Dody, who was Jan's widow.

CG Did you know them, and what can you tell me? They were leading figurative expressionist artists. You work in that manner.

TV No, my work developed when I was in Italy in 1952. I was very close to Steve Pace. He was older than me and moving into abstract expressionism. I started working in that manner, and when I got back to New York, was hook, line, and sinker into the de Kooning splash thing.

CG Is the small black and white painting in the gallery indicative of that?

TV Right. It developed out of what I had been doing in Italy. I was very involved with landscape. I was still painting that way when we came here. After getting married I was drawn to the figure. I developed as a figurative artist around when we came to Provincetown.

CG Was your wife the model?

TV I guess she was, not directly, but indirectly. I was also interested in painting as a mythological idiom.

CG How did you meet Elspeth?

TV We met at Monhegan Island, Maine. I went there one summer to paint and shared expenses with Steve Pace and another artist, John Collins. On our second night we went to a dance. I started dancing with Elspeth and that was it. Six weeks later we married. We've been married for 30 years. I was then about 27 or 28.

She had studied at the New School and Art Students League. When Stephanie was born in 1955, she decided to be a full-time mom, which was the case for 15 years. Then she took up photography and sculpture. She shows in Wellfleet at Visual Images Gallery, as well as in New York. She has a very busy career.

CG Can we get back to Thompson, Müller, and figurative expressionism?

TV When we came here, one of the first things we heard about was Sun Gallery, which opened that summer (1955). The people who ran the gallery, the artist Yvonne Andersen and poet Dominic Falcone, came to see my work. I showed at Sun Gallery. (1955–1959).

I was included in a couple of group shows. I had already met Jan Müller through his fiancé because they both knew Steve Pace. I got to know them and the Sun Gallery artists; that included Lester Johnson, Alex Katz, and George Segal. Red Grooms joined later.

CG Did you know Earl Pilgrim?

TV I met him later in New York. The Sun Gallery space was originally his jewelry shop. He also painted. Sun Gallery was unique because they said they weren't interested in making money. They believed in art that was expressive but not that much abstract. I was a part of a number of young artists who used the figure but respected and admired abstract expressionism.

There was a second generation of abstract expressionism and even a third which included Alfred Leslie, who I got to know quite well. He was here in the summer of 1956. He drove up in a jalopy bringing Franz Kline with him. He had a great time and stayed the summer. There was a party every night. Dick Bellamy came in '57 or '58. It was a terrific summer with lots of picnics.

(Richard Bellamy, 1927–1998, ran the seminal Green Gallery from 1960–1965. Then he ran Noah Goldowsky for several years before founding the vast Oil and Steel. He first visited Provincetown in 1949. In the early 1950s he was director of Hansa Gallery, a cooperative gallery that included members Allan Kaprow, Alfred Leslie, George Segal, Richard Stankiewicz, Jean Follett, Robert Whitman, and Jan Müller. He was the long time representative for Provincetown's Myron Stout.)

CG Quite different from winters.

TV We felt starved for action. It was wonderful to see our New York friends. That kept us going as we stayed here year-round for eight years. Those first years I was very wound up with Sun Gallery.

At that time Jan knew that he only had a few years to live. He was a refugee of Nazi Germany and went to school in Switzerland. He contracted pneumonia, which damaged his heart. He had one of the first plastic heart valves. You could hear it. I remember sitting behind him in the movies and hearing it click-click. The doctor said that if you give up painting and lead a quiet life you could live another five years. In the summer of 1956, he married Dody James and participated in our social life.

He was a bit older, 32, while we were 28. He came to our parties, but had to lie still. He was very productive, painting bigger and bigger. He died suddenly in New York in 1958. He was having dinner with friends, laughing and having a good time, and just fell over dead. It was a great tragedy. He was buried in the North Truro cemetery.

CG You created the painting Jan Müller's *Funeral.* Can you talk about that? Where is it today?

TV Jan was buried here on a cold winter day with snow. Friends came from New York. Paul Resika came, as did Al Leslie who we had breakfast with. There was Jan's sister and mother, a young painter and disciple, and Miles Forst. There were about 20 on a very dark and dismal afternoon. As the minister spoke, the clouds broke and a great ray of light came through. It was very moving and everyone cried.

I was haunted by the funeral and did a series of studies and sketches. I did the painting which is now in the Hirshhorn Museum. It was in my first Provincetown show in 1958 at Sun Gallery. (Joseph H.) Hirshhorn was passing through and bought it. That was the first of a dozen pieces I sold to him in the late '50s and early '60s. It has been a very important painting for me coming from direct experience. It was the first experience we had with mortality.

CG Has the museum shown the painting?

TV I don't think they've shown it, but I've borrowed it a couple of times. The price was 400 bucks. It's 30 x 36 inches. At the time, Sun Gallery artists didn't make big pictures because the space was small. Jan, however, painted big pictures. Which, by today's standards, aren't that big. Pollock was working large, but that's another thing. Alex Katz was painting tiny images like 10 x 6 inches.

CG The consensus is that figurative realism began with Alfred Leslie, Jack Beal, and Philip Pearlstein in the 1960s, but there were a lot of artists painting the figure well before them.

TV I should mention Bob Beauchamp (brother-in-law of Lester Johnson). A lot of people say that Sun Gallery was the center and provided the spark. I remember Jan's paintings in New York were squares evolving into people. I remember talking about the figure with Marcia Marcus and Sherman Drexler. The figurative artists were from all over the country. I never met Sherman until the 1960s. It's interesting that we were all from the same generation moving toward the figure. It was a strange phenomenon.

I've thought about it a lot. There is definitely the sense of moving against the grain of the prevailing movement. One of the reasons why I wanted to leave New York is because abstract expressionism had become a formula. Everyone was painting à la de Kooning or à la somebody else. It was boring with all the same brush stroke and color, with the same kind of space. It became very boring.

We were all married or in relationships, which was not the case with the abstract expressionists. When I went to New York in 1952, there were no women on the scene. There were a few: Joan Mitchell, Grace Hartigan, Elaine de Kooning. Lee Krasner was on Long Island with Pollock. Women were noticeably absent, not just as painters but as companions. It was a time of male togetherness and women were supposed to be homemakers.

A woman who was very much around was Louise Nevelson, hanging out at the Cedar Bar. I remember feeling strange when I got married. Most of my friends were not married or living a kind of monastic life. There was a noticeable lack of friendly companionship.

CG That's why you held on tight to Elspeth and wouldn't let her go.

TV Looking back what strikes me is that the Sun artists were either married or with a mate. That made us different. There was Bob Henry and Selina Trieff, Bob Beauchamp and Jackie, Jan and Dody Müller, George Segal and his wife. They were all married or the equivalent, which made us different. We all had figures to be with or around. The sense was not rebellion, but rather validity in reworking the figure.

CG The mainstream of critical thinking was that abstract expressionism and rejection of figuration was, as Irving Sandler put it, "The Triumph of American Art." The conventional wisdom was that a return to the figure was reactionary and counter revolutionary.

TV That's a common problem. Critics and art historians forget or neglect that de Kooning always had a figurative base. (Late Pollock returned to the figure.) We were all impressed by Karl Knaths, Milton Avery, and Edwin Dickinson. They had gone their own way, but were all working with the figure. That's especially true of Avery, who was admired by Mark Rothko. Personally, I was very inspired and influenced by Avery.

CG Would you say that Karl Knaths, Edwin Dickinson, and Milton Avery were a link to the younger figurative artists?

TV I don't think so. I got to know them by living here. The others were aware of Avery because he was a part of the art scene. Most of them, I think, had probably heard of Knaths, who lived in the West End, but he was rather aloof. What influenced us was that we saw how Avery had gone his own way and was creating beautiful work while independent of any movement. That was very impressive.

CG Did you know Knaths and have any interaction with him?

TV I knew him, but he was much older. He was a rather withdrawn person who didn't go out much. He led a regimented life.

CG Were you aware of his color theories?

TV I was aware of his use of space because it was post-cubist. I knew that he followed a system and used a prearranged color formula. He mixed paint ahead of time and put it into clam shells. He had people who were closer to him than I was. Jim Forsberg, for instance, and Judith Rothschild were close to him.

CG Did you have contact with Dickinson?

TV No. They were there but nobody knew them.

CG Who was exerting leadership and influence in the 1950s?

TV That's hard to say. Bob Motherwell started coming here in 1957. Prior to that, he had been in East Hampton. One had the sense that he was one of the most important artists. Milton Avery was here from 1958 to 1965. He summered here and we were certainly aware of him. Hofmann, of course, his school was still running. He stopped teaching in 1966, when he turned 65.

CG Did you know Larry Rivers when he was here?

TV Larry stayed just down the street from us. I didn't know him well, but previously had met him in the city. Claes Oldenburg was around and showed at Sun Gallery.

CG He did happenings here?

TV No, the happenings were works by Red Grooms. He was the first to use people. Prior to that Alan Kaprow had staged static happenings where he just walked through an environment. That simply involved a physical space. Red was the first to use people and actors.

CG Talk about Sun Gallery high jinks and how locals reacted to them.

TV I was talking to Mary Jo Avellar, an early selectman for the town. She was a kid at the time and recalls being forbidden to go near Sun Gallery. It had the reputation of being a wild place, not among artists, but among townspeople.

CG There was the scandal of a nude in the window.

TV That was mine. Actually, it was after the founders, Anderson and Falcone, had left the gallery. Sun Gallery was picked up by the artist Bill Barrell and his wife Irene.

(Provincetown's figurative artists included: Yvonne Andersen (Born 1932), Bill Barrell (Born London, 1932), Robert Beauchamp (1923–1995), Gandy Brodie (1925–1975), Emilio Cruz (1938–2004), Red Grooms (Born Charles Rogers Grooms on June 7, 1937), Mimi Gross (Born 1940), Wolf Kahn (Born in Stuttgart, Germany, 1927), Lester Johnson (1919–2010), George McNeil (1908–1995), Jay Milder (Born 1934), Jan Müller (1922–1958), Peter Passuntino (Born 1936), Earle Montrose Pilgrim (1923–1976), George Segal (1924–2000), Bob Thompson (1937–1966), Selina Trieff (Born 1934), and Tony Vevers (1926–2008).)

He rented it for two more years. In 1960, I had a one-man-show of nude monoprints. In a few of them, pubic hair was indicated. They were quite small. One was in the window, and you could look in and see the gallery. The cops came and demanded that the show be closed. It was just after McCarthyism, and there was a strong reaction to the curtailment of human rights. I went to Fritz Bultman, and he suggested I talk with John Snow, a leading local attorney. He told the police that this might escalate into a national scandal and to lay off. A compromise was reached. We put a curtain across the window so kids couldn't see into the gallery. The result of that was that the show got a tremendous amount of press and publicity.

CG So you were a celebrity.

TV For awhile I was. Hofmann came and wrote a manifesto about the freedom of artists and how the nude was a part of art history. About 300 people signed his petition. It's one of my prized possessions. I sold out the show. In a way it was rather frightening and not a happy time for me. I remember feeling very harassed. The lawyer suggested that I not be there for the opening. There was an unpleasant feeling although it entailed some notoriety.

CG So you didn't exploit the situation and were quite innocent.

TV I think I was quite innocent. Of course, today one would send out a press release and hope for a front-page story in the *New York Times*. In those days we were more naïve, which is ok. Of course, a week later there was another show and by then the whole thing blew over. Of course everyone remembers it. The Sun Gallery was fantastic; you never knew what would happen next. Every show was exciting and people jammed in for the openings. It was very electric.

CG Do you remember who was showing?

TV Jan Müller had a show each year. Lester Johnson showed more often than anyone else. Yvonne Anderson, who co-ran the gallery, also showed there. Bob Beauchamp and Alex Katz showed there. Three years ago, we did a Sun Gallery show and catalog for PAAM. Irving Sandler did the introduction because he was part of the scene. He was a graduate student during Sun Gallery days. I wrote the text.

CG That's surprising, because he never gave credit to figurative expressionism.

TV I know. The neo-expressionist movement is now prominent but there is the feeling that it was anticipated by Sun Gallery artists. Bob Beauchamp was a figurative expressionist, as were Jan Müller, Bob Thompson, and Jay Milder. They were all working in an expressionist manner. They are making a big deal about neo-expressionism coming from Europe then launched in America. It's a bunch of baloney. The Art Association is planning an exhibition in a couple of years to make that point

In the catalog, I stated that many things that have come up in the past 20 years were anticipated by Sun Gallery. The only thing they didn't do was minimalism, which was the opposite of humanism.

CG What about Myron Stout? Did you know him?

TV He was here but certainly didn't show at Sun Gallery.

CG He was an early minimalist.

TV That's a good point. I think he was earlier than Ellsworth Kelly, and surely before Kenneth Noland.

CG He hasn't gotten much credit for that.

TV No, the bias of official art history is always staggering.

CG Did you know Bob Thompson? What can you tell me about him?

TV I met him when he first came as a friend of Dody Müller. That was the summer when Jan died. Bob immediately showed at Sun and was seen as an important artist.

CG Did you like his work?

TV I wasn't crazy about it. I found it perverse and there was something willful about it. He was a terrifically talented painter and I had enormous respect for him. Some of the things I liked very much, like the piece that Reggie Cabral bought. It's maybe his best piece. I think some of the work wasn't as resolved as it might have been.

CG He was a heroin addict and troubled person. He died young in Rome. What do you remember of him in the Provincetown mix?

TV During the time when he was here, I was working as a laborer remodeling the Chrysler Museum. I didn't participate much in the social scene that summer. I was simply working day and night. I didn't get to know Bob as well as I did other Sun artists. The last time I saw him was when we had a house warming for the home we now own. It was 1963, and I remember he crashed the party. He happened to be in town and I remember I felt ticked off, as I hadn't invited him. We weren't that close. He was somebody who was around but I didn't know that well.

CG He was black.

TV He was one of the very few black artists I knew at the time.

CG Earle Pilgrim was black and part of the Provincetown scene as a painter and jeweler. He was different from Thompson and could be flamboyant.

TV He was the Earle of Pilgrim.

CG So colorful with his hats and canes.

TV A dandy. He wasn't from New York. I believe he was from Boston. I believe from a West Indian family. He inherited that heritage.

CG Earle was a Bostonian but I knew him in New York. Bill Cardoso spoke of him and the loft that was full of Day Glo paintings and theatrical sets. By the time I knew him he was in morbid decline. His wife Lily, a lawyer, looked after him. I would visit their loft, which was under that of minimalist musician Lamont Young, who we could heard droning on and on. I would take Earle for a night out at Max's Kansas City. She would give him a bit of spending money. Later he folded his clothes neatly and drowned.

TV There was another very good black artist from that era, Emilio Cruz. He showed during the final years of Sun Gallery. If you want to know more about Bob, you should talk to Dody Müller. She didn't come back here for years because she had such poignant memories. Finally, she came for a summer about ten years ago. She came for the Sun Gallery show at the Art Association (PAAM) as well as last year.

CG I understand a lot of people came for the show that hadn't been here for years.

TV That was August 1981. A lot of artists came but not as many as we had hoped for. They had dispersed.

CG Did Red Grooms come?

TV No, he didn't. Red came to my studio in the spring of 1958. Yvonne (Anderson) had come around and said I want to show your work but you're not ready for a one-man show. Then Red came with Yvonne and saw my work. He liked it and they immediately agreed to give me a show.

CG What did Red have to do with that decision?

TV They were close at that time. They were living and painting together, the three of them Val, Red, and Yvonne.

CG Who was Val?

TV Dominic Falcone, they called him Val. Red was much younger, only 19 or 20. We were all about 30, but realized that Red was a very talented artist. At the time he wasn't doing much painting. He was mostly doing line drawings. Within a year he was doing happenings and paintings. Eventually he was evolving into making constructions.

CG The Provincetown art world was dead until the founding of Long Point Gallery. How do you explain all the activity in the '50s and '60s then the morbidity of the '70s?

TV I've thought about that. The art schools closed. For one reason or another, galleries closed. The '70s were generally a bad time. I think of the '70s as being a bummer. The '50s were wonderful for me and the '60s, until Kennedy was killed. Things were just bad after that.

CG Vietnam.

TV Yes, things like that. There was incredible growth of the art world in New York. It stifled everything outside. There was a black hole and impossible to function outside that. Provincetown became negligible. Why would Martha Jackson continue to have a gallery here? The main gallery in town was HCE and Nat Halper decided to close it. All the main galleries closed, the last was Tirca Karlis.

(In her initial season, 1958, according to the Provincetown Advocate, Tirca "selected a diversified group of painters and sculptors. Many on the roster are known internationally and are featured in leading museums and private collections in the United States and abroad." Tirca Karlis Gallery represented Milton Avery, William Baziotes, David Burliuk, Peter Busa, Ed Giobbi, Lester Johnson, Franz Kline, Lillian Orlowsky, Theodoros Stamos, and Bob Thompson.)

CG Initially rents were affordable but that changed by the '70s with a surge of tourism. The gay presence greatly expanded. The character of Provincetown changed substantially. Is it fair to say those factors caused the demise of galleries?

TV The seasonal rent for Sun Gallery was about $300 to $400. Yvonne and Val lived in the back. The landlord Harriet Abrams supported the arts and gave them a break.

CG Now, a storefront rents for $15,000 to $30,000 for a season.

TV So it was no longer feasible to rent a space for the season. What people miss is that it wasn't a destination for rich collectors to come and stay. What attracted visitors was the old Seascape House, which is where Surfside Arms is now. It was an idiocentric place where people could reside elegantly. When the motel scene started, that discouraged collectors from coming here. Pat Lannan, a very wealthy collector from Chicago, came here for years. He came for a month and loved to be around artists. That entailed buying their work.

(Lannan lived in Palm Beach and established his Lannan Museum in a former movie theater in Lake Worth. That space was later gifted to Palm Beach Community College. From his estate, the Lannan Foundation was established.)

CG Was Joseph Hirshhorn a regular visitor?

TV He had just gotten divorced and came to see his kids. I recall a time when he came during the winter. He dropped by my house and bought several pieces. He was always jumping around.

CG Do you sense that he had good eye?

TV He knew exactly what he was looking at. You could show him 20 works and invariably, he'd chose the best picture. He was absolutely decisive. Sometimes he would bargain with you, but I always felt he was an ok guy. Walter Chrysler, on the other hand, would work you over for weeks to get the price down. He was terrible. After my show at Sun Gallery, he wanted to buy work at a discount, and we said absolutely not. He came to my house on three successive Sundays and tried to get me to sell him three for the price of one. Finally, I said stop screwing around and buy one for $400. He said ok, and bought one. That's how he dealt with artists. Hirshhorn wasn't like that. He would pick two and then say let's make a deal. So why not?

CG Chrysler seems like quite a character. Is he deceased?

TV No, his wife is.

CG There are stories about questionable provenance.

TV He had an art historian who made all the attributions for him. Walter had an eye and feeling for Victorian paintings and Sandwich glass.

CG Why did he leave Provincetown?

TV He didn't get what he wanted. The town wasn't as interested in his gallery as it should have been.

(In 1958, Chrysler moved a portion of his collection to an abandoned, nineteenth-century church in Provincetown creating the first Chrysler Museum. The collection quickly outgrew the space. When Chrysler searched for a new home for his collection, his wife, Jean, steered him toward Norfolk, Virginia, her hometown. In 1971, Chrysler gifted much of his collection to the Norfolk Museum of Arts and Sciences and the institution was renamed in his honor.)

He was tight. For example, he never let high school students in for free. He was bored and wanted more action. He liked to get things riled up. His wife, Jean Chrysler, was from Virginia. The Norfolk Museum was willing to make a name change if he brought his collection. He liked the idea of starting over with a new community.

I was on sabbatical leave in 1971. At the time, Elspeth was working at the museum. He gradually was moving then stealthfully one night. He left owing a lot of bills with legerdemain.

CG How did your job at Purdue come about?

TV In 1963 a friend of mine, the art historian John Sedgwick, was teaching at the

University of North Carolina. There was an opening for an academic year for a professor who was on sabbatical. They called and asked if I wanted to come and I jumped on it.

I had been teaching a summer class at Barnstable, mostly to seniors. I had offers before, but never felt mature enough to do it. I really like teaching immensely. When I left North Carolina, I had three job offers, the best of which was Purdue.

CG Was that when your life became more stable financially?

TV It was the first income I could count on, having gone from job to job. After ten years of carpentry, there was nothing left to learn, and it was becoming repetitive. Twenty years ago, teaching was different from how it is now. There were no faculty meetings. On the down side, it took me away from the East Coast. It was a very different kind of life, but we came to know Chicago very well. We were there in the winter and here in the summer. In the winter, we usually rent the house to people from the Fine Arts Work Center. The kids don't have an interest in staying here year-round; though Tabitha was here last winter for the first time.

CG By the way, where does the name Tabitha come from?

TV It's a Scottish name that Elspeth discovered.

CG I saw her work at Bromfield Gallery (Boston) and liked it very much.

TV That's good to hear.

(She lives in Wellfleet and Cambridge with her husband, the artist Daniel Ranalli, who was my boss at the Metropolitan College at Boston University. Dan curated a show of Tony, Tabitha, and Elspeth for the gallery I ran at New England School of Art/ Suffolk University.)

CG What can you tell me about Irving Sandler and Provincetown?

TV The last time he was here was '55 or '56. He feels that Provincetown was part of his youthful period, and since then he has become an art historian. I've run into him from time-to-time in New York and when we were doing the Sun Gallery catalog for which he wrote the introduction. At first, he said that he didn't want to do it, but came to realize that it wouldn't be that demanding.

CG Overall, few critics and art historians have summered here.

TV For years the only guy was John Sedgwick, who got me the job in North Carolina. Now he's at the University of Georgia, but has never done anything about Provincetown. Part of that is because Provincetown has a reputation as a party town. The misinformation is that nothing serious gets done here.

CG Long Point has a show of new work that is done here.

TV Actually, this year is the first time we are doing that. Fritz Bultman, for example, comes up from New York with nothing. Everything he shows is done during the summer. A lot of people are like that. Budd Hopkins works that way.

CG This has been helpful. Thank you for your time.

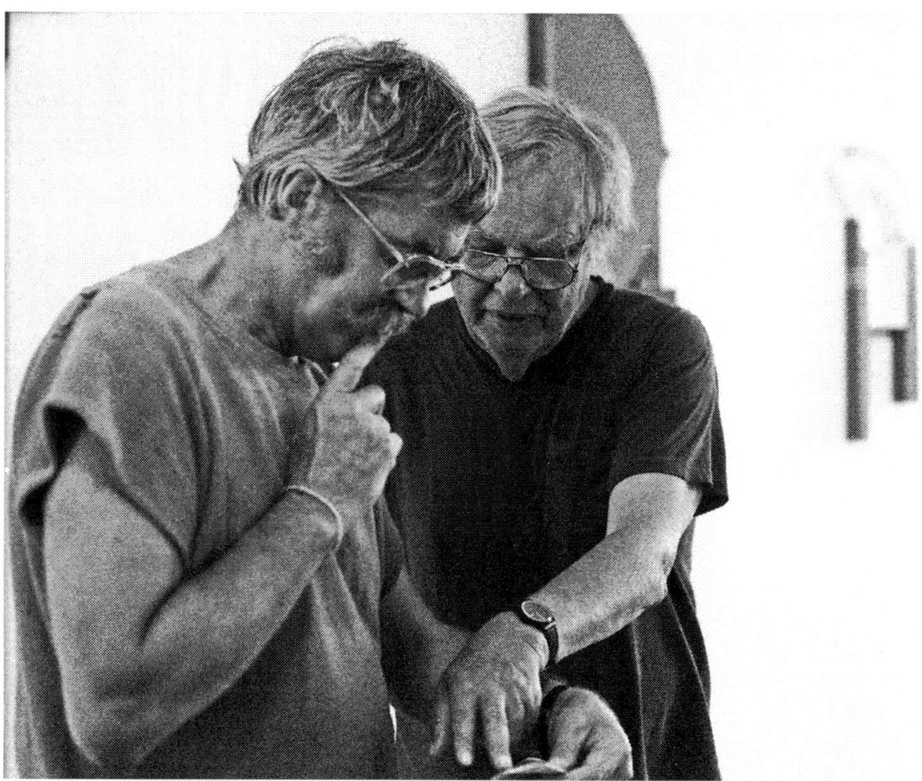

Vevers and Motherwell installing at Long Point Gallery. Giuliano photo.

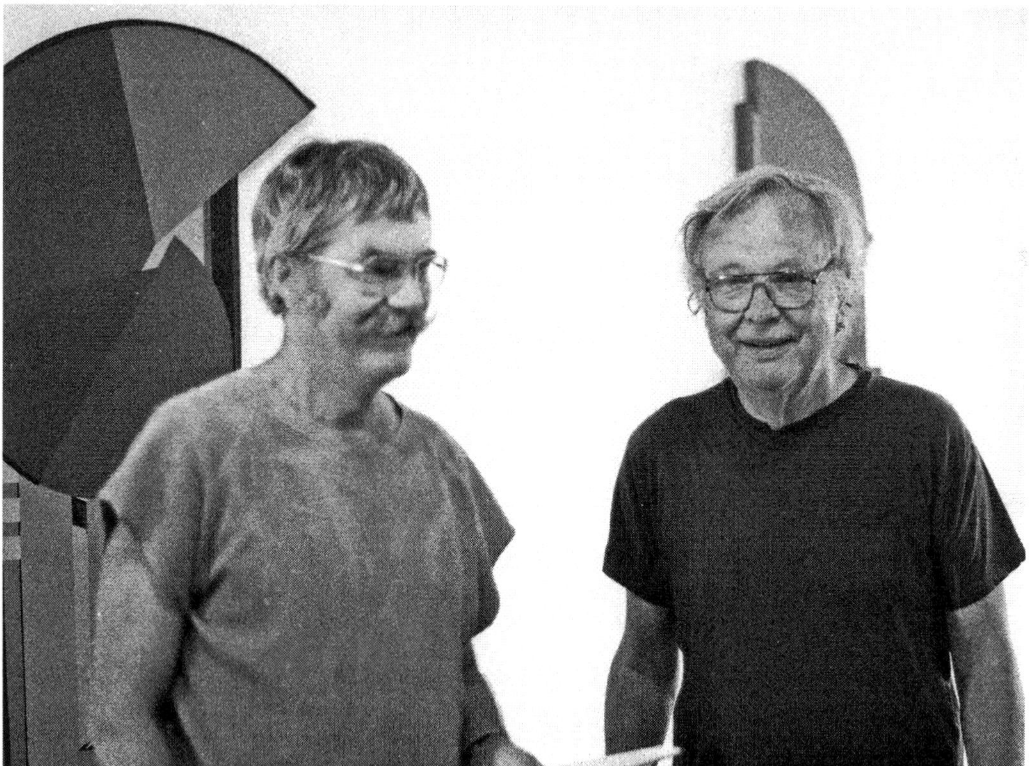

Tony Vevers and Robert Motherwell at Long Point Gallery. Giuliano photo.

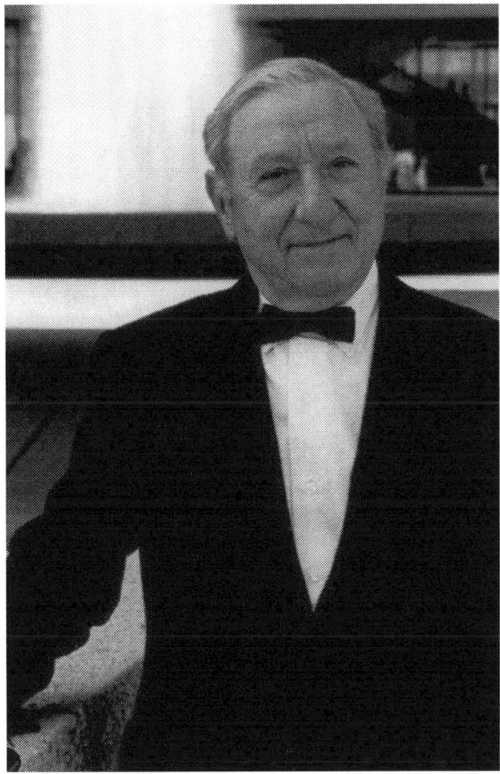

Collector Joseph Hirshhorn bought directly from Vevers's studio. Courtesy of PAAM.

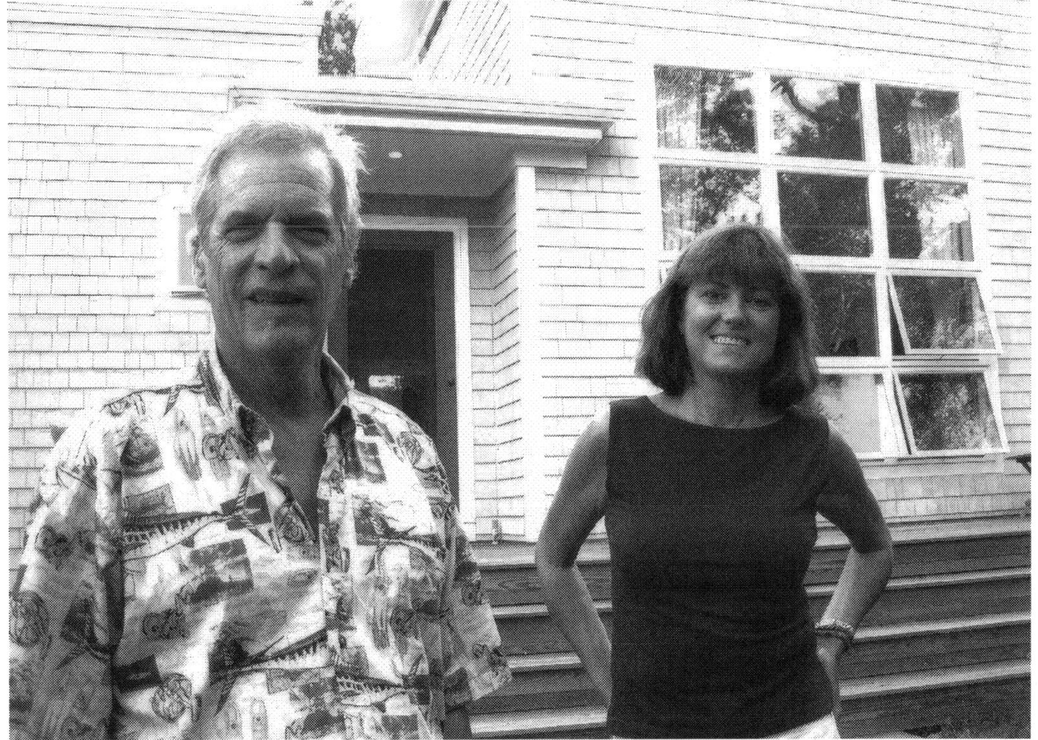

Tabitha and Dan at home, Giuliano photo.

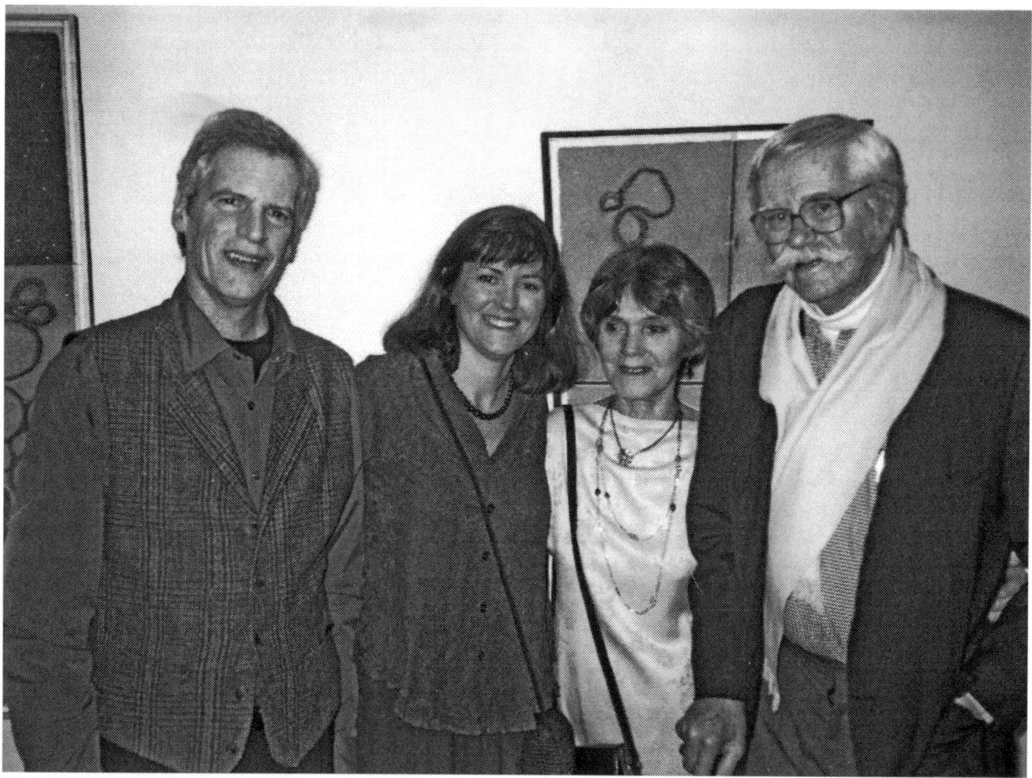

Dan Ranalli, Tabitha Vevers, Tony, and Elspeth at NESAD. Giuliano photo.

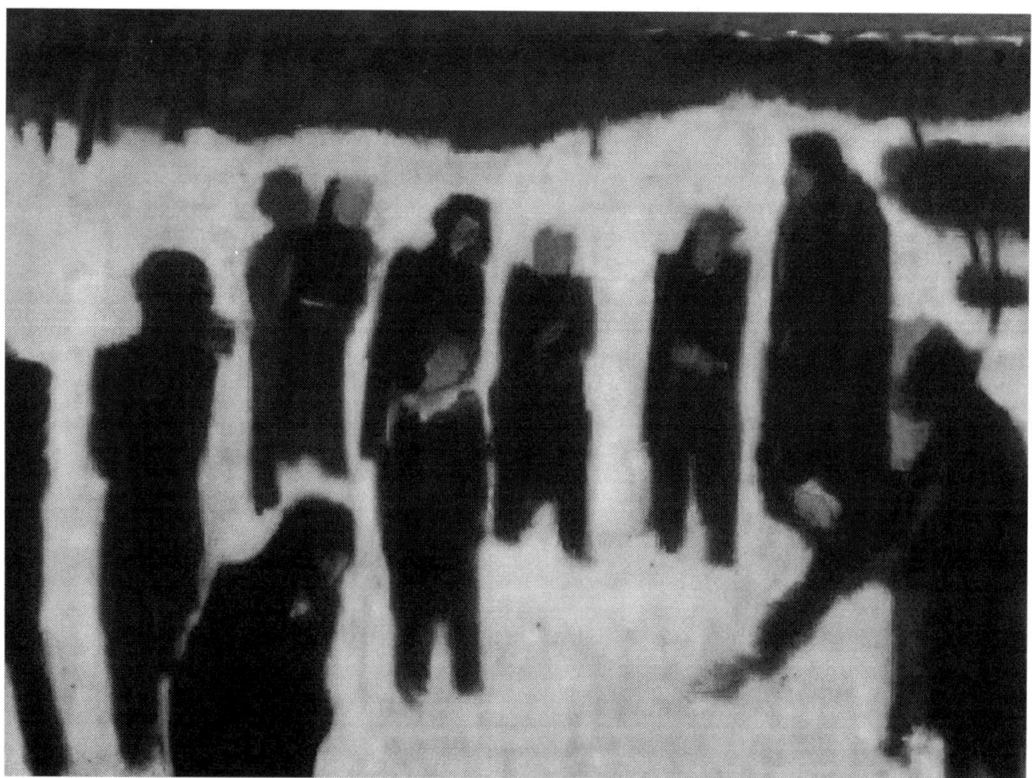

Tony Vevers, Funeral in Truro, 1958, Hirshhorn Museum.

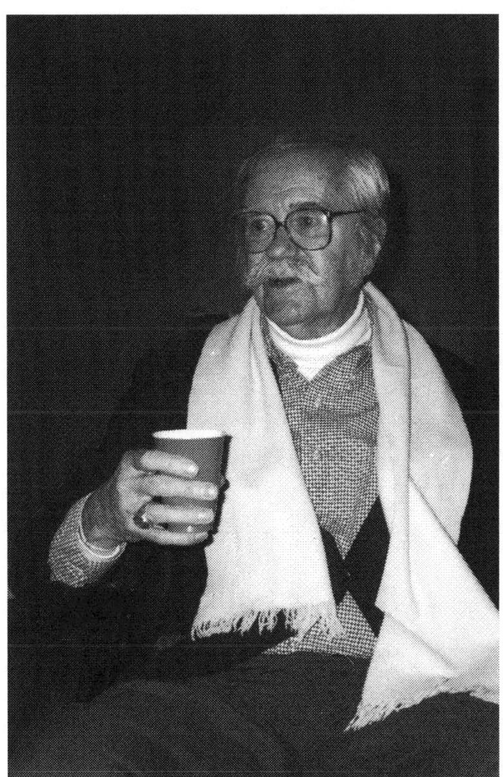

Tony Vevers at New England School of Art & Design. Giuliano photo.photo.

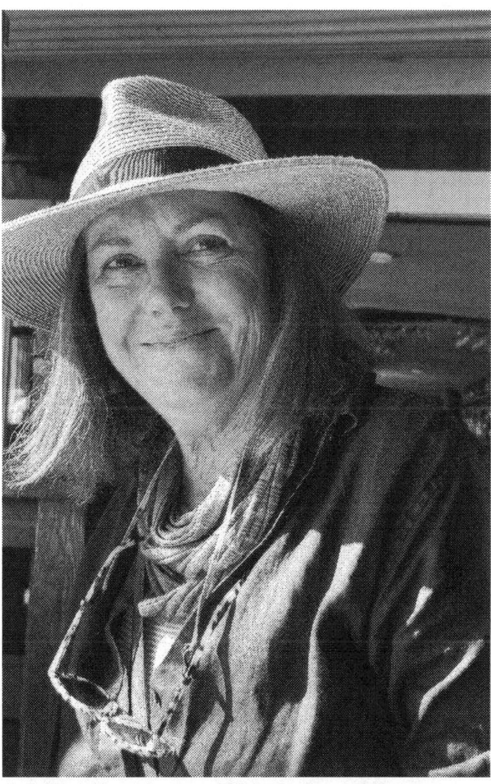

Artist Tabitha Vevers, 2024, Giuliano photo.

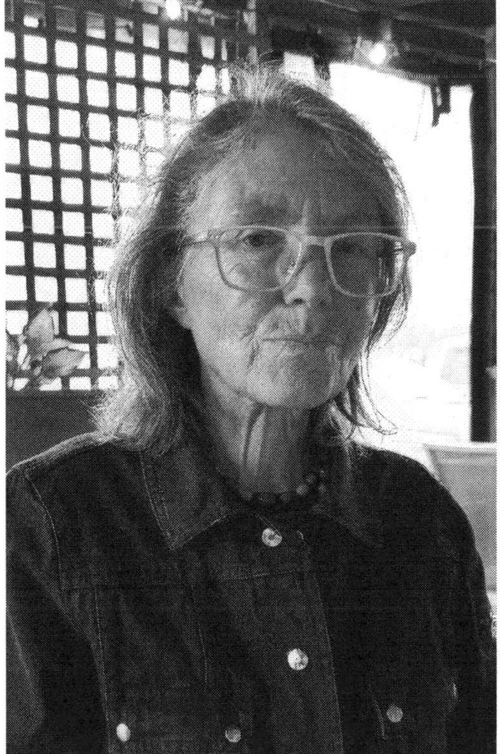

Video artist Stephanie Vevers, 2024, Giuliano photo.

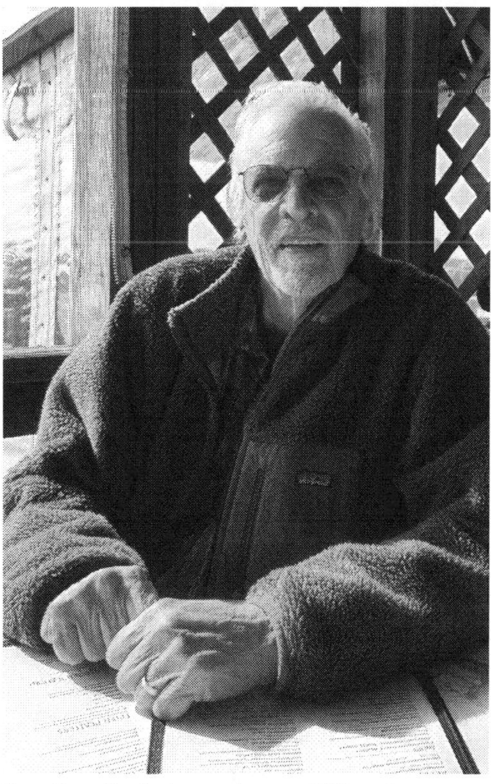

Dan Ranalli, photographer and BU professor, 2024, Giuliano photo.

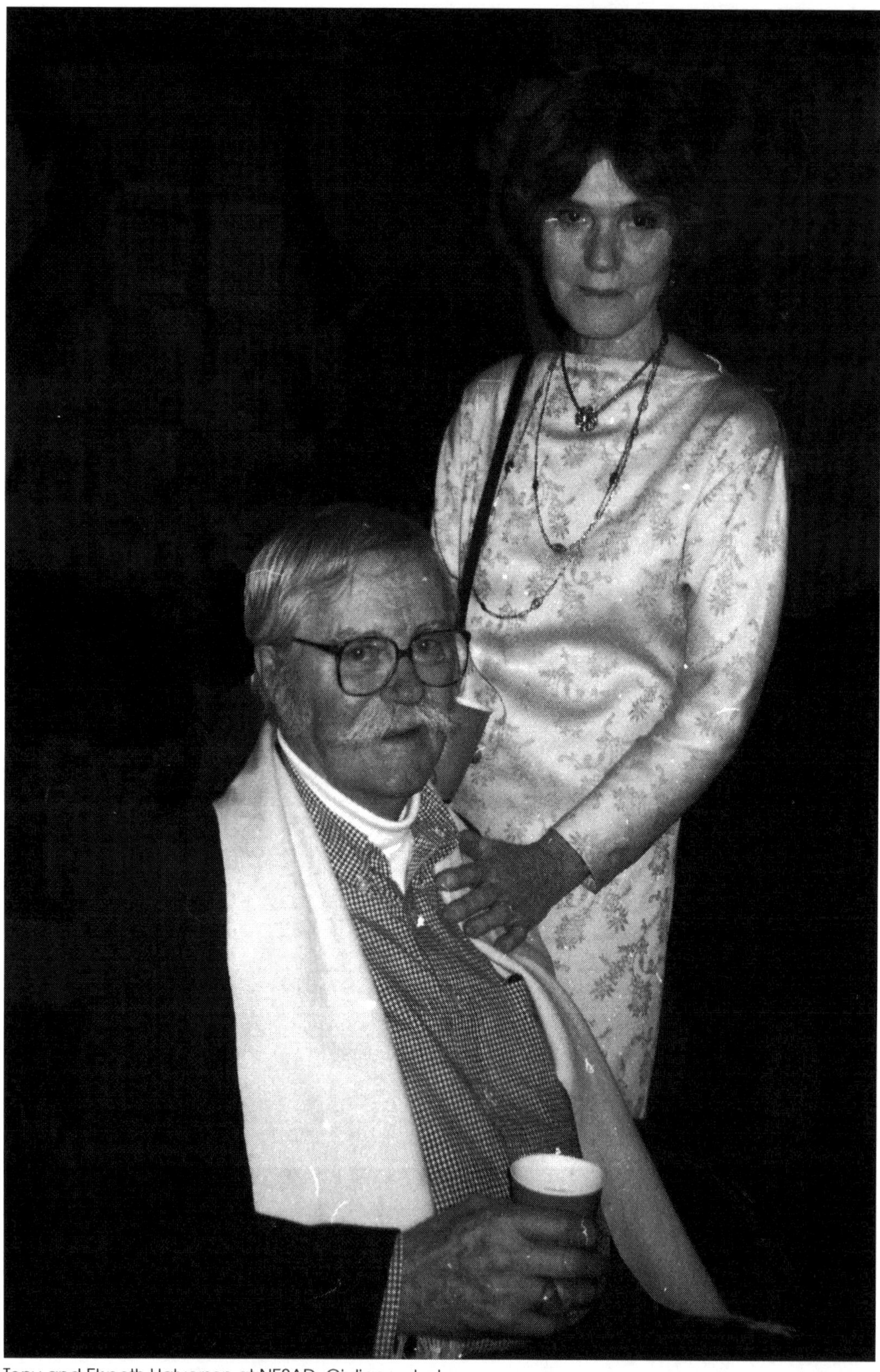

Tony and Elspeth Halvorsen at NESAD. Giuliano photo.

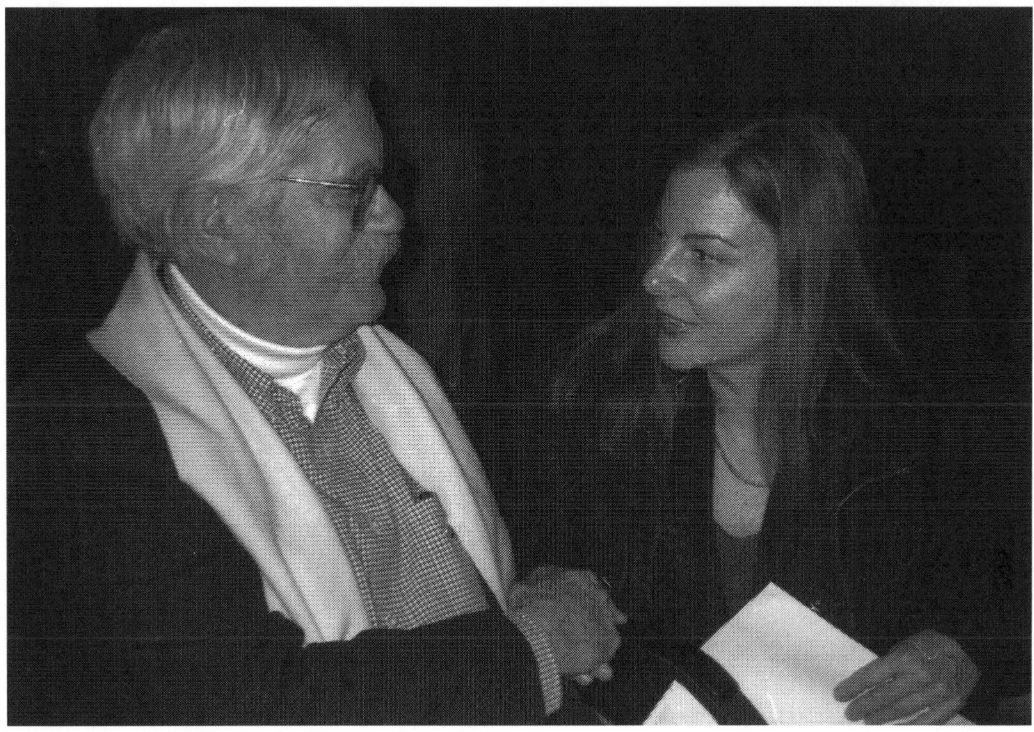

Tony with Jeannie Motherwell, Giuliano photo.

Leo Manso, "Master of Collage," a Founder of Long Point Gallery

Leo Manso (1914–1993) was widely regarded as a leading influence on the art of collage. Robert Motherwell called him "one of collage's masters." Dedicating an exhibition of Manso's works in Provincetown in March 1991, he said, "Seductively beautiful as the work is at first sight, it holds its own like iron, a visual poetry that never compromises, never loses its inner life."

In 1947 he started to spend summers in Provincetown. With Victor Candell he ran a summer art school for 18 years, beginning in 1958. Rather than give up the magnificent space, in 1977 Manso recruited several like-minded artists to form Long Point Gallery. He joined other influential cooperative galleries including American Abstract Artists (AAA), which was founded in New York in 1937. It was notable for the leftist politics of its members.

His son, Peter Manso (1940–2021), was an American writer and journalist known for definitive biographies on Jackie Stewart, Norman Mailer, and Marlon Brando.

While Manso participated in major Provincetown events, during a contentious interview, he dismissed them, as well as other artists, with a focus on commitment to his own work. "I'm 70-years-old and still painting like hell," he told me. For many years he served on the board of the Provincetown Art Association and Museum, championing the work of younger artists.

Interview with Leo Manso
August 27, 1984
The artist's home in Provincetown

Charles Giuliano When and why did you come to Provincetown?

Leo Manso I came to Provincetown in 1947.

CG The same year as Paul Resika.

LM I don't know about Paul, but that's when I came.

CG He came to study with Hofmann that summer.

LM I didn't come to study. I came to work. If Paul came, or Moses, or Jesus Christ came doesn't make any difference. I didn't come because of Paul. I came looking for a place. I had been in Mexico in 1946 and then had gone to Monhegan Island, which I liked very much. It was an island without cars and way out in the Atlantic. It was very beautiful, rugged and masculine in character. By then we had a child and were looking for a place that was suitable for family and working. Many of our friends had been coming here.

CG Who were they?

LM There was an older painter, Saul Wilson, who had been here by way of Gloucester. He has a studio next to mine in New York and said, why don't you try Provincetown? My studio was on 6th Avenue near 16th Street. Peter Busa was an instructor with me at Cooper Union and we came together that summer. I bought a house and he bought a house.

CG How old were you at the time?

LM If I get the math right, 33.

CG Were you an established artist at that time?

LM No, I was a young painter and had a one-man show.

CG Where had you studied?

LM I studied when I was a good deal younger. I went to the National Academy at night. When I was in high school, a teacher assigned us to go the museum and copy a painting. I chose Renoir's *Madame Charpentier and Her Children* but never completed it because I discovered El Greco. I found Renoir boring and was interested in a more expressive approach. I discovered that the visual arts could be as powerful as music. I was already very moved by music. By 15 I had discovered that art could be very expressive. I began to look at art, mostly at the Met. Every time I went to paint the Renoir I took a different route. I discovered the Italians and Spanish. I went nights to the National Academy until we were expelled because of an eraser fight. It happened because we were bored with a teacher who was late. We were bad schoolboys amusing ourselves. In walked our teacher to a barrage of erasers and we were thrown out.

Then I went to the New School to study with a man who wasn't much of a teacher but who had the sexiest models. I drew all the time. I used to draw on the subways and in the streets. I loved being on the Lower East Side, so the subject matter was what I saw. It was expressed with a sympathetic point of view. I discovered aesthetics, form, and so on. As you know, it's a long story.

CG Was there an artistic tradition in your family?

LM My father was a craftsman, and my mother's brother was a woodcarver and sculptor and stage designer. My mother sang beautifully. Her father was a carpenter.

CG So it wasn't unnatural for you to be an artist.

LM It's never unnatural for someone to follow their instincts. What's unnatural is to deny them. I don't know if it's genes or whatever, but my intelligence is oriented to the visual.

CG Your family was supportive?

LM My father would have liked me to be a dentist or doctor or a lawyer. Being hit by the depression, he didn't have much choice. I was on my own and went my own way.

CG When you arrived in 1947 can you give an impression of what you found here?

LM Impressions are always marred by the momentary necessities. Nostalgia is a liar. I remember Provincetown being far less crowded. That's obvious. It was far more relaxed. If you wanted to make a campfire in the dunes you could do it without restrictions. As a young artist, I recall that there were many of us in the community. The energies released by the end of WWII were abundant everywhere, and this place was a nexus.

CG Were you in the army?

LM I'm glad to say that I wasn't. This place was very open and gave you a sense of freedom. The Art Association was the center. It was also like the Academy, as those who didn't make it in juried shows were out. So, we started a cooperative gallery called 256.

I was in *Forum '49*, which was separate from the Art Association. Larry Kupferman brought me into that. Through the publishing business I knew an organizer, Cecil Hemley. I made a buck designing the occasional book cover. Cecil Hemley and Weldon Kees were the primary instigators of the thing.

CG What about 256?

LM That happened the next year, in 1950. It was in the lower floor of what later became a movie house. I think there is a café there now. It's close to town hall.

CG Café Blasé.

LM Yes, that's it. Judge Welch owned the property and said, "You can have it for $400." When we went to sign the lease, he tried to raise the rent to $500. So, we had a big lawsuit. Anyway, the artists were Myron Stout, Kenneth Campbell, Peter Busa, myself, Harry Botkin, Seong Moy, and later Will Barnett. I don't remember all of the artists.

CG Isn't that where Ivan Karp later had a gallery?

LM He worked for Sam Kootz for awhile and had that space, Nat Halper's space (HCE), which is now a guest house or hotel. Later it was taken over by artists, but for a time, it ran for three years with a new show every ten days. It was a co-op. I brought John Frank up, who became the director. He slept in the back. We put in a cot and a curtain. That's where he stayed. It was run as a *Salon des Refusé* showing artists who couldn't get into the Art Association. We had forums and jazz concerts, as well as a very good photo exhibition of Arnold Newman's work. It was very lively. He has a place up the street. Shows often, sold well.

CG So you've been here every summer since 1947.

LM I had a very good school here. It was known as the Provincetown Workshop. In, I think, 1952, there was a big spread on Provincetown in *Horizon Magazine.* It covered the Art Association, groups, and individual artists like Hofmann, Dickinson, and Hopper. We were featured as a major school. It was after Hofmann stopped teaching, which was in '54, so the article had to be dated to '55 or '56.

CG When did you start your school?

LM 1954.

CG Was it in the space that is now Long Point Gallery?

LM Yes, we ran it for 18 years. My partner was Victor Candell. When he died, I tried to have someone come in to work with, but a third of the school was on scholarship. We had a marvelous school. It was one of my great experiences.

CG Who were some of your students?

LM Melissa Meyer, who won a Prix de Rome. Generally, I don't remember our students.

CG Most teachers have that problem.

LM We had very good students, including Fulbright winners. We had students from Boston University, the Art Students League, The Art Institute of Chicago, Cooper Union. They came from all over.

Victor was Hungarian, with a very delicious accent. He had a relatively formal personality. I met him through a friend who was into classical music. We both enjoyed the music and got started talking about art. I knew him since 1940.

I taught at NYU and he taught at the Brooklyn Museum School. We started the school partly to subsidize our summers here. It seemed like a good idea at the time.

CG What did you make?

LM It's hard to recall. That first year we made perhaps $800 bucks.

CG What did you charge students?

LM We charged $300 for the season. There were about 40 students. We never took a raise and 18 years later, we were still charging the same money. It wasn't a money-making venture. For us it was an act of love. The school was open seven days a week from 8 a.m. to midnight. We each taught two days and we had a monitor system.

Let's talk about something else as that part of my career is past.

CG What was your involvement with *Forum '49*?

LM Only to be invited to show paintings. It was a way to become acquainted with certain people. I knew Adolph Gottlieb very well. Beyond that I can't say much. It wasn't a big thing in my life. Other things were bigger.

CG Such as?

LM That I'm 70 years old and still painting like hell. I don't think that *Forum '49* was the greatest thing that happened. It was pretty good and a symbol of post war liberation. Provincetown was a kind of center for advanced art for a short time. You knew that abstract expressionism was burgeoning. But what was happening in New York was far more important. I've always been involved in cooperative groups because I believe that artists have to take their destiny into their own hands. Leaving it to dealers is a lot of garbage.

CG What were the NY co-ops you were a part of?

LM Here we had 256 and in New York in 1948, I was a member of American Abstract Artists (AAA). It had John Ferren and people you don't know because they have passed out of the picture. It was a very good group and we showed at the New School for a couple of years. Philip Guston came to our shows as he was very interested in the group. There was a lot of circulation and contact with vigorous ideas. It was an exciting time.

(AAA held its inaugural exhibition in 1937 at the Squibb Gallery in New York City. This was the most extensive and widely attended exhibition of American abstract painting outside of a museum during the 1930s. The majority of AAA members worked in either a cubist-inspired idiom, a geometric style with biomorphic forms, or neoplasticism. The group officially rejected expressionism and surrealism.

Ibram Lassaw was the only sculptor to be represented in the first AAA exhibit. For the 1937 exhibition AAA produced its first print portfolio of original zinc plate lithographs, instead of documenting the exhibit with a catalog. George L. K. Morris, an exhibitor and founding member of the AAA, purchased 10 pieces from the show. Morris had established the Gallery of Living Art in 1927, a public collection of modern art in New York City. Future exhibitions and publications would establish AAA as a major forum for the discussion and presentation of new abstract and non-objective art.

There was extensive hostile criticism of AAA exhibits in New York City newspapers and art magazines of the time. The most influential critics dismissed American abstract art as too European and therefore "un-American", a term that meant suspected of having communist ties. In the 1930s American Abstract Artists was divided on political grounds with disagreements among Communist Party members who demanded AAA advocate political positions. Some artists who joined AAA were interested in Trotskyism, and there was turbulence between the group's Trotskyist and Stalinist members. AAA still exists.)

CG You and Bob Motherwell are approximately the same age. Did you know each other then?

LM No, I met him here. I met him a long time ago here in the 1950s, but we kept our distance. That's the way life ran. When we formed Long Point, we became pretty good friends.

CG You mentioned Weldon Kees bringing you into *Forum '49*.

LM Cecil Hemley. I mentioned Kees, but it was Hemley and Larry Kupferman, a painter from Boston.

CG I've met him and his wife, the artist Ruth Cobb. Their son is also an artist.

LM He had a show recently in Wellfleet.

CG Did you go to any of the symposia of *Forum '49*?

LM I didn't go to any of them. Socially, I'm pretty solitary.

CG The following summer, they invited the "Irascibles," the artists who protested against the Metropolitan Museum.

LM It helped them like a hole in the head. It was just a way of getting action.

CG In 1950, they were invited to show at the Art Association. Do you recall what you showed in *Forum '49*? Do you have any recollection of that work?

LM No, none at all.

CG In the Long Point show this summer you included early work.

LM That's a work from '56. My work, like everyone else's shifted over time. Not only are you affected by what's around you, but by styles, movements, and concepts. My work has gone from an abstract impressionist, nature-based orientation to a kind of abstraction, toward what you saw in the gallery.

CG Has anything of the early period survived?

LM I have some things in the studio.

A lot of important people were in Provincetown over a long period of time; if you were to go back to when Stuart Davis (1892–1964) and Morris Kantor (1896–1974) were here. It was an important part of the release of post WWII energy. Housing was relatively cheap and you could make a summer of it. That drew a lot of artists to a relatively free environment.

CG In 1954, when you founded a school, how many artists were there at that time?

LM Hofmann had already given up his school. I think Davidson was still going, as was Henry Hensche. There have been six or seven schools in Provincetown.

CG Mervin Jules is thinking of doing an exhibition based on the schools.

LM That was my idea, which I have been talking about for three years. It's an impossible job. It would be interesting if they did it because the history goes all the way back. If someone undertakes it, they do so with my blessing and gratitude.

CG Can you describe the differences between the schools and the kind of students they attracted?

LM Our school was one-to-one. There was no house style and you could work however you pleased from figuration to abstraction. We were dealing with ideas that were current at the time. Morris Davidson taught a form of truncated cubism.

Hensche taught concepts of color that derived from Hawthorne. He had been his class monitor. About the others I don't know.

CG It's amazing that these schools existed simultaneously.

LM There was a larger art following then. The change has a lot to do with cost of living and housing. It's very expensive to stay here, which is one of the reasons why I gave up the school. Scholarship students had to spend too much time outside the school making a living. I didn't see myself bringing indentured labor to this place. It was time to end it and start Long Point.

CG Was it your idea to start Long Point?

LM Essentially, it was. I spoke with Budd Hopkins and Fritz Bultman. We decided to invite a few other artists.

CG What were your criteria for inclusion?

LM People we respected. Not necessarily liked, but respected.

CG Can you explain the difference?

LM There are artists in Long Point who I feel no affinity with but respect their endeavor and professional attitude.

CG Everyone I've spoken with refers to it as comradeship.

LM Yeah, we've become good friends, right.

CG People make the point that Long Point has done a lot to revitalize the art scene.

LM Frankly, I don't give a damn. I'm interested in my own work. If Long Point gives me incentive, not that I need it, but if I have a few friends who I respect and they respond to my work, that's quite satisfying. That's a stimulant, but I would work anyway. That wouldn't make a difference. There's a lot of misinterpretation about that. We didn't found Long Point to revitalize Provincetown. That would be sanctimonious. We got together because we wanted to have a good gallery. Everything is cause and effect, so I suppose that's what happened. To assume that we are saviors of Provincetown is nonsense. The presumption that we uplifted Provincetown is untrue.

CG In fact, it has exerted leadership.

LM Well, as I say, it's a part of all that.

CG But it was not the intention.

LM How could it conceivably have been? It was too good a space to give up for yet another nifty gifty shop. We just decided to make a gallery of it. I'm afraid I'm debunking something but that's all right.

CG Do you make a habit of debunking things?

LM Not particularly.

CG From the 1950s to the present, are there changes in the Provincetown scene that you care to comment on?

LM You have to go beyond the Provincetown scene. I think we are in an era that is regressive intellectually and artistically. It's manifest in a political sense and filters down into society. There is a lot of artistic regression back to safe anti-intellectual positions. That has happened in Provincetown as well.

CG Can you be specific?

LM Not particularly. We don't have as many young people involved and coming up. The winter program at Fine Arts Work Center is helping. Overall, it was just easier in the past to survive a summer in Provincetown. It's more difficult now, if not impossible.

CG You mentioned being on the exhibition committee. What has been your involvement with the Art Association?

LM I've been a member since 1947. It's an important association in the community and I have been involved in one way or another. As a member, at times I have been active and at other times, not so. For the past few years, I have decided to throw whatever skills I have into the hopper to help them.

CG Are you encouraged by the direction it has taken?

LM It has improved.

CG Along what lines?

LM I think in every way. The standards are higher and the exhibitions are better. Mervin Jules is doing a bang-up job and Ellen O'Donnell is doing a hell of a job. Committees have been enlarged to involve more people. The problem is that we don't have any money.

CG Do the fights between abstraction and figuration continue?

LM I don't feel that way, perhaps because I am aloof and don't get involved with that nonsense. The only thing that counts is quality and intelligence.

CG Over the years who have been artists you felt close to and inspired by?

LM He didn't come here.

CG Who?

LM Caravaggio. There are artists I drew inspiration from, but they are not from Provincetown. My inspiration came from artists greater than those that have lived here.

CG What has been your relation with peers?

LM Moderately friendly, with standoffish attitudes on the part of both of us.

CG What was your take on Hofmann?

LM I liked the man and hated the work, which was bombastic and crude. I prefer work that's more refined and possibly more intellectual.

CG Did you ever sit in on one of his crits?

LM Yes, I sat in on them. He had a lot of magnetism and a dynamic personality. His greatest power was an ability to get students to respond. His explanations were impossible to understand because his language was difficult. He was a nice man and great father figure for a number of people. But I must say that I saw a lot of his exhibitions and never liked any of them.

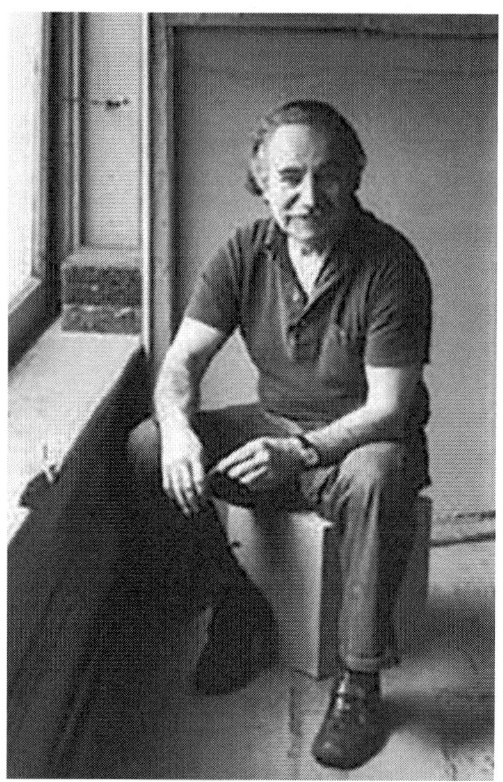

Artist Leo Manso founded Long Point Gallery. Photo by Norma Holt. Courtesy of PAAM.

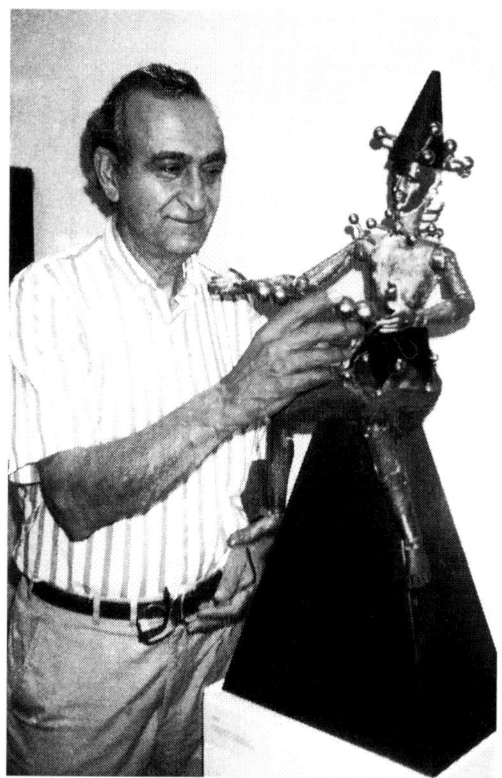

Long Point artist Varujan Boghosian. Giuliano photo.

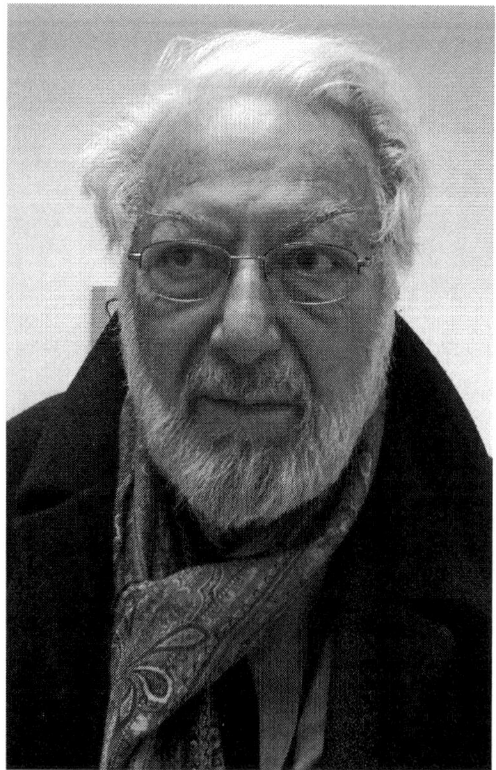

Artist Paul Resika. Giuliano photo.

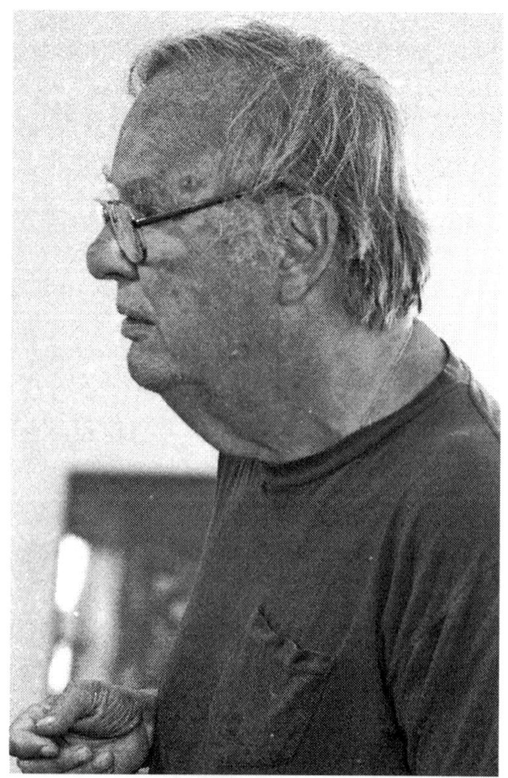

Robert Motherwell. Giuliano photo.

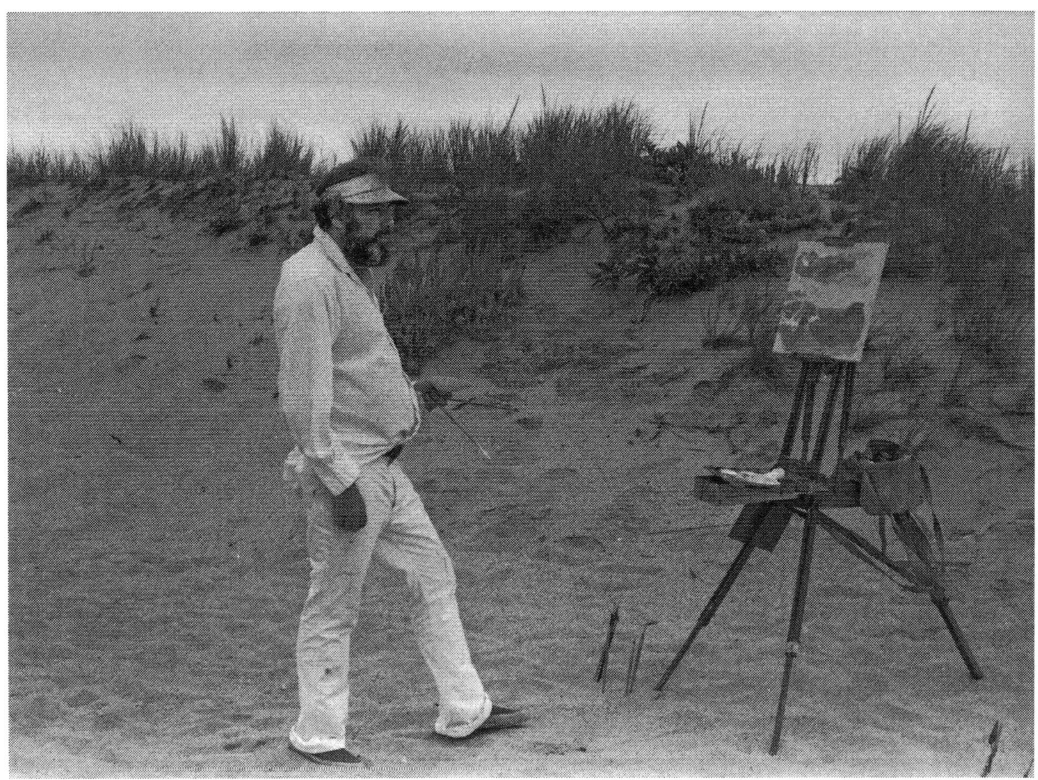

Resika painting. Courtesy of PAAM.

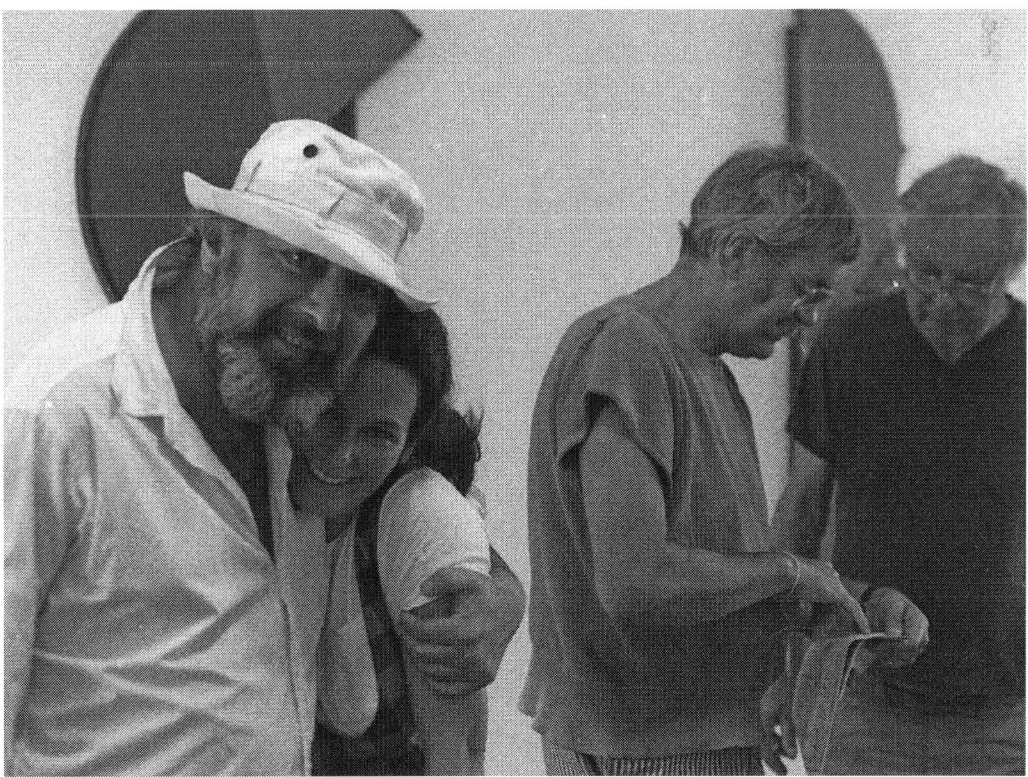

Resika hugs O'Donnell, Vevers and Motherwell. Giuliano photo.

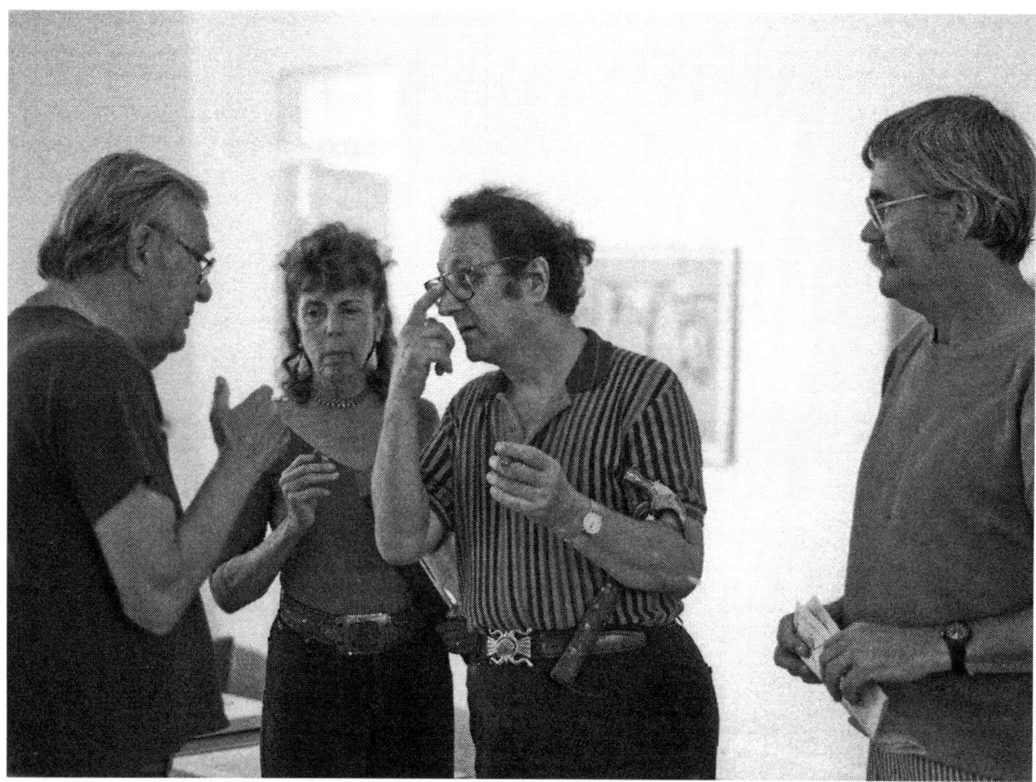

Motherwell, Speyer, Fromboluti with hammer, and Vevers. Giuliano photo.

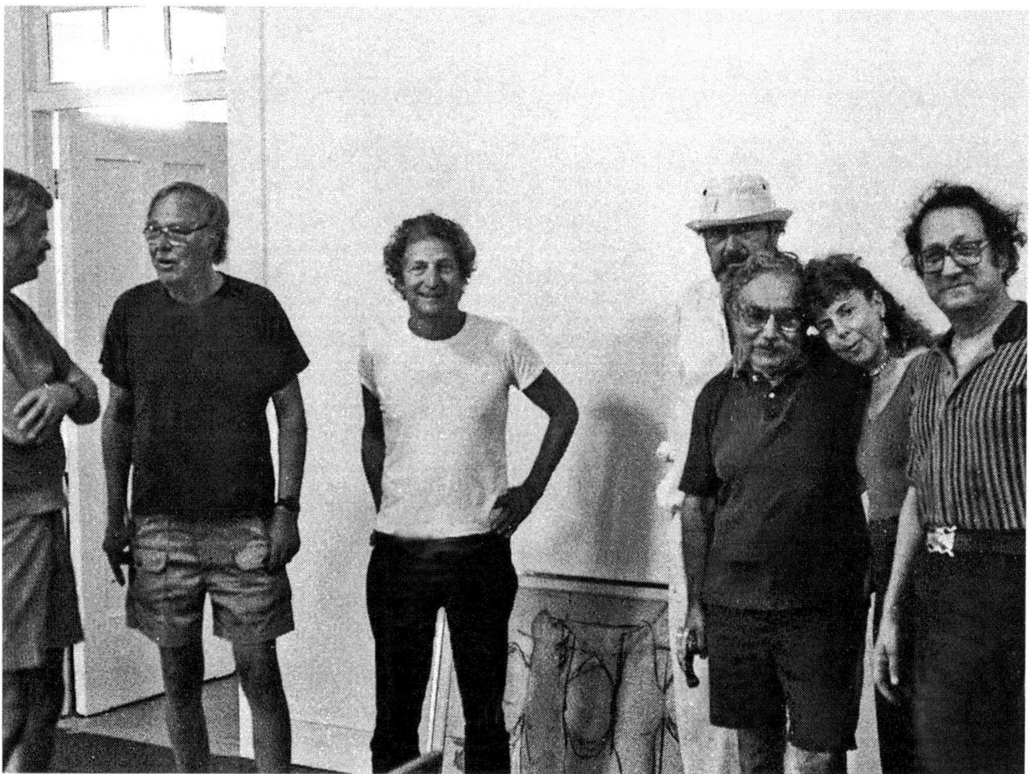

Long Point artists, left to right, Tony Vevers, Robert Motherwell. Carmen Cicero, Paul Resika, Leo Manso, Nora Speyer, Sideo Fromboluti, Giuliano photo.

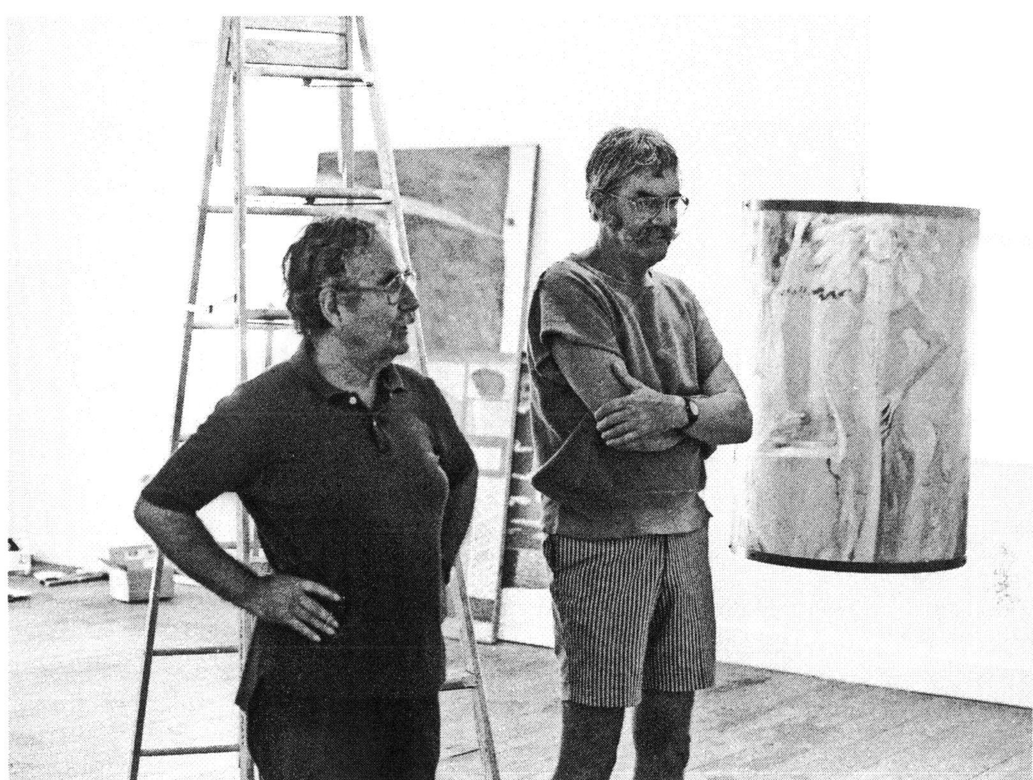
Manso and Vevers. Giuliano photo.

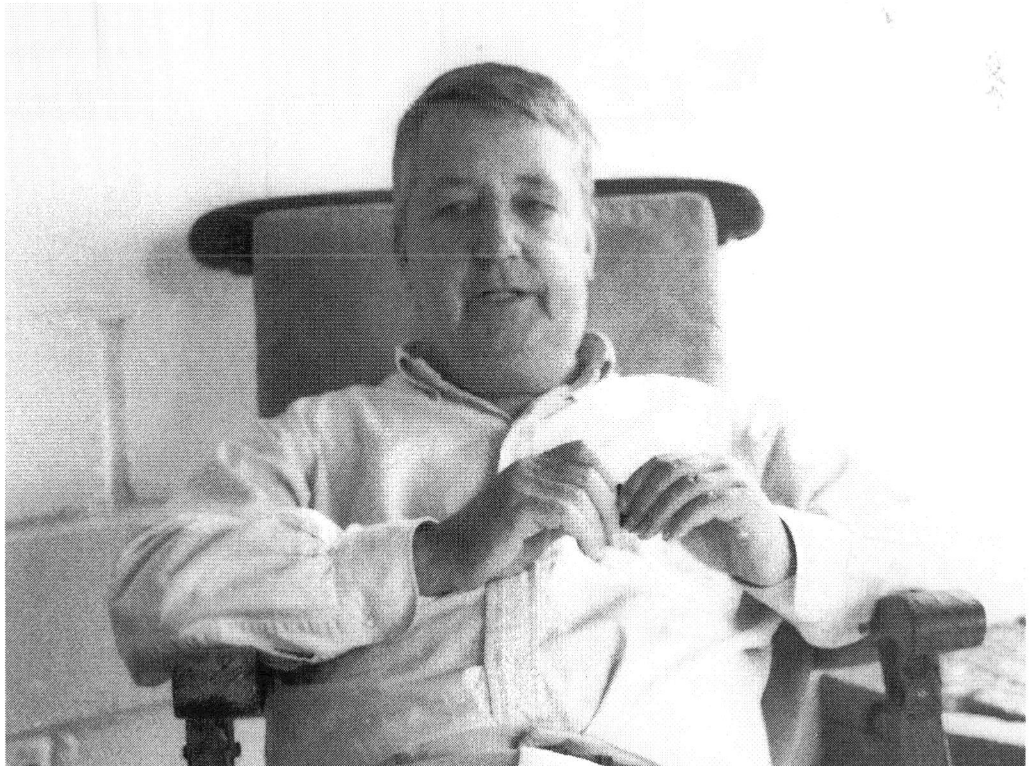
Fritz Bultman was a Long Point artist. Giuliano photo.

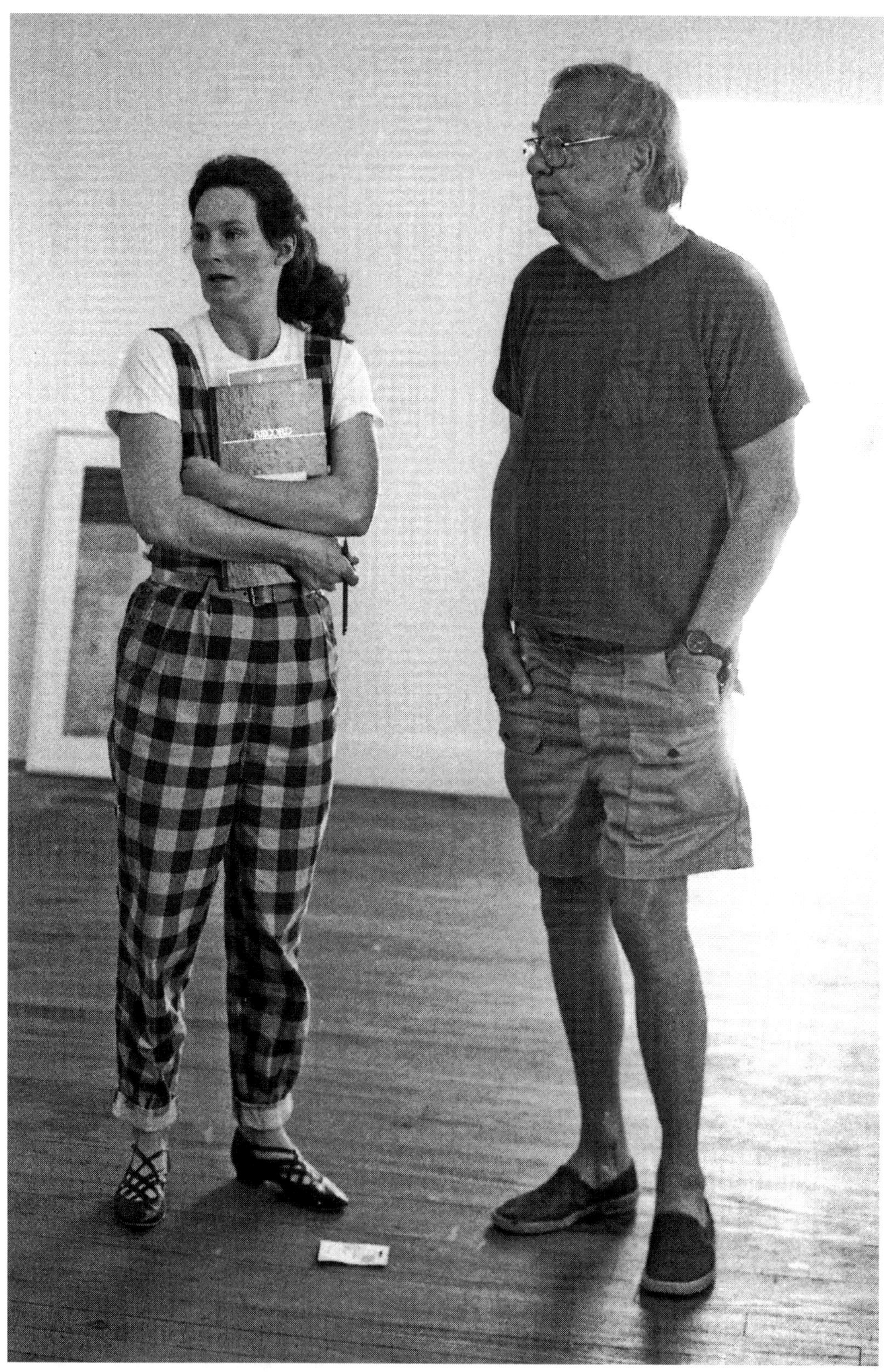

Gallery director Elizabeth O'Donnell and Motherwell. Giuliano photo.

Long Point Artists Sideo Fromboluti and Nora Speyer

In 2015, the Provincetown Art Association and Museum presented the exhibition *Nora Speyer and Sideo Fromboluti: A Shared Life in Art, 1975–2008*. They met at Tyler School of Art, and with remarkable longevity, shared a passion for painting. They were founding members of Provincetown's Long Point Gallery. In 2024 she passed away at 101, while he died a decade previously at 94. I interviewed them at their secluded home in Wellfleet.

Sideo Fromboluti and Nora Speyer
August 5, 1984
The artists' home in Wellfleet

Sideo Fromboluti In the summer of 1940, I came with ten guys. We rented a whole house for $100, so it was $10 each. Commercial Street was nothing but picket fences and flowers. There were very few shops. I put up an easel in the middle of Bradford Street. A car drove by about every ten minutes. Hans Hofmann was also on Bradford Street. I didn't study with him. He was maybe 30 feet away with a five-foot canvas in the middle of the road. It was so magnificent.

Charles Giuliano Were you in the war?

SF I was drafted in 1943 while I was in college. There were three years of war left.

I stayed in America running an art department producing war manuals. We were married by then. We met at Tyler when she was 19 and I was 21. We married in 1944. We have two children, an architect and our daughter, who is a painter married to a painter.

I came from South Philadelphia, which is a slum area. When I married Nora, I said that after the war we are going back to Provincetown. We returned in 1952 and it was so disappointing. It was no longer a quaint fishing village. By then there were a lot of galleries and the fishing industry had changed. When I was first here there were nine piers jutting out into the harbor. You can see that in a Karl Knaths' night scene of the harbor. There were fishing boats tied to the piers.

Nora Speyer Every year we did landscape paintings during the summer and figure paintings during the winter. We lived in Woodstock and were able to commute to New York. From New York to the Cape was a long drive. In those days it was about ten hours. Sideo was freelancing. We would go to Woodstock for three or four days then come back. I was participating in the freelancing. The result was that we always went to very rural places with lots of trees where we could be inspired to work outdoors. We had developed a feeling for landscapes and felt it was vital to our work. We needed a place with nature and after a day's work the camaraderie of other artists. We found that in Provincetown.

CG Who did you show with here?

NS Tirca Karlis, when we finally got here. We made a circle around the Cape and stayed on Martha's Vineyard. With our freelancing we stayed in Woodstock for about ten years. We went to Martha's Vineyard because we knew artists there. We stayed there for ten years. Some of the artists were Alice Yarmon, de Kooning was staying there, Herman Cherry, Paul Georges, Wolf Kahn. It was a small community.

SF Then they started disappearing.

NS The Hamptons were a huge community. We went out there but found it disappointing for landscape as well as associations. We got fed up with the Vineyard because the artists were disappearing. It became a rather lonely position. People told us about this area so we came here. We rented a house in the woods, where we are now. Sideo could drive into Provincetown and we could work out here.

CG You like to be isolated?

NS We do.

SF When we are working, we like to be immersed in nature.

NS I stress that this is a small community.

SF It's a repeat of our New York life because there we're involved with hundreds of artists, hundreds of galleries, hundreds of activities. Everything we do is related to the artists we know.

CG Who do you show with?

SF The last gallery we showed with, for about ten years, was Landmark in SoHo. We showed with Virginia Zabriski. We both arrived in New York in 1948. In 1950, I showed with Artists' Gallery. There were very few galleries, so it was important. Adolph Gottlieb and John Grillo showed with them as well as Michael Low and Lester Johnson. I showed there three times. then a few of us went to Zabriski.

CG I loved what you showed at Long Point (early work) and the thick paint you were using at that time.

SF I studied with Alexander Abels in Philadelphia. He was a descendant of Max Derner the German scientist of color. He was the Freud of pigment. He was tremendously knowledgeable and advised the WPA on their mural program; what to use and what not to use. We became close and I learned a lot from him. I got to know the properties of thick paint. You can't paint thickly if you don't understand the drying qualities of colors. Some dry more quickly than others. If you put yellow ochre into cadmiums there will be curling because of their different drying qualities.

I keep my palette very small, just four of five colors which dry evenly, so I can put them on any way I want. The other thing that's dangerous is the medium. If you use dammar varnish as you build up heavier and heavier, it's a perfectly good medium. But if it's heavy, it causes curling problems, but not cracking. Then you can go on with that. Nora and I worked together all these years and it came down to just turpentine. There's enough linseed oil in the paint to control this, so it's a perfect medium. In those early paintings I could paint as much as an inch thick and never had cracks. Those oil paintings are as good as new.

CG They are remarkably fresh.

SF We still paint heavy, but nowhere near as much as we used to. The reason was that we came out of an academic tradition. We studied with Franklin Watkins, Alexander Abels, Alexander Brooks, Louis Boucher, people who were old-time academicians. When we got to New York, there was so much excitement about abstract expressionism, the freedom of paint, and so on. Nora and I felt it was shaking up the deadness in art. We joined, but all I can say is that it wasn't our revolution. It was something we loved and accepted, but it wasn't our revolution. We both retained a love of imagery. I continued on with it, but our stock was expressionist with heavy paint.

NS We were inspired and challenged by the opportunities of someone like Jackson Pollock. It opened the possibility of working in the freest possible manner. We adopted a manner of central expression in paint.

CG Nora can you talk to me about the painting of two figures in the Long Point exhibition?

NS It's from 1962. It was an expulsion theme which I am still working on. People who were driven out, like the hippies. On an emotional level.

SF As you can see (from slides) I kept the figure within the paint. That was important and a vital meeting of the two thought processes; the paint world which I adored on its own terms, and the figurative which I am extremely involved with. Those two things are interlocked.

CG With the rise of abstract expressionism the figure was largely abandoned but never disappeared. The figure was being reexamined on its own terms.

SF There is a traveling show curated by April Kingsley on just that point. At that time there was Nora and myself, Lester Johnson, Bob Thompson, Emilio Cruz, Larry Rivers. They had a private love of the figure.

CG At that time, who were you in contact with that was painting the figure?

SF Nicolas Africano.

NS We were always outsiders.

SF We had each other and didn't need whatever it was.

NS We weren't that outside. We knew everyone but the critics. The attitude in our work is different from most people. Even in the early days this (points) looks free. It's from 1962, but is considered and orderly compared to what was going on. Even with all that paint, if you look at our work, it has nothing to do with Hofmann. We have huge, brilliant colors which come way off the canvas. Although the plane is flat, it's not an evenness.

Our work has a solid well-knit system. There isn't that dichotomy which goes on with abstract expressionism. Even with the figure, like Nicolas Africano, who is a fine figurative painter. He is closer to abstract expressionist free-flowing use of drawing, with a back and forth, extreme use of contrast. Our work had a higher rate of finish.

SF There are several important things that we felt involved with that's different from other artists. I felt an involvement with the figure in a brand new, abstract expressionist spatial image. Space was no longer reality, rather, an invented space. It made the image much more interesting.

I've got paintings of the figure sitting in front of a window which is all around and envelops the figure. It's a contemporary way of looking at space. There is something else about invented space which is the modern Freudian age. I did a series of sleeping women. If you took a Titian sleeping woman, if you can put the head into the space and the space comes out in front of it. You sink it deeper into mystery than if it were lying on the surface like a Titian woman, who is lying on a couch. You start playing psychologically and create great mysteries. Giacometti really capitalized on that marvelously with great drawings and paintings. It's a twilight world where people are in or out. You don't know exactly where they are standing.

CG You both work in a similar manner.

SF That's true and it never bothered us. It's wonderful to be married to an artist that you agree with.

NS It's been nothing but helpful. As Sideo said, it wasn't our revolution but we loved it, ate it, digested it, and made it our life. We developed this together. It was personalized and projected into the work. It was more a school of thought than that we paint alike. When I or Sideo have a solo show, it's a different attitude. If you are not familiar with the art, it's because it's not a school of art that has extended its tentacles to other people. We stand alone, which makes it more similar than if you have a group of people who have been influenced by us. Neither of us has ever taught.

SF In the end what makes great art is individual expression pouring through. I was stunned by a show of Seurat and his followers at the Guggenheim Museum. I never got over the fact that I could walk around and immediately spot a Seurat. Not because he was using dots. They all did that. It was a matter of his intensive personal poetry pouring through that nobody else had. That's what informed the artist. It was not about his technique.

People would find it interesting if they could see us drawing the figure. Nora is five inches from the model. They have become so nervous that they quit because they can't take it. Me, I sit back and don't give a damn about the model, although I am completely aware of her. I'm totally involved with myself.

CG You support yourself entirely on the work?

SF No, we have an income which we rely upon, but that only started when I was 45 or so. Until then, I supported myself by selling paintings and through commercial work. We were raising two children. After that, I quit commercial work and devoted myself to painting.

CG It's interesting that you have never taught.

SF I have two teaching degrees, a BFA and an MFA. Today, if we needed money, I would rather teach than do commercial art. At the time I was dividing my time with great care. In the morning, I would work for three hours on commercial art. Nora would be getting jobs for illustration. In those three hours I made enough that the rest of the day I could paint.

CG Did you share your interests with Jan Müller and other Provincetown artists?

SF I knew Jan Müller, but didn't know Bob Thompson. I knew Lester Johnson and other artists from our time in the city. In those days, we were all members of the Artists' Club.

CG Did you know Peter Grippe? (A sculptor and my Brandeis professor.)

SF Yes, I knew him. We were in Zabriski Gallery.

CG Did you discuss the figure with those artists?

SF With most of the artists we talked very little about the figure. We were all going in our own directions. But we allied ourselves in a very quiet sort of way.

The artists went to the Cedar Bar every night. We went about once a week when we could get a babysitter. That was our only night out. On Fridays, we went to the Artists' Club then the Cedar Bar.

NS We loved all of the new concepts. We sat around for hours talking about them. We did not talk about the figure as such. Although we kept it, we didn't feel that it was an important part of our work. Now we talk about it a lot because we realize that it was a big difference. It isn't something to forget in terms of construction. We had our landscapes, which were never totally abstract.

It was an important part of our work because we went outside and painted. You tried to match yourself against the elemental feeling of nature. It was the paint quality where you were trying to give yourself a surprise. Matching your sense with what was out there caused very unexpected sensations. We developed a lot of things in our work that we could carry through.

That's a very good point. If you look at a Pollock, it's a tangled mesh. There's a strong subconscious there even if he was not involved with it. A strong feeling of nature lies there. He used to go to Martha's Vineyard where there are scrub oaks and bramble meshes. I always believed that the three barber poles (*Blue Poles*) were those trees. In the tangled mesh one could see that there was nature in Pollock. You can also find nature in Rothko. My studio has a bar across the window. I could see the different times of day in terms of light coming in. You can become quite spiritual looking out a window. Through abstract expressionism, we were able to develop the sensory qualities through paint that we were able to absorb from nature. How, for instance, do you paint dampness? When you're dealing with nature, it's just a still life object like an apple. What makes it meaningful is smells and wind. There's light pouring over it and on your skin. Those elements come together and become almost religious in a way. You develop an awe which, with respect, unites you into a creative being. Not in a powerful sense, but in a humble one. When we work out there on landscapes, you feel quite humble. In the city, we paint figures in our 22nd Street rat trap studio which we work in all winter long. We've had the same studio for 40 years.

CG Don't you get tired of each other?

NS As I said, it's a very good relationship. We're always talking about art and our headaches.

SF I was having dinner with John Grillo and Al Jensen. They turned to me and said, "How can you paint with a woman?" They just couldn't believe it was possible. I said, "I don't know how you can feel that way. If it's a matter of competition, I'm competing with you as much as I'm competing with her." Art is not about competition, it's a matter of finding your own way and expressing feelings about the life you are living. That's what's important. Our relationship wasn't the issue. Of course, were she not equally talented, there might have been problems. Nora's a fighter. If I got ahead, she got ahead. There was always a united effort moving forward.

CG Lee Krasner was a great artist overshadowed by Pollock.

NS We didn't know she was working. We didn't know them as a couple. She didn't seem to work as much as her husband. I don't know what happened between them, but after he died, she knuckled down more.

SF We don't know that.

NS No, we don't. I remember Pollock as running to the bathroom at Cedar Bar to let out more of his liquor. From what I remember, he was always drunk. He was a very difficult man, a sweet man, a lovely person.

CG Who did you know at the Cedar Bar?

SF We sat with John Lester and Ray Heller, Philip Pearlstein, Wolf Kahn. They were people our age. Pollock and the abstract expressionists were twenty years older than us. They were artists we looked up to. I knew de Kooning but he didn't know me. Ones I knew better were Rothko and Franz Kline.

CG They were heavy drinkers.

SF Everyone was.

CG Were you drinkers?

SF No, because we had kids. We kept that secret because people wouldn't associate with us if they knew we had children. It was a period when you sacrificed everything for art and we did.

CG It's been said that there were few women on the scene.

SF That's not true. There was Louise Nevelson, Louise Bourgeois, Joan Mitchell, Grace Hartigan, Nora.

NS It's my opinion that women were looked down upon. They were not taken seriously because up to that time there had not been any important women artists. The men felt that the women artists were not serious or committed. That changed when a group of us came along; Marisol, Helen Frankenthaler, Louise Nevelson, Louise Bourgeois, Joan Mitchell, Grace Hartigan.

When they started, these women had a difficult time. They managed to impress themselves on the hard-boiled male artists. There was Mary Frank, and Dody Müller was a serious artist. There were strong women who really worked and carried the ball. They were every bit as serious and committed as the male artists. Galleries didn't change their attitude for a long time. That's changed today except, perhaps, for Mary Boone.

SF We were at a restaurant this winter and Mary Boone was there with five of her male artists. Perhaps she doesn't want the competition of another woman. She likes being surrounded by the boys.

We built our life around art. We were good parents, but didn't force our ambitions onto our children. Our kids were raised well and are happy. We gave them the tools to go out and succeed on their own. You can't pass the buck. Each of us has to contribute.

CG Can we talk more about the figure?

NS I've always dealt with myth. In terms of content, it opens avenues for me. It creates truths that I can put down that reveal my feelings about people. I like to draw people and get their inner psychological being. Then I like to take that and out it into a theme. That creates a greater dramatic attitude; sexual passions, sorrow, nightmarish foreboding. It's a way of bringing a whole world into your work.

CG Is Balthus an influence on your work?

NS It's interesting that you ask that. We have been compared to him a lot. A long time ago, we saw a show of his and don't know the work that well. It was early on for us, and I don't think we liked it that much. Then we saw a very fine show at Matisse Gallery about ten years ago. We saw a huge retrospective at the Metropolitan Museum. I now realize that he shares many of our thoughts. As an important contemporary artist that we relate to, that makes us less mavericks. We belong to attitudes that exist in contemporary society.

SF He came out of cubism but made his own way. Nora and I came out of expressionism and yet maintained our own individuality.

NS That's very important to our work, the feeling of contemporary concepts of pain. Balthus had a great feeling for the past and brought that into his work.

SF (Shows his catalog) This could be Balthus-like but I had no direct connection.

CG Everyone seems sad in these pictures.

SF It's the models, they were all girls with serious problems, and I absorbed their sadness. I have always had a feeling for the plight of women. I dressed them in costumes like Pagliacci the sad clown. The models were dolled up to look sexy, jazzy, and everything else. But they would come and pose feeling miserably unhappy, worried about their boyfriends or where they were going to get the rent.

CG You don't exploit them as erotic objects?

SF Not at all. That's the last thing on my mind. I just don't care.

NS Scale plays an important role.

SF I have a respectful attitude toward women and can't stand men who talk about them with hostility.

CG Is it erotic to work with models?

SF It's the difference between Titian and Matthias Grünewald. Titian is not painting a beautiful woman. He is conveying a beautiful attitude toward life. Whereas the view of Grünewald is disturbed. I think what's important is not the subject matter but the emotions you are pouring out. Chardin could paint a still life that conveyed more despair than the social realists of the 1930s. There's one person who left an impact on me, he is a social realist. I won't mention his name because he is a friend. He painted a man with one leg sitting in a door of a Bowery flophouse. The problem with the painting was that it was painted like a beautiful Renoir still life. He wasn't feeling it at all. He was pouring out his love and the image was just a superficial part of it. In most art the image is a superficial part.

NS From the beginning I adored painting the figure.

CG You just paint women.

NS No, I paint males as well, but not as many as I would like to. I draw from the figure then paint them. Male models are harder to come by. I can't find as many men to paint. I paint couples, as well as lone men and women. I work on a painting for a long time.

SF Neither of us paint from models. We just use them for drawing.

CG The drawings seem more observational and detailed than the paintings.

SF Very true.

CG Do you have individuals who respond more to the drawings or paintings?

SF The drawings are a different trip. You have a line, then a blank, then another line. To create the form, the lack has to be accounted for. Automatically that makes it a different world. It's two entirely different things. Look at the quick and spontaneous way that Rembrandt draws. Then consider the layer upon layer, plodding of the paintings. That sucks out all the psychological force that the paintings have. Nora and I can do a drawing in an hour, whereas it takes a month or more to do a painting.

CG What about the drawing in the gallery?

SF That's a drawing for a large painting, so it took me eight hours over two sessions because I become exhausted. It takes tremendous tension.

CG Do you and Philip Pearlstein use any of the same models?

SF We criss-cross because we're close friends. We used to draw together. With time, our approach and attitude changed. He got more involved in the subject than either Nora or I did. He went more to the tradition of it. I don't think of it that way and have no feeling for realism.

NS I have no feelings about realism and don't think you can be realistic. I'm not even interested. When I paint, reality doesn't come into my mind. I may work on all kinds of descriptive areas to focus on something. You can get a sense of what I'm trying to put on canvas. Reality does not enter my mind.

CG How did you get involved with Long Point and what does it mean to you?

NS To begin with there was Tirca Karlis and other good galleries. It does a lot for artists and the community for artists to have places to show, places to gather and talk about the work. When Cape Cod National Seashore (U.S. National Park Service) came here, that brought additional blight. There was increased tourism and a real estate boom. The galleries were closing. There was little left in terms of what we wanted as an artists' community. That was eight years ago when a group of us got together.

CG After Karlis died there was no major gallery.

SF Motherwell has been here for 40 years and Budd Hopkins has been here a long time. At 17 years, we are relative newcomers. Three or four artists got together, Leo Manso, Hopkins, Fritz Bultman. They started choosing artists and called us.

It's a versatile group, but we are mature enough not to quibble. Nobody storms out of the room over something petty. We have been through that when we were younger. Now we let things slide.

NS There were all these galleries showing candles, seagulls, and sailboats. There was a desire to set standards. That was one of the reasons for Long Point.

CG What has Long Point meant for you?

SF It brought together some very fine people who we all have respect for.

NS It's very stimulating because we have all kinds of shows. We bring our work each summer and plan a season.

CG Liz (Elizabeth O'Donnell, the gallery director) said that there will be a "red show" next summer.

NS We have a lot of red paintings.

CG During abstract expressionism there were emerging artists painting the figure which was anathema to Clement Greenberg and mainstream critics. These artists have been marginalized.

NS Outstanding work can be overlooked during any period. Even when everyone assumed that they knew what's going on. It's easy to ignore what you're not interested in.

CG What do you think of the neo-expressionists, Chia, Clemente, Schnabel, who are now prominent?

NS I have mixed feeling about the work, but glad because I did not support Pearlstein and the realists who were arid and dull.

SF I would say that if it is not coming from a past tradition, they are pushing a new image onto the scene. De Kooning put it well when he said, "When I came to art, art was already there. All I could do was add something onto it." The artists of significance are always the ones that carry on. Cezanne carried on with what came before him and Picasso took it from there. I have to add to what came behind me.

NS If you were involved with the abstract tradition, there was no way to be involved with what Sideo and I were doing.

CG How were your reviews?

NS The earlier ones were interesting. In the 1950s the critics liked our work and we got good reviews. But they would say things like that we were confused between abstraction and subject matter. They always wanted a clean package.

SF It reversed itself with the Philip Pearlstein school in the days of Hilton Kramer with the dry and cool school. There was too much emotion and paint. We never fit in. The Europeans came through the gallery system, and blew up a lot of concepts which had been hanging heavy. Now we have a ridiculous art scene with a lack of judgment or standards. Compared to the way it was going, which I didn't like at all. I prefer it now.

CG Carmen Cicero (Long Point artist) is responding to what's going on with neo-expressionism.

NS He's very much into the new way of working.

CG Looking at the work, you would assume the artist is in his 20s.

SF He's a jazz musician and very young in spirit. He had a lot of recognition in the 1950s. I didn't know him, but we were showing at the same time. He was with Peridot and I was with Zabriski. All of the Long Point artists have had reputations. Leo Manso was a very popular artist and Fritz Bultman has always been respected. Budd had been respected, as have been all of the artists. We are artists past 50. The shows are interesting because we are all good painters. We have a complete understanding of each other.

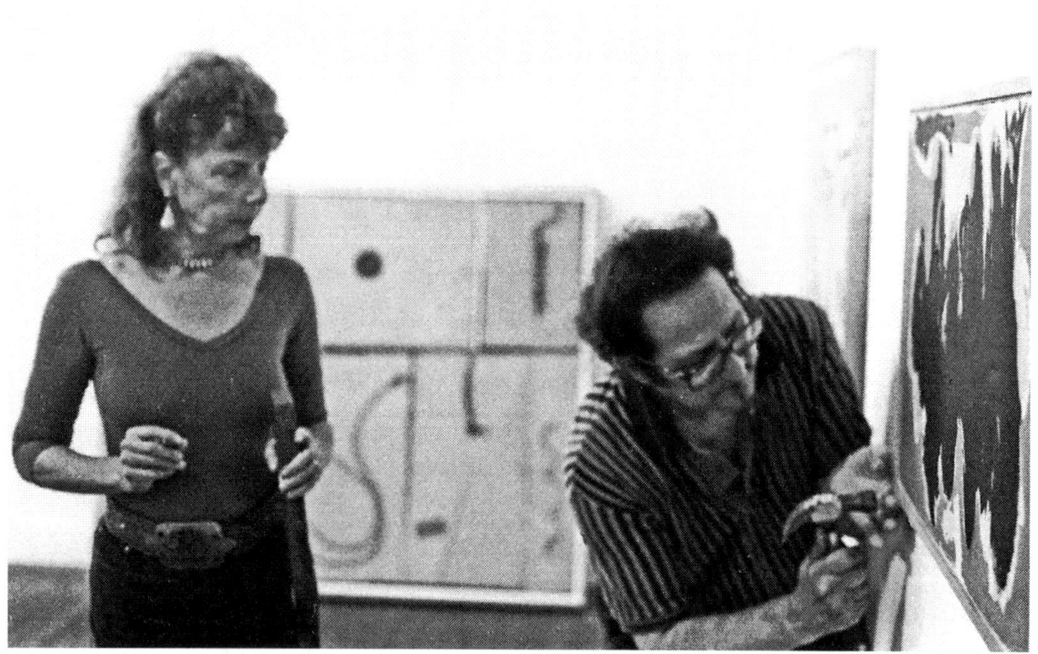

Nora Speyer and Sideo Fromboluti installing at Long Point. Giuliano photo.

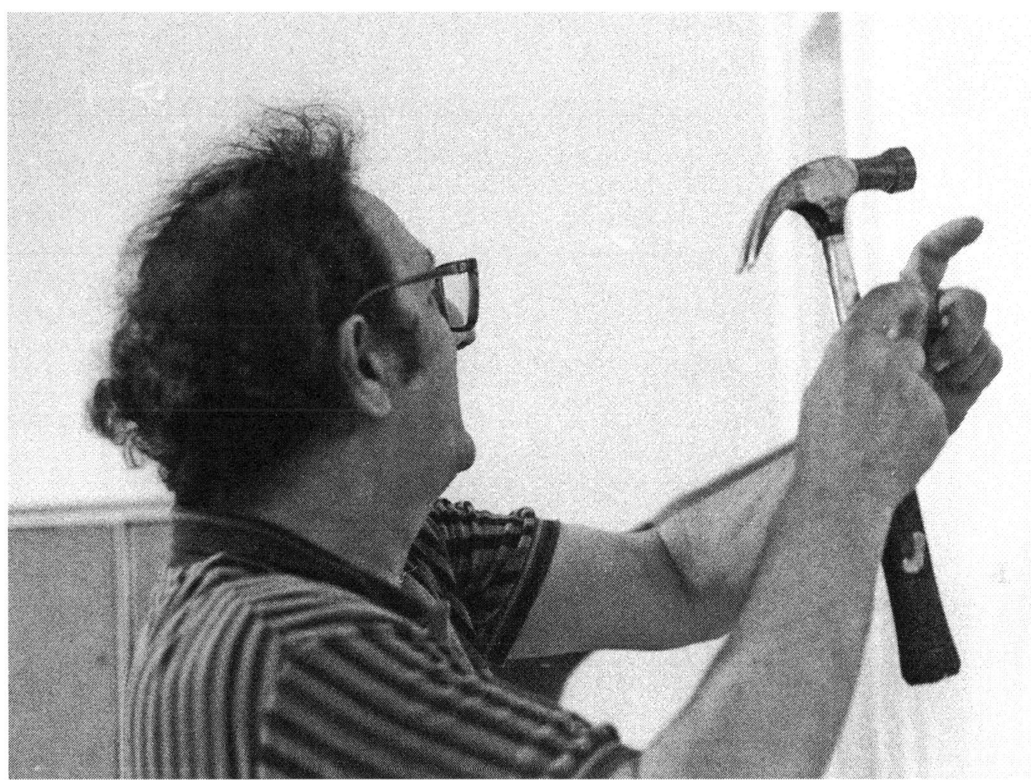

Sideo hanging a picture. Giuliano photo.

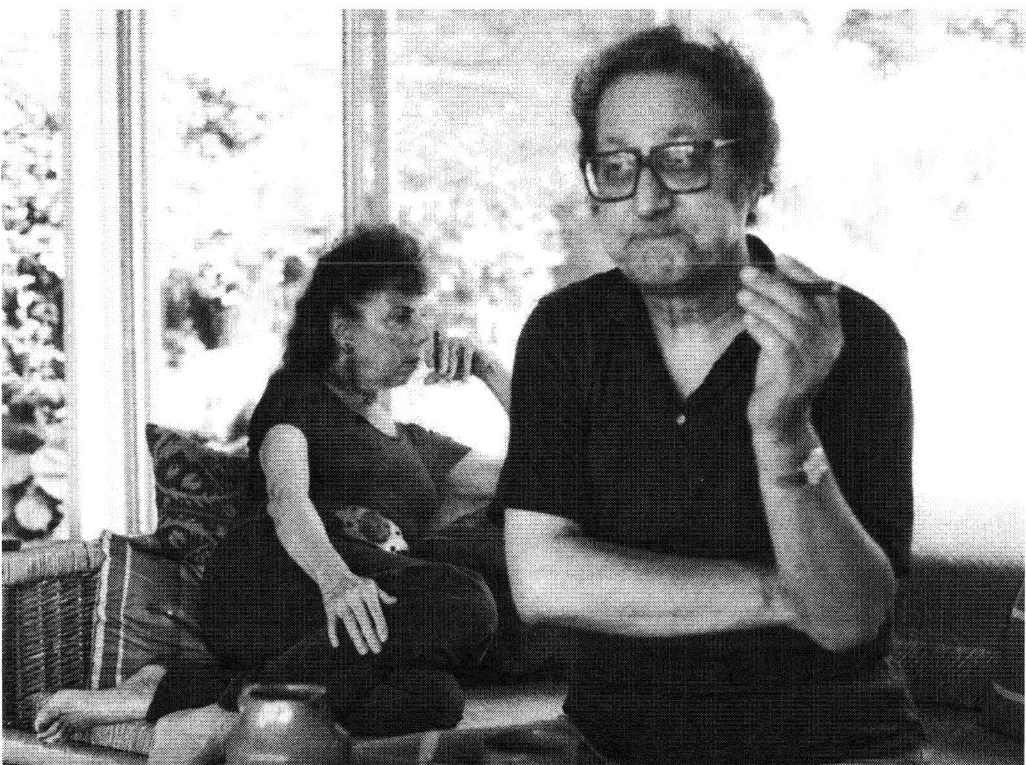

The artists at home. Giuliano photo.

Sal Del Deo, Artist and Chef

We viewed the stunning 2017 retrospective, *Salvatore Del Deo: A Storied History* at the Cape Cod Museum of Art in Dennis. In 2023, then 95, he was the subject of national news when there was an attempt to evict the renowned artist and chef from his historic summer Provincetown dune shack.

In the 1980s, I first interviewed Sal who, with Ciro Cozzi (1921–2013), started a sandwich shop which expanded into the most renowned of Provincetown's many-storied restaurants, the still-running Ciro and Sal's.

By the 1970s, they had parted ways and Del Deo opened his own restaurant, Sal's Place, in the East End. I have been regaled with many colorful stories by the artist Vico Fabbris, who worked for Sal and shared a passion for Italian cuisine. For a time, Cozzi expanded the restaurant into a franchise with a second Provincetown restaurant, The Flagship, and another Ciro's in Boston.

In addition to expanding, as Peter Manzo revealed in *Ptown: Art, Sex and Money on the Outer Cape*, the front-of-house staff was running a lucrative football pool. When Cozzi bet on the Sunday games, losses were routinely subtracted from the till. That's not good for business. Sal proved to be less flamboyant but more level-headed restaurateur.

In 2017 the Cape Cod Museum's former director, Edith Tonelli, informed me that Sal, then 92, was in great spirits and had enthusiastically worked with her to select paintings that covered the range of his oeuvre from figurative triptychs, to saturated, high-chroma landscapes, still life paintings, and abstract canvases. He is represented by Berta Walker Gallery in Provincetown.

Over the years, I have seen individual works in exhibitions of the Provincetown Art Association and Museum, but viewing them in depth was remarkable.

The artist's wife, the poet, musician, and arts activist, Josephine Couch Del Deo, passed away at 90. Over a period of 20 years, she researched and published *Figures in Landscape, The Life and Times of the American Painter Ross Moffett.*

During the era of WWI, Moffett was a part of the generation who joined the artists' community that was formed around the summer school of Charles Hawthorne. Moffett was a third of the artist's triumvirate that included Edwin Dickinson and Karl Knaths.

Both Provincetown Art Association and Museum and CCMOA have been crucial in preserving the heritage of generations of Cape Cod's renowned artists.

When Ciro and Sal settled in Provincetown after WWII they, like many on the GI Bill, came to study with famous teachers. They enrolled in the school of Henry Hensche. He had been an assistant to Hawthorne and continued in the tradition of plein air painting with saturated color and emphasis on the play of natural light. They pursued a conservative, naturalistic form of modernism compared to the radical approach of Hans Hofmann who attracted nascent abstract expressionists to his New York and Provincetown classes.

That influence of Hensche is richly evident in the landscapes of Del Deo. The surfaces of canvases are flatter, more abstract, and explode with saturated color. Here the famed Cape Light has been juiced up with riveting intensity.

Particularly striking is a painting of fishing boats tied up to the town dock. The silhouette of a warehouse anchors one end. There are accents of color in the patterns of several boats parallel to the picture plane. Both sea and sky have been flattened into an electric expanse of intense cobalt blue. There are several typically P'town distant views of flat, parallel stacks of sand, sea, and sky.

Del Deo is a part of the long tradition of artists who remained "true to nature" as John Ruskin stated, but played along the evocative cusp of non-objective painting. What intrigues about the work is pushing the limits of site specific, plein air painting which have been finished and intensified in the studio. Tonelli described it as abstract realism.

Early on, Sal did odd jobs to pay the rent, and one summer went to sea with a scallop boat. It's that experience which resonates in the poignant triptych *Homage to the Patricia Marie.* It memorializes the sinking, in 1976, of the scallop boat of that name off Eastham. Seven men were lost.

The central figure in the three panels is a boy looking straight out at us. There is pain and loss in his expression. While staring at the viewer he appears to be looking into a beyond that will comprise a future without his dad.

The space of the panels is compressed by a cluster of several fishermen. One whets his scallop shucking knife. Another is huddled over a newspaper that reports the disaster at sea. In a panel we see the boat sinking in an imagined background with sailors foundering in pounding surf.

The exhibition synched with the artist being given the museum's annual MUSE award for outstanding contributions to the artistic community.

Interview of Sal Del Deo
August 1982
At his restaurant

Charles Giuliano When did you meet Karl Knaths?

Sal Del Deo In 1937 I was a student at Vesper George School of Art (St. Botolph Street, Boston). During lunch, I would walk to Newbury Street and visit galleries. I saw a Knaths at Boris Mirski Gallery. I was impressed by it. The following year, I came to Provincetown. As a student I wrote to Knaths and he answered inviting me to his studio. I later learned that he frequently did this with young artists who admired his work. There were weekly invitations for certain people to come see his latest work. There was always something to look forward to. Even though along in years, he was always interested to listen to someone else's point of view. He was a very humble guy.

He was reclusive, but when he knew you, he was friendly and jovial. He loved having young people around. He woke up early, painted, and then took a walk in the afternoon. He did his creative work around seven a.m. He would come by my restaurant, sit on the patio, and chat. He was reclusive but had close friends.

CG Who were they?

SDD Jim Forsberg and his then wife, Joan Wye. They could read German. They spent the winter translating, reading great works in German.

CG In the Archives of American Art there are translations of Mondrian, Kandinsky, and Malevich (from German).

SDD He was of German ancestry growing up in Wisconsin. He could read German, but not that well. But Joan knew it and they struggled through. His sister-in-law, the artist Agnes Weinrich (1873–1946), figures prominently in this narrative. It's too bad you weren't here earlier as there was a wonderful show of her work at the Heritage Museum. They own a few small woodcuts.

Agnes was a great influence. She and Helen, Knaths' wife, spent time in Paris, Munich, and Berlin. It's where the action was. He never left the States. Agnes opened his eyes to cubism while her sister Helen was a musician.

CG While a student at the school of the Art Institute of Chicago, he was employed as a guard for the touring *Armory Show.* So, he saw cubism (Duchamp) before he came to Provincetown.

SDD She studied with the cubist Albert Gleizes and knew the futurist Gino Severini. He was a major influence on a lot of Provincetown painters. He wrote prolifically and took on students. He worked in a neo-cubist manner.

CG Did you know Agnes?

SDD She died before I came here. Karl thought highly of her as a painter.

CG I understand that you were with him when he died.

SDD I was with him the day before he died. When he was pronounced dead, I rushed to his studio to assure that everything was there. There were exquisite works that related back to his early subjects.

CG Do you know the self portrait that Nat Halper owns?

SDD Yes, but it's not by Knaths. It was painted by his friend Ross Moffett.

CG Nat Halper said that several years before he died, Knaths asked him about the Milton Avery estate. Halper concluded that he was concerned about his health.

SDD He had bad attacks of kidney stones. I was with him at the hospital on a couple of occasions. We had long discussions about his estate. There was a collector, Emil Arnold, who bought from him and donated to museums as tax write-offs. Karl was under contract to Rosenberg but could sell anything that they turned back.

CG They were not his best works.

SDD I wouldn't say that, but Rosenberg didn't think they were his best paintings. The story of the estate is fascinating, but makes me sad. This guy Arnold told him to put the work in a bank. They would handle it and take care of Helen. You won't have to worry about the financial end of it. I cautioned him not to do that. I spoke with people at the bank (Ken Demaris, Cape Cod Bank and Trust) and I was not impressed by their knowledge of art. They had no interest in the preservation of the paintings. After he died, I was vindicated when they had a show of his work at the bank. They had taken everything from Rosenberg Gallery and had it all there.

CG Do you recall what was there?

SDD There was a lot there, but not the best work. There were the big paintings of *Moby Dick and Ishmael.* One of the best works was a still life that I got them to donate to PAAM. I also got the Deer which is in the Heritage Museum. Actually, Mrs. Knaths gave the still life to PAAM.

CG There are no dates on *Moby Dick and Ishmael.*

SDD I think they're from the 1940s.

CG How many works were in the bank? A hundred?

SDD Not that many. I wouldn't chance a guess. There were about 20 works in the bank's show. What appalled me is that they were all over the bank on cheap easels. They had large cardboard labels tacked to the canvases. I was so angry I took them all off. The bank manager came to me and said, "What are you doing?" I said, "This is a disgrace." He told me to come to his office. We talked and he asked, "What should we have done?" (The bank served as sole executor with nobody from the art world to advise them.)

I told them that they had no right to treat the work in this manner. "If it were jewelry, you would have it appraised and properly protected," I said. "If you are going to be executors of an artist's estate, you need to retain consultants in order to do things properly."

CG Are all the paintings gone?

SDD Yes, because they got rid of them.

CG The independent dealer and collector, Ed Shein, bought in bulk from the bank, then immediately met with Jim and Jean Young of Woodstock, New York, who bought a number of works from him. They made a serious investment in Knaths and acquired interesting pieces, including a portfolio of early abstract monotypes, circa 1919, with about half signed Otto Knaths, his birth name. Reggie Cabral may have acquired sketch books and drawings. The bank was pulling pages from sketch books and giving them estate stamps. You see them show up at Provincetown auctions.

SDD Karl was working on a book (*Ornament and Glory*) that he never published. I read it. He had a couple of versions in sketch books. Ferol (Sibley Warthen) could help because she learned his system.

CG She is now 92 and it is difficult to get the specifics.

(There was the exhibition *Ornament and Glory: theme and theory in the work of Karl Knaths:* October 9–November 21, 1982, Edith C. Blum Art Institute, Milton and Sally Avery Center for the Arts, the Bard College Center, Annandale-on-Hudson, New York. The catalog included a version of his text. Over the years a number of his artist friends read and suggested edits.)

Why didn't you learn his system?

SDD By then I was a mature artist and it would have entailed orchestrations of color.

CG Did he discuss with you the grid that he used?

SDD I learned a lot from Karl, including the orchestration of a color scheme in a painting. He talked a lot about the picture plane. He was very tough on other painters. He would take down a book of Old Masters and go through it with me. He would identify works which he thought were successful, as well as ones that were not; which ones violated the picture plane with confusion between two- and three-dimensional space. That was always very exciting for me.

CG There are notebooks in the Archives of American Art in which he would paste a reproduction of a painting then write comments around it.

SDD Those are the notebooks which I recall from the bank vault. When he was alive, he let me borrow them. There were a lot of things that he did which were similar to *Klee's Pedagogical Sketchbook*.

CG Did he plan to publish that critical analysis?

SDD Mira, an elderly lady friend of Ferol's, planned to publish them.

CG Did you ever buy his work?

SDD He gave me some things, but I didn't think that way. I own a restaurant which is open during the summer. Overall, we live frugally. We are not wealthy by any means. We were here as Ciro and Sal's for 20 years, but split up in 1961. Ciro still owns Ciro and Sal's and has a branch in Boston.

CG Why did you split?

SDD For many reasons. I thought I wanted to get out of the restaurant business. That just lasted for two years. I did construction work but couldn't make ends meet. I took over this place and after three years had a chance to buy it at a very good rate. Some friends helped. That was 20 years ago. You couldn't do it today, not by a long shot. The season is short, but I wouldn't want it any longer. That's the way I like it. I no longer have to work behind the stove, so I have the summer off.

Ciro and I were art students. He had a scholarship to Art Students League in New York where he studied with Mahonri Young (1877–1957, a social realist painter and sculptor). Later he trained as a sculptor with Piccirilli and studied fresco technique with Jean Charlot (1898–1979). We came here to study with Henry Hensche (1899–1992). It was 1946 when we studied with him.

CG Hofmann was here and why didn't you study with him?

SDD I wasn't that interested in the modern approach. When we came in the late 1940s, Provincetown was very alive. There were a number of galleries, prominent New York galleries with summer branches like Samuel Kootz and Virginia Zabriskie. There was the Saltpeter Gallery. Overall, there were at least a half dozen New-York-based galleries as well as the local ones.

I've been here long enough to know that the art scene is cyclical. There were great artists here: Karl Knaths, Edwin Dickinson, Ross Moffett, and Hans Hofmann. When they passed, a new cycle started with a lull in between.

It's just beginning to come back again with Long Point in Provincetown and Cherry Stone Gallery in Wellfleet. These galleries show artists of national stature.

CG What attracted you to Karl Knaths?

SDD His use of color, which I'm interested in. I always thought he was a great colorist. It was rather unique at the time because it was a deviation from local color. He told me, however, that his color was based on nature. We had a marvelous show of his work at the Art Association. I wish you had seen it, one of the best shows ever. Do you have the Charles Eaton book *Karl Knaths Five Decades of Painting*?

CG Yes.

SDD He's the poet in residence at Chapel Hill in North Carolina. They used to have a house in Connecticut and came here in the summer. They have a dozen or so works that they bought from him. He's in his 60s, a gracious man and supporter of Karl.

CG Was he prolific? There seems to be a lot of work floating around.

SDD He was diligent, working every day of his life with no deviation from his schedule.

They had no children or family life. He went to bed after supper and was up at the crack of dawn. He loved any excuse to go out. We would go to galleries together.

He loved to talk about baseball and had been a decent player in his youth. I asked if he played and he said, "Third base." He was a very human kind of guy, which was what I loved about him.

When he first came here there were very few artists around, Dickinson and Moffett.

CG Did you know Moffett?

SDD Very well. My wife is writing his biography.

(Figures in a Landscape: The Life and Times of the American Painter, Ross Moffett, 1888–1971 Limited Edition Hardcover–January 1, 1994 by Josephine Couch Del Deo (Author), Ross Moffett, and Ross Moffett 1889–1971, January 1, 1975 by Josephine Couch Del Deo)

CG I would love to see some of that material.

SDD I doubt that she will show it to you because she's working on it. She has a great deal of stuff. She has written something about Dickinson as well. Dickinson, Moffett, and Knaths represented the modern jury for the Art Association when there was a big split.

(At the time I asked Bob Brown the Boston branch director for Archives of American Art about the Moffett material. He said it was on extended loan to Mrs. Del Deo. The AAA branch later closed and since then it has been ever more difficult to deal with them. I even had a lot of trouble gaining access to files I donated to them. They are plagued with budget and staff cuts.)

CG Can I talk to her?

SDD She's not well.

There's something else I want to say about Karl. In the early stages he was very opposed to the war in Vietnam, as were my wife and I. One of the first petitions against the war was created by artists. It was published in the New York Times. Karl and Helen were listed, as were my wife and I. There was a protest in August 1962 against America and nuclear bombing of Hiroshima and Nagasaki. There was a published photo of Karl and Helen walking through Provincetown denounced as traitors. That brought us together with shared political views. Until the day he died, Karl was a tremendous spirit.

CG Did he discuss (Emanuel) Swedenborg with you?

SDD He gave me some things to read. Did you see the little book on Knaths that Duncan Phillips published? Of course, Phillips had the largest collection of his work.

CG About his philosophy?

SDD He quoted from Swedenborg *The Book of Psalms*. He also read the Bible, as did his friends Moffett and Dickinson. Each of them had great knowledge of the Bible. Karl and Moffett came from the Midwest and Dickinson from upstate New York.

CG What did he tell you about Swedenborg?

SDD I didn't understand any of it other than as a pantheistic appreciation of life, which I share. Karl was raised Catholic.

CG Did you hear him lecture?

SDD Yes, at the Fine Arts Work Center. He cut through the crap. When there was a lot of double talk in a discussion he would say, "Let's cut all the baloney and get down to the facts." He was a very matter-of-fact kind of guy.

CG How did you get into the restaurant business?

SDD As an art student you learn to fend for yourself. It turned out to be something I enjoyed doing and close to painting.

CG Karl was a panelist in *Forum '49*.

SDD I recall one at a gallery founded by Weldon Kees. He was an avant-garde poet. He and another poet, Cecil Hemley, started a gallery here. (Gallery 200) It was the first to show a Jackson Pollock drip painting. That was in 1949, just up the street from here.

He lived here early on when he was struggling, before the move to the Hamptons. The studio he lived and worked in was bought by Franz Kline. It's a famous place just up the street from here.

CG You and Ciro worked together?

SDD He had a bunch of kids and there was the chance to buy a house very cheap. He said, "How the hell are we going to stay here in the winter and support ourselves?" It was a wonderful life, so beautiful here. There wasn't a crowd. It was a painter's paradise.

CG One hears that the fishermen were tolerant and kept to themselves.

SDD They are simplistic in their needs. Their vessels are ship shape and their homes are the same. They tolerated the artists and gays. In the beginning it was like a small European village.

Karl was proud of how little it took for him to live here in the winter. The fishermen on the docks gave us fish.

CG Was he poor?

SDD In the beginning, yes. When I knew him, he was under contract to Rosenberg Gallery, but it took many years to reach that point. I have no idea what the estate is worth. His wife had relatives in Wisconsin who were beneficiaries. I met them when they came here from Wisconsin. When I saw paintings in the bank vault, they were priced from $3,000 to $12,000.

(The Knaths' will was divided in three. The Art Institute of Chicago, where he trained was willed a third. Another third went to the Phillips Collection in Washington, D.C. in appreciation for all that Duncan Phillips did for him. The final third went to their heirs.)

CG So you think that *Moby Dick* sold for $12,000?

SDD It was very large, 8-foot by 4-foot on masonite. I don't think he sold it and the painting went into the estate. It was over the bank president's desk when I saw it.

CG So Knaths never made a lot of money.

SDD He was frugal but never rich. They were modest people. We went clamming together, so he had his bucket of clams, a glass of beer, and occasionally wine, and that was it.

CG Did he say why he didn't travel other than to New York and D.C.?

SNN On a number of occasions I asked him about that and he said that it just didn't interest him. I don't know why he never went to Europe because he was very excited about what Agnes told him. I would say, "I'm going to Italy, would you like to come with me?" But he wasn't interested, by then he was too old.

CG You can see a change in the works of the 1960s. They are less structured and have more high key color.

SDD I think he flirted with the ideas of abstract expressionism but never fell in with them.

CG Did he discuss Hofmann?

SDD Yeah.

CG You smile. He didn't think much of him.

SDD There, you said it.

CG We've talked about cycles.

SDD Hensche took over the Hawthorne tradition and ran a very successful school, which Ciro and I studied in. Dickinson was here as a part of the Hawthorne tradition.

CG Dickinson was close to Karl.

SDD Not really. He was linked to Hawthorne, but was a friend of Karl and developed a great respect for him. He called him Otto because he knew him well. Very few people called Knaths Otto.

CG By the time Hofmann arrived, Knaths, Dickinson, and Moffett were the Old Masters of Provincetown.

SDD There had been a split. On one hand was abstract expressionism headed by Hofmann. Then there was modernism derived from cubism which Knaths represented.

CG You would think that Hofmann and Knaths shared commonality.

SDD They respected each other. Karl never downgraded anybody. He liked something or he didn't. He didn't care for Hofmann's color, which he felt wasn't orchestrated.

CG Do you know anything about the Knaths' grids?

SDD You mean (Jay Hambidge's) *Dynamic Symmetry*? Moffett and Knaths knew it very well. I've been trying to read it. He was the great exponent of the Golden Section. Everyone in the 1920s was using it, but I don't see why it's necessary. The selectivity of the eye can put everything in place. Karl gridded off his pictures.

CG In general, Karl was tough on other artists, but he liked Nicolas de Staël (1914–1955) and Milton Avery. Did you know him?

SDD Very well. Avery was quiet, but urbane. Knaths was also quiet, but rustic.

CG Did he have a sense of humor?

SDD He was great. Underneath I suspected was a really lusty soul. He had a lusty appetite. His wife was older and that's where he toned down.

CG Did he have students or assistants?

SDD They had a housekeeper who cooked. She stayed on after Karl died, taking care of Helen. There was this kid, Bob Johnson, a student who stayed with him for a number of years. He helped and stretched canvases. I think he's now in Virginia or North Carolina. Bernie Beckmann also did odd jobs for Karl. There was another kid who helped.

CG He was under contract to Rosenberg and seemed to have steady income.

SDD Yes, for the last 20 years of his life. He was having success winning first prize at the Carnegie as well as The Met. He had paintings in major museums.

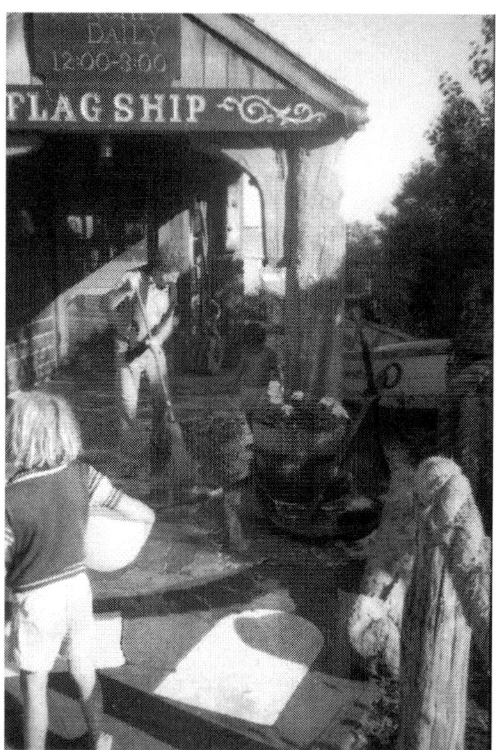

The Flagship was not a good investment for Cozzi. Giuliano photo.

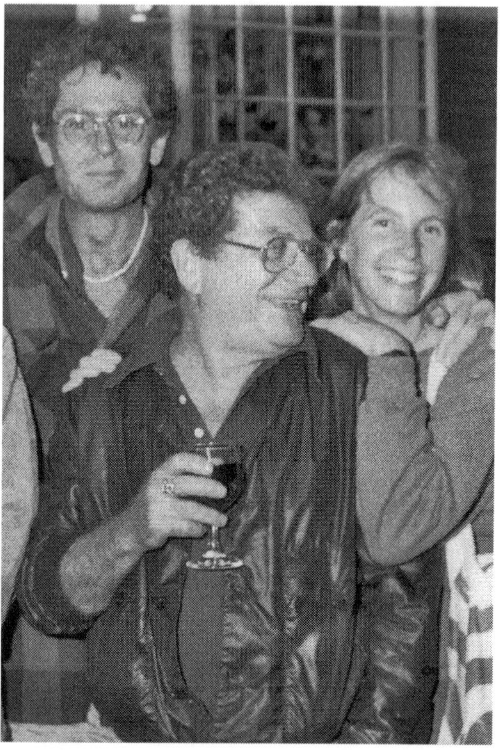

Chef Ciro Cozzi with artists Peter Plamondon and Necee Regis, Giuliano photo.

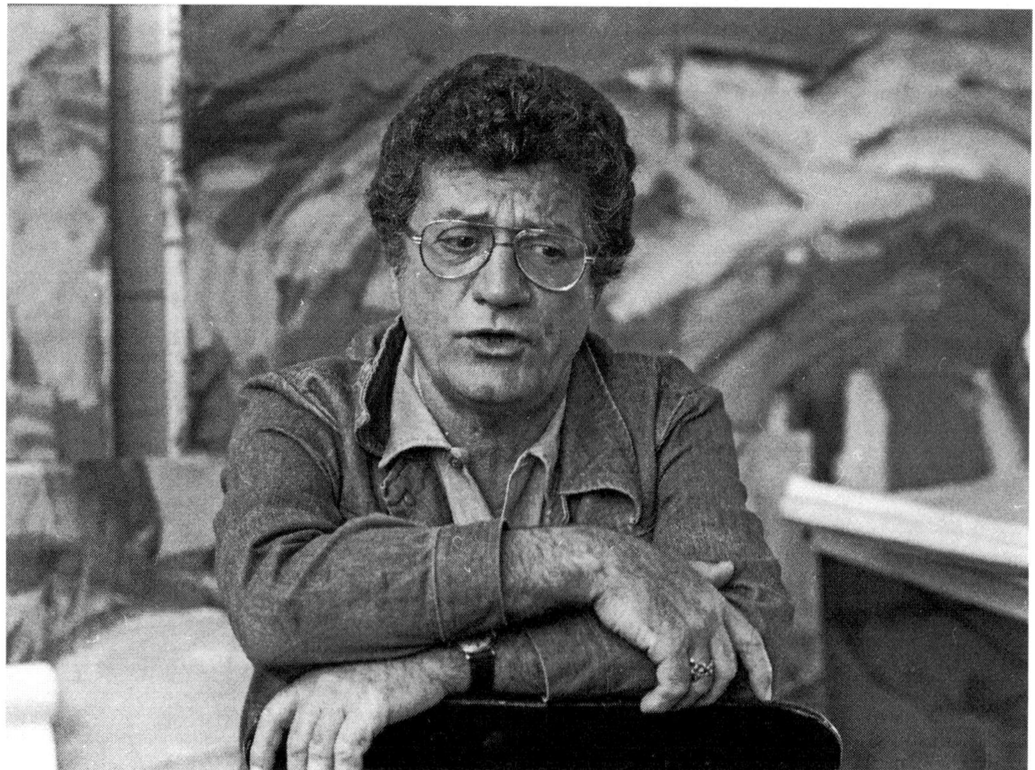

Ciro Cozzi, Norma Holt photo. Courtesy of PAAM.

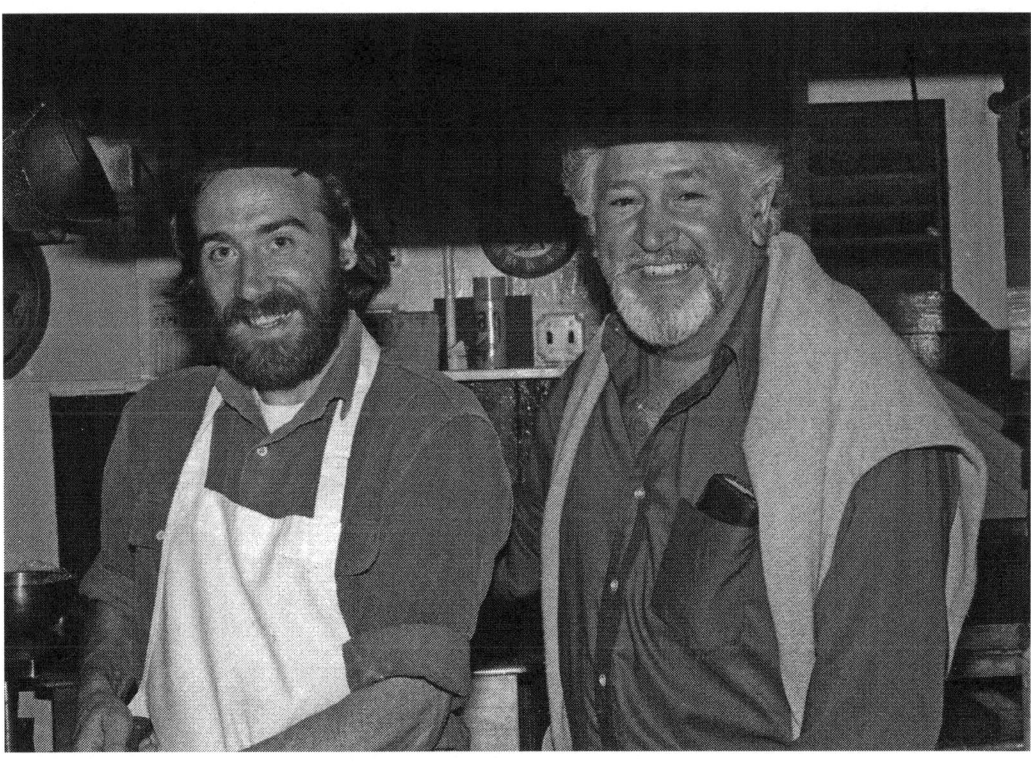

Sal in the kitchen with Vico Fabbris, 1980s, Giuliano photo.

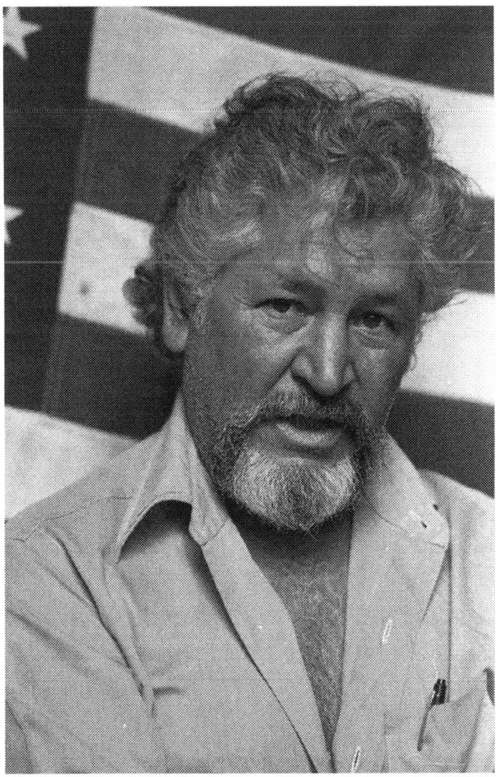

Norma Holt photo of Sal. Courtesy of PAAM.

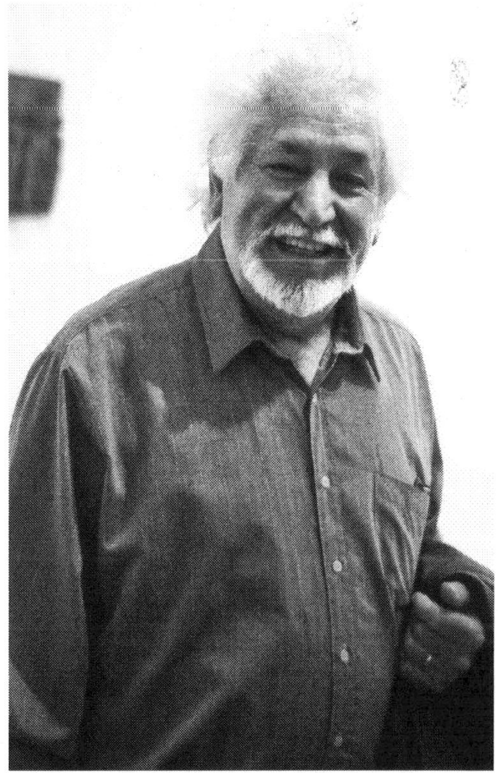

Sal Del Deo, 1995, Giuliano photo.

Forum '49 Moved the Cultural Needle

"Now about the series of programs for this summer. At a meeting last night, I made the suggestion that, to get a double-barreled effect, we should not only have a big opening on July 3, but also on that evening, present the first of our programs. The series, incidentally, is to be called *Forum '49*, and we plan to plaster the Cape with posters and flood the press with publicity releases within the next few weeks. We all agree that the panel you are going to do is a natural for the July 3 opening." Weldon Kees in a letter to Adolph Gottlieb, June 8, 1949.

In 1899 Charles W. Hawthorne moved to Provincetown and founded Cape Cod School of Art. Artists came to study with him. The outbreak of WWI resulted in artists relocating from Europe. Needing space to show their work, the Provincetown Art Association was founded in 1914. For decades it reflected the conservative naturalism of Hawthorne in conflict with artists who had brought home modernism from their study in Europe.

There was a second post war influx of artists in the late 1940s. Many of this new generation came to study with Hans Hofmann, including those on the GI Bill. In contrast to its small population, there was an increasing critical mass of progressive artists, creators, and intellectuals that placed Provincetown at the epicenter of radical cultural change. The ambitious, summer-long exhibitions and weekly meetings of *Forum '49* was an attempt to capture lightning in a bottle.

When Cecil Hemley, Fritz Bultman, and Weldon Kees were organizing *Forum '49* there was opposition. The Provincetown Art Association, under the leadership of Hawthorne, refused to host it. Donald Witherstine, whose Gallery 200, a popup in a renovated garage, would be the *Forum's* venue, forced Kees to include several traditional artists. Witherstine also limited the show's run to a mere two weeks, prompting Kees' wife, Anne, to describe him as "a class-A son of a bitch for my money."

Arguably, that brief exhibition may have been the first dedicated to a core of the emerging abstract expressionists. It included two works by Jackson Pollock, who had previously visited Provincetown but was not there that summer. Not all of the artists were present, there were loans from New York galleries, but the checklist of exhibitors is formidable. It included then "emerging" and established artists: Jackson Pollock, Robert Motherwell, Adolph Gottlieb, Karl Knaths, Judith Rothschild, Fritz Bultman, Weldon Kees, Perle Fine, Kahlil Gibran, William Baziotes, Byron Browne, Richard Pousette-Dart, Bradley Walker Tomlin, Mark Rothko, Lawrence Kupferman and others.

The bi-weekly exhibitions that followed focused on established and salable artists selected by Witherstein. The venue also hosted the ambitious summer-long program of weekly panels and lectures.

Kees ensured that the inaugural event on July 3, titled "What Is an Artist?," included opposing views, with two abstract painters, Gottlieb and Hofmann, alongside architect Serge Chermayeff, and the representational painter George Biddle. 500 people were turned away that first night.

Biddle's correspondence with his former classmate (and recently elected president) Franklin Roosevelt, contributed to the establishment of the Federal Art Project, an arm of the Works Progress Administration that produced several hundred thousand pieces of publicly funded art. Biddle himself completed a mural titled *The Tenement* for the Justice Department building in Washington, D.C. He was a strong advocate for the conservative status quo.

"Adolph Gottlieb, much-publicized of late as a leading figure among avant-garde painters, held the fort for so-called 'unintelligible' art. To Mr. Gottlieb, the process of creation is guided by an element of mystery...the artist by strong inner compulsions that force him to express what he feels, come what may. The ensuing violation of accepted patterns of thought were indicative, not of chaos, Mr. Gottlieb stated, but of the evolution of new ideas. Defending the maze of rhythmic shapes and riotous color that surrounded the audience, he described them as the true art of today...the logical outgrowth and humanistic blend of the great traditions of cubism and surrealism." *The Provincetown Advocate,* July 7, 1949.

Hofmann, the final speaker of the night, closed with a defense of modern art and democracy: "Our constitution is a great work of art; it must not be destroyed by mediocrity. Let the youth of America speak. Let a free press and a creative critic speak. Long live the arts and the artist in a free future."

Gottlieb was asked to organize a panel on the topic "French vs. American Art." Fritz Bultman and Hans Hofmann drafted a manifesto objecting to the forum, which they distributed outside of the hall. Later that evening Gottlieb met Hofmann at a party and asked him what he thought of the panel discussion. Hofmann said it was fine. Gottlieb asked him why he put out the circular. Hofmann said that he objected to the title, "American vs. French Art". The French should have come first. Gottlieb told him it did in the title. "Oh," Hofmann said, "Then it's O.K." Irving Sandler's Conversation with Adolph Gottlieb at the HCE Gallery, August 15, 1957.

"No one now creates with joy; on the contrary, with anguish," announced Robert Motherwell during that panel. György Kepes, speaking on "Directions in 20th Century Architecture" a week later, said, "In this incredible chaos, we are almost lost people. We have lost our inner seismograph."

There were other flashpoints. Negative response prompted a change to Dwight Macdonald's lecture "The Dream World of Soviet Bureaucracy." It was modified to read "Speaker: Dwight Macdonald, editor of *Politics,* on a new theory exposing the lies of the Russian dictatorship." The promotion of Macdonald as a "vociferous opponent of Communism" was misleading. For Macdonald, this was a recent political posture, having moved from his Marxist position of less than 10 years before. And while Kees, Macdonald, and many others had protested against a Communist-backed Waldorf Conference in New York in the spring of 1949, the political landscape entailed confusing polarities, with artists and intellectuals taking various and sometimes conflicting positions.

It was an intense summer for Weldon Kees (1914–1945). A polymath, artist, poet, critic, traditional jazz musician, composer, and filmmaker, he was uniquely qualified to plan an overview of cultural issues of the day. He died young, an apparent suicide. There have been mixed assessments of him in critical studies and biographies. While advocating radical change in the arts, his featured *Forum* presentation was a reactionary, conservative survey of traditional jazz. He clung to the past while ignoring the importance of bop which was the emerging force of postwar jazz.

With the inclusion of psychoanalysis, leftist politics, traditional jazz, and the new architecture, *Forum '49* took on changes in contemporary culture along a broad front. Its great accomplishment was as harbinger of the New York School and Abstract Expressionism.

The global focus of the fine arts shifted from Paris to New York. The emerging artists gathered at New York's Cedar Tavern or debated at their Artists' Club. The later was managed by Irving Sandler who chronicled the the emerging generation of artists in his book *The Triumph of American Art.*

What the German born Hofmann and his associate, Bultman, had objected to was the chauvinism of discussion of post-war American art. They argued that in matters of aesthetics there are no winners and losers. The commercial dynamics of the art market which influenced critical thinking, however, enforced the notion of combat. The emerging avant-garde pushed aside the dominant movements of Regionalism, the American Scene and Social Realism. In the new paradigm Hawthorne, Biddle, and even Knaths were old hat. Provincetown danced to the beat of a different drummer and for at least that summer defined the cutting edge of cultural change. Kees and *Forum '49* had its finger on the pulse.

The headline of a 1950 *New York Times* article read "18 Painters Boycott Metropolitan; Charge 'Hostility of Advanced Art.'" In a letter to the museum, it was reported that "All the advanced artists of America will join us in our stand."

The artists who signed the letter were Jimmy Ernst, Adolph Gottlieb, William Baziotes, Barnett Newman, Clyfford Still, Richard Pousette-Dart, Theodore Stamos, Ad Reinhardt, Jackson Pollock, Mark Rothko, Bradley Walker Tomlin, Willem de Kooning, Weldon Kees, and Fritz Bultman. The letter was also signed by ten sculptors with the notation that they supported the artists' stand. The sculptors were Herbert Ferber, David Smith, Ibram Lassaw, Mary Callery, Day Schnabel, Seymour Lipton, Peter Grippe, Theodore Roszak, David Hare, and Louise Bourgeois."

While Knaths was a prominent participant in *Forum '49*, his work had been accepted for the Met exhibition which prompted protesting artists. He found himself on the wrong side of the decisive moment of post war American art. As momentum shifted to the new work, his status as a leading artist began to decline.

A group photo of the dissenting painters was published in *Life Magazine* identifying them as "The Irascibles." These artists came to be known as the abstract expressionists, action painters, or simply the New York School.

The *Forum '49* exhibition committee stated, "It ought to bring out, if nothing else, the roots of vital abstract work that had its beginnings in Provincetown not long after WWI. The vanguard work of (E. Ambrose) Webster, (Oliver Newbury) Chaffee, (Agnes) Weinerich, and (Blanche) Lazzell is part and parcel of the international aesthetic revolt that took its cue from the School of Paris, a revolt not unconnected with that of the poets, playwrights, and novelists who made Provincetown famous in the Twenties." Of these only

Lazzell (1878–1956) was then living.

For seating, pews of a razed church were purchased. With a capacity of 200, most of the programs were sold out with crowds outside. As an honorarium, speakers were given a bottle of scotch. There were lively after-parties during which Kees played piano and sang amusing songs. All that summer it was party time in P'town.

In a July 17, 1947 posting of *Provincetown Art Association Notes* there is a heading *Weekly Forum*. It states, "The Tuesday weekly art forum which has been a popular feature of the Association for the past several years was resumed Tuesday evening. Lawrence Kupferman, instructor of painting at Massachusetts School of Art…The topic for Tuesday's forum was 'The Position of Non-Objective and Abstract Painting Today…'"

So, the notion of *Forum '49* was not unique. But scheduling weekly talks and panel discussions was innovative. In creating the programming, organizers Kees, Hemley, and Bultman drew on the local community. The series of ground-breaking evenings were locally sourced. What follows is the complete schedule of events.

Forum '49 Panels
Every Thursday at 8:30 p.m.
Admission 60 cents including tax
Gallery 200, 200 Commercial Street

July 3rd (Sunday) *What Is an Artist?* Speakers George Biddle (1885–1973) ran artists projects for WPA, Hans Hofmann (1880–1966), Adolph Gottlieb (1903–1974), Serge Chermayeff, architect, (1900–1996).

July 7th *The Dream World of the Soviet Bureaucracy,* Dwight Macdonald (1906–1982) Editor Politics on a new theory exploring the lies of the Russian dictatorship.

July 14th *American Jazz Music: the 1920s,* Weldon Kees (1914–1955) Famous records by Jelly Roll Morton, Louis Armstrong, Bessie Smith, Kid Ory, etc.

July 21st *An Evening of Films,* Joseph Cornell Movie Theatre, featuring rare American and European Films. "First public showing of *104th Street: Notes for a Documentary,* by Helen Levitt (1913–2009) and Janice Loeb (1913–1996)," the team who made the prize-winning film *The Quiet One.*

July 28th *Francis Beverley Biddle* (1886–1968), a federal appeals court judge, solicitor general, and U.S. attorney general.

August 4th *James Joyce and T. S. Eliot* recordings of their readings with *Finnegan's Wake* commentary by Nathan Halper (1908–1983) with Howard Nemerov (1920–1991) on Eliot.

August 11th *French Art vs. U.S.A. Art Today,* speakers: Karl Knaths (1891–1971), Paul Mocsanyi (1900–1993), Stuart Preston, (NYT art critic died at 89 in 2005), Frederick Wight (1902–1986) played a significant role in transforming Los Angeles into a major art center. At the University of California, Los Angeles, curated shows for what was later named The Wight Art Gallery), chaired by Adolph Gottlieb (1903–1974).

August 18th *Directions in American Architecture,* Marcel Breuer (1902–1981), Gyorgy Kepes (1906–2001 founded Center for Advanced Visual Studies at MIT).

August 25th *Finding Yourself Through Psychoanalysis,* Speakers Gerardus Beekman, Dr. Wilfred Bloomberg, Dr. Leo Spiegel, Dr. Clara Thompson, Chairman Donald Slesinger.

September 1st *Everybody's Forum,* End of season retrospect with many of the speakers on previous forums participating. Individuals were given a few minutes to speak. Elaine de Kooning read remarks and was described as shaking and nervous.

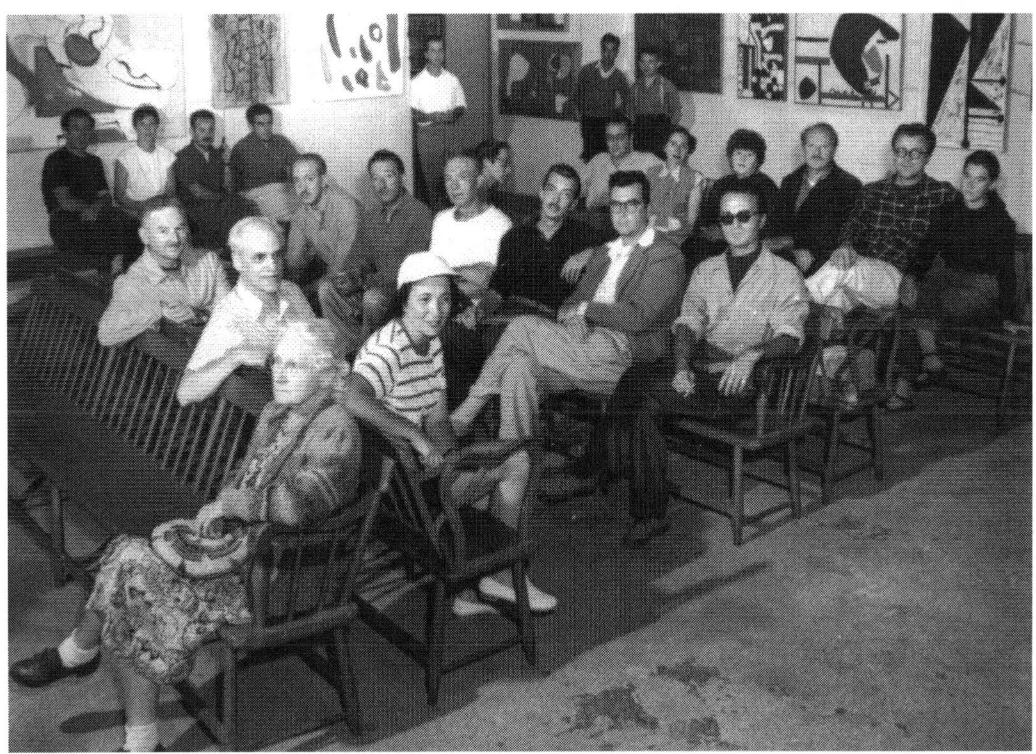

Attending Forum '49. Front, Blanche Lazzell. First row bench: Morris Davidson, Fritz Pfeiffer, Perle Fine. Second row bench: George McNeil, Adolph Gottlieb, Karl Knaths, Weldon Kees, David Heron, Giglio Dante. Kahlil Gibran behind Knaths. Back row: Lawrence Kupferman, Ruth Cobb, Lilian Ames, Howard Gibbs, Kenneth Campbell, Judith Rothschild. Against the wall, sitting left: Boris Mango, Minna Citron, Leo Manso, Peter Busa, Standing in rear Fritz Bultman, John Grillo, William Freed. Photo by Bill Witt. Courtesy of PAAM.

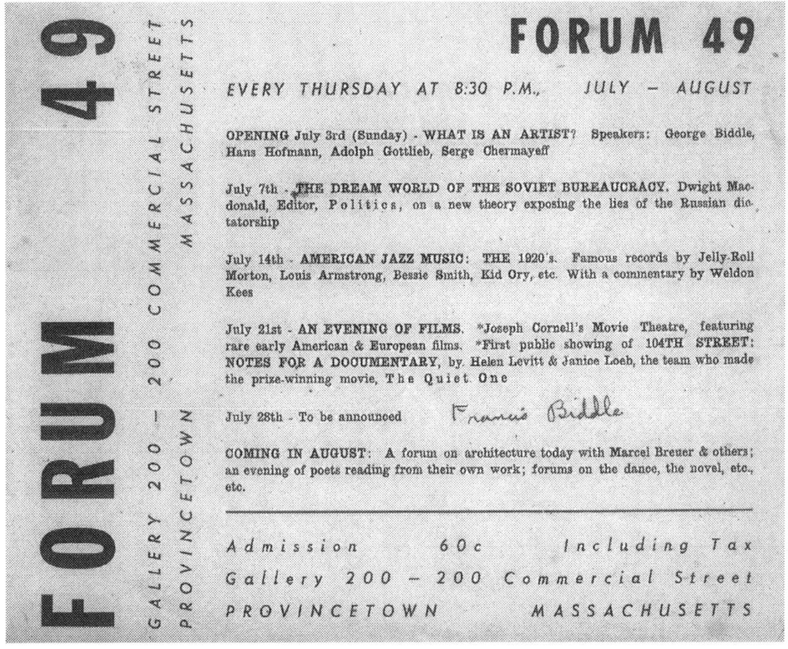

FORUM 49

GALLERY 200 – 200 COMMERCIAL STREET

PROVINCETOWN MASSACHUSETTS

FORUM 49

EVERY THURSDAY AT 8:30 P.M., JULY – AUGUST

OPENING July 3rd (Sunday) - **WHAT IS AN ARTIST?** Speakers: George Biddle, Hans Hofmann, Adolph Gottlieb, Serge Chermayeff

July 7th - **THE DREAM WORLD OF THE SOVIET BUREAUCRACY.** Dwight Macdonald, Editor, Politics, on a new theory exposing the lies of the Russian dictatorship

July 14th - **AMERICAN JAZZ MUSIC: THE 1920's.** Famous records by Jelly-Roll Morton, Louis Armstrong, Bessie Smith, Kid Ory, etc. With a commentary by Weldon Kees

July 21st - **AN EVENING OF FILMS.** *Joseph Cornell's Movie Theatre, featuring rare early American & European films. *First public showing of **104TH STREET: NOTES FOR A DOCUMENTARY**, by. Helen Levitt & Janice Loeb, the team who made the prize-winning movie, The Quiet One

July 28th - To be announced Francis Biddle

COMING IN AUGUST: A forum on architecture today with Marcel Breuer & others; an evening of poets reading from their own work; forums on the dance, the novel, etc., etc.

Admission 60c Including Tax

Gallery 200 – 200 Commercial Street

PROVINCETOWN MASSACHUSETTS

Program for *Forum '49*. Courtesy of PAAM.

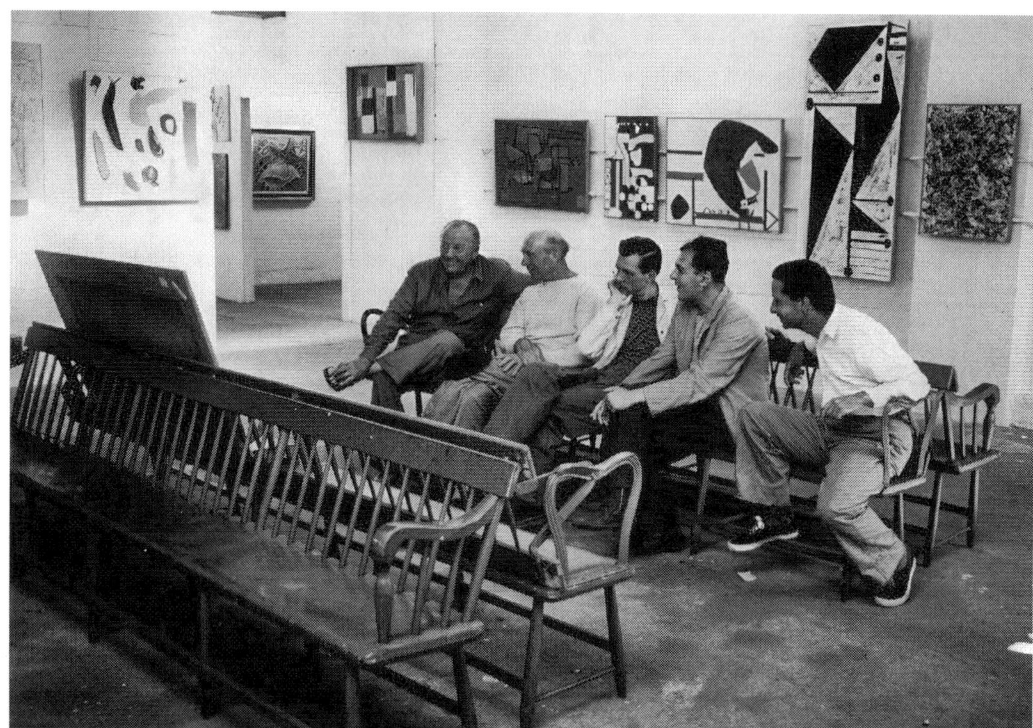

Jury for an exhibition. Left to right: Hans Hofmann, Karl Knaths, Weldon Kees. Cecil Hemley, and unknown. Witt photo. Courtesy of PAAM.

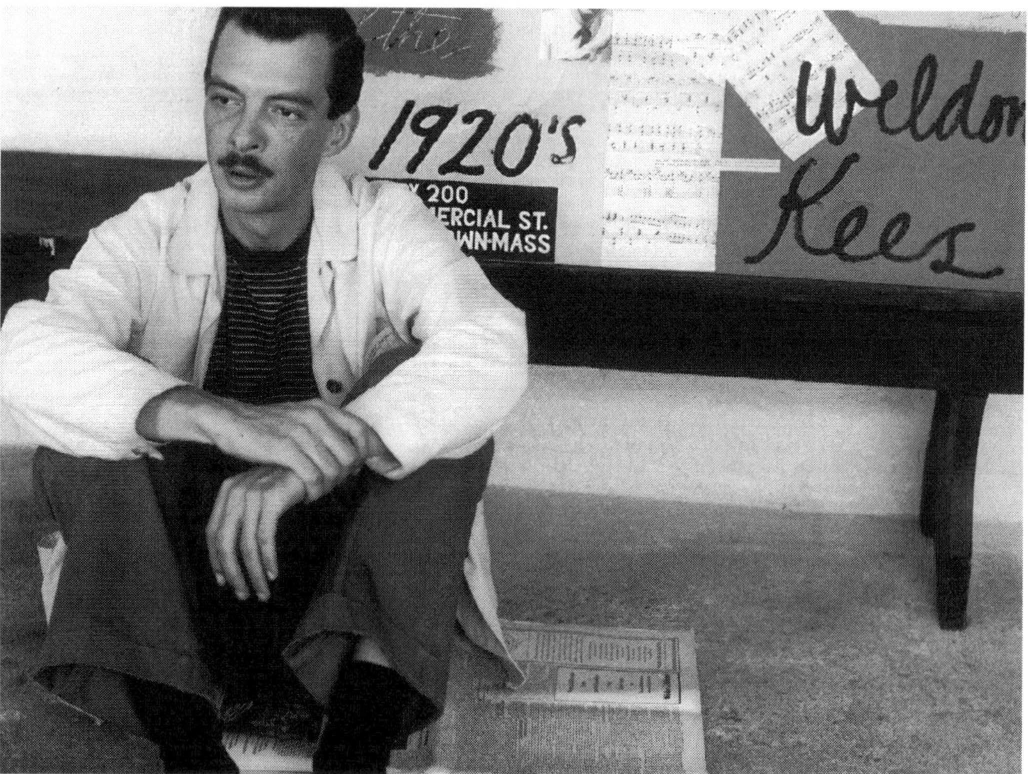

Poet, artist, and musician Weldon Kees was the primary organizer of Forum '49. Photo by Bill Witt. Courtesy of PAAM

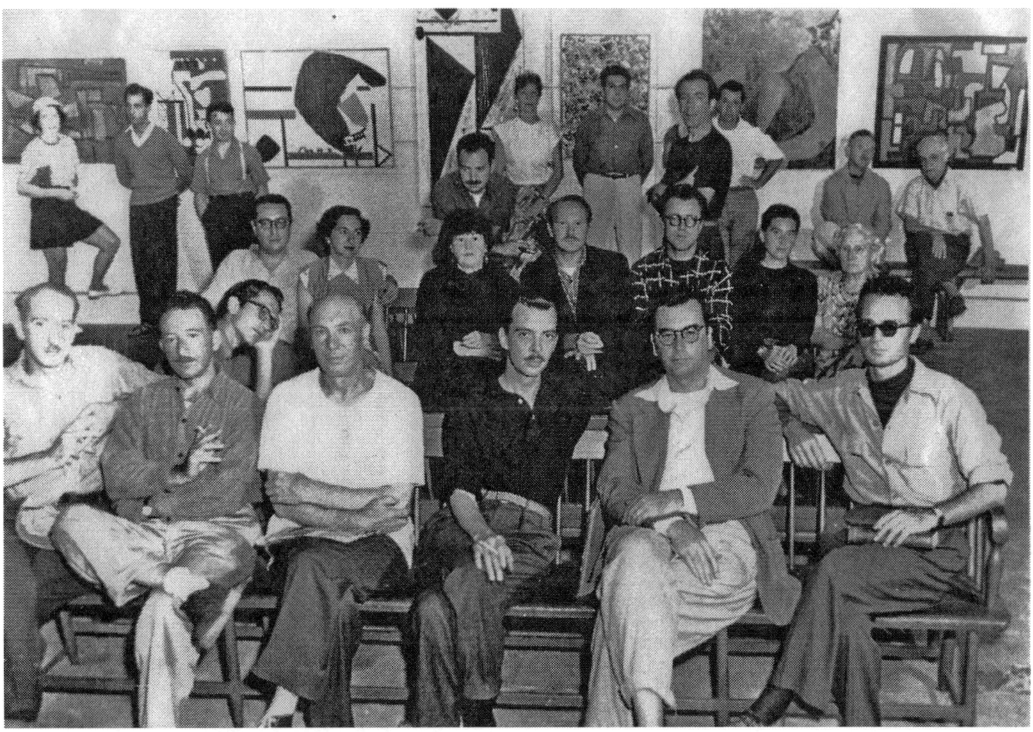

Another group shot. Witt photo courtesy of PAAM.

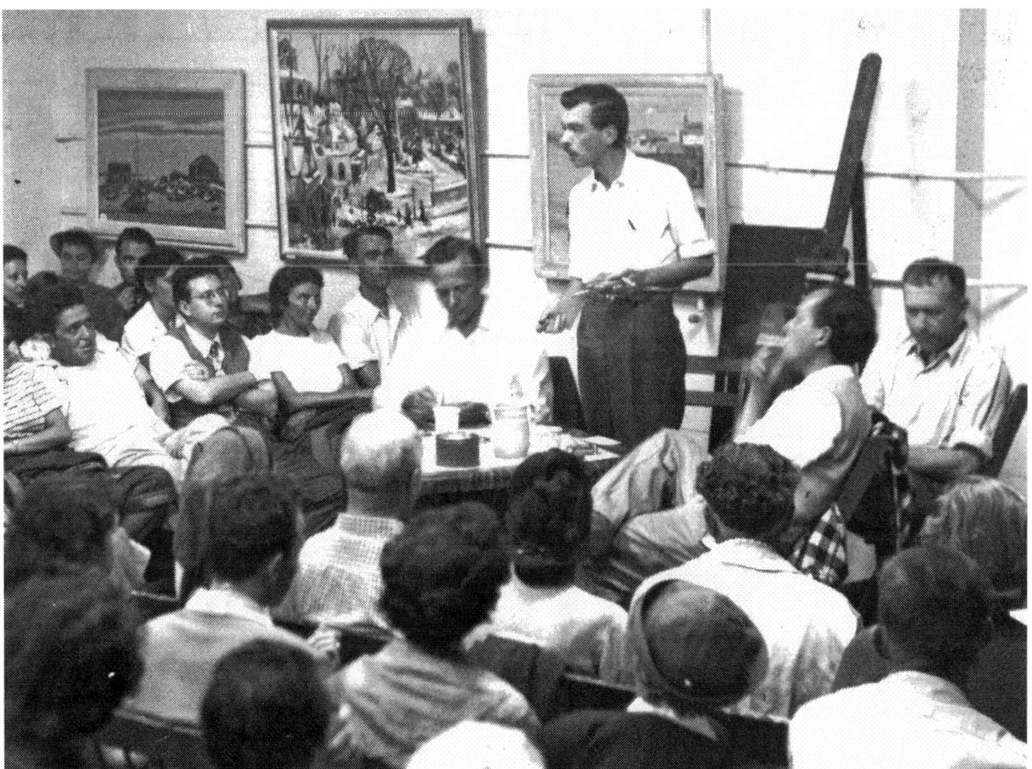

Kees lecturing on jazz, Witt photo. Courtesy of PAAM.

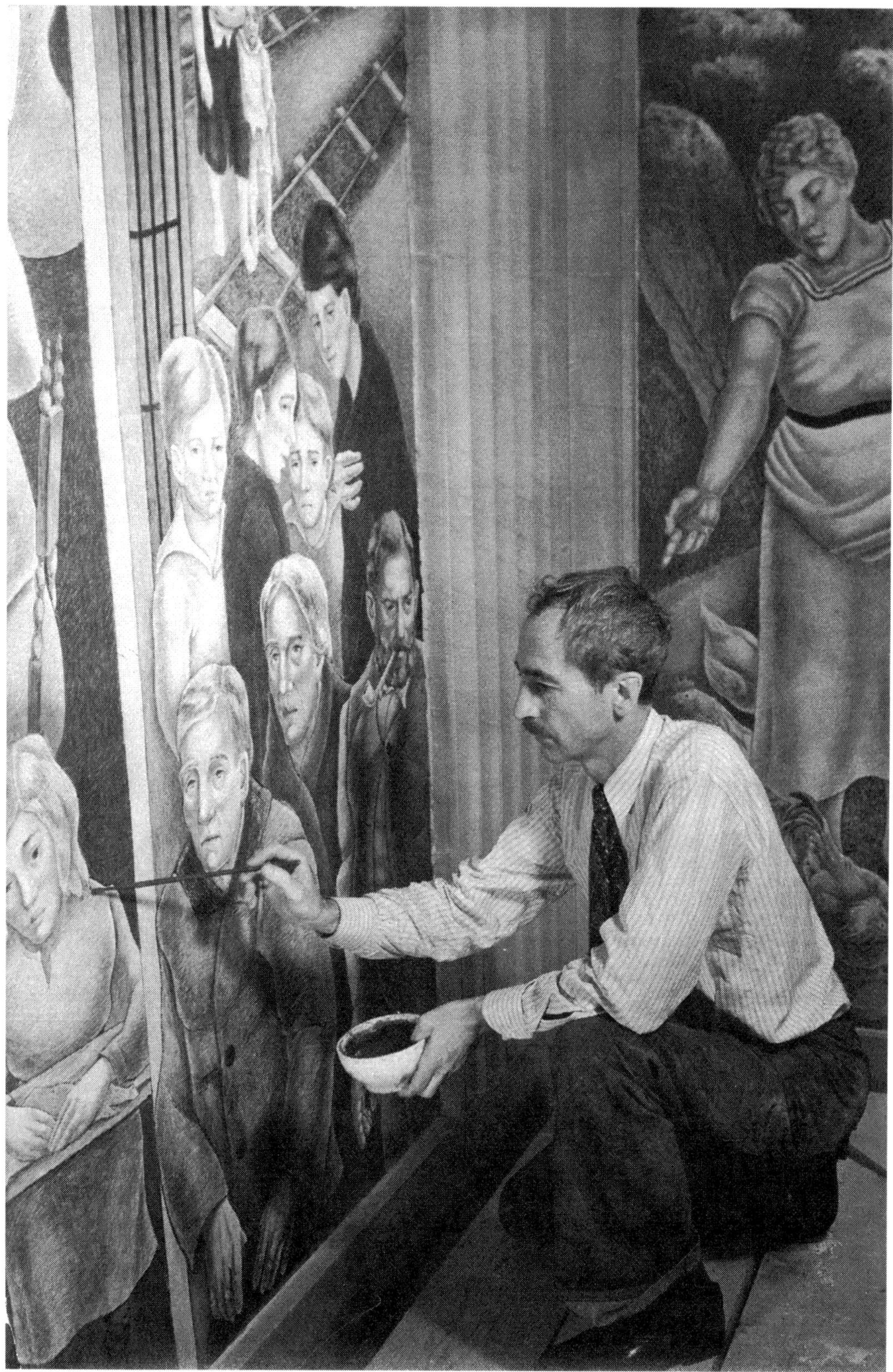

Mural painter George Biddle, who ran the fine arts division of the WPA, spoke for traditional art. Courtesy of PAAM.

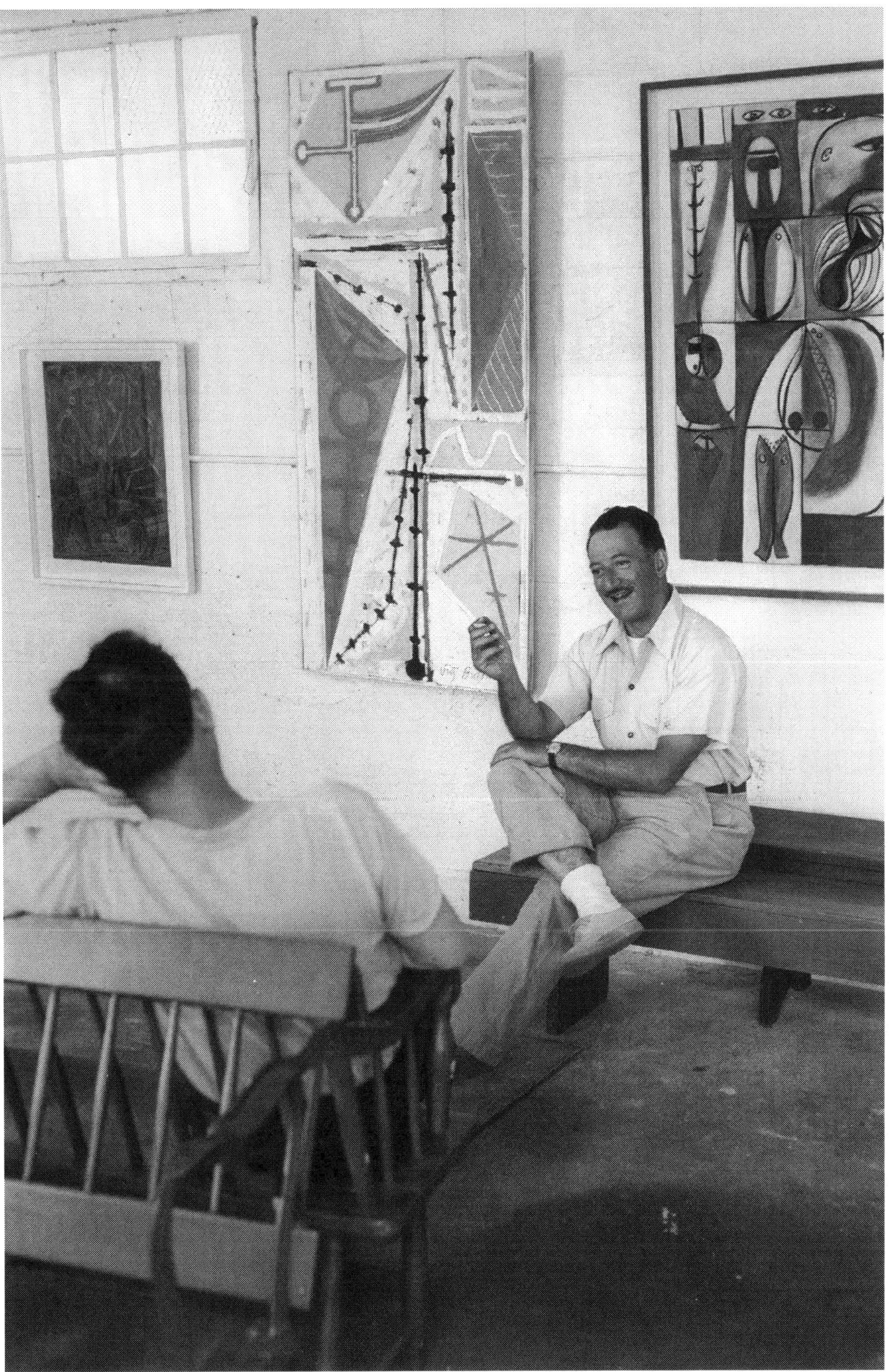

Adolph Gottlieb with Cecil Hemley's back to the camera. Witt photo. Courtesy of PAAM.

Long Point Artist Judith Rothschild

Judith Rothschild
August 5, 1984
At her Cape Cod residence

Judith Rothschild (1921–1993), a brilliant colorist with a keen eye for composition, gained success as a young artist in New York in the 1940s. Following her graduation from Wellesley in 1943, she studied at the Art Students League with Reginald Marsh, at Stanley William Hayter's Atelier 17 as well as, in Provincetown with Hans Hofmann and Karl Knaths. She married and later divorced the novelist Anton Myrer. Relatively unrecognized in her lifetime, a foundation to promote undervalued artists of her generation was created. The asset to create it was her personal collection, then valued at $33 million. There were also properties, including a Park Avenue complex, sold eventually for $15 million, which housed the foundation for a number of years. A country home in Kinderhook, New York, sold for $4.1 million in 2008. She owned works, among others, by Pablo Picasso, Henri Matisse, ten by Piet Mondrian, a portfolio by the futurist Giacomo Balla, and *Muse* by Brancusi. She appointed a friend, Harvey S. Shipley Miller, as sole trustee.

The catalog, by Jack Flam, was published in 1998 by Hudson Hills Press for a major traveling exhibition: Metropolitan Museum of Art, New York, New York: *Judith Rothschild: An Artist's Search,* May 19–September 6, 1998. Traveling to The Phillips Collection,

Washington, D.C., May 15–August 15, 1999 and San Francisco Museum of Modern Art, California, October 25, 2001–January 2002.

Charles Giuliano We are looking at a group shot from *Forum '49,* can you identify the individuals?

Judith Rothchild On the back is the identification of everyone. But let's not take tape time now. The paintings on the wall, right to left are, mine, the next Weldon Kees, Pollock, one of the first he included in a group show, then two by Karl Knaths. It was an invited show, mostly from New York galleries, Charles Egan, Sidney Janis, Samuel Kootz, Betty Parsons, and Rose Fried, where I showed. Karl, as one of the most important local artists, was included in what was an old garage (200 Commercial Street). It was an anti-Art Association project. There was still the effect of terrible battles of the 1930s that Karl would tell us about. He didn't have much to do with the Art Association and considered it pretty much old hat. It was very antique.

That was the idea that motivated Weldon Kees and Fritz Bultman. The concept was to have a kind of weekly forum of various aspects about, not just the arts, but the culture of our time. There were important people from various fields: psychoanalysis, architecture, film. There were readings of James Joyce and T.S. Eliot. There was a panel on painting with Knaths and Hans Hoffmann. Then Weldon hosted an evening of jazz. He was the driving force behind it. He kept it all together with tremendous energy, sweetness, and enthusiasm.

CG He designed the poster and Reggie Cabral owns the original.

JR Do you have the photo of him seated in front of the poster?

CG He is included as a formative member of the abstract expressionists. (He was one of the Irascibles who signed a letter of protest against the Metropolitan Museum for shunning emerging artist from its annual juried exhibition.)

JR I wouldn't say he was formative. I would say that he was absolutely secondary, not at all central. But he was accepted and showed with them, and was a part of the group. But he was far from being seminal or an influence on other people. Visually, I don't think he was. He was a force because of a very wide range of knowledge, tremendous enthusiasm, and a sense of the importance of the arts and communication of the arts. He had the ability to get people, in this situation, to get people to participate.

For the last *Forum,* at the end of the summer (September), I don't think anyone else will tell you about this, at the very end of the summer we had an extra week somehow. Some people had defected (gone home from vacation) and we didn't know what to do. So, we decided to call it *Everybody's Forum.* And anybody who wanted to could speak for three minutes. To make sure it was lively, we invited some people to speak. I remember Elaine de Kooning was down at the end of the summer. Weldon asked her if she wanted to speak on the role of women artists. I had never met her and didn't know her at all. I had met him (Willem) but didn't know her. She stood up and was very nervous. She had written a paper. Her hands were shaking and she sounded like a little school girl. She read this kind of history of women in art. It is incredible now to recall her being so shy and diffident and sort of nervous about presenting that subject.

I don't know if Weldon chose the subject or she did. If you know her, it would be fun to ask her about it. I don't remember the whole thing. It was kind of a free-for-all.

CG *Forum '49* had nothing to do with the Art Association?

JR Absolutely not. Two Hundred Commercial Street was a garage in the center of town. They painted it all white. It was so popular. We sold tickets. (sixty cents). Ester Gottlieb and I were at the gate. We had to ask a guy to help because people were forcing their way in, because we were sold out.

For the speakers, we offered a bottle of liquor of their choice as our thanks. They did it for nothing. Afterwards, we would have a party and go out to drink somewhere. It was incredible.

CG How did you come to participate in *Forum '49*?

JR We had been in California and came East. When we arrived, we were new to everything. Nobody knew us. Nobody knew my husband (best selling author, Anton Myrer). So, we didn't get into *Forum '49* until it had been settled. Weldon asked me to participate. There was a lot of physical work to do. My husband also participated. There was a lot of crating to handle, carting things around, and managing guests. There was a lot of arranging to do.

CG Do you recall who was in the show? Was Lawrence Kupferman involved?

JR Yes, he and his wife, Ruth Cobb. Lawrence Campbell was sitting next to me. Hofmann was in it. Pollock was in the show, but not in Provincetown at the time. Franz Kline was not in the show, but came later. Some of the work we got from New York dealers. Adolph Gottlieb was active in *Forum '49*. His wife, Ester, and I worked a lot together. He had an uncle or cousin or something, who had a house on the West End and may have given some money to help it out.

We invited Paul Mocsanyi, who runs the art program at the New School for Social Research.

CG He wrote on Karl Knaths.

JR The very same. There was a battle during the course of the summer, which I wasn't a party to, and only learned of it through Weldon. It was the question of the position of advanced American vs. European art.

CG Was that the theme of *Forum '49*?

JR No, but that's what they had a great argument about. Fritz (Bultman) and (Hans) Hofmann had an argument about that. Fritz pulled out around the beginning of August.

(They issued the following statement.)

Protest Against Ostrich Politics in the Arts

The estate of the arts should never be narrowed to a national basis—particularly by the artists.

The greatness of Paris is to offer an invitation of participation to the spirit. If the United States has assumed, as in the past few years, the same free and open attitude, this warrants great promise in the arts. Paris's humanism has given the opportunity for free development of the artists as the Spaniards—Picasso, Gris, Miro; the Swiss—Klee, Corbusier, Giacometti; the Russians—Kandinsky, Chagall; the Rumanian—Brancusi; the Irishman—Joyce; the Americans—Stein, Man Ray, Carles; the Pole—Lipschitz; and many others.

Still today, many of them are living masters of Paris. We earnestly hope that the artistic creation in America will develop the same fruitful ground to equal such a great example.

Hans Hofmann, Fritz Bultman

CG What was the purpose of *Forum '49*?

JR At that time there was a great sense of real excitement in many of these fields. Everything seemed to be opening up.

CG I understand that Norman Mailer and Robert Motherwell came that summer.

JR I didn't hear Mailer but Bob gave a very good talk. I had met him in New York. After the talk Weldon and Robert came back to our place in the West End, an old net-mending shack opposite the Hofmanns. We had drinks together. Bob was likely in East Hampton. He probably rushed back. Probably gave the talk and rushed back. They came to our place for drinks, but not for hours and hours. I suppose he had a plane to catch.

CG Kees appears to have committed suicide in San Francisco. (His abandoned car was found next to Golden Gate Bridge. A body was never recovered.) Did he strike you as a depressed person?

JR No. I've talked a lot to both men who are working on his biography. Weldon, I think, was a person with an enormous love of life and appetite for life, which you could see when he played jazz. He made up incredibly funny songs. He was a very good jazz pianist. He composed, like when driving in the country, he made up funny, ridiculous songs. "Newton had a trauma/ Got it from his mama/ a woman who distorted many lives/ and the family water closet/ she used to deposit objects/ like cleavers and knives…"

Then he wrote a wonderful song when he was living in Point Richmond. That was when Ford Motors was expanding. There was a little town, Mill Pete, which had been a nothing town until Ford took it over. He wrote a sweet little ditty based on *Manhattan.* All I remember is, "Now town is sweet/as that Old Mill Pete is." He had a great sense of fun.

CG People say he killed himself. Was he depressed?

JR The measure of his despair was the height and intensity of his hopes. I don't think he was at all depressed. The human condition being what it is, and he being as sensitive as he was, Weldon was increasingly despairing at what was happening in the arts.

CG He was very handsome.

JR Like Zachary Scott. People were attracted to him. I never thought of him as sexy, and I don't think people did. Not that anyone thought he was homosexual, but you felt warmth, electricity, and involvement. When we met, I was newly married and not into that kind of thing. But I don't think that was his quality. He was not a macho guy. He was gentle and his movements were gentle. He was small.

CG What was he painting?

JR They tended to be abstracted biomorphic forms, from '49 to '50, on dark backgrounds, usually with quite a bit of texture involved; sometimes using a lot of palette knife.

CG Do you own one?

JR No. Fritz bought one recently and I saw a slide of it. I don't think it was great, but it's not fair to judge from a slide. Then he was in California. Jim Reidel, who is working on a biography, has been trying to collect some. (*Vanished Act: The Life and Art of Weldon Kees,* 2003.) He has four or five. There are some in the University of Nebraska. What I liked best of Weldon's were a large group of collages that he did in the early 1950s for the Palace of the Legion of Honor. They were luminous, wonderful, mostly yellow and white. They were not at all unhappy and full of sunlight. Charming. A little like the early Motherwell collages which were shown at Peggy Guggenheim's gallery. Probably, actually, a lot like that. He was probably influenced a lot by Bob's early work.

CG Was Pollock around in 1949?

JR He had left. He had been here, I think, in '45 or '46. There is uncertainty about that. Franz Kline bought the same property. Pollock rented it, and then the next summer I rented it, or the summer after. By the time I was in the West, Kline bought the whole property and built his studio there.

CG Was Kline around for *Forum '49*?

JR No, Kline came after that. I never knew him because he wasn't here. Barnett Newman was here. I know because I'm a good friend of his wife.

CG Was he in *Forum '49*?

JR I don't think so.

CG What about Edwin Dickinson?

JR I don't imagine he was. In those days he was rather aloof. He was not a part of this kind of mood. I think that Nat Halper showed him at HCE Gallery. Milton Avery wasn't here that summer.

CG But Knaths was.

JR What everyone thought in those days was that there were two important artists in town; Karl Knaths and Hans Hofmann.

CG Not Dickinson. He was often linked with Knaths and Ross Moffett.

JR Dickinson was in Wellfleet, not Provincetown. Hopper was also here, but I don't recall much talk about him. That's my opinion and other people may think differently. We tended to think that Hopper was a part of the past. Even though Knaths was somewhat figurative, there was a lot of feeling in town of a polarity between Hofmann and Knaths. They were competitors and had to be kept apart. They did not dislike each other and both were very shy, really. They were not averse to seeing each other. It was a curious thing.

You have these two men who were both German, they spoke with German accents and both were hard of hearing.

It reminds me of what Pierre Matisse told me about arranging for Joan Miro and Henri Matisse to meet in Paris. He tells it charmingly. It was a big deal to get these artists together. They met in a café that was decided upon and introductions were made. They ordered drinks. They discussed the weather and events going on in Paris. They finished the drinks then politely shook hands and left. Miro was overjoyed and delighted to have met Matisse, whom he greatly admired. That was it and a bit like when Hans and Karl were together. While always polite, I don't think they had much of a conversation.

In the fall of'59, we rented the house across the way from here, Jack Hall, and stayed for the winter. We had been all summer and decided to stay on. That winter we went once a week to see Karl. All summer we just had three sessions, translations, that sort of thing.

CG You were in the group with Myron Stout, Joan Wye, and Jim Forsberg.

JR That's right. There was someone I wanted to ask you about, Max Gould. He had been chairman of the Securities and Exchange Commission and a Marxist. He was a complicated, interesting guy. He was fired. He was head of the SEC during the Roosevelt administration, but probably not for long. Max was basically a linguist. After he was fired, he had enough to live on, but under a cloud. He was around the summer of '49 when we met and did translations. We used to meet at our place. I was wondering if he or his wife Ester studied with Knaths? They lived in Washington. Ask Myron Stout if he knows what happened.

CG What were you translating?

JR I'm trying to remember. It wasn't all translating; we were also reading. I wonder if we were reading Joyce that summer. There was usually a final version typed by me or my husband. That meant deciphering people's handwriting.

We were working on Carl Einstein from a series in German on cubism. Einstein was a friend of (Daniel Henry) Kahnweiler (Picasso's dealer) and there's a lot that's significant. People were interested in what Einstein said about Juan Gris' method. What Karl always clung to was that Gris said he started with the abstract and worked toward the concrete. Toward the specific, I should say. It's a very complex thing to decide; if that was the way Karl worked, or he wanted it to be true. I think, if you look at his work over a period of time, the period when charts were made, what I see is that he started with something much more concrete, more real, let's say a rooster, a real rooster, then tried to relate it to a method. Later the whole process became much more one. But until way after the war I think, that wasn't true. I don't know when Karl encountered that quote from Gris. When I knew him, this is how he worked, the way that Gris did.

Will Barnett was also in those sessions which were a lot of fun. But nerve racking because we all considered Karl to be the center and bowed as much as we could to his preferences, except when it came to something that was actually intellectually important where you couldn't. His understanding of German was hit and miss. Sometimes it was very good and other times not so. My husband majored in history and lit at Harvard, specialized in German lit, and had had a lot of German. So, he knew the language pretty well. Max Gould knew the language very well. On the other hand, those two people didn't know the art side. So, there was a terrific battle among people who were ill-equipped for the task at hand.

CG So you met every Thursday evening?

JR No, in the afternoon, because Karl went to bed early. Sometimes we met at Jim Forsberg's. Then there was a summer when we didn't translate, but did readings. We met at different places and read a lot of Blake. Someone who liked to read would do so aloud. One was Gloria Linner who knew Karl and later married Dwight McDonald. Her then-husband, Linner, was a poet.

The first show I had was at Jane Street Gallery, a cooperative in the Village. Karl and Agnes (Weinrich his sister-in-law) came to see the show. I didn't know him and it was before I met Anton. He liked my work and I was very excited. I didn't know his work very well.

Nurendorf, who introduced Paul Klee to America, bought a work from my first show and his friend Neuman from my second. They came down to this little gallery and made that commitment. I didn't know them.

By chance that Spring, I went to the Guggenheim, which at the time was run by Hilla Rebay (1890–1967). You could present work to her, and if she liked it, receive a little stipend around $20 a month. I had a commercial art job and thought this would help, so I went for it. Agnes Weinrich brought some work for her to see. You went at an arranged time and she would do this periodically. I showed her my things and she liked them very much. At the end of the session, she said, "Go to my secretary." That was tantamount to saying that I was on the "A" list.

Agnes was late. It was very informal. We were all standing around and she would say, "OK, you're next." One of the last people, a woman, presented a small work. She was telling a long story about Kandinsky not working on painting for ten years so he would know the exact thing to do. Rebay was drawing on the woman's work to illustrate her point. By this time, I didn't like her at all. I said, "I don't think you should be drawing on someone's work without their permission." I could see that the woman was upset and this was a terrible thing to do.

There was a terrible silence and she went on to the next person. At the end of the session, she came over to me and said, "You needn't see my secretary." Agnes came over, deeply moved, and introduced herself. She probably told Karl about the incident. I always thought that Helen (sister of Agnes and wife of Knaths) had a nervous breakdown and Agnes saw herself as a protector. I think Agnes was in love with Karl. When he spoke about Agnes there was a lot of emotion in his voice.

Agnes died in the Spring of '46 of a heart attack. I didn't know her very long. I got married and we moved West.

CG Joan Wye recalls that Karl was involved with Agnes and asked her to marry him. Her reply was, "I could never marry you because it would take me away from my career as an artist. Being married would mean that I would have to take care of you and that would take me away from my work. But why don't you marry Helen? She would make the perfect wife. She's more the kind that would marry." He said to Joan, "So I married Helen."

That sense of "So he married Helen" is such a lack of psychological insight, typical of Knaths' bumbling primitivism. Even telling that story decades after the fact, who else could say that without any introspection?

JR There is the tale of a man who married the oldest daughter in a family. Of four girls he fell in love with the youngest. The mother and sisters manipulated him into marrying the oldest girl. Karl, I always thought, had been manipulated into marrying Helen for whatever reason. Subsequently, he had no introspection about that. He just took it as it happened at the time.

They were very nice people and decided to be together in some way. Certainly, for instance, he was very protective of Helen as a pianist.

CG Did you ever hear her perform?

JR Not perform, but I heard her practice. During our Thursday meetings she would never play if she thought someone was listening. I took piano lessons, so I knew about music. She usually practiced in the afternoon when Karl took a nap. It was arranged when we would arrive, say 2 p.m. Sometimes he would be upstairs finishing a nap and she would be playing. The first time I heard her play, I thought it was the radio. She had amazing manual facility. Helen had a repertoire of things she knew. The way her fingers tripped over the keyboard was manually quite good, but skittery. She would play Mozart in the most ladylike, unprofound way, but surprisingly well. That's what's interesting and her phrasing was good. It was intelligent, but not interesting, playing, I would say. I never heard her play an entire piece from beginning to end.

CG I heard that when she was supposed to give her graduation recital she froze and couldn't perform.

JR Who told you that?

CG Joan Wye. Karl insisted that she continue to play.

JR He got very interested in music theory. I might be explaining something about music, about harmony or something, and I would say, "Maybe we should ask Helen?" He would say, "No, no, no." He did not want to involve her in any way, which I still don't understand.

CG He was living with sisters, one an artist, and the other a musician. They had studied in Europe. There is the sense that Agnes introduced him to modern theory. Her work was more advanced than his. It's said that Agnes got him interested in cubism. Imagine the three of them sitting around at night talking about art and music.

JR That reminds me of his early days and his stories from before he met them. I don't think he was a virgin and there were women before them. There was a wealthy woman in Chicago who encouraged him in some way. As far as what started (cubism) he saw the *Armory Show* in Chicago and it was a revelation. (He worked as a guard for the show.) It was seeing the Cezannes in that show that started it. By the time he came to Provincetown he was committed to modernism. I think he was drawn to Agnes and those two women because he felt that this was his contact with the big time and what he admired. I don't think that Agnes introduced him to cubism. She did introduce him to the specifics and the whole Juan Gris thing.

CG Because she had studied with Gris?

JR That's right. I got from him, through her, the Gris notes.

CG Do you still have them?

JR I may. I know I loaned them to some archive. I'll make a note to look for them before we break.

CG Do you have a Weinrich in your collection?

JR No, I wish I did.

CG When we were talking on the phone, you said that you have three works by Knaths. Can you tell me which ones?

JR One you saw at Wellesley called *Dusk.*

CG That was shown at the Whitney. Was it in the annual?

JR No, that show of Knaths'.

CG The *Four Americans* show?

JR Yes. One was called *Spearing Eel,* which I can get you a picture of if you need it.

CG There's another version of that which Henry Delawrence owns. Did you see the movie on Knaths? He tracked it down. Three of us saw it; Henry and Bob Brown from the Archives of American Art. The screening was at the Boston Public Library. It was awful. It started with views of the docks and fish with schmaltzy music. Unfortunately, it was not an interview. Interestingly it had a version of *Eel Spearing.* Henry knew of it sitting in someone's cellar.

JR Is that the green one? One that he did was very green

CG I couldn't say because the color of the film was so deteriorated. It was all red and purple. It was a very disappointing Knaths' incident.

JR He had bad luck. Like when Arnold Newman was going to photograph Karl. (*Karl Knaths, Provincetown Studio.* Photo by © Arnold Newman, for the article written by Robert Hatch, "At the Tip of Cape Cod" July 1961 issue of *Horizon,* a hardbound magazine.) He got a stye in his eye and was very upset. I don't know if it shows in the image. He felt unhappy about that photo being taken at that specific time. He had a lot of that kind of bad luck. The third painting I have is an unfinished portrait of the man I was married to. He did very few portraits. They were not like his other paintings. They were portrait sketches.

CG Marcel Duchamp came to your show.

JR He came to my first show at Jane Street Gallery. He liked the show and we talked. I guess he was excited about it. He asked if I knew the work of Kurt Schwitters? I don't know by chance how he came to my show. The night before, I had seen a book with collages by Schwitters. His collages excited me. I had collages in that show, perhaps just one.

He said, "There's a gallery uptown that has Schwitters and you should go see them." It was the Rose Fried Gallery. As you know, at that time he was helping Katherine Dreier assemble her collection (later donated to Yale University). He was helping prune the collection. I had sold something from the show for $115. She had a very nice 1920s Schwitters for $135. I told her all I had was $115, so she sold it to me for that price. Subsequently it was sold because we needed money. It was a small cubist work.It was a very good classical one. Actually, that's how I got into Rose Fried Gallery, through Duchamp. She really listened to him. The Schwitters was the first modern thing I collected.

I was going to talk about Karl's method. The reason that he chose Ostwald over others' color theories was because Ostwald based his system on pigment not light. As you know, he was a painter.

(Friedrich Wilhelm Ostwald 1853–1932 He recommended a systematic arrangement of colors and a standardization of colors used. He believed colors should only be used and selected from a finite collection. He acknowledged that his system left out some intermediate colors between the ones he selected, but he did not work to include them in his color space. The system provides a single, midpoint interpolation between adjacent colors. It does not have an easy way of recording millions of colors.

The *Color Harmony Manual* is made up of charts of colored chips representing a color space. The overall shape of a chart is an equilateral triangle made up of 28 samples. Each chart is made up of samples of approximately the same hue. Each chart has one sample with the greatest purity. This sample is the far point of the triangle. A series of five samples with increasing reflectance and decreasing purity are on the upper edge of the triangle. It ends with an almost-gray modification of the original pure hue. A series of five samples with decreasing reflectance and decreasing purity are on the lower edge of the triangle. It ends with an almost-black modification of the original hue. Between these light and dark series are other samples of intermediate reflectance and purity.

All color samples on the same chart have almost the same dominant wavelength. All color samples in the same vertical row have almost the same dominant wavelength and purity, making the only difference the reflectances.

Color samples made from clear cellulose acetate sheets with one side coated with an opaque colored lacquer. This ensures that both sides are the same color while one side is glossy and the other is matte.)

> Ostwald wanted to make a useful color-step manual. It is more useful than other systems because it is based on the actuality of twenty-four steps around the color circle. It was a natural progression for Knaths, as we have a twelve-tone scale to connect it to the Western keyboard. I made a little sketch of it before you came just to show you simply. If you take the color circle as full intensity, this being the circle, one would be yellow and 13 would be its opposite, a bluish purple. Numerically one is the note C. C-sharp would be 3, D would be 9, F being a half-note would be 11, and G being a half-note is 13. It's one octave and G, 13, is the tonic. Seven would be 23 up here, the 7th on the keyboard.
>
> C is the tonic, the note C. Let's say you want to do a major chord in C in music, it's C E G. So, C is here or 1. E is here, which would be 9. G is here, which would be 13. Let's start and keep it simple. Let's not talk about the geometry, which is another complication. That's what he worked out much later and I have a chart of it somewhere. If you look at his work there is a pinpoint and lines radiating out. That's all connected with this.
>
> (Knaths used the Laws of Dynamic Symmetry. Convinced that design was not purely instinctive, Jay Hambidge (1867–1924) searched for the technical bases of design. He found his answer in dynamic symmetry. The study of Greek art convinced him that the secret of the beauty of Greek design was in the conscious use of dynamic symmetry—the law of natural design based upon the symmetry of growth in man and in plants. He worked out a series of root rectangles that the

artist, using the simple mathematics supplied in his book, can apply. Part I sets forth the fundamental rectangles with their simple divisions based on the proportioning law found in nature; Part II explains compound rectangles, many of which were taken from or suggested by analysis of objects of Greek art.)

Let's say this is yellow. or C, in Karl's musical system. This would be pure yellow of the maximum intensity. This is pure black and this is pure white. This would be the scale of gray. There are 27 steps of this mixture being of less and less hue and more and more white with no black. This would be the same thing going toward gray with no white. Each of the 17 steps is numbered. If you knew the Ostwald system, the green, it's mostly 24. You could identify everything in the room. Anything you see.

CG Did he teach you this? How did you learn?

JR By osmosis. That winter, when we visited him each week, I knew a certain amount by that time, but I learned by osmosis as much as anything else. This is not what he was using later on. He was using a more simplified geometric thing. He was also interested in various relationships like the Fibonacci sequence.

(In mathematics, Fibonacci is a sequence in which each number is the sum of the two preceding ones. Numbers that are part of the Fibonacci sequence are known as Fibonacci numbers, commonly denoted Fn. The sequence commonly starts from 0 and 1, although some authors start the sequence from 1 and 1 or sometimes (as did Fibonacci) from 1 and 2. Starting from 0 and 1, the sequence begins 0, 1, 1, 2, 3, 5, 8, 13, 21, 34, 55, 89, 144, ...)

He used the Golden Sector a lot. (A ratio, observed especially in the fine arts, between the two dimensions of a plane figure or the two divisions of a line such that the smaller is to the larger as the larger is to the sum of the two, a ratio of roughly three to five.) It related to the color harmony he set up. What I just described would be like a melody. It has nothing to do with the harmonic structure. Let's say it was a particular five notes. That would determine what colors around the circle he was using; which hues. Then you have to discuss what gradation or intensity, which has to do with the harmony within it.

In other words, they were not all equally important. And when you looked into his chest of drawers, or closet, you saw the clam shells. (In which he mixed paint.)

Elaine de Kooning must have seen it when she did an article on him. Maybe that was the occasion when he did the portrait. ("Knaths Paints a Picture," by Elaine de Kooning, *Art News*, v. 47, n. 7, pt. 1, November 1949.)

The subject (in the article) is a woman, but it isn't identified as Elaine de Kooning. In the article she didn't discuss his color or compositional theories. I think she says, "If you open the chest you see."

CG I would have to go back and check, but it's not an insightful article.

JR I don't think she was drawn to his style or his method as it was alien to what she was used to.

CG Florence Grippe (wife of my Brandeis professor, sculptor Peter Grippe) told me that she wrote an article on Knaths and submitted it to *Art News,* but they chose Elaine's.

JR There are several paintings that he did in the 1960s with a horizon line motif which is three or four colors horizontally. That would be like a chord. In some cases that chord pulled against a huge amount of movement on the other side. Those colors might be yellow, nine being a blueish-red like a cerise which would be 9 on the Ostwald scale, which would be 3 musically. And maybe a blue would be 5. Then maybe a very strident green, a yellowish green which would be a 7 leading back to the tonic like a very important chord pulling back to the harmony, on the other side of which, you might have the same tones in it but presumably would not be, at this point might all be in the triangle, because you have very small amounts of it in it. There's tremendous contrast and it's meant to hold against all this complexity. The other part would move around, very likely, in the gray scale and in the other area of the circle. The only way you can analyze it is, maybe take a couple of the pictures, and identify all of the colors. Then you'll see clearly what the structure is.

CG Can you identify this picture?

JR It's not a good example because it's too over simplified. It's unusual for him, as there is no blue in the picture. He used blue or bluish purple a lot to anchor things. There's a little shadow on the face but it's minimal. It's almost an either/or kind of thing. It might be almost, very atypically, a sort of red contrast. If you are going to do a circle of it, I've never looked at it this way before, the red is probably 5. Of course there are all these greens. All this pinkiness is probably 9. It is unusual for him to have all this contrast. The gray was probably 13. The gray was probably 13, but it's all very minimal. I think I have analysis I did of *Adam Zero* and a couple of other things that would be useful to you. (*Number Zero Adam,* Karl Knaths, 1948, Albright Knox Museum)

CG It's one of his most important paintings.

JR This is all about his method. We used to tease him because he would work on a picture for a very long time. Certain colors which were prominent in the beginning, would gradually disappear. I would say, "Karl, wait a minute, I thought this whole thing was based on a wonderful Russian melody. Now I don't see any of that." He responded by showing me the underpainting and how he had to work some things out. When his work went well, he used it, then forgot it, as he painted. It was like a security blanket for him. He would get all this out, then when he got into it, he felt pretty free doing whatever he wanted to do. It is kind of a very strange process. I don't think it always worked for him. At times it really trapped him.

CG Did anyone try his system?

JR All of his students in Washington (Phillips Collection) tried with little success. It really wrecked my painting for awhile. I remember once we decided to use the same exact notes, use the same exact structure. I still have the painting which is not a disaster. We selected a Russian melody. Karl had a lot of interest in numerology. The melody had exactly 21 notes. That had mystical significance. We made a deal. I said that he picked such bad music that nobody could make a good picture. We were good enough friends that I could say that jokingly. Nobody could make a good picture out of those bad melodies. So, we made a deal that we would both make pictures based on a Mozart motif that I would pick out, and that winter we did.

When we went over, he would show me what he had worked on that week and we discussed it. I could never get over how impersonal he could be discussing his work. It was so different from the Hofmann romantic thing in which it's all very mysterious and the process comes from the unconscious and who knows what else. His attitude was that it all may be happening but the other thing is something you can talk about. So, we would look at it and I think he came to rely a lot on my judgment because he really looked forward to showing me the work. I don't think he had much of a sense of an audience at that time. He was so isolated here. When he came to New York, he didn't have a lot of artists that he had a great rapport with.

One of the sad things that happened to him during the years that I knew him was how his old friends, like de Kooning, became so successful. In New York they used to get together at the old Waldorf cafeteria. De Kooning was one of his regular contacts and they always met at the Waldorf. When de Kooning really hit it there was a rift. Deeper than Hemingway and Fitzgerald, a real cleavage. Sometimes Karl met with Mondrian.

CG Among the Knaths' materials in the Archives of American Art are manuscripts that show up. There's a Mondrian manuscript and de Kooning lecture. There's a Malevich piece. There is no explanation of what they are doing there.

JR That's likely something we worked on translating. Was it on Neo Plasticism?

CG I don't recall.

JR When I was in New York during the war, most of those writings had not yet been translated. We started translating all that stuff from Europe. I had the idea that it should be available to other artists. In those days you could go to MoMA, and if they knew you, take anything home. I would take things out, translate them, and then bring them back. If they knew you that was okay. I got things from the New York Public Library. Of course that was subsequently translated by other people. The Mondrian and Hofmann I'm sure I translated. The Malevich, I don't know. That was probably in Agnes's papers. I'm sure somebody has told you about the chimney.

(Knaths inscribed the names of important artists and influences on it.)

Are you going to interview Anton Myrer because he would know the names on the chimney? He's difficult to reach but I urged the men who were researching Weldon Kees to contact him. He had the letters between Weldon, Anton, and I. When I left, I didn't take them.

CG I'm trying to get through his book.

(His first novel, *Evil Under the Sun,* published in 1951, was about a war veteran convalescing at a Cape Cod artists' colony...The artificial worlds-within-worlds of narcissism, sexual obsession, and license among a group of artists, which are examined through the eyes of several Greenwich Villagers, seasonally transplanted to a summer colony.)

JR I think the protagonist in the novel is a combination of Knaths and Hofmann. The book had some really good writing in it. You should contact Anton but it's best if you do it on your own. He knew Knaths ever since he was a little boy. His mother studied with Knaths.

I think until 1955 or so Knaths looked on him as the closest thing to a son. I think Karl became more fond of me as time went by. What I didn't see at the time was that Anton was pulling away from what Karl thought was the point of the game of art, wanting more money and things. I think his attitude changed a lot.

(Off the record observations.)

CG You have so many interesting things in your collection like the little Picabia.

JR That's one of my favorites.

CG You had Gris and futurism, like the series of prints by Balla.

JR Actually, they're not prints.

CG I had a tour of Lois Torf's print collection with MFA curator Cliff Ackley. For futurism there was a Severini and a Boccioni, which was redrawn at the Bauhaus, so it was not really a Boccioni. I asked him why don't you have more futurist work? He said "The futurists didn't make prints." I told him that I knew of a series of prints by Balla. He said that he had never heard of them.

JR He was right they are not prints, though they look like lithographs.

CG Which is what I assumed they were.

JR Balla had a portfolio which I have the cover of, which he made himself. Every now and then he made something to put into the portfolio. It started in 1911 and continued, I think, until 1919. We did not get all of them, which I tried to do. I know a woman with two of them and I think that's the complete set. She won't sell them. It's interesting how he did them. I think it's fascinating.

CG I like the collection because it's so personal and eccentric. I'm not sure what word you would choose.

JR I know what you mean. They are all the things that are absent from the collection now. We gave the largest Mondrian to the National Gallery.

(There were ten works by Mondrian in the estate.)

CG You had early Mondrian landscapes.

JR When I was elected into American Abstract Artists, I was the youngest member at that time. Then it was a really great thing, though now AAA has fallen on sad times. Mondrian was a founder, as was Burgoyne Diller. He showed with Rose Fried, which was before she took me on.

(The Rose Fried Gallery (1936–1972) was instrumental in introducing the American public to many abstract painters, including Mondrian and Kandinsky. The Gallery remained operational until Fried's death in 1970.)

Hofmann used to talk to me about Mondrian (1872–1944). That was before his show at MoMA. At that time, it was only artists that thought about him. James Johnson Sweeney had a great Mondrian.

(James Johnson Sweeney (1900–1986) was an American curator and writer about modern art. He graduated from Georgetown University in 1922. From 1935 to 1946, he was curator for the Museum of Modern Art. He was the second director of the Solomon R. Guggenheim Museum, from 1952 to 1960.)

CG In his personal collection?

JR Yes. Do you know how he got it? They were friendly and Sweeney invited him to dinner. At the last minute, Mondrian thought that I can't go there without anything. Should I bring a bottle of wine? So, he brought a painting. That's the way it really was.

CG What will you do with the collection?

JR I haven't decided.

CG Do you have children or heirs?

JR No, not really. Nothing compulsive that I have to do. I've thought about it a great deal. I'm not sure what's the right thing to do. For instance, museums change so. In some ways they are so dependent on the human situation at some time. I'm a great believer in teaching museums. I think what has happened to museums is apocalyptic and horrifying. Did you read the Hilton Kramer piece in the *New*

Criterion?

CG About MoMA?

JR He touches on a lot that's significant. I mean we are now in the mass-oriented museum setup. It's really impossible to see paintings in the typical museum. The next thing they will do is put you on a moving belt. You are being programmed in such a way that you can't change the order, can't stay with one thing. There's only one room with seats in MoMA. It's very scary because the pictures that we study, that I most love in art history, the more time that they take, the more I love them. As an artist, there are very few pictures that I like and draw upon, that matter to me. But the whole process is making it impossible to see those pictures. So, are you going to give them things like Gris who said that every picture was an idea and it wasn't completed until the idea was completed? Nobody is looking to see what the idea is. Can you see it that long now? The new wing in Boston is deadly that way.

CG I don't agree. I own the Juan Gris *Portrait of Picasso*. I bought the print when I was in college for $50. It's a beautiful print which I love and look at every day.

JR Sure, you're seeing it at home, which is how it is meant to be seen. You're saying the same thing as me.

CG Let's get back to Knaths. When did you arrive in Provincetown?

JR I visited in '46 but my first summer was '47. I had met Karl and Agnes in New York, so I went to see him. I think I went by myself. I was supposed to go with Anton's mother but that didn't happen. At that time, I didn't know him well, and then we went West returning after a year and a half.

CG People comment that he didn't like company.

JR Oh, but he did. He was embarrassed by all that "stuff" as he put it. When visiting you would walk into this narrow room. It was the only living room that they had because the larger room was where Helen had her piano. It was very stiff there with an arch over the fireplace.

CG I visited him once in 1966. I was hired by Paul Haldeman of the United Church of Christ. He was putting together a portfolio of biblical images to distribute to the churches. I was hired to select and visit the artists. A mandate was that they be figurative, though I included Jules Olitski and Esteban Vicente. Paul rejected Olitski. Karl was one of the artists, as well as Sister Corita Kent, William Gropper, Balcolm Greene, and others. I knew Karl's work from *Lilacs* in the MFA. (Later deaccessioned by Ted Stebbins.) I remember Helen looking in from another room. The stone was shipped to him and Paul liked the print. I believe it inspired Knaths to do other lithographs.

JR I witnessed their will in, I believe, winter 1959. Before signing, they had a discussion about items in the will. Karl was convinced that Helen would outlive him. That was weird as she was 15 years older than him.

CG She died at 103.

JR I know. So, they were discussing the will. There were quite a few important things that were not resolved. He would say, "See Helen, what are you going to do?" She would say, "I don't care. Let them fight over it." She had an incredibly tough side. I was really shocked. She was talking about her niece and his nephew. It was completely unclear who would get what when they died.

Karl managed the home. He washed their clothes. He had an incredible thing about cleanliness and was extremely neat. He always got the exact same things. He knew what they were and washed well. His clothing was cotton or wool and washed well. It was only in later years that they had help. They didn't have a washing machine; he washed in the sink.

Once when we were there, he was so tired. I asked a personal question, "What are you eating?" He told me and it was low fat yogurt, cottage cheese, and lettuce. He had a woman once a week before Joan (Wye?) and she cooked. We persuaded him to eat some meat. Then he felt better—more lively. He was fading away, not that he was losing weight, but very low in energy.

CG I got the impression that Helen didn't do much.

JR She didn't and became weaker and weaker, a little leaf.

CG Joan (Wye) described that he would take a morning walk then start work. When I asked what she did, the answer was, "sit."

JR She blinked slower than anyone I ever saw in my life. Her blinking was like opening and closing her eyes. It was incredible. At the same time, she exerted a lot of possessive pressure on him. He worried about being away from her for very long. She would frighten him about what he could eat and drink. He got this idea that he couldn't drink coffee, so he had no stimulants.

When we were in New York, in the same building that Weldon and Ann were in, Karl would see us once a week. We lived on Stanton Street in the Lower East Side.

He and Helen would come for about six weeks in the winter. They stayed at the Albert Hotel (23 E. 10th St, the hotel and apartment complex was popular with artists.) Later they stayed on the West Side in the 90's. I remember trying to get them something more comfortable. I think we once persuaded them to stay at the Adams. (1049 Fifth Avenue is a 23-floor luxury condominium apartment building located in the Upper East Side, New York City. Built in 1928 as the Adams Hotel, the building underwent extensive renovation in its conversion to residential condominiums during the years 1990–1993.)

That's how he got off on Mondrian. His various friendships changed as other people became more successful. I don't think Karl was ever bitter about his lack of success. We certainly talked about it a great deal. The trips to New York became less and less rejuvenating because he didn't have wonderful times with his colleagues, which is maybe why he became very fond of me.

Occasionally we would introduce him to artists who admired him. There was an artist, Hy Solomon, who I had known since Jane Street days, who admired him enormously. Karl came to Stanton Street and we traveled by subway over to Hy's. In his studio he must have shown us 40 pictures. Karl didn't say a single word. Finally, he said, "It's a matter of interest," and we left. Karl obviously thought the pictures were horrible. Hy was heart broken and I was furious. He couldn't even thank him (for showing his work). It was just horrible. In some ways Karl was gauche and very obstinate.

I was talking about food. Stanton Street was in a Jewish neighborhood. The first time Karl visited I had gotten a really gooey coffee cake which he loved though it was off limits. I made coffee and he got this idea that I did something different with it. That was his story to Helen. So, all the bad things were filtered out and it was okay for him to drink my coffee. So, from then on whenever he came, he would say, "I can drink your coffee because you do that thing with your coffee." I think it was leftover coffee and that was it, the dregs had settled. The interesting thing was how nervous he was that he would have coffee and Helen would disapprove. He was much in bondage to her views. Maybe that was what he wanted.

CG People have commented that marrying Helen was not a bad deal. The Weinrich sisters were well off and could take care of him. Later his work began to sell. In the beginning he did odd jobs and built their home from wood scavenged from abandoned buildings.

JR People say that. But before the Weinrichs, there was a crazy Chicago woman (Zona Gale from Wisconsin) who was very wealthy and in theater. It was through her that he briefly came East. Then back to Chicago (New York) then finally here for good. It wasn't as though he was a poor farm boy who had never had a woman and thought, "Hey, I better latch onto one." I don't think that was Karl's way at all. He was not an opportunist, to a fault, he was incapable of that.

His whole relationship with (gallerist Paul) Rosenberg, for instance, was pathetic if not tragic, as far as the life of an artist went.

CG Can you elaborate.

JR Rosenberg liked Karl's work passionately. Neumann (his third gallerist) had been emotionally generous. Rosenberg was more business like and got him when he was ascending and winning prizes. (1946 First Prize, Carnegie Institute International Exhibition). Rosenberg had a tight contract with him. Karl called him Rosie. I thought that Rosenberg was bad for Karl. When collectors came, he held back the best pictures. Perhaps he viewed them as long-term investments. When that subject came up, I would encourage Karl to push the gallery to sell more work.

CG Some good works ended up in museums.

(Whitney, *The Mexican Blanket,* MoMA, *Giorgioni Book*, 1941. Duncan Phillips was an avid collector. The Albright Knox acquired *Adam.* The Metropolitan owns *The Blue Platter.* In the 1980s I saw his *Day of Atonement,* a large, two-part 1939 work on Masonite in the basement of the MFA. It now hangs in the Lane Gallery.)

JR You have to look at the whole oeuvre for important works that are not yet in good collections. There must be a lot of inventory held back by Rosenberg Gallery.

How many times have I suggested his name when there is something coming out about Provincetown. The list always includes E. Ambrose Webster, Charles Hawthorne, and Hans Hofmann, and I will add Knaths. By the time it gets into print, more often than not, Knaths has been left out. There is always a reason why his name didn't make it.

I am concerned that his manuscript for *Ornament and Glory* (a summary of his theory) may no longer be intact. I was corresponding editor for *Leonardo.*

(The journal, *Leonardo*, was established in 1968 by artist and scientist Frank Malina in Paris. Since 1968, *Leonardo* has published writings by artists who work with science- and technology-based art media. Journal operations were moved to the San Francisco Bay Area by Frank's son, Roger Malina, an astronomer and space scientist, who took over operations of the journal upon his father's death in 1981. In 1982, the International Society for the Arts Sciences and Technology (*Leonardo*/ISAST) was founded to further the aims of Leonardo by providing avenues of communication for artists working in contemporary media.)

The main thrust of *Leonardo* was to publish articles by artists without any critical intervention. It didn't always work out as purely as was hoped, but that was the general idea. We invited artists to write about their work.

I got the idea that little by little, unedited, we could print the entire *Ornament and Glory,* in the exact way that Karl wanted. That meant the pages facing each other in the exact format and size that he had designed. It was the size of his favorite sketch pad with spiral binding. Here being the spiral and two pages facing, like this.

He created many versions of *Ornament and Glory.* And we worked with him many times on versions. We helped him to rewrite, as much of it was very, very cryptic. He started out doing it for himself. Then he started to use it as a teaching manual when he was in D.C. at the Phillips, or Bennington. (He taught there during WWII. I later visited Paul Feeley (1910–1966) who was director of the Art Department at Bennington College during the 1950s and early 1960s.) I wrote to Karl and asked if *Leonardo* might use it? I had contacted the publisher who was enthusiastic.

(1982 Bard College, Annandale-on-Hudson, NY, *Karl Knaths: Ornaments of Glory,* curated and edited by Linda Weintraub, published his manuscript in its catalog. An edited transcription includes facsimile reproductions of about half the manuscript pages published by Jean and Jim Young, in the Bard catalog. Jean had studied with

Knaths and they bought a number of works in the estate from Ed Shein.)

Frank Milina, the owner of *Leonardo* died suddenly three years ago. His son came to see me and it may be revived. The son is a scientist who lives in California. It's a very expensive thing to do and a full-time job. I don't know if it will be reborn. The founder of the magazine was a fascinating man.

Frank had agreed. We met in Paris and it was all set up. I wrote to Karl and he granted the rights, me, or the magazine. I don't remember which, but I had the letter, rights, and two pages of the manuscript that he sent to me. I have it at home (New York), but I'm not sure whether they are original or Xerox. By then there were a lot of versions around. My father-in-law, Raymond Myrer, was trying to get Harvard University Press to publish it. I am sure he was going to put some money into it, but then Harvard reneged.

The young man who was running the press moved on and the new man didn't want to do it. So, it was more bad luck. When Karl died it was all set for *Leonard*o but I had concerns that publishing it in a magazine would keep a commercial press from doing it. I spoke to a friend (Whittemore) about doing it but he wasn't interested.

I wrote to the bank executor, whoever this man was. (Ken Demaris of Cape Ann Bank and Trust). I asked if they would go forward with funding this as it was in the best interest of Karl. I got back a very cold, brief response, just a short note on a small piece of paper saying that they would prefer not to have anything published. They had a lot of plans and this might disrupt anything they might do. By no means should we proceed. So, we didn't, and of course nothing ever happened. (It was around the time of the Bard show and publication that she didn't mention.)

CG Demaris mentioned to me that you had approached him. He said that he had made the decision not to be in the art business. The bank decided that they had the option of promoting his career which meant organizing exhibitions, publishing catalogs, things like that. Basically, they opted to liquidate assets including his work and properties.

JR In this case, they wouldn't be promoting his career. I didn't even need permission from the estate. I had permission from Knaths.

CG He said you wanted money to do the book.

JR That's absolutely impossible, you're not to trust that man.

CG I can show you on tape that they were asked for funds from the estate to publish the book.

JR They might have me mixed up with somebody else. I think that's what it is.

CG The Youngs also asked him for money.

JR That's what it is; very likely.

CG He said, as I recall, that several individuals had approached him about publishing catalogs. So, it's possible that several projects were conflated into one statement. I don't think the bank officer was pulling any hanky panky. He acted in what he viewed as the best interest of the estate.

The estate was worth more than a million dollars. It seems that Helen owned a farm with several hundred acres in Wisconsin, as well as the house in Provincetown. Knaths wanted a third to go to the School of Art Institute of Chicago, where he studied, a third to the Phillips Collection, which supported his work, and the rest to their heirs and relatives.

JR As far as my part it was concerned, *Leonardo* was funded by Frank Milina. It was a super idealistic non-profit venture. Nobody on the masthead including Nobel Prize winners got money for anything. Frank paid for everything, and I want that to be clear. There was no thought about money. There would be no increment (honorarium) from publishing as to who would get money from the magazine. My concern was that there be a first-class publication of *Ornament and Glory* as Karl had intended it. I didn't want it published on less beautiful paper. With *Leonardo,* which was a quarterly publication, it would have taken about two years, because they weren't going to commit the whole magazine to it.

We were going to have four pages per issue. In those days Leonardo had wonderful color reproductions. I thought it would be a dignified presentation.

CG Overall today how do you evaluate Knath's position in the art world?

JR When I met him, he was in the position of an eminent older artist. If you had to say who was more important between say Knaths and Milton Avery, at that point (1950s), it would have been a toss up. Knaths was part of the mainstream, and to me, more important. He was more true than Avery and unsentimental, a tougher kind of artist. It is impressive that Knaths never became bitter or self-deprecating—or distrustful of his talent.

He would see old friends like de Kooning, who no longer had the same feelings toward him. It became bitter tea for Karl to see old friends in New York. 57th Street was a different world than it had been ten years before. His idealism and generosity to other artists remained unwavering. He had a stack of gallery postcard announcements that he would go through. Some of those cards were relegated to the bottom of the stack when the artists didn't continue to live up to his expectations. He believed that what was good would be seen and what was not would fall by the wayside. He didn't loose that sense of belief.

CG When a mediocre exhibition is mounted it takes a generation to set the record straight. That was true for the 1973 traveling show *Karl Knaths: Five Decades of Painting* curated by Charles Eaton and edited by Isabel Patterson Eaton.

The Bard show was dense and fascinating, but did not have the budget to secure major loans. That was the case for the show that I curated in 1986 for the Boston University Art Gallery. Most of the work was borrowed from the Fuller and Danforth Museums, with a prize-winning work loaned by Henry Delawrence. On short notice I was given the slot when another show was cancelled. My curatorial essay was published in *Provincetown Arts Magazine.*

(On the occasion of its 100th anniversary in 2014, the Provincetown Art Association and Museum mounted *Karl Knaths: Between Form and Freedom.* David Maril, wrote in the exhibition catalog, "(He) was a person you knew you could trust. He had a strong, distinctive, slightly gruff, but reassuring voice. Although he was a rugged looking individual, he had a laid-back, gentle demeanor, almost like a deer in one of his cubist paintings." Josephine Del Deo wrote in the catalog, "Nothing could be more true of Karl Knaths than that he was a man of matchless diligence in the pursuit of his art and his way of life.")

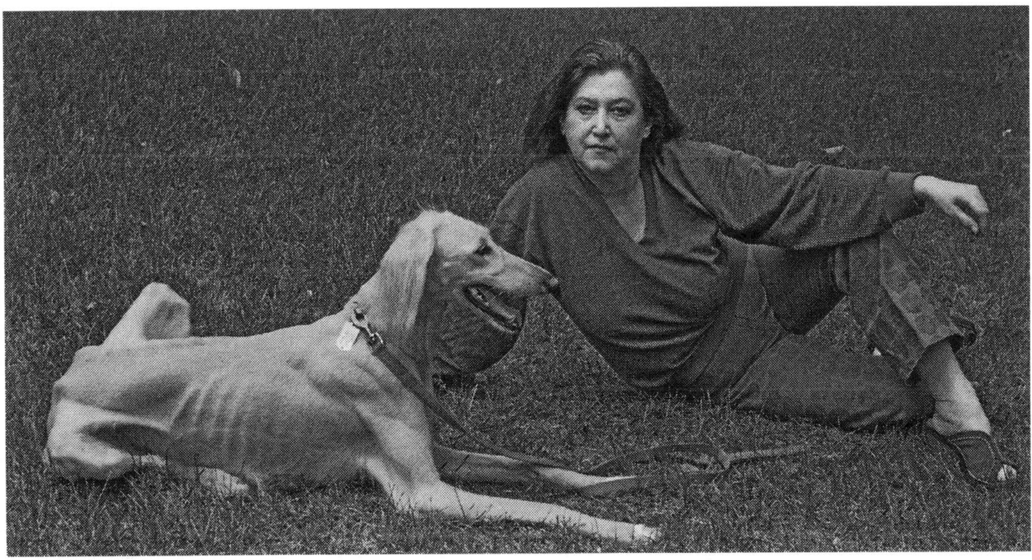

Artist. Collector, philanthropist, Judith Rothschild and her borzoi. Norma Holt photo courtesy of PAAM.

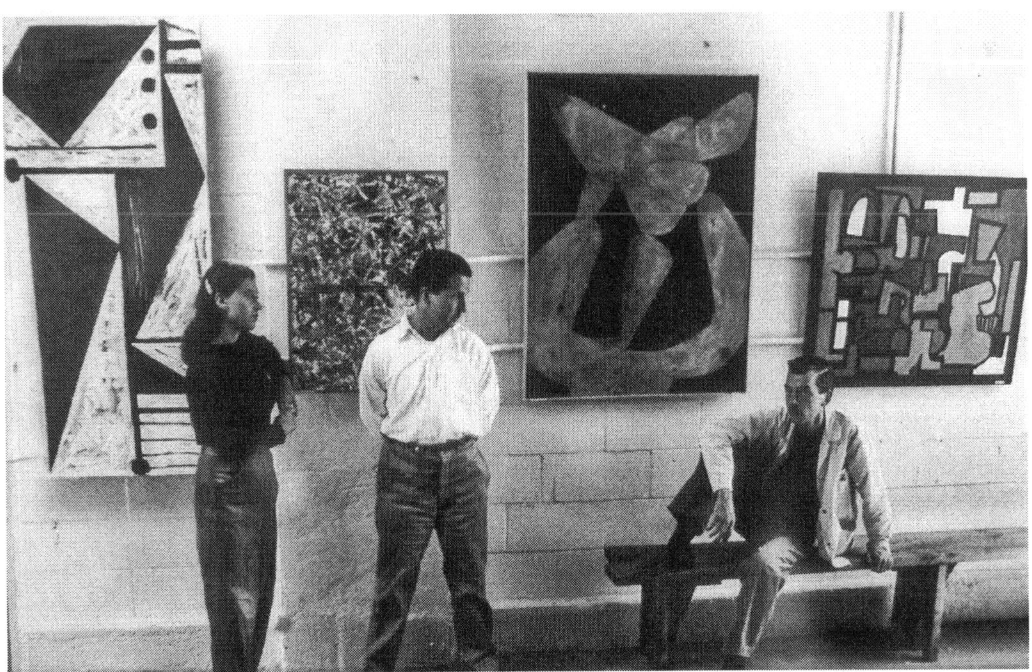

A young Judith Rothschild, with Fritz Bultman and Weldon Kees, helped with *Forum '49*. Photo by Bill Witt. Courtesy of PAAM.

Ellen O'Donnell Rankin Was Director of Provincetown Art Association and Museum

Ellen O'Donnell Rankin was executive director of the Provincetown Art Association and Museum from 1983–1986. She left to take that position at the Aldrich Museum of Art, 1986–1992. She holds an MFA in fine arts from NYU where she has taught arts administration. She taught at the University of Toronto from 1988–2003. She has been executive director of Eorankin Fine Arts Advisory since 2005. She continues to lecture at NYU in the graduate Arts Administration Program. Presently, she is an historian for the New York Yacht Club and writes about their maritime collection, history, and architecture of the historic club houses.

O'Donnell Rankin was enormously helpful in launching my Provincetown research. We collaborated on a major exhibition, *Kind of Blue: Benny Andrews, Emilio Cruz, Earle Pilgrim and Bob Thompson.* It featured the work of four African American artists. With no money for a catalog, the curatorial essay was published by Chris Busa as a feature in his *Provincetown Arts Magazine.*

Ellen O'Donnell
May 1984
At PAAM

Charles Giuliano How did you come to be associated with the Provincetown

Art Association and Museum?

Ellen O'Donnell I was a long-time summer resident. I graduated from Regis College in 1976 as an economics and art history major. I took a year off and traveled. In 1978 was hired by the PAAM to organize education programs. That lasted for a year and a half. Then I became assistant director under Annabelle Hebert. In 1982, she left to become director of Guild Hall, a small museum in the Hamptons. It's an organization very similar to ours. They have two galleries and the John Drew Theater (now The Hilarie and Mitchell Morgan Theater). This past January I went to NYU to work on a master's degree. It's a program that combines arts administration and 20th century art history.

I had a terrific significant knowledge of the history of Provincetown before I started working here. That came from living here, research, and reading a lot. That's why I had a good grasp of the institution and caught on as a good administrator. A lot of people in town knew me and things just happened.

CG What's the mandate for PAAM?

EO It was founded in 1914 as a kind of club. At first it was in the Town Hall and in 1919 it acquired this building. The membership bought the property for $3,000. It was a home that they converted into an exhibition space. It was conceived as an organization for artists, run by artists. It was intended to help artists to show their work. It continued like that with open and juried shows. They were a year-round organization for a long time. During WWII they became a summer thing. After the war, Provincetown became a resort. Artists were a part of the attraction. William Merritt Chase (1849–1916) and Ambrose Webster (1869–1935) were artists who had come here in the 1890s. They came early, and Charles Webster Hawthorne (1872–1930) came later. They were integral to forming the art association as there was no place for artists to show their work.

CG Later there was the Chrysler Museum.

EO It's now in Norfolk, Virginia. Chrysler collected many works by Provincetown artists. He collected pop art and had some fun shows. I remember seeing Warhol's soup cans there.

CG When did your family first come here?

EO 1958.

CG So you had an overview long before you were officially connected. What was it like then as compared to now?

EO An early recollection was of a lot of street artists. In the late 1950s, you would see a lot of people painting landscapes. An early memory was the Chrysler Museum, which had fabulous shows. There was sculpture in front of the museum, so you were introduced to new things. I have vague memories of Sun Gallery. There were all kinds of happenings and parties. Sun Gallery was important with artists like Jay Milder, Claes Oldenburg, Red Grooms, and Bob Thompson. It wasn't just a gallery, with all kinds of things going on, including poetry readings. People were still talking about *Forum '49*. There were fabulous galleries. Ivan Karp and his wife had a gallery in what is now Metro Café. It was a small space in back, underneath the café.

CG Tirca Karlis Gallery?

EO Her son Aaron runs it now. There was Nat Halper's HCE. I don't know what it means but it has something to do with Joyce. Nat had everyone in his gallery. When he closed, Sam Kootz picked up his artists. There was also Virginia Zabriski's gallery. There was a lot going on.

The turning point was the 1970s. As a resort, there was a real estate boom. The nature of the town began to shift. More commercial galleries opened and the economy had a lot to do with that. When real estate went up, nobody could afford the rent for galleries. Summer rent for a shop is now $15,000 to $20,000.

Artists and galleries could rent for $500 for the summer. That changed. A waterfront home now goes for $160,000 and $100,000 for one with no view. Norman Mailer's home sold for $250,000.

There is a resurgence now, with a lot of young artists. Part of that is the Fine Arts Work Center, which brings them in. Some of them leave during the summer and return for lower winter rents. Some of them work in restaurants during the summer and have the winter to do their own work. Winters are wonderful here.

CG What is winter population like?

EO There are 4,000 registered voters. A wild guess is 8,000 to 9,000 winter residents. There are 80,000 permanent summer residents; people who come for a couple of weeks or the whole summer. Then you have day-trippers and weekenders. Depending on weather, at any given time, there may be 120,000 to 150,000 people in town. They come in excursion boats. Whale watching is a major attraction. There are four or five boats. That's a new thing which has brought a lot of people to town.

CG So Provincetown is an accordion that shrinks in winter and expands in summer. What do locals think of that?

EO Of course there are people who object to that. But the economy depends on it. The fishing community is not what it was. They are in the process of rebuilding the town wharf. The town is trying to build a marina like the one in Nantucket. We have a great harbor but people can't dock their boats. There may be a marina in the next ten years.

A lot of these people will live on their boats, so there won't be a housing issue. The season now starts in April and runs through Christmas.

CG Who are some of the prominent artists today?

EO Motherwell is here from June through September. Myron Stout is here year-round. He had a wonderful show at the Whitney three years ago. Jack Tworkov died recently. Raphael Soyer comes for six weeks. He always wears a suit and tie. He and his wife promenade the streets.

CG Did his brothers also come?

EO I remember Moses. I never knew Isaac, but I'm sure they all come as did Chaim Gross. He will jury one of our shows this summer. (His daughter Mimi was the first wife of Red Grooms. She worked on his installations.) As far as writers, there's Norman Mailer and the poet Stanley Kunitz. In Wellfleet, there's Grace Paley. Of the younger artists, there's Paul Bowen. He's having a show at Graham Contemporary. Paul was born in Wales.

CG Who is emerging from the Fine Arts Work Center?

EO Paul Bowen. Dan Rice is big in California. The writing program is very strong and they seem to have more success than the artists. Quite a few of the visual arts fellows have won Guggenheim and Fulbright fellowships.

CG Provincetown has been known for its schools.

EO In the early publications of the Art Association there were ads for 20 to 30 schools. Today we have a school here. In June, Xavier Gonzalez teaches painting. We have Bill Behnken, who teaches at New York State College. Now in his 80s, Henry Hensche still teaches and has demonstrations. He has an incredible following. Leo Manso and Victor Candell had a school here in what is now the Long Point Gallery. There are people who teach privately, but as far as schools, there aren't any. We are trying to revitalize with our school.

CG Is it because students can't afford to come here?

EO That's part of the problem. Years ago, when people came here to study, housing was affordable. Our enrollment would be very high, but students can't find a place to stay. A studio apartment for the season is $2,500. Everything is expensive, including groceries. When I was in New York this year I was struck at how much more affordable food was.

CG What are the plans for the coming season?

EO We are open year-round other than a couple of weeks in May, when we refresh galleries. Our winter season starts October 1, and we just keep open the main gallery. That's the Richmond Gallery. During the winter, we have open shows and invitationals. Last winter, I curated a show of six photographers.

We are the artistic hub for a radius of sixty miles. We have theater in the Murchison Gallery. The Provincetown Theater has its home there with a winter average of four or five plays.

In the Hawthorne Gallery, we have students from Parsons School of Design. They are MFA students in a workshop setting. It's part of their curriculum, and four or five come and work independently. We arrange to have artists who live here come and crit their work. Mostly they are landscape painters. We have openings and talks. In the back, we have painting and sculpture classes. Groups use our facility for their meetings.

The summer season starts at Memorial Day and ends on October 1. In four galleries, we have an average of 16 shows, each lasting a month. Every year we have a young artist's show, which had 187 applicants this time. Of those 30 percent are from the Cape. We've had a young artists' show for the past six years. We want young artists to feel that they can participate in our shows.

CG How many visitors do you have, and what is the admission price?

EO We don't charge anything. I did away with fees last fall. During the summer, I experimented by not charging for a week and our admissions tripled. Now we have voluntary contributions. During the summer, attendance is 20,000, not counting lectures and special events. Including those, our attendance is about 50,000 to 60,000. Our winter shows get excellent media coverage. We get about 75 visitors a day for winter shows. The gallery gets a lot of exposure because of the theater program. They usually sell out their performances. People come from as far away as Hyannis as it's the only theater on the Cape.

CG Discuss the 16 summer shows.

EO We try to achieve balance. In each time slot, we do a members show. In the first slot, we have a juried show. We have 800 members, of which 70 percent are artists. Membership is $40, which is a bone of contention because it used to be $25. I didn't raise it, the board did. Our operating budget is about $120,000. We don't have a mortgage, rent, or pay taxes. Everything is paid for, which is fabulous.

Through fundraising and careful management, over the past few years, we have paid off the bills and are in the black. I'm good at projecting a budget and sticking to it. This is, perhaps, something that prior administrations lacked. I have managed to increase programming without additional expense.

We have jurors coming this weekend and we don't pay them. Instead, we provide four days in Provincetown. We offer a nice place to stay. There is an edge we can bargain with. If someone comes in summer and they stay at a house on the beach, they love it. We don't offer an honorarium.

CG What impact have you had as director?

EO Under our prior director the mortgage was paid off. We had an auction. Our next task was to pay off our bills. We were carrying about $25,000 in bills. One of my objectives was to get rid of the deficit and to initiate year-round programming.

Each fall we have a fund-raising event in New York, and in spring, one in Boston. It keeps people in touch, as well as raising a substantial amount of money. For our first New York event, we bought a hundred tickets to *Gandhi.* That came with an Indian dinner following the screening. We sold out at $50 each. This year we went to *La Cage aux Folles,* followed by a party. People love to get together with their Provincetown friends. Each year we have an event at Ciro's in Boston. These events create revenue.

CG Can you break down the budget of $120,000?

EO Heat and utilities 20 percent, salaries 50 percent, exhibitions and programming another 20 percent.

CG About $21,000 for exhibitions?

EO It's not a lot of money. During the summer, 4 of the 14 shows we put on are from the collection. Two are member shows. So those 6 shows don't cost us anything. The endowment, just $7,000, is very small. Last year we got an endowment of $25,000. From the interest 50 percent provides scholarships to our school. The other 50 percent goes to operating expenses.

CG Let's talk about the permanent collection.

EO It revolves around Charles Hawthorne. We have about 25–30 of his works. We have William Merritt Chase. He was an American impressionist who Hawthorne studied under, as well as Childe Hassam, who came around 1900. We have works by both of those artists. Hawthorne also studied with Ambrose Webster. Recent auction prices for Hawthorne have been $50,000 to $75,000. We have three works by Edwin Dickenson, two paintings and a drawing. The Wadsworth Athenaeum recently purchased one for $250,000. We have one (Hans) Hofmann. There was a schism in Provincetown at that time. The Art Association was conservative and classically orientated. There was opposition to abstract expressionism. When, at that time, Hofmann offered work to us, it was not accepted. He was then a trustee of the museum. He was a frequent juror for our shows. In fact, I picked up the Hofmann in New York just ten days ago. We have a Gottlieb, but no de Kooning, Pollock. or Kline.

CG So you will never have a truly representative Provincetown collection.

EO I think we will. There are major collectors in this area.

CG Have you broached them, and what is the response?

EO Very positive.

CG These are works that every museum is looking for. Why would they give them to the Art Association?

EO If they get the same tax reduction, what difference does it make? Why not fill gaps in our collection. Provincetown has been important to their lives? It is more valuable to give work to small museums than big ones. That's how I feel. Our collection is worth about $1 million. We have excellent facilities, which were designed and approved by John Hofstetter, who is chief conservator for Williams College. We have had other conservators advise us on our facilities. When Vose came to appraise the collection, he was amazed at what we had. Our cataloguing system is one approved by American Association of Museums.

CG Have you thought of putting together a traveling show?

EO We did that in 1977 with Ron Kutcha's *Provincetown Painters 1890s to 1970s* show. (Everson Museum of Art, April 1 to June 26, 1977.) The Hawthorne watercolors show has been to five museums so far, and is coming here. It includes several works from our collection. In the *Provincetown Prints* exhibition five or six works were from our collection. We want to make our collection more visible and accessible to other museums. As far as initiating a traveling show, that's very expensive. It's better if another museum does that and we assist them. The Guild of Boston Artists covered everything in 1978 and we haven't done anything since the Everson show.

CG When was your last major Hawthorne show?

EO We have to do one every ten years, which is part of our bylaws. This summer we're having the Hawthorne watercolors. It was organized through us by the National Museum of American Art. We've gotten grant money, as well as corporate support. We've gotten money from the Mass Council, though we didn't apply this year. I'm sure we will find support for our show on *Forum '49*. Reggie Cabral and Fritz Bultman are ones you want to talk to about that. There might be an outside curator. Cynthia Goodman, who curated our Hofmann show, wants to do it. A show of Provincetown's art schools is another show we are planning.

CG What else are you planning?

EO We have a photography show with (Annie) Liebowitz, (Joel Peter) Witkin, and (Cindy) Sherman. Last summer we showed Renata Ponsold, who is Motherwell's wife. And we had (Joel) Meyerowitz's *Redheads* show. That was our second show of his. *Cape Cod Light* came to us from the MFA and was a great success.

Last summer, a lot of people came to see our shows of (Jack) Tworkov and (Robert) Motherwell. There was strong attendance for the Judith Rothschild Collection. There was also a show of her work at Wellesley. We try to have collector's shows, but this summer nothing is scheduled.

This summer we're having a Chaim Gross show. He has been coming here for 40 years and has been in group shows, but never a one-man show. That's a major oversight. The show will have paintings, sculpture, and drawings. On March 17, he turned 80 and is in good health and still teaches.

CG The Zorachs have also been here for a long time.

EO We recently got a nice work for the collection.

CG What part did you have in last summer's *Provincetown Printmakers* show?

EO Nat Halper and Mervin Jules worked on it for a long time with Janet Flint. They helped track down works and gathered archival material. It brought in so many people that I wish we could have it back.

We have four different shows because there are such rich resources here. There are so many artists to deal with. We try to have a balance of group shows and invitationals.

CG Bob Thompson would be an interesting person to show.

EO Sure, or Red Grooms. There are so many interesting artists that we might show.

CG Thompson, Grooms, Jay Milder, Lester Johnson, Tony Vevers, and Jan Muller, who all showed at Sun Gallery, returned to the figure at the height of abstract expressionism.

EO Lester has been in our group shows. He lives in Greenwich and teaches at Yale. Some of those guys come now and then. When we have a particular show there is an amazing reunion of people. Certain shows generate that.

CG What will be the main attraction this summer?

EO Last summer we had Tworkov, Motherwell, and *Provincetown Prints*. Those were major shows, as was the Judith Rothschild Collection. Chaim's show is significant. That and *Hawthorne Watercolors* are the big shows this summer. The photography show includes individuals who might otherwise not be seen here. It's important to bring work to Provincetown to again establish that it is a major art center.

CG So it's a rebuilding process.

EO Exactly. Bringing someone like (critic) Grace Glueck to judge a show. People will enter a show based on the juror. Even if the work is accepted or not, it's the chance to be seen by a major critic. It's also a way for the Art Association to be known by artists. That's why those shows are important.

CG Who chooses the shows?

EO We have an exhibitions committee. Part of our mission is to collect Provincetown's artists. That includes artists who have lived here for a number of years, but may not mean much to most people. We are not here just for the big names, but to have overall representation.

CG What are your goals for the collection?

EO To fill in the gaps for the abstract expressionists. There are a lot of collectors, both summer and year-round, who have that work. We can cultivate and court them. We have an edge because many of them are already a part of the organization.

Last summer, we did not have a single exhibition based on our collection. Those decisions are made by the exhibitions committee. Things came up which caused us to reschedule. During the winter, I curate a couple of shows from the collection, which allows us to be creative. I want to start collecting young Provincetown artists.

CG How do you do that without funds?

EO We have some. People donate works to be auctioned. I think people would be pleased to give work to the collection. Even though funds are limited, you can collect these artists. I believe in purchasing and supporting these artists. Nat Halper was interested in that idea and Reggie Cabral has been helpful. It's less a matter of numbers than filling gaps. Numbers are less important than the quality of acquisitions.

CG Can you tell me about the Heritage Museum?

EO They have exhibitions of hooked rugs, sandwich glass, things like that. They have some nice works in the collection.

CG Sal Del Deo is involved?

EO Sal's wife, Josephine. They are owned by the town with a historical emphasis.

CG When was the Fine Arts Work Center founded?

EO Last year was their tenth anniversary. It came about as a means to bring young artists and writers to Provincetown. Hudson Walker was behind it. He's from Minnesota and a major collector. (In 2024 his daughter, Berta Walker, celebrated 35 years of her gallery.) Berta is now chairman of the board. They moved into the former Day's Lumber Yard in 1975. Artists had studios there, including Hofmann, Peter Grippe, Myron Stout, Fritz Bultman, and Robert De Niro, Sr.

When we showed Motherwell last year, a lot of the work went to a show in Albany. The insurance costs were staggering, thousands of dollars. We don't have the money to travel shows unless someone pays for it.

CG Isn't that where grants come in?

EO Sure, but we can't organize well enough in advance to apply for them. Also, much of our staff leaves during the winter, so we don't have people to work on them. For the *Forum '49* show, for example, we are pushing to meet the NEA deadline. We missed the deadline, so we are rescheduling. The woman who is doing the show just had a baby and wasn't able to work on the grant. We have to plan as far out as possible. In the past, we didn't fix our schedule until April and then summer was right on top of us. We used to open on June 15 and instead of 14 shows we had just seven or eight. We have doubled our exhibition schedule.

CG How many works are there in the collection?

EO We have 800 works; paintings, sculpture, works on paper, and photography.

CG Do you have archival material like photos and documents of the early years?

EO Tons, boxes of them, but we don't count them as part of the permanent collection. When people say, why don't you have this or that. I say, ok, help us to organize our archives and photographs. We have photographs of exhibition installations, as well as numerous photos of Hawthorne's classes on the beach.

CG Has anyone curated a show of that material?

EO No, but the potential is unlimited.

CG What limits the unlimited?

EO Energy, manpower, finances. There wasn't anyone working year-round until a few years ago. We're making strides. The material is there, but it takes time. The fact that we are now in the black is hopeful. We constantly have students and art historians requesting to come see our archives. These are people doing thesis research and organizing exhibitions. Galleries request information on specific artists. We try to keep up with that. There are ongoing attempts to document this rich history. There was a lot of activity around 1912–1914. In addition to the fine arts there was the literary and theater development. That was the era of The Wharf Theater, Provincetown Playhouse, Beachcombers, and when the Art Association was formed. There was so much going on.

CG And yet so little has been documented. There's Ross Moffett's *Art in Narrow Streets*, a slim volume, and Ron Kutchs's *Iverson* catalog. There are artist monographs and exhibition catalogs, but little in terms of comprehensive research and publication.

EO Bradley Robinson (1914–1984) was working on compiling this information. He started on the project a year and a half ago and wrote a thousand pages. I talked with him about how there might be a major book about Provincetown, not just Provincetown, but the whole lower Cape. Not just the artists, but all of the arts, including literature and theater.

What Bradley had started doing, but didn't complete, was compiling biographical information. People who came through Provincetown, their education and style of work. He wanted it to be a resource book, an index of artists with some story telling. He was thinking of it as a long-term project and we were planning to apply for grants. He was an experienced writer who published several books. He wrote on Admiral Robert Peary, who explored the North Pole. (Bradley Robinson, *Arctic*, Vol. 36, No. 1 (March 1983), pp. 106–107 Arctic Institute of North America.)

He was a retired writer living in Provincetown and totally engrossed in this project. Now we need someone to pick up the pieces. That was a terrific project. He just passed away a month ago.

I am surprised there are not more people doing this kind of thing. It's something I would love to do, but I am overwhelmed by my job here. That's one of the reasons I went back to school to become more involved with art history. There is so much here with great potential. I just wish there were someone here to share that history.

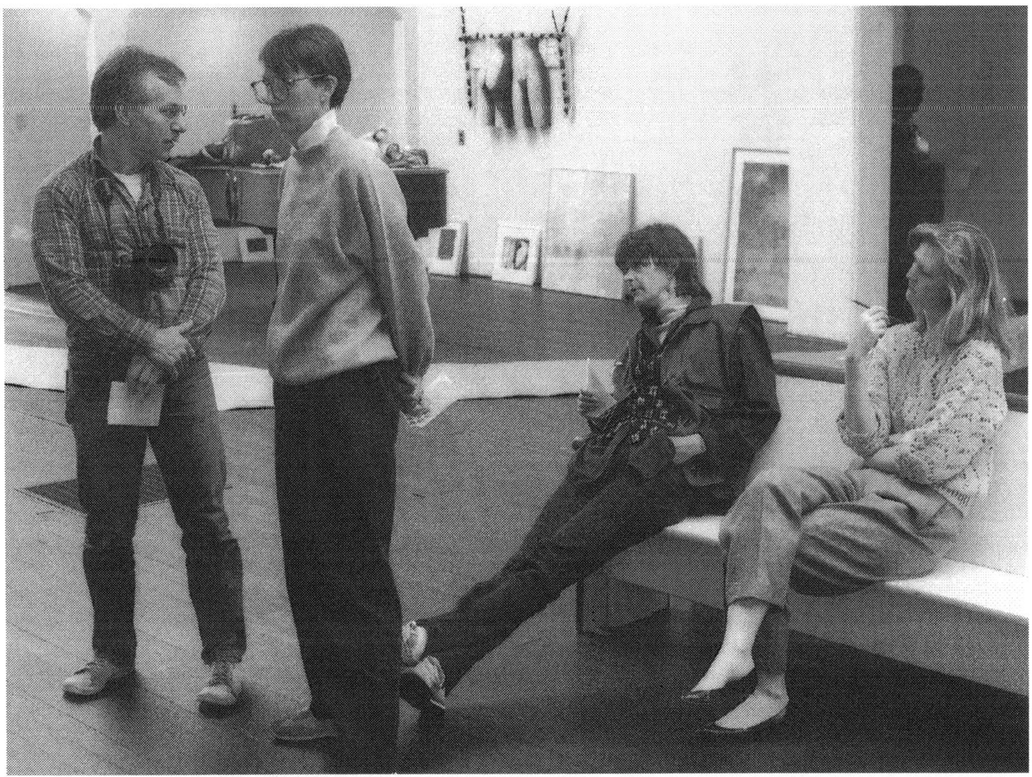

Ellen with a PAAM exhibition jury. Giuliano photo.

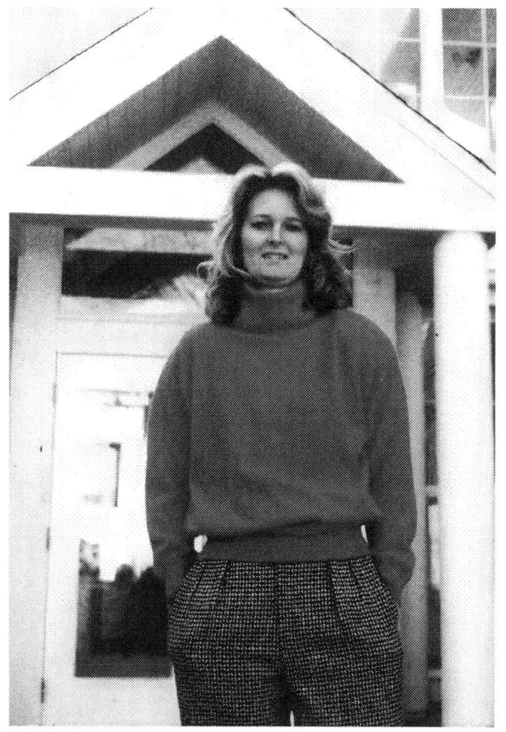

Ellen while director of the Aldrich Museum, Giuliano photo.

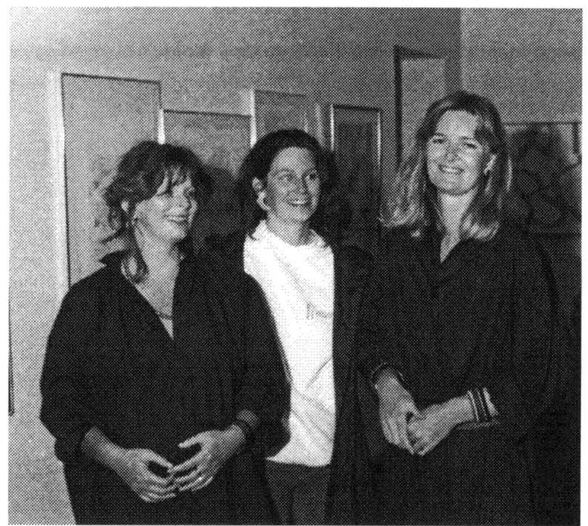

Left to right, Moira, Elisabeth, and Ellen O'Donnell. Giuliano photo.

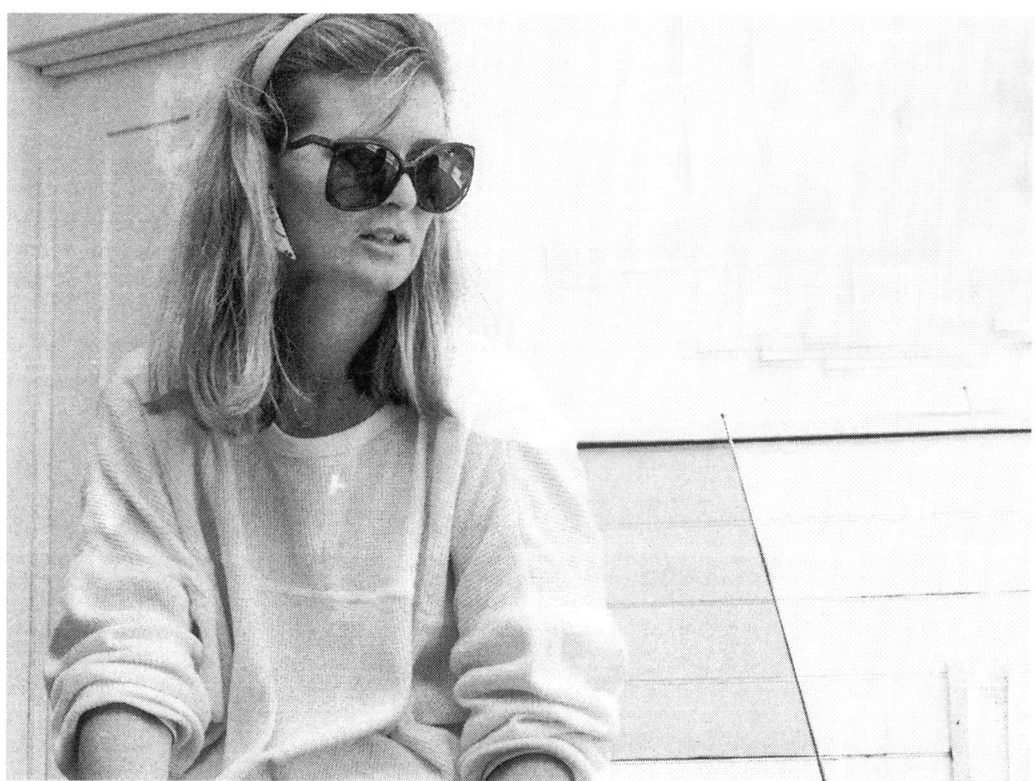

Ellen O'Donnell Rankin, 1980s, Giuliano photo.

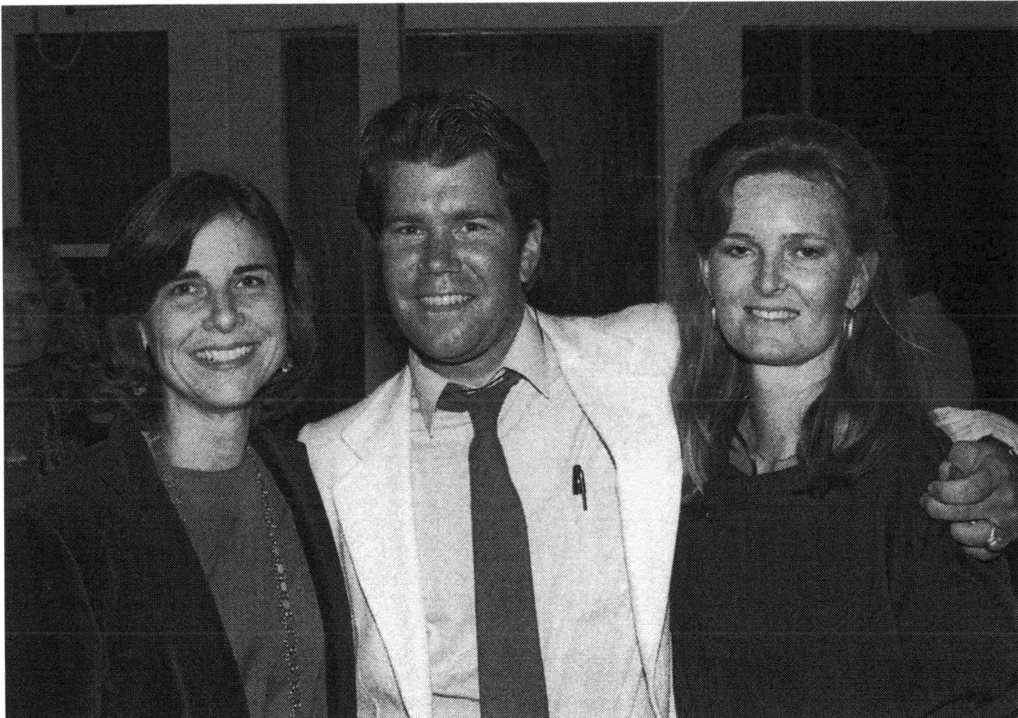

Anne Hawley, Mass Council/Gardner Museum director, and later PAAM director Bill Evaul, and Ellen O'Donnell Rankin. Giuliano photo.

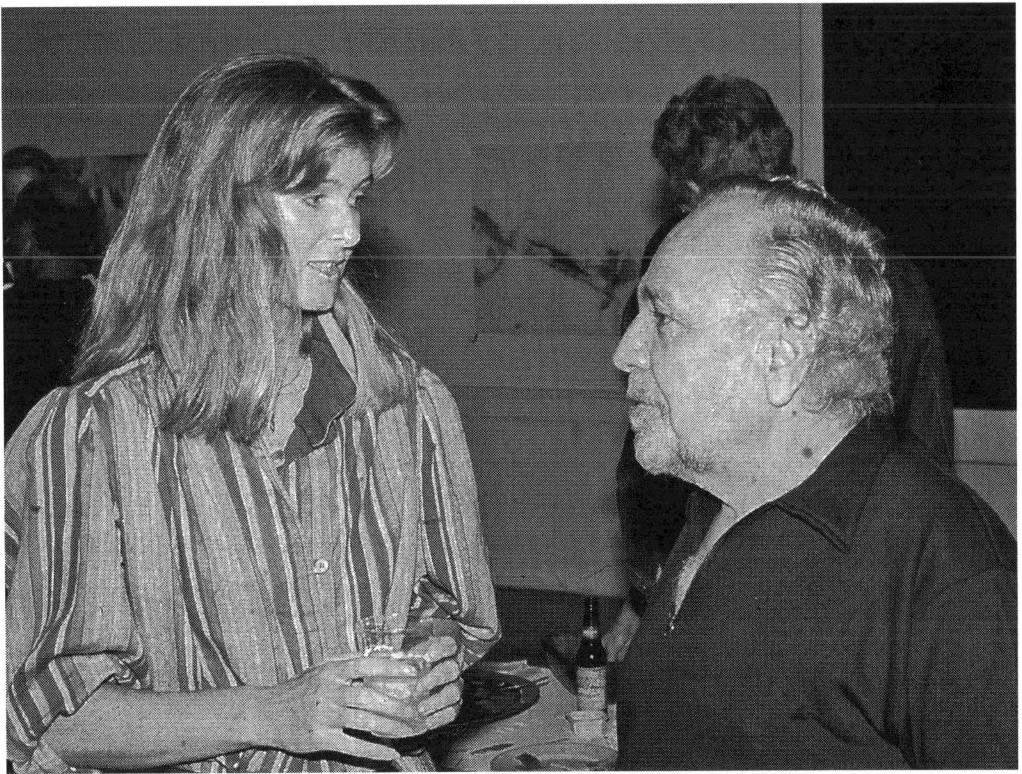

Ellen with A House owner, collector and trustee, Reggie Cabral. Giuliano photo.

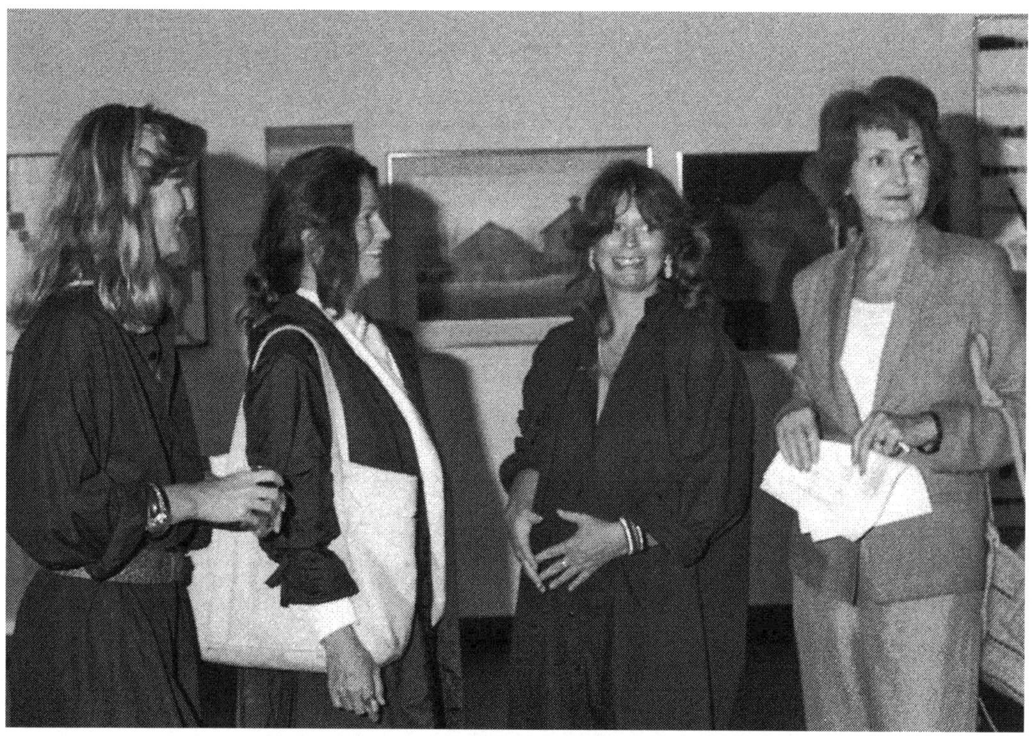

Long-term Provincetown residents Mrs. O'Donnell and her daughters. Giuliano photo.

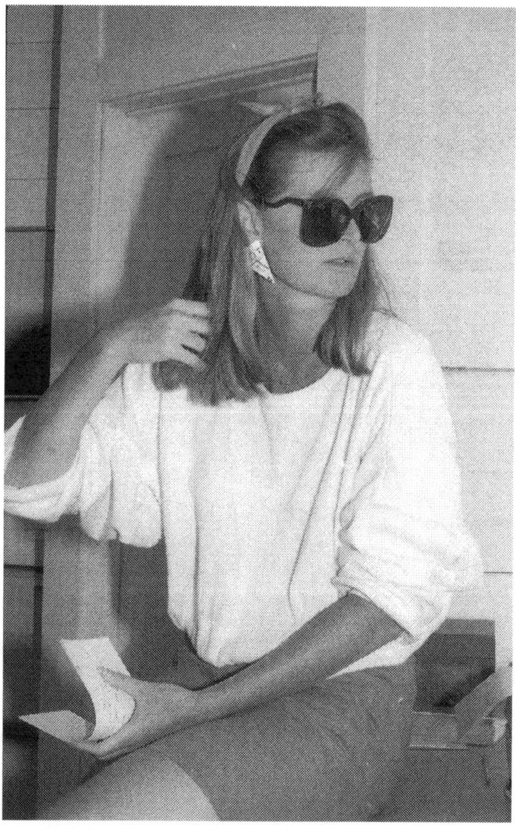

O'Donnell Rankin. Giuliano photo.

Sun Gallery Was Small But Enormously Consequential

From 1955 to 1959 the artist Yvonne Anderson and her husband, the poet Dominic Falcone, operated the legendary Sun Gallery in Provincetown. In one-week shows over five seasons, with a combination of group, one-man, and two-man shows, they displayed work by about 100 artists, a selection of whom formed the nucleus of the figurative expressionist movement.

The Sun Gallery took over a small space that had previously been the gallery and jewelry shop of Earle Montrose Pilgrim and his wife Lily.

Anderson documented the exhibitions of the Sun Gallery. With an "eleven-dollar camera" she has at least one photograph of each show. Also, she shot film of the shows and studios, which has been compiled as a DVD.

When they left Provincetown, the Sun Gallery was operated in the seasons 1960–61 by Irene Baker and Bill Barrell. They added the artists Emilio Cruz, Rosalyn and Sherman Drexler, Claes Oldenburg, as well as film-makers Ken Jacobs and Jack Smith.

From 1962 to '63 the gallery was run by Nat Halper, who added Eben Given Jr. (who designed the covers of Boston's publication *Avatar*), John Frank, and George Segal.

Interview with Yvonne Andersen 2013 By phone

Charles Giuliano Over the years I have written about Lester Johnson, Bob Thompson and Jan Müller, among others. This summer I have been invited to write a catalog essay for an exhibition curated by Adam Zucker at the Provincetown Art Association and Museum.

Yvonne Andersen Those are our guys. Not so much Bob Thompson. Bob was in a three-man show. We had two one-man shows for Jan Müller. And five one-man shows for Lester Johnson. Did you mention someone else?

Here's the situation. We opened Sun Gallery, my husband and I, Dominic Falcone. It was his idea, by the way. He went to work as a dishwasher at the Moors Restaurant to pay for it, while I ran it. We did this for five years.

We did a lot of what was called innovative things. After a while, I thought we had done everything I could think of to do. We had poetry readings and all kinds of stuff, including the first *Happening* with live actors. So, we left. Meanwhile, some of the painters who showed in the gallery didn't want us to leave. So, one of them, Bill Barrell, talked to some of the other people we had showed, and they opened the gallery again for a year. We were not there for the last year and it is quite possible that George Segal was included. (Segal was shown at Sun Gallery when it was run by Irene Baker and Bill Barrell.)

I have pretty good notes on everybody who was there. Tony Vevers (and Irving Sandler) wrote a catalog for a Sun Gallery show at PAAM in 1981 (July 24 to August 30). In that catalog he mentions a few of the people who showed after we were gone. I think that's where he is if you want me to confirm that.

CG What were people thinking about the figure? Of course, people came to Provincetown to study with Hans Hofmann.

YA Me included.

CG But people were pulling away from that. Artists like Red Grooms and Lester Johnson. Jan Müller was European. Artists were talking about a return to the figure.

Do you recall people talking about that?

YA Yes. Hmm. Let's see. I'll tell you what happened to me. Actually, if you want me to send it to you, I have a video on the Sun Gallery. We became filmmakers after we left the Sun Gallery. We ran a film series and I showed a lot of these people who I shot with documentary footage, Tony Vevers, Alex Katz.

As to this particular question, I can tell you about the years we were in Provincetown. Val (as Falcone was known) was interested in art. He was a poet. But I remember him not being very comfortable about modern art. For myself, both abstract and modern were fine. I went to L.S.U. on a band scholarship, but quit the music department and moved over to fine arts. My instructor was Peter Kahn. He was the brother of Wolf Kahn. Both of those guys were students and teaching assistants of Hans Hofmann.

Peter Kahn, by the way, was a great teacher, probably the best teacher I ever had. I asked him where he studied and he said, "Well I studied with Hans Hofmann." So, I said, "Well I guess I'll go study with Hans Hofmann." I was over at his house at the time because he had invited me for a Sunday dinner, a number of times. His younger brother, Wolf Kahn, was there. He said, "You know if you want to go study with Hans Hofmann, I can find you a place to live there."

He got me a place at Sunny Tasha's house. A lot of artists lived there. Alan Kaprow lived about ten yards from my spot. She made all these little houses and constructions in her backyard. John Grillo also lived there.

My roommate and I went to Provincetown. We studied with Hans Hofmann. My roommate was Betty King, who lives in Brazil. She's also an artist.

When we started the gallery, my husband had a certain vision about it. We wanted to concentrate on showing new people, young people who we thought were very interesting. I guess we sorta got a reputation for picking out good new people.

Everyone was welcome to show at the Sun Gallery. Anyone who came by and asked to show, I showed. We had group shows, one-man shows, two-man shows. We had a five-man show once. So, everyone could participate.

It was different in those days. If we wanted to have a program that night, we put a poster in the window, maybe a day before, and everyone would come.

CG It was a very small space.

YA A very small space. We had a new show every week. On Sunday night we took down the old show and put up orange curtains. We would hang the new show and on Monday night there would be a big crowd of people across the street at nine o'clock when we opened up, and they would all come in. One time it was so instantly crowded that I had gone outside and couldn't get back in. It was always controversial. People would come by to see what was our latest outrage.

CG Coming back to the question, what about the figure?

YA The figure? I myself was a Hans Hofmann student. He seemed to like everything I did, which was fairly abstract, maybe semi-figurative. I was there for awhile with him and nothing seemed to be happening. I realized why he didn't work for me was I had already learned it from his student. I learned all of that stuff.

I don't know, we just seemed to be going in that direction. My husband was certainly not interested in abstract art. He was very much an expressionist. He gave a number of readings when we were having our gallery.

There was a lot of talk about this going on all the time. I didn't participate in intellectual discussions. Myself, I was a very practical person. I was the one that got everything done. Got it hung and got the people to come. Of course, it was a place for me to show my work, which was kind of a cross between abstract and figurative. My husband got to give readings and show his poems and art.

It just sort of grew. We arrived in Provincetown and put a sign in the window.

CG Is it just a coincidence that the artists you showed were figurative? Is it just that these were the artists who were around?

YA We gave one-man shows to the artists we liked.

CG What was it that you liked?

YA We liked a strong expression of emotion, which was pretty visible in the human figure.

CG Now that art historians are interested in figurative expressionism the Sun Gallery had become a center for all that.

YA Yes, we were. People seemed to think that new stuff was happening. After the first two years a lot of people wanted to show at the gallery.

Jan Müller had a one-man show at the Hansa Gallery in New York. Then he had a one-man show at the Sun Gallery. It made such a strong statement that the next year he got a show. I think it was at the Whitney. People we were showing started catching on in New York. So, everyone wanted to show at our gallery.

(There was a strong Provincetown connection to Hansa Gallery, 1952–1959. 70 East 12th Street: Fall 1952–Fall 1954, 210 Central Park South: Fall 1954–Summer 1959. Directors of the Hansa Gallery were Richard Bellamy and Ivan Karp.)

CG Would you say that the most important artist was Jan Müller?

YA No. I hate to say that he was the most important artist, but we had five artists we liked quite a bit. We liked Jan. We showed him and then he was dead. (1922–1958) I can still remember when his friends brought over this huge painting. They carried it over from his house. It went across the whole back of the gallery. A monster painting. I think it was called *Of This Time of That Place.*

We liked Lester Johnson (1919–2010).

Then my husband was washing dishes at The Moors. The Fourth of July came and they hired his young kid from Nashville, Tennessee. My husband stayed late to help him survive. Then he found out he was a painter. He asked me to come over and look at his drawings. I was flabbergasted. So, we started having Red Grooms (born Charles Rogers Grooms on June 7, 1937) in many of our shows.

We finally gave him a one-man show and that show I remember being very criticized. People were saying, "Why are you showing a 21-year-old guy? You should be showing more established people." But we all know what happened with that.

CG You said that you liked five artists. So far; Jan Müller, Lester Johnson, Red Grooms.

YA Tony Vevers was one.

CG That's four.

YA Let's see. Joan Wye. She was married to Jim Forsberg. I worked in his Studio Shop in Provincetown in the mornings. He was the manager of the shop. He was in a two-man show at the gallery.

CG What was Alan Kaprow doing?

YA When I met him, I had just moved to Provincetown. My roommate and I were living in a basement apartment of Sunny Tasha's. Facing out to a back, she had a space that was kind of like a garage and Alan Kaprow was living in that. He was a friend of Wolf Kahn. John Grillo lived upstairs. There was a community garden we all worked in. If you pulled the weeds, you could eat the food.

We were friends with him (Kaprow) and it was very interesting a few years later. I was finishing school at L.S.U. with one more course to take. I wasn't going to be in Baton Rouge. They said, we know you're going to Provincetown. If there are any college professors there, they can give you your test. That's what Alan Kaprow did for me.

CG Was he painting?

YA Yes, he was painting.

CG Do you remember what the paintings looked like?

YA No. I was going to the Hofmann school. My roommate and I were working. We had no money. We used to go get free fish from the fishermen. We saw Alan and were in his place a lot. But I don't remember exactly what he was doing.

CG Do you remember his performance in Provincetown?

YA The first showing of Alan Kaprow that I saw was in New York City in the Hansa Gallery when he had something that he called "Happening." This *Happening* didn't have any actors in it. My husband Val, Red, and I were sharing a loft in New York. We went to the Hansa show. They had music playing. They had this big thing called a "Veronica." Like a big piece of cloth. Cut up things were sewed to it. There were sort of artworks with things moving, from a breeze from a fan, I think. Music was playing. That I believe is considered the first *Happening.*

CG Did he do a *Happening* at Sun Gallery?

YA That was by Red Grooms. It had live actors.

CG So Alan Kaprow did not do a *Happening* in Provincetown.

YA No. He did show at our gallery, later.

CG What did he show?

YA Well he showed the "Veronica" for one thing. We had him come pretty much right after his (Hansa) show. I think in the spring he had the "Veronica" shown at the Hansa Gallery. That summer, we showed it at our gallery along with some other stuff. (Veronica collage and paint on canvas, 1956, 145 x 120 cm). I have at least one photograph of each of our shows. I had an eleven-dollar camera at the time.

We do have a picture of Red and Val (Falcone) standing outside the gallery. I think we have a sign saying "Welcome to Alan Kaprow."

CG What did Claes Oldenburg show?

YA That was after us, and Bill Barrell set that up. He was very connected to Tony Vevers. One of their shows was visited by the police, as was one of ours. It was a Vevers show, and he had a great painting of himself, nude with a wolf-like thing on his back. We didn't put it so people passing by could see it. This was the '50s. We put it on a side wall. People managed to see it anyway. Also, they were upset about one of my husband's poems. That's when the police came. They tried to get our landlady to close us down but she refused.

CG How much rent did you pay?

YA $500 for the whole summer.

CG Was that a lot of money?

YA It was for us. I was working part-time in the morning at the Studio Shop and my husband was working full time.

CG I imagine you didn't make any sales.

YA Oh yes, we did occasionally. But that wasn't our main interest. We treated the whole thing as a form of theater. One night we came back to the gallery after it was closed. There was this man with his nose pressed against the glass. He was smoking a cigar. My husband walked up to him and asked if he would like to go in. It was the Tony Vevers show. We went in the gallery and he bought a painting. Tony had done a really terrific big painting called *The Funeral.* It was Jan Müller's funeral. I didn't know who Hirshhorn was. The next day a painter came by and I said, "This guy, Hirshhorn, said he was going to give us a check. Do you think it will be good?"

Hirshhorn, by the way, did not give us that check immediately. We shipped the painting. It was part way into the summer and Tony said, "What happened?" I sent a letter to Hirshhorn. Three days after he left Provincetown, he was on an airplane that crashed. He was a hero who saved a lot of people. He said his memory was completely wiped out. He forgot that he had to send us a check for $400.

CG Did Walter Chrysler buy anything from you?

YA No. He tried to buy things through the artists but not through us. He was trying to save money.

CG He was famous for that.

YA It wasn't our main interest. For Jan Müller, we sold a couple of his small pieces to a guy who had quite a bit of money. We gave Jan the money. They were very inexpensive for which we didn't take any fee. Our fee then was 20 percent, which was lower than galleries, which was about 30 percent. Then this guy gave us back the paintings and wanted his money back. We said, "We already paid him." That was the end of that.

CG Did you acquire any paintings? Did you collect?

YA We had a lot of paintings. In 1981 PAAM did a Sun Gallery show. Then they did another one in 2003. We took a lot of stuff down there. We have works by Red Grooms, Lester Johnson, Alex Katz, Tony Vevers. I did have one small Jan Müller. A very nice painting that he gave me. A couple of years after we left Provincetown, we were trying to build a house here in Lexington. The contractor ran into rocks and would have to use explosives to build our bathroom. Nat Halper, who ran HCE gallery at the other end of town, had been trying to buy that Jan Müller painting from me. It had been up for sale in my gallery for $100. He offered me a thousand, and I took it. I figured Jan would want us to have a bathroom.

CG When I was working with Lester (Johnson) for a museum catalog he gave me a video of him in the 1960s working on huge heads. Did you shoot that?

YA No. I have several videos of Lester. One was shot in his studio when he was on the Bowery early 1960s. The place was just filled with paintings. We sort of interviewed him and looked at the paintings. We don't get him actually painting. While we were there with Lester, Angelo Ippolito, in the same building came down and invited us to come up afterwards and see his stuff. Angelo's place was spotless. It was like going from a mud hole to a hospital. He was a very good friend of my husband. When we first set up our gallery, he would come for coffee every morning and visit with us.

CG What about Jay Milder. Did he show with you?

YA This is what happened with Jay and Bob Thompson. Val and I lived with Red in a loft in New York in 1958 and did a number of projects together. Then we went to Provincetown. At the end of the summer Red returned to New York and started a gallery in New York with Jay Milder.

Red wasn't in Provincetown too much that next summer (1959). He came in time for his show. When he arrived, he said he didn't want to have a one-man show. He wanted to have a show with his friends. I said okay. His friends were Jay Milder, who I had not met before, and Bob Thompson, who I had met. Bob is actually in my documentary for a few minutes. I have a very nice closeup on him. So, the three guys, who were penniless at the time, as was everyone in those days, crashed on the floor of the gallery for the night. Then they hung the show. A three-man show.

It was particularly spectacular because Red had a black and white drawing that went from the floor to the ceiling, of a face, a man's face. I never got a really good shot of the gallery from outside but someone sent me a terrific photo outside the gallery at night with all those paintings in there and Red's huge startling portrait.

CG What do you remember about Bob Thompson?

YA I remember him as having a very nice personality, handsome guy. I can't remember too much about his artwork. I didn't study him. He was very well thought of by other artists. Our last project at the Sun Gallery occurred a month after the three-man show. It was *The Walking Man.* It was the first *Happening* with live actors. Red, Sylvia Small, his girlfriend at the time, Bill Barrell, Val, and myself were the actors. We made a 20-minute presentation that night, twice. It was so popular that we had to run it 5 more nights. Then we left town.

CG Did you ever know an artist and jewelry maker who had a gallery in P'town named Earle Pilgrim?

YA Oh God. We were in his place. That's where the Sun Gallery was. It's that same building. When I was in Provincetown for the two years before we made the Sun Gallery, that was his place. It was very strange. Very dark. Sort of a slight feeling of evil about it. Unique. Earle Pilgrim would be down in one corner. He made jewelry. I bought one of his rings. A wonderful double ring with a snake coming out of it. His wife (Lily) did these dark strange puppets. I did not know them well but I bought a ring there. I liked the place.

CG Did you ever show him?

YA He was gone. We were shocked to see his place dark when we got there. Val said this is our place. We gave the landlady $500. Not all of it immediately.

Let me tell you a little bit more about Earle Pilgrim. For at least one or two summers he was showing artists there. I remember mostly they were outside on the sidewalk. I'm sure he had stuff inside also. He had Lester Johnson's stuff. That was the first time Val and I saw Lester's work. He had John Grillo. Possibly Wolf Kahn, but I don't know. I remember distinctly. It was very informal. It was one of those wonderful unique places.

CG By any chance did you know Emilio Cruz?

YA Yes. My husband worked in the restaurants. When I first got to Provincetown, that's when Ciro and Sal started their restaurant. They had mostly sandwiches. I couldn't afford to go there. I was a waitress at the time. I had no money. Emilio was sort of around. I made a documentary film at Sal's Place in the early '60s that featured an artists' party.

The two restaurants, Ciro and Sal's and Sal's Place, competed with each other in baseball games. The losing team had to give a party for the team members of the winning restaurant. Many of the team members were artists. Sal's Place lost the tournament, so the party was there. I do a slow pan across the party. Emilio is there, along with, let's see...wow, I'm 80-years-old now and I'm having to take a little time with remembering all the artists. I can see their faces, but not remember their names.

CG Tell me about your film and photographs. What were you shooting with?

YA On that day I had a 16mm Bolex camera, handheld, filming with no lights in a pretty dark room. Forty years later I was able to lighten it up and slow down the footage a bit. Val and I were showing films in Provincetown even when we had the gallery. The reason I started filming in Provincetown was because we were running a film series. I couldn't get good animated films. I wasn't interested in cartoons. I was interested in animation as a fine art. So, I said, I know what I'll do. I'll just make them myself for the program.

So, I bought a camera. Then I discovered that it wasn't as easy as I thought, but I taught myself and made my first animated film with Red Grooms. That was probably about 1962.

CG Tell me about RISD (Rhode Island School of Design). You were in the video department.

YA I've been retired from there for ten years and I worked there for 23 years. Before that Val and I started the first children's animation production courses in 1963. The children made films, which got a lot of publicity and they were frequently shown on television programs. What we did had not existed before. I've written three books about it. I had sort of a reputation and I had gone to RISD to do a couple of show-and-tells. Later, they called and asked me to come there to teach animation. After five years as a part-time animation instructor, I was asked to be the Department Head of Film/Animation/Video.

CG Were you one of the early people to shoot video? Did you go from film to video?

YA I'm an animator. Video was something I had to learn. I was very experienced in film when I got to RISD. I had shot live-action films and made animated films and taught film animation all over the country, but I knew nothing about video. Video was new for me. As department head, I made it my business to learn a reasonable amount about video.

RISD wasn't too thrilled about computers in the beginning, but I was one of the five department heads who said computers were going to be useful. I suggested that we get them. Someone from the purchasing department told me that they were just toys. Wouldn't I rather use a very good expensive typewriter? I said, "Oh, but this little Macintosh is a very nice toy. I can get my work done on it." It was one of those early tiny Macs. Then we had Amiga computers for a while, and I organized a few classes for the department. Our students immediately made some prize-winning animated films on those, and the department gained more computers as prizes.

CG Are you still in contact with Red?

YA Yes. There was a big show in New York at the Pace Gallery on *Happenings.* (February 10 to March 17, 2012) They have a new book on *Happenings* written by Milly Glimcher. If you open up the first few pages you'll see us at the start of it. She considers us one of the innovators.

(The Pace Gallery *Happenings New York: 1958–1963* was the first exhibition to document the origins and historical development of the transient, yet pivotal, *Happenings* movement from its inception in 1958 through 1963, when its originators abandoned or moved beyond it. The experimental performances, which began in Provincetown and unfolded in New York City in a number of alternative exhibition spaces and galleries, forever changed the definition of art and the possibilities for what it could be. The exhibition was accompanied by an illustrated book (304 pages, hardcover) published by The Monacelli Press and authored by Milly Glimcher. *Happenings: New York, 1958–1963,* capturing more than thirty of the original Happenings and the contributions of the main participants—Jim Dine, Simone Forti, Red Grooms, Allan Kaprow, Claes Oldenburg, Lucas Samaras, Carolee Schneemann, and Robert Whitman.)

My husband, Val, was always coming up with ideas at the Sun Gallery. Once he decided that Red would make a painting in front of an audience. There is a photo in our gallery where Val is handing a paintbrush to Red. I had stretched a big canvas for him. It was one of my jobs at the Studio Shop. A lot of people came to see Red make the painting. All we had to do was put a sign on the door and everyone was there the next night.

CG What did the Hofmann crowd think of the gallery?

YA Hofmann came. Hofmann was such a really nice man. He had a thick accent and I couldn't understand him all the time. He and Jan Müller connected because they were both German. Hofmann would be at an opening and he and Jan Müller would have arguments. (laughs) I didn't get into them. Friendly arguments of course.

We preferred to be outsiders. Because as outsiders you can do anything you want. We did a number of things. We had the first environment there. A big show called *City* in which everything was in black and white. I made sculptures of black roofing cement and chicken wire...black city streets, cars, a big tar head with red eyes, and a 5-foot tall, free-standing tar man. Lester Johnson had charcoal sketches. Red Grooms had drawings. Val had large poems that we printed on our own small printing press. Robert Frank had black and white photographs. People took photos of their children standing next to my tar man. It was a popular show.

CG How are you archiving all of this material? You mentioned that you have at least one photograph of all of the Sun Gallery exhibitions. The films. Now some of them collected on DVDs which are for sale.

YA One of the first things I did was to start making a scrapbook after the first year of the gallery, not realizing it would be important later. It was just for fun. Now many of the Sun Gallery people are dead. For the last few years people started calling me for photographs and information about that time. Some people want the information for their books, or their advanced college degrees, or the exhibition they are going to set up.

So, let's see. We were innovative with the gallery. Then we became internationally known for what we were doing with children. Now animation classes for children are everywhere. Then we did a number of things at RISD. It was a very small department when I got there. Now it is much larger. Our former students at RISD have won academy awards in Hollywood.

CG My question was how are you archiving the materials?

YA (laughing) It's very, very hard work. Every once in a while, I try to clean things up. Your friend Adam (Zucker) called. He sent a message yesterday that he wants high rez pictures. A lot of our stuff is on the computer now in JPEG.

I spent most of yesterday looking for stuff that was in Photoshop rather than

JPEG. A pain in the ass. But I'm going to get them for him.

CG I'm sure he's asking for the catalog.

YA For publications, it's good to have those things.

CG We spoke with Christine McCarthy (director of PAAM). She said that you had given a set of videos to the museum.

YA We revised them a couple of months ago, largely because we had run out of prints. We don't distribute films anymore, just videos. Instead of having three little separate discs on Sun Gallery, they're all now on one DVD.

CG It seems that Sun Gallery showed a hundred artists.

YA That could well be. I would have to count them up. PAAM and Tony Vevers made a small booklet of their first Sun Gallery exhibition, which has all the names and the schedule of our shows.

CG Was George McNeil one of your artists?

YA No, he wasn't, but Lester Johnson talked about him quite a bit. He may have been a part of the afterward group.

CG Thanks for your time and memories.

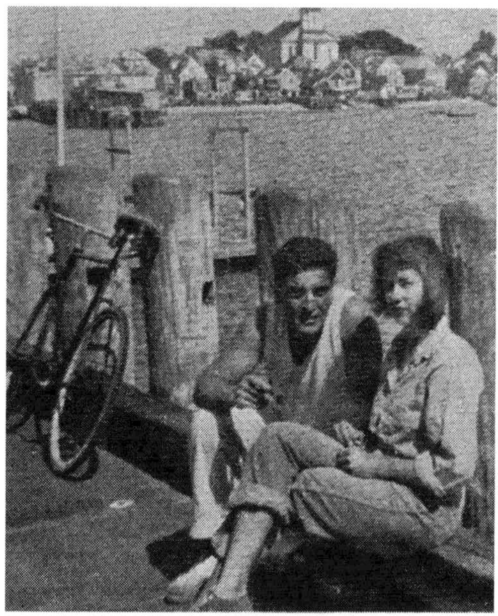

Artist and filmmaker Yvonne Andersen with her husband Dominic (Val) Falcone, who together ran Sun Gallery for five seasons. Photo courtesy of Andersen.

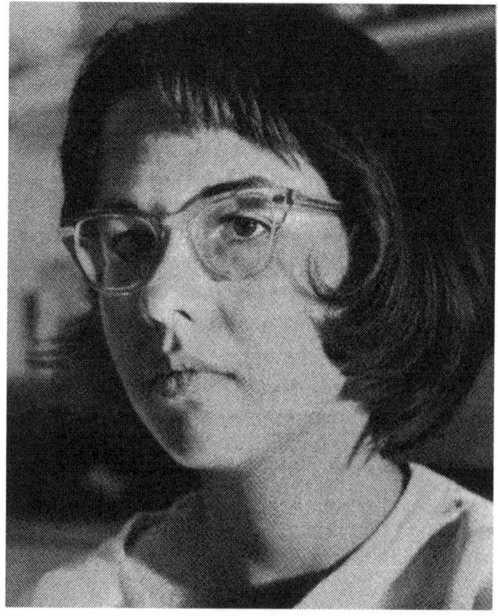

Yvonne Andersen. Photo courtesy of Andersen.

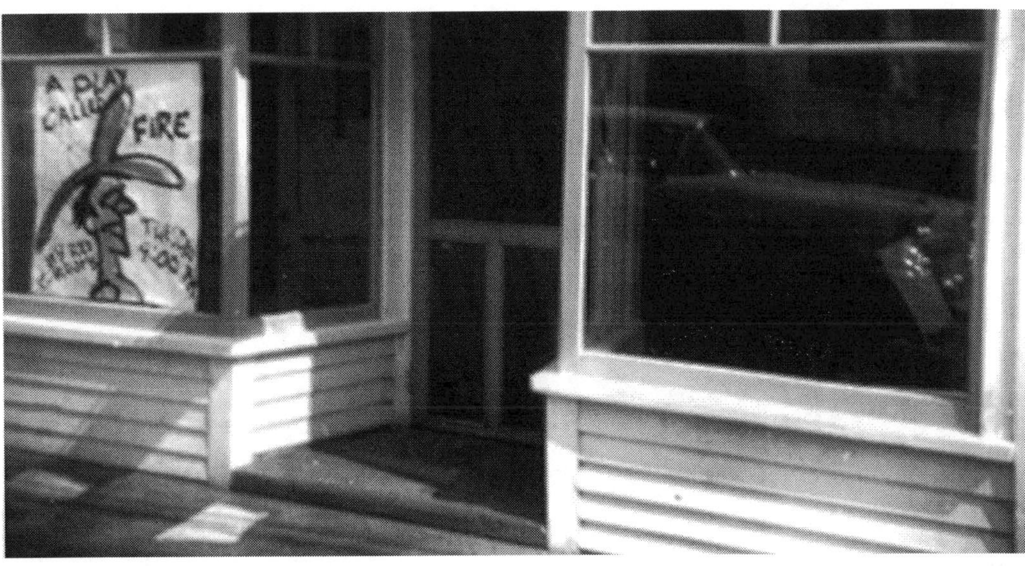

Sun Gallery. Photo courtesy of Andersen.

Yvonne Andersen
Ann Avalotis
Helen Avlon-Daphnis
Irene Baker
Bill Barrell
Robert Beauchamp
Dan Bernstein
James Bilmeyer
Nieves Bilmeyer
Alexander Bing
Connie Black
David Brisson
Jack Calderwood
Mirhan Chobanian
Ciro Cozzi
Jack Cuddihy
Vivian De Pinna
Josephine Del Deo
Sal Del Deo
Al DiLauro
Lynne Drexler
Roslyn Drexler
Sherman Drexler
Dominic Falcone
Jackie Ferrara
James Forsberg
Joan Wye Forsberg
Mary Frank
Robert Frank
William Freed
Laurie Freedman
Ovid Freedman
James Gahagan
Leah Gold
Blanch Grady
John Grillo
Red Grooms
Mimi Gross
Bob Hallett
Myrna Harrison
Robert Henry
Henry Hensche
Carl Hofer
Angelo Ippolito
Dolores James
Lester Johnson
Josephine Valenti Johnson
Allen Kaprow
Alex Katz
Mickey Kaufman
Betty King
Frank Keller
Oskar Kokoschka
Bernard Langlais
Jack Larned
Toni LaSelle
Ronnie Lion
Irene Legendre
Rudi Lesser
Marcia Marcus
Virginia McCall
Jay Milder
Margret Millickan
Morton Mintz
Rudi Mueller
Jan Muller
Robert Munford
Hei-Goon-Na
Manuel Neri
Henri Osborn
Vernon Osborn
Earle Pierce
Belle Politi
Clair Rabe
Emy Roeder
Gloria Roloff
Mary Sants
JoAnn Schidlo
Paul Scott
Max Spoerri
Neil Stark
Rudy Stern
Joy Stuttman
Barbara Swan
Fred Tasch
Selina Trieff

List of Sun Gallery artists.

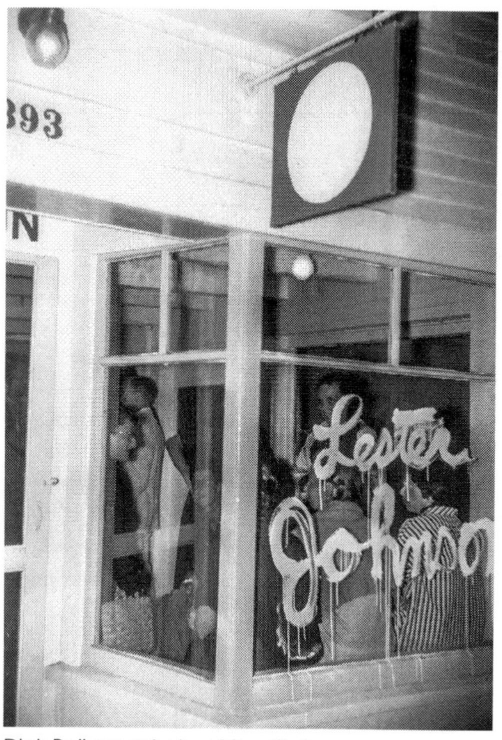

Dick Bellamy photo of Sun Gallery.

I WEAR YOUR CLOTHES.
I LIVE IN YOUR HOUSES.
I PAINT MY RED FACE WHITE.
I AM AN INDIAN WHO DOES NOT DRINK.
I HAVE NO BUFFALO.
I WAS NOT KILLED AT THE LAST MASSACRE.
I STILL REMEMBER THE SACRED EARTH AND THE EARTH REMEMBERS ME.
WE RENDEZVOUS AT NIGHT IN A SECRET PLACE WHERE WE TREMBLE
WE MAKE PLANS AND RIDE BAREBACK IN THE MOONLIGHT.

Poem by Falcone. Courtesy of Andersen.

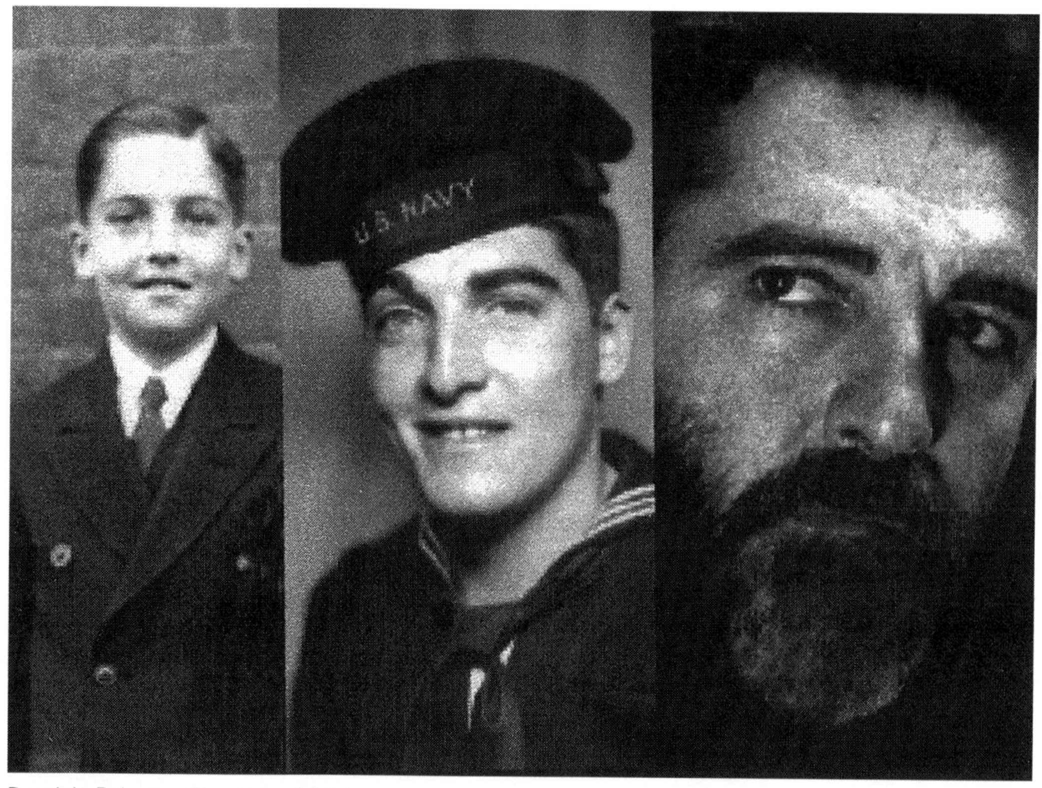

Dominic Falcone. Courtesy of Andersen.

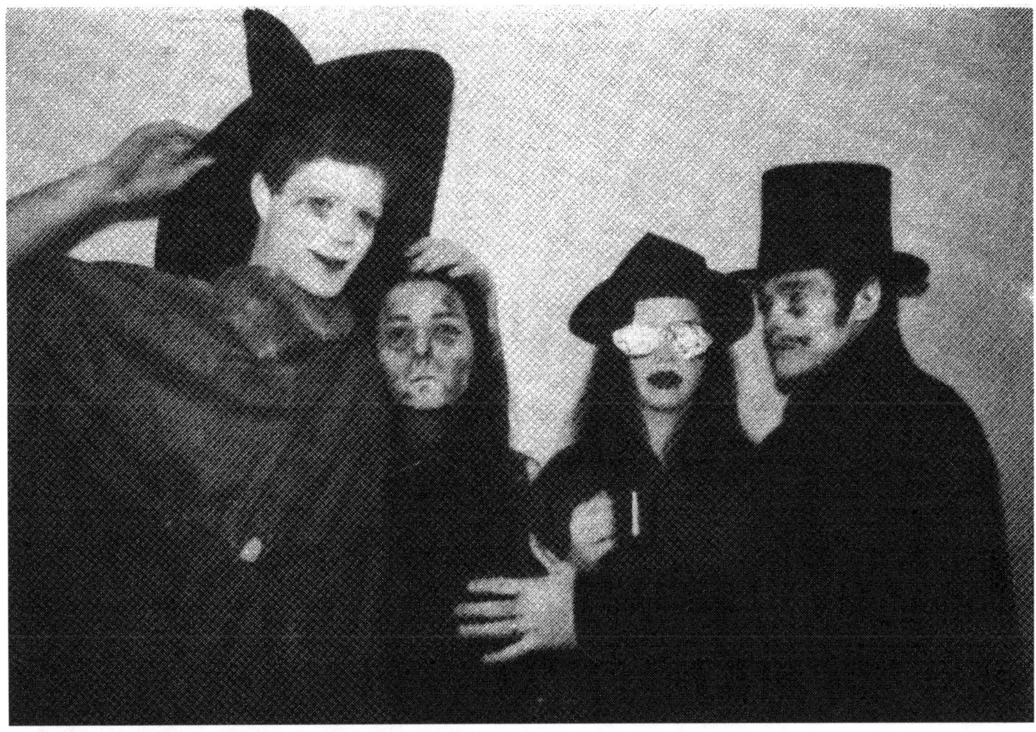

A Red Grooms' Happening. Courtesy of Andersen.

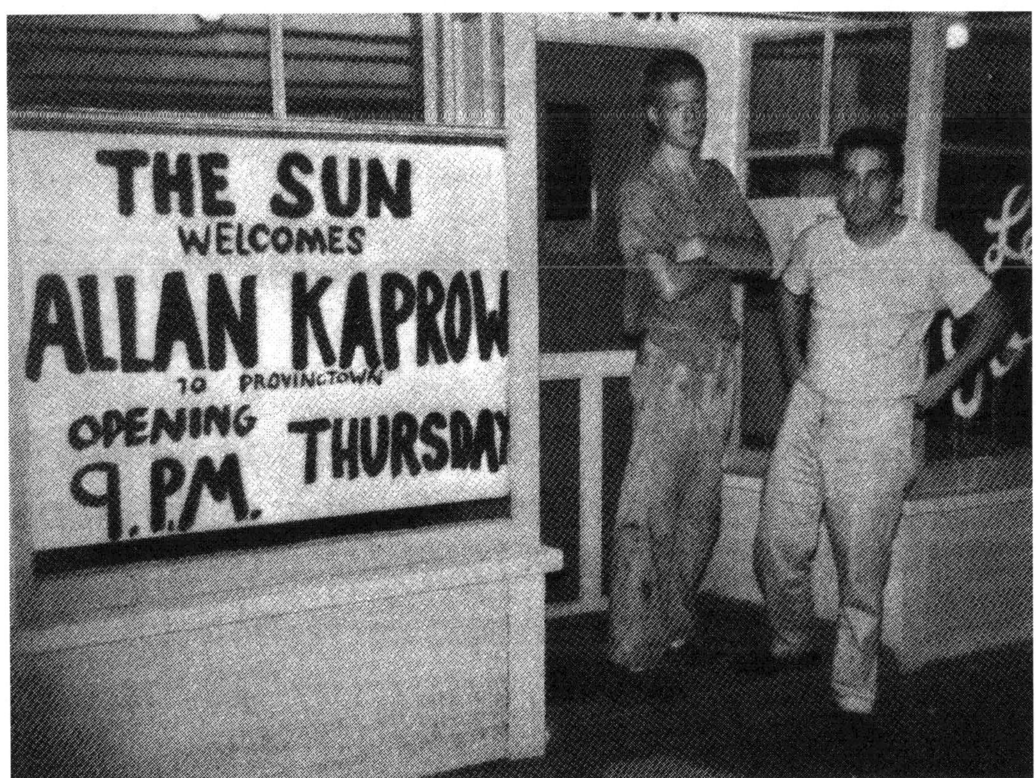

Val and Red Grooms in front of the gallery. Courtesy of Andersen.

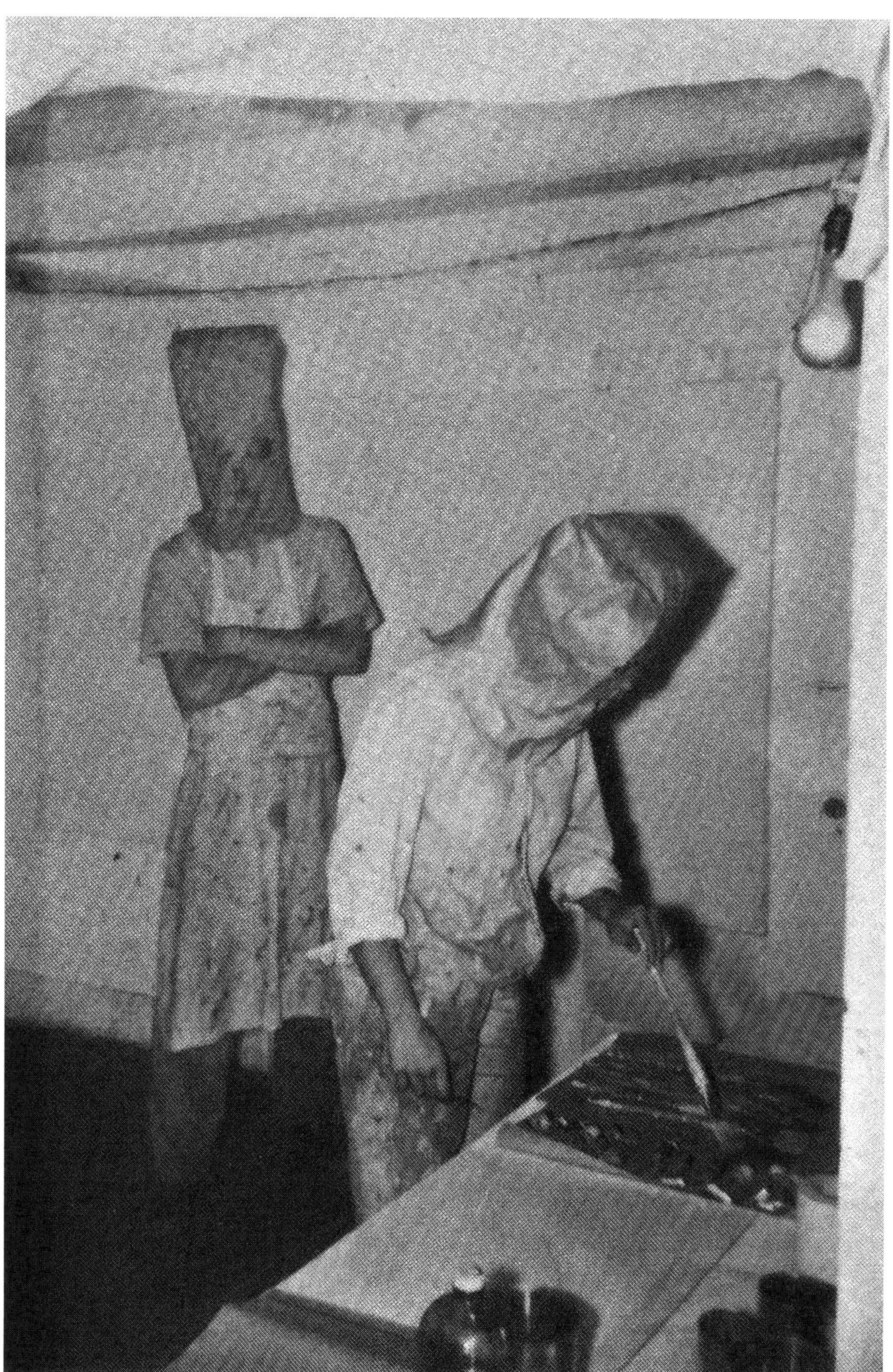

Happening. Courtesy of Andersen.

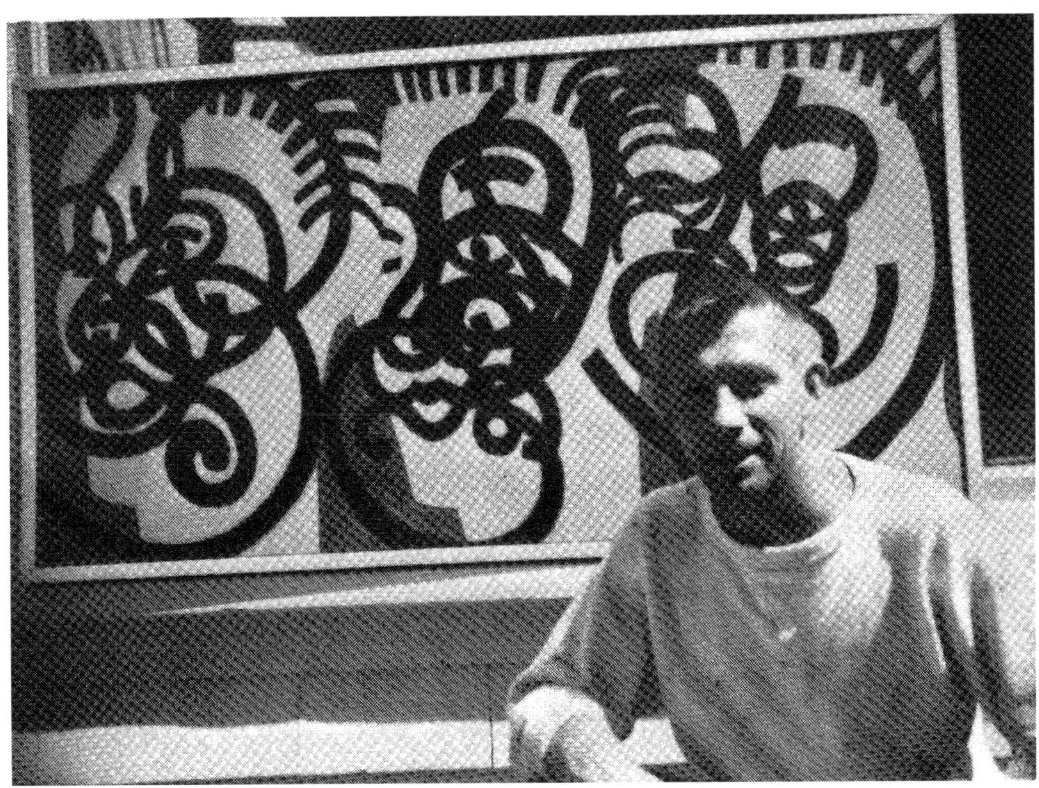
Lester Johnson at Sun Gallery. Courtesy of Andersen.

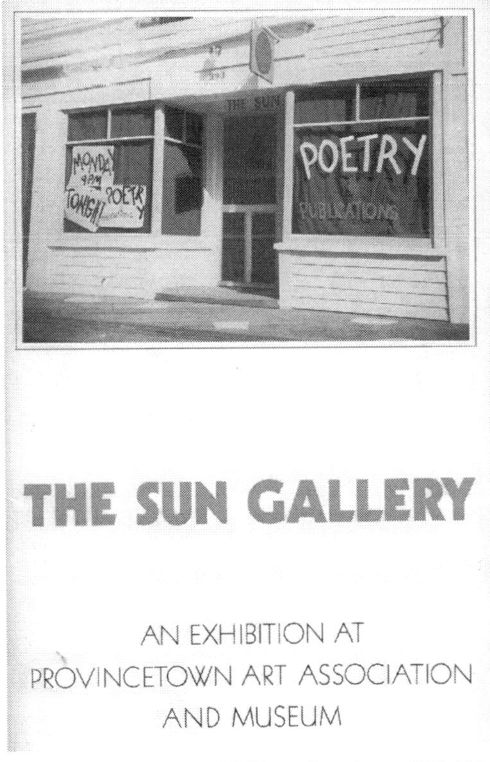

Catalog for PAAM exhibition. Courtesy of PAAM.

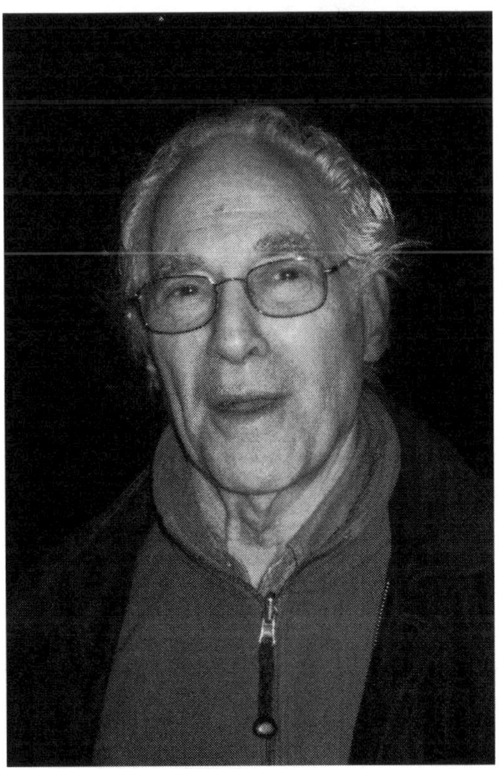
Jay Milder,.Giuliano photo.

Benny Andrews, Artist and Activist

He was born in a family of ten, the son of sharecroppers in Plainview, Georgia. His father, George, was a renowned self-taught artist. While needed for labor, his parents encouraged education and he graduated from high school. He received a two-year scholarship to go to Fort Valley College, a Black state college in Georgia. He joined the Air Force and served as a staff sergeant in Korea. After four years in the military, he attended the School of the Art Institute of Chicago on the GI Bill.

In 1958, he moved to New York where his exhibitions were praised and led to awards and fellowships, including several residencies at MacDowell, where he joined the board in 1987. Early on he summered and exhibited in Provincetown.

Andrews co-founded the Black Emergency Cultural Coalition (BECC) in 1969, an organization that protested the *Harlem on My Mind: Cultural Capital of Black America, 1900–1968* exhibit at the Metropolitan Museum of Art. No African-Americans had been involved in organizing the show, and it contained no art—only photo reproductions and copies of newspaper articles about Harlem. The BECC then persuaded the Whitney Museum to launch a similar exhibition of African American artists, but later felt compelled to boycott the Whitney show for similar reasons.

From 1982 to 1984, Andrews served as the director of visual arts for the National Endowment for the Arts. In this position, he had the chance to advocate for fellowships and grants to go to talented Black artists.

There were collaged elements in his paintings in the figurative expressionist style which developed among the Sun Gallery artists in Provincetown. We met as dinner guests and initiated an ongoing dialogue. With the support of Ellen O'Donnell, then director of the Provincetown Art Association, I curated *Kind of Blue: Benny Andrews, Emilio Cruz, Bob Thompson, and Earle Pilgrim.* It traveled to Northeastern University. The curatorial essay was published by *Provincetown Arts Magazine.* The Andrews estate is represented by Michael Rosenfeld Gallery in New York.

Interview with Benny Andrews
1980
At his New York Studio

Benny Andrews (1930–2006) A heavy social problem is obvious and conscious for Black artists, or anyone Black, to deal with representational things. So, a lot of the ways you say things, it would be a lot easier and understandable to deal with the figure. Being abstract means bringing something else to it.

Even Sam Gilliam (1933–2022), when he talks about his work, talks about representational things, Mississippi and stuff like that. For most of us, what we are working is a natural extension of us. In a sense it's unfortunate because it (Gilliam's work for example) is a luxury we cannot afford. I'm not talking individually but as a group. Black artists are not looked at for anything that they do other than representation. We're pigeonholed.

Jacob Lawrence (1917–2000) is the best example. He would be put into exhibitions and that would integrate them. If his work wasn't representative of something identified as Black figures, he wouldn't have served that purpose because of just blending in. If he had been an abstract expressionist, what good would it have done for curators to have him in there, for the general public too, but you at least have one.

Charles Giuliano The intent is not just to include a Black artist, but one that clearly reads as Black.

BA I had an experience that a lot of people had in the 1960s. At first, by and large, nobody was interested in the Black people I did. I started to show at Forum Gallery with exhibitions in '62, '64, and '66. All along, I have depicted both Black and White people. Nobody was interested in the Black people. Black awareness evolved in the mid-1960s and (then) nobody was interested in the White people I did. They would come to my studio and pick all the Black people, but they weren't interested in my White people because they were trying to make a point about Black people and Black art. There was an irony that what remained in the studio was the exact opposite of what was being shown. In the exhibition there were all the Black people, and in the studio, what remained, were all the White people. That's an example of when social consciousness outweighs whether the work is good or bad. That's an underlying problem for most Black artists.

It's the same in theater. The presence of a Black actor on stage has to be dealt with. Do you want to put two Black actors out there or have an all-Black cast? That starts playing around with the question of quality. Is that person the best actor, dancer, or artist? Are you dealing with quotas in one way or another? That plagues the artists.

Often, they come in and like the other work. They like (images of) my father who is nearly White, but it wouldn't serve a purpose to show that. They would take a painting of my mother because she is so Black that it would serve their purpose. If they like the painting of my father, but don't take it, that's racism.

When people come to the studio they're not interested in my landscapes. That's not what they have in mind for representation in a show. That's changed a lot as people have gotten to know my name. I have a show called *Completing the Circle* where I finish the monuments in Washington D.C. There's the George Washington Monument which extends from the Capitol. When I studied (Pierre "Peter" Charles) L'Enfant's (1754–1825) plan for Washington D.C., I learned that he had a plan for a circle, so I designed three other monuments. One for the struggle of the country, another for beauty, and a third that I can't remember right now. There has been a lot of interest in the show, which is traveling right now. When exhibitors found out, they wanted a show of Benny Andrews the Black artist in their museums and exhibition schedules to have a Black artist. The show includes maquettes and drawings through my conceptual interpretation. I do what I want to do.

Consider Henry Ossawa Tanner (1859–1937) and people like him. In retrospect they became collectable, but they don't serve the long-term purposes of people who are talking about Black artists. What Tanner was showing was that he was an artist. He incorporated being Black in some of his work, which is a healthy thing.

CG The painting we all remember is *The Banjo Lesson.* If you visit the Philadelphia Museum you encounter Tanner as a brilliant student of Eakins.

BA It doesn't satisfy that need. In the case of Horace Pippin (1888–1946) some of his works are fantastical representations of race, but in other works he goes into something else. Pippin was known and collected for a long time with nothing to do with being Black, which is as it should be.

When it comes to the general public, there are needs to serve certain quotas, and unless that individual represents that quota in a certain way, he doesn't qualify. You know, when we are talking about the figure. I like to do the figure.

CG In curating this show *Kind of Blue,* I have dealt extensively with Black artists through a career of covering jazz, rock, and blues. I have been involved extensively with Black culture as a critic, teacher, and record collector. But prior to this show I have not dealt with Black visual culture on a professional basis. It strikes me that a lot of Black shows in museums have been curated more from a political than cultural basis. For this show I find it challenging to work apolitically and feel no pressure other than to create an outstanding exhibition.

BA Prior to the show that Barry Gaither organized for the MFA (*African American Artists; New York and Boston* included 158 works by 70 Black artists, May 19 to June 23, 1970.) they had never before done any such shows. It's like when the Metropolitan Club let Jews in for the first time. What happens when it's for the first time is totally different from what happens when it's a routine thing.

CG What has happened now that the political pressure that spawned those shows has subsided?

BA For me, it was not just restricted to Black artists. It's something that happened all over the country and throughout society. It created a climate in this country where other non-traditional groups were included in the cultural arena.

You have to exclude entertainment because even when people were in chains, they were allowed to travel in minstrel shows to entertain White people. They would make things funny, like court jesters. You can look at the entire White entertainment industry and compare it to the entire world of painting and sculpture and it doesn't hold anything. It's nowhere near it. When you talk about Sinatra and Prince, the entertainment business, then turn around and talk about artists and museums, well they are just nothing. The entertainment industry represents billions. Then you look at Frank Stella and other leading artists, the general public has no idea who they are. They may know about Warhol if it has to do with fashion. But there are no artists who are really well known. Maybe Andrew Wyeth.

CG Because the entertainment industry is a business, you can quantify it. You can see how a music release charts in *Billboard* or the box office for Hollywood and Broadway. It's possible to compare critical reviews and how the product sells. There is no such information in the fine arts. We don't know what shows are selling in galleries. Is Stella, for example, in the top ten this week, or has he dropped? What about Benny Andrews charting at 78 with a bullet? The art world is remote and inaccessible. The public has no access to information or its influence. Only a handful of individuals are capable of purchasing work and influencing an artist's career. That's in the hands of a few influencers, which makes them more important in establishing matters of aesthetics and taste than they should be. At the academic level, movements and individual artists are not evaluated. There is no dialogue about why Pollock, for example, is more important and influential than Motherwell. Museums do not disclose what works in their collections are worth. There is an academic lie that all work is equal. Which is not true, of course, for the collectors who buy from galleries and auctions. Then we see the real dollar value of the work, which is never discussed in the classroom. In the teaching of art history, all movements and individual artists are treated as equal. The introduction of feminism has further flattened the canon. In the new textbooks Judith Leyster gets equal billing with Rembrandt and Vermeer.

BA To the general public. the art world is insignificant. For us, it's pretty big. We are impressed because we are a part of it. People in the poetry world are impressed though the public could care less. In the real world, nobody knows any poets. In the entertainment world, if you ask people who they like, there are ready answers. I'm saying this to put into perspective a show like the MFA's *African American Artists: New York and Boston.* In the enclave of the art world, it was the first time that happened. It didn't matter what happened compared to the fact of Black people coming to an opening and drinking out of tea cups that was unique. To come as guests and not as servers was a phenomenon. It was a breakdown of segregation and so much more than just an exhibition. Before they had the first woman on a space shuttle there was never a conversation of where she was going to go to the bathroom. It wasn't an issue until she went and I don't know what they did. Until things happen you don't have a problem. The MFA didn't have a problem of what to do with Black people who are guests at an exhibition.

CG Did Black people visit those shows?

BA They came in droves. But the Met was a fiasco. Not many Black people visited *Harlem on My Mind.* It wasn't something that Black people were interested in. It didn't reflect them in the way that they felt they should be. A lot of White people went because it was kind of an exposition. It was something that should have taken place at the coliseum. It was like a trade show. The same was true about the one that took place at the Whitney, about which there was so much controversy, because we worked with them on that show and then they reneged on it. Of course, the MFA show was the definitive one of its kind and the public attended in droves. It's a historical show in that it occurred at that venue at that time with input from Black people. It was the only one at that time with Black input.

CG Were you involved with the selection?

BA At a distance. It was Barry Gaither who made the selection. At the Whitney there was no Black involvement. They had no Black people they were able to consult with. The Black historians they claimed on the brochure were not consulted. So, there was no Black input for the show. The MFA show was the only one at that time with Black input. You were asking about the status of Black artists today. That goes with all the pluses and minuses of society. There has been a transition of attitude.

Black people who have been included are doing well and that includes artists. The ones that are still out, and that's the largest group, are still having a hard time. The pressure that created the MFA show no longer exists.

CG That's part of why I want to do a Provincetown show, because there is no pressure to do it other than to curate a compelling exhibition which says something about Black artists in Provincetown.

BA That's the plus and there are more of these shows. More people are interested in what you are saying about the aesthetics or dramatics. That's healthy and how it should be. It's like poor people. It's understood that people should eat better. But a lot of people are eliminated from getting food, which is a bad thing. That's what's happening with artists and not just black artists. There's a stronger emphasis on financial and critical success. People are getting the rewards. We are seeing it happen in Soho and the East Village. It's happening for a few Black artists. But there's less effort being made to assist artists in areas like alternative spaces where artists don't have to prove that they are trying to be successful.

(On April 6, 1971, Grace Glueck reported in the *New York Times*. "Fifteen black artists out of a scheduled 75 have withdrawn from the Whitney Museum exhibition, *Contemporary Black Artists in America,* opening today. Their action is in sympathy with a boycott called by the Black Emergency Cultural Coalition, a group of black artists that initiated the show nearly two years ago.

"The Coalition, which claims an active membership of over 150, charges that the Whitney reneged on "two fundamental points of agreement"—that the exhibition would be selected with the assistance of black art specialists, and that it would be presented 'during the most prestigious period of the 1970–71 art season.'

"At a press conference called by the Coalition at the Studio Museum in Harlem yesterday, a number of black art specialists from across the country issued a supporting statement. It demanded, among other things, that 'black art experts and consultants and/or institutions must be involved in the preparation and presentation of all art activities presented by white institutions and involving the black artist and the black community.'

"A separate statement issued by Cliff Joseph, co-chairman with Benny Andrews of the Coalition, said in part that in order for the show to have authenticity, 'it is essential that it be selected by one whose wisdom, strength, and depth of sensitivity regarding black art is drawn from the well of his own black experience.' The show was organized by a white curator, Robert M. Doty.

"Yesterday John I. H. Baur, director of the Whitney, said he had a basic philosophical difference with the sentiments expressed by Mr. Joseph. 'It's more than a matter of our wanting to take full charge of our own show,' he noted. 'The Coalition stands for a kind of separatism I don't believe in. The black artists don't have backgrounds in tribal art—they're part of the American experience. And they should be judged by the same yardstick as other American artists.'")

CG What's happening to organizations like the Studio Museum of Harlem or African American Artists in Residence Program at Northeastern University?

BA That bears out what I am saying. The Studio Museum is doing fantastic. It's the nation's foremost Black cultural organization. Other kinds of organizations that would have helped are dying on the vine. There is adequate. if not plentiful, support for the Studio Museum. It has raised itself by its bootstraps to become a first-class institution.

CG Give me some other examples.

BA There's Barry Gaither's National Center for African American Artists in Boston.

CG It has very low visibility.

BA It suffers what Boston suffers on a lesser scale. The Studio Museum benefits from what happens in the New York art world. The National Museum suffers in that sense. The MFA and ICA get a certain amount of publicity but a fraction for that of the Met and New York museums.

CG Are there other institutions around the country?

BA There is the DuSable Black History Museum and Education Center. It's named for the Black French pioneer who established what became Chicago. I believe he was a fur trader. In Philadelphia, there's the Museum of Afro American Art and Science.

The museum in Chicago is funded by the city, as is the Art Institute of Chicago. It's a success because it receives a certain amount of public funding, as does the Studio Museum. So, it is not existing hand-to-mouth. There's an Afro American Museum in Los Angeles which was built by the state. It was legislated into the state budget. The institutions which I mention are the only substantial ones that are mostly oriented to the high arts.

The rest of the organizations are like AAMARP which has survived because of the support of Northeastern University. (Which is no longer the case.) Artists spaces, if they exist, would be like PS1 and things like it but they are almost nonexistent.

CG Is this Reaganomics?

BA Reaganomics have played a part. He and his staff are reflecting on what the people want. There hasn't been any attempt to impeach him. The voting population is quite happy with Reagan. He and his people are the mechanics for this because it is what the country has wanted. Look at what's happening with food stamps and social security. Roosevelt didn't make social change by himself. There was a demand in society for social security. We're in an era of survival of the fittest for society. The poor and unfortunate are being shunted aside. It's happening to Black artists as well.

CG Is that what you felt in Washington, D. C. at the National Endowment for the arts? (Andrews taught art at Queens College for three decades, and from 1982 to 1984, served as the Director of the Visual Arts Program for the National Endowment for the Arts.)

BA I was trying to level out fairness with distribution all over the country. That was a different approach. Utah and Maine were being looked at for what they were doing. We tried to get more of them involved in making decisions reflecting what they saw instead of having one group decide what everyone saw. You have New York people deciding for a Georgia or Texas person. That this is Georgia or this is Texas. Or, this is not Georgia or this is not Texas.

I was trying to get more involvement of experts and people who were trained in those areas, who had an affinity for what they were about or not about. I tried to encourage more tax payers' money to go to diverse places.

CG Did that agenda succeed?

BA Yes, very well.

CG How did that impact you with your New York friends?

BA It was never written about in any art publications. I was never mentioned. It was seen as anti-New York to do something like that. When I was there it was never mentioned in newspapers or magazines. They didn't mention me because I was attempting to make a more democratic NEA.

CG You were not interested in rewarding the already established and celebrated.

BA I was not the only one but I was trying to get more and more people from all over the country to speak and talk. The jurors were trying to see that more of an experimental nature would be done in areas where this would not normally happen.

CG Still the best artists move to New York.

BA That's changing because it's no longer possible to come to the city and find an affordable loft. It's very hard to live here but that's another thing.

CG Are more artists staying home?

BA They are trying to or going to other areas. There's coming to be more and more support. When they said that about Paris it wasn't true. Artists went to Paris because it was the best place to get attention for their work. But when America progressed socially and economically people developed art here in New York. People started to come here. Now there are a large number of people moving South because there are jobs there. They used to come here for jobs. In the arts you have to go where you have the best chance to survive. It's not just being an artist, it's to find a place to survive and create.

Right now, New York is so expensive that it's almost an impossible place to live. When they are starting out artists need cheap space to live in order to survive. If you can't find that there's no way to be an artist.

CG A couple of years ago I visited Skowhegan School (in Maine). Art critic Hilton Kramer happened to be in residence. I attended an informal session with students. He fielded questions including how important it was to live in New York. He responded that they would never be successful artists unless they lived in New York as that is the center of the international art world at this time.

BA Kramer plays an interesting game. That makes him very appealing as a lecturer. We're on the same circuit and have had some interesting debates. It's set up like throwing red meat to hungry lions. People know it's not the truth but can't argue against it because he has all the right credentials. There are art world powers.

It's like the Metropolitan Club with fat cats sitting in huge chairs. They have the money and power. They guard the doors that lead to opportunities. They're not right because out in the street other things are happening that they can't control. If you look at the art world there are the heavy hitters and gallerists like Leo Castelli and Mary Boone. In criticism there's Kramer, Grace Gleuck, John Canaday, and John Russell. They greatly influence things for the general public. Robert Hughes tries to see it differently. Because he writes for *Time* he has a larger audience with a great advantage and can knock them. It's like Boston playing LA. They are both winning a lot and making money. When you think about it. the power brokers are all millionaires. Hughes is doing this with Kramer and Kramer is doing it with whoever.

CG *Clash of the Titans.*

BA That's right. What does it matter if Ali beats Frazier? That's what we've got on a small scale because the art world is so insignificant.

CG As someone who has served in the NEA, what would you say to a young artist other than go to New York and find a loft?

BA None of us are at the stage where we can tell others exactly what is good or bad. But the basic thing for anyone aspiring to be an artist is that you are doing the work and want to be an artist. Trying to be one should be your primary goal. If you find a way to do that, you're successful and you should see that just being that is a success. Anything beyond that is at the mercy of fate.

Be it Hilton Kramer saying you have to come to New York, or, someone else saying that these people should have a chance; things that sell and things that don't sell. You have these problems and they are a part of the profession.

It's like being a cab driver who has problems with wrecks and flats. If someone tells you to go to the barn and pick up a cab be prepared for what it entails. You can't start complaining about the issues. You won't even get to start the ignition, which is your mission as a cab driver. A great many individuals set out to be cab drivers and succeed. They don't become famous like movie stars. They don't meet producers who put them into movies. That happens once in a very great while.

It's the same with people aspiring to be artists. The problem with discussion of insidious plots and schemes is that they have nothing to do with making art for the vast majority of artists. It's like gossip of the Tylenol scare (1982). It killed ten people but all of us were involved. It's like when Leo Castelli shows up at Sotheby's and buys something or sells a Johns for $2 million. Or Andy Warhol wears a tuxedo backwards at an event. All that has nothing to do with being an artist. It has nothing to do with me and my work. It doesn't impact my art, possibilities, or opportunities.

That's the problem when you start talking about what Hughes said, or Kramer said, or what Castelli and Mary Boone said. It has nothing to do with being an artist.

CG If you have a speaking engagement in Iowa or Wisconsin, and visit students and artists, is what they are making reflective of what they have seen in art magazines? Young artists tend to take very seriously the influencers you have mentioned.

BA For a young person trying to be creative whatever is going on is by and large over. If you know about it in Wisconsin it's over by the time you get the news. It's like yesterday's paper. If you learn about Keith Haring or Neo Geo, by the time you learn about it, then it's too late to work in that manner. It's been done.

CG That's what's wrong with art schools. Instructors get hired when they have established careers. With that security and tenure there is less pressure to develop new ideas and work. They pass on their outdated approach to students. My professors taught social realism and abstract expressionism in the 1960s when Pop, Op, Minimalism, Conceptualism were emerging. What we were taught was outdated. That's the plague of art schools. Very few of my colleagues are still trying to develop and exhibit.

By that standard are you over?

BA No, I am talking about being influenced. When I was a student (Art Institute of Chicago), we would be getting material from MoMA or what have you roughly a year late by the time they put the show together. It was over. That's what I would tell students. When it comes to (David) Salle or (Julian) Schnabel that's ok to read about but has nothing to do with your own creativity. You can't try to do something in that manner.

CG During the 1960s during Spring break I visited New York museums and galleries. I went to the Cedar Tavern expecting to find artists. It was just a bar. I had a beer then left.

What is the current status of Black art?

BA I don't accept that there is quote "Black Art." Not in the way that you or we are talking about it. Now if we talked about Voodooism. Or if you talked about Africa in the context of the art of Africa. Or if you wanted to slash and say Africa/ Black. I think you could generalize a lot more about Africa or Black art. Unless an individual is kept in a barrel or down in a well it is impossible for him or her not to be affected by what the country is. It would be like saying Polish Art or Irish Art or Jewish Art. Of course. there are things that the Jewish people, if they are concerned about it, they can affect the way things are done. There can be Yiddish Theater, Ben Zion, or Chaim Gross. They do things that stem from a Jewish or Hebrew basis.

That distinguishes it from what a Sean O'Casey would do on an Irish basis. Nobody pigeonholes his as "Irish Writing." They talk a lot about Irish writers that write and give it a lot of room. It can be romantic, social, or abstract. You can talk about French writers or American writers. You can talk about Black writers in America or talk about Black painters in America. But if you expect that when a Black person creates a work of art, and you come to it expecting to see Black art, that's asking to see too much. There are a lot of Irish writers who don't write in such a manner that you can distinguish them from a Scottish, Welsh, or English writer.

CG What about Jean Michel Basquiat (1960–1988)?

BA I'm not really critical of him. I think it's fair that he gets what he gets. But it is a typical thing in America that he is not, in the eyes of those who make the decisions, an Afro-American artist. He comes from an island and things like that. And that's been the history of acceptance in the United States. It is much easier for White people to accept people from other areas. People who, in their eyes, did not come from slavery. That's the logical thing.

When they did the *Conflict and Controversy* show at the Studio Museum, they selected work from the decade 1960–1970 when there really was a social thing at that time. As a gesture the *New York Times* put Basquiat on the cover of its *Sunday Magazine*. They simply would not deal with any of the African-American artists in the exhibition because they just can't handle that. But exotica they can handle and chose someone like him. He reflects the living style of that magazine. He dresses in a manner similar to styles advertised in the magazine. It's a classic example. The social implications of putting a Dana Chandler (Born 1941, an artist activist who founded AAMARP at Northeastern University) on the cover, or even in the magazine, was too much for them. Basquiat had nothing to do with that decade. He wasn't even working then.

CG So it was tokenism. Did the *Times* review the exhibition?

BA It was reviewed. But what I am saying is that this was an example of not being able to deal with it. It would be like the magazine running an article on the Holocaust and putting Mr. Bloomingdale on the cover.

CG Can we talk about Provincetown. Is it a coincidence that I am doing a show with Benny Andrews, Emelio Cruz, Earle Pilgrim, and Bob Thompson, four Black artists who lived and worked in Provincetown?

BA Provincetown was different then from what it is now because the social circumstances have changed. Provincetown offered greater opportunities for Black artists not only to enter the arts but society for Black artists, for Black people actually. I first showed in Provincetown in 1960 at Paul Kessler Gallery. I had about twelve shows there from 1960 to 1972. Then I moved to Tirca Karlis's gallery. What happened for people like me is that people who would be interested in you, artist-to-artist, would very often be in places like Provincetown. The town had a very diversified group of people because they were coming from someplace else. There's so much freedom in that. I guess that's why homosexuals do so much better there. Because you don't have an established community there or established taboos. You have people who are from somewhere and they tend to be much more tolerant. It's like Vegas conventions where people chase prostitutes, stay out all night, and do things they would never do at home. You have a freedom thing which includes race and everything else. Chaim Gross (1904–1991) was instrumental in helping me. He was always there, liked my work, though I didn't know him. Bella Fishko, founder of Forum Gallery was there. Chaim recommended me, which is how I got into her gallery. Later I met Raphael Soyer who was with Forum Gallery. I remember a lot of people from that time; Bob Thompson, Nat Halper had a gallery, and Martha Jackson (gallerist) was around.

CG Do you recall Sun Gallery?

BA They were on the way out.

CG Did you know Bob Thompson (1937–1966)?

BA He came to Provincetown in '58 or '59, which is when I met him. I knew him very well. I was one of a few (figurative expressionist) like Bob, Red Grooms, Mimi Gross, Emilio Cruz, Jay Milder who were all there at that time. I came from New York in 1958. Jay and Red had a loft in the Lower East Side. Bob Thompson came in '59 and met Red and Jay. Walter Chrysler (1875–1940) bought works.

Bob came in a big car, which I'll never forget. I was living on Suffolk Street and he was looking for me because they had been telling him about me. Eventually we got to know each other. I was the only one married with children. The others were single. That summer Jay Milder, Bob Thompson, and Red Grooms went to Nebraska. All three planned to get married, but only Jay did. They all knew women there. Jay was from Omaha or Lincoln.

CG Is he still married to her?

BA No, but they had three children. Then Red returned and he and Jay set up the Delancey Street Museum, which was on the corner of Delancey and Suffolk. Mimi and Red moved in there. Red and Jay had been living together in a loft downtown. They would babysit for me. They would sleep and I would bring the kid in a carriage. They would get up at three in the afternoon when I returned. Then Bob moved in and Red was doing his happenings. He did *Burning Building* which premiered in Provincetown.

That's when a lot of people were coming from the Village looking for drugs. There was a joke at the time that people were leaving New York to look for drugs in California and Californians were coming to New York for drugs. They would meet somewhere in the middle and say, "Go back." People were abandoning their lofts, just putting on their hat and leaving. It was that *On the Road* Jack Kerouac time.

CG Earle Pilgrim and Lily did just that—left suddenly for California.

BA You could just go around and pick up books and stuff off the street. I loaded up the baby carriage. That's when Bob left for Louisville where he married Carol.

They settled on Rivington Street in the Bowery. He was always painting. I would drop by with my kid but Bob was so into drugs that it would take and hour or two for him to wake up.

Eventually Bob would be up and we would shoot the breeze. Then some famous jazz musicians showed up and they would be doing drugs. They would kid me but I would just leave.

(Several are depicted in his large masterpiece *Garden of Music* in the collection of the Wadsworth Athenaeum.)

CG So he was part of the jazz scene.

BA There were recordings dedicated to him. Jackie McClean and those guys were dedicated to him.

CG It sounds like a scene from Jack Gelber's play *The Connection.*

BA He played the drums. I have a poster of him performing as the drummer. They played in the Lower East Side and St. Mark's Place. He existed in a world probably the freest world of race of any of us because he always had an entourage. We kidded that he was like Jack Johnson (1878–1946 World Champion boxer). He wore Italian silk suits with bowler hats. He would have shows and take people to Harlem. Not like Johnson in the 1920s but much nicer and more respectable the way Bob was doing it.

He joined Martha Jackson Gallery, but he got into drugs, which was unusual for an artist. In general artists smoke pot but don't get into heavy drugs like he did.

CG That was the jazz world.

BA I used to do a lot of jazz sketching and would be out late at the Sagamore Café which was opposite to Cooper Union. I have drawings of Thelonius Monk and musicians at the Five Spot. At two or three in the morning people came in and the drug trafficking would start. Bob was into that but none of the rest of us. It got to be worse and worse like a bottomless bucket. He didn't bother me about it because I had a wife and kid. There were artists who stopped being around him because he was always asking for money. He sold work but it was a bottomless bucket and he begged for money.

CG How did he keep working?

BA I don't know but he just did. It took him longer and longer to get up during those days. It was afternoon when he dragged out of bed but he was always working.

CG How important was Bob Thompson?

BA It's hard to explain how important he was because he did not have a vision that was restricted to what you say would be Black art.

CG With its Italian renaissance influences few would recognize the work as Black art.

BA Think of artists like Ensor who did subtle surrealist inspired paintings. He came from a very healthy family background in Louisville. He didn't have a sense of oppression about being Black. Kentucky is a very difference state than where I came from in the deep South in Georgia. Alabama, Mississippi, South Carolina, Georgia are real heavy southern states. Kentucky, North Carolina, Delaware, they're light. People who come from those states didn't grow up as oppressed as those in air-tight segregated societies. It shapes an individual differently. Bob was less scarred by racism than I was. That was reflected in his work.

CG The interest in Piero.

BA That's what I'm saying. He didn't feel as hard pressed to reflect on Black American concerns as a lot of us did. So, he was less identified with it. Not only that, but he was never involved, though he was a bit early on for it, in any Black-awareness social activities, in terms of any political activities.

In the eyes of Black people, he later suffered for that because they weren't interested in him either. Jacob Lawrence and Charles White (1918–1979) especially were always given credit for being very self-conscious about race and doing all they could to identify with it. Bob didn't do that one way or the other. In a sense, Sam Gilliam is similar to Bob. Today Sam is doing well and people are proud of him in a way. But, in his actions he doesn't reflect what I do in my work. So, there is not much insistence on including him in Black anthologies. That's changing now because the concept of it is different. It's not required today in the way that it was in the ten-year stretch between 1965 and 1975 when it was a given that you had to pay your dues, without anyone consciously thinking it. There is no way to associate that Bob paid his.

CG He paid the ultimate price, he died.

BA I'm not talking about that. Martin Luther King also paid the ultimate price but he was a martyr.

CG Bob Thompson wasn't a martyr but he was a victim.

BA There are some Black people whose art work is less respected. Dana Chandler's work is less respected than Bob Thompson's. But in the community (Boston) where people know him, they feel that he has made a greater contribution to Black people than Bob did. This is not to say that Bob should have acted differently. There are a lot of people who have no concern for things like that. In fact, there was a time when people were penalized because they painted abstractly. The point is that we are as diversified as anyone else.

CG The Boston artist Ellen Banks told me that she was chastised as a traitor to her race by another artist because she painted abstractly.

We have been talking about your work as well as other figurative expressionists who worked in Provincetown and New York: Lester Johnson, Jan Müller, Tony Vevers (not a New Yorker), Red Grooms, Jay Milder, Bob Thompson, Emilio Cruz. Clement Greenberg declared figurative painting to be reactionary. When the figure returned, it was identified as the new realism of Pop art. The figurative expressionist movement was weakened because major figures like Müller and Thompson died young. Johnson, a leading artist, was out of New York on a teaching gig. Isn't it true that this major movement never received proper recognition?

BA When you discuss Greenberg and the world he operated in, you are not talking about any recognition of Black artists. There's no reason for you to concern yourself with that. The artists you are talking about just did what they wanted to do. There were no critics with interest in them. They were not interested in what artists like us had to say.

CG When Thompson died in 1966 the Martha Jackson Gallery mounted a retrospective. They arranged for me to meet his widow Carol and view a number of works as well as those in the gallery. Rare for that time, I reviewed Thompson for the New York supplement of Boston's *Avatar*. I was surprised when Judith Wilson found the review and included it in her Thompson bibliography.

Is lack of critical support still an issue for you?

BA For most of us it remains a problem, and I am a big problem for critics. For many reasons, one of which is that I write Black. That helps in a way because they can't knock you down, but they won't come near you. It works both ways.

It's hard for critics to take criticism. That's the first thing. They insist on being able to do the most despicable things to a practitioner, then take immediate offense to anyone who tried to objectively criticize them. John Canaday would write humiliating, belittling reviews. Anyone who tried to speak back was dismissed as a cry-baby. Not all, but the majority of critics behave this way. What we do and the way we behave, in the eyes of a lot of them who don't know us from Adam, to them we are flaunting the law.

When you look at Thompson, Grooms, Johnson, people like us, they always have a problem. Are we primitive or what? If we are primitive, how the hell did we get through art school? That's a problem they have. They can't figure out that maybe you can do something else. In my case they can't reconcile that I can also be an administrator, or that I'm a strong advocate for the rights of Black people. I am also in a strong position to do something for everyone's rights. When I was at the Endowment there were times when I argued against giving preferential treatment to any one group. I was going against what was best and I felt you shouldn't do things like that.

CG Do you believe in a quota system?

BA Yes, I do believe in a quota system. But there are ways to best do that. I try not to accept generalities.

I feel there should be a quota system for school bussing. I believe in bussing. We must try to make up for, compensate and assist any group that has been deprived. When I grew up no matter how far we were from schools there were no busses for Black students. No matter how close to schools White kids lived, however, there were busses. That took them a long way past our schools which they could have walked to. I'm just giving you an example of racial inequality. If you are going to wait for the system to include Black people, it's never going to happen.

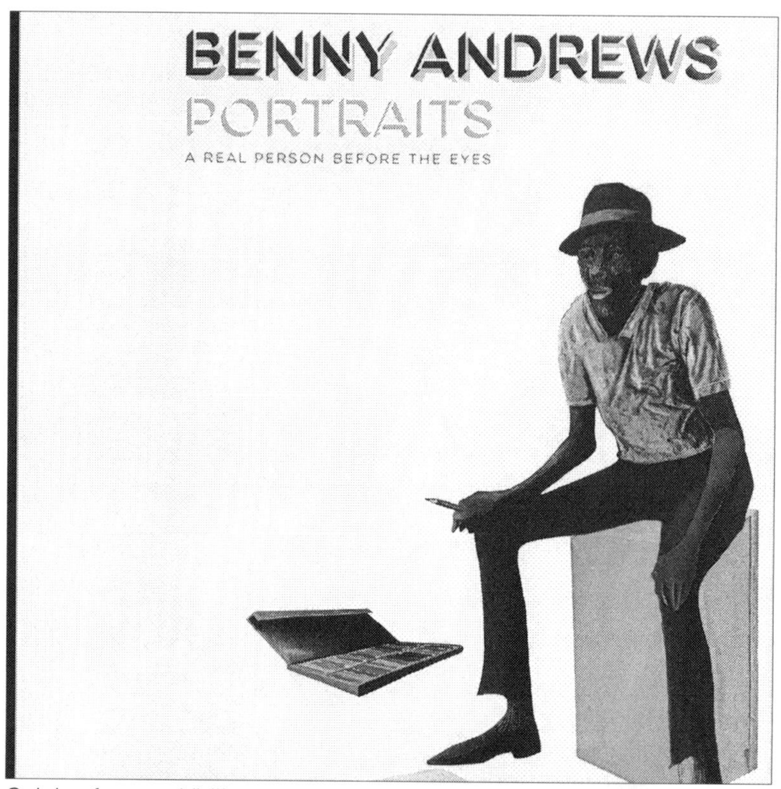

Catalog for an exhibition.

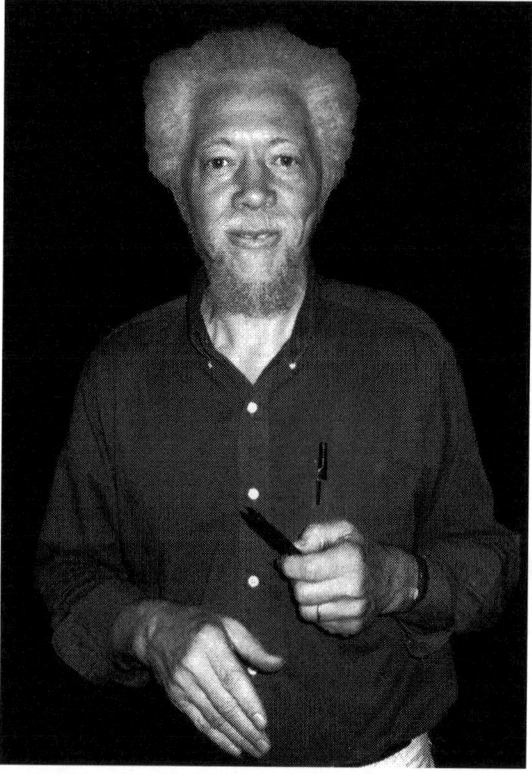

Benny Andrews, 1980s, Giuliano photo.

Kind of Blue:
Benny Andrews, Emilio Cruz, Earle M. Pilgrim and Bob Thompson

In 1986 I organized an exhibition of four African American artists who lived and worked in Provincetown. I was given the opportunity by Ellen O'Donnell, then the director of the Provincetown Art Association and Museum.

That fall my exhibition, *Kind of Blue,* traveled to the gallery of Northeastern University at the invitation of fine arts professor Mira Cantor. In Boston there was a panel discussion chaired by Edmund Barry Gaither, then the director of the National Center for African American Artists and an adjunct curator for the Museum of Fine Arts, Boston. In addition to myself, there were two other panelists. Patricia Hills was then a professor of art history at Boston University. She has long championed issues of social justice and wrote a monograph and curated an exhibition of the work of Jacob Lawrence. Dana Chandler is an artist and activist. His actions impacted changes at the MFA. Several years ago, one of his major works was acquired for the museum's permanent collection. In 1974, he founded the seminal African American Master Artists-in-Residence Program (AAMARP) at Northeastern University.

Judith Wilson, then working on a dissertation on Bob Thompson, traveled from New Haven to attend and record the panel. With Thelma Golden, she was later co-curator of the Bob Thompson exhibition mounted by the Whitney Museum of American Art. Two cassettes of that recording were among papers Wilson donated to the Archives of American Art. They were transcribed by the Lily and Earle M. Pilgrim Art Foundation through the initiative of its director, Peter Stebbins. I edited the following transcript for clarity and continuity. It was judiciously abridged.

Edmund Barry Gaither I think the first order of business would be if Charles could share with us his thinking in putting together the show, and his vision of its impact, and what his intentions were. So, you'll share that with us, Charles.

Charles Giuliano This exhibition started in 1968, and I was reminded of that in a very curious way by Judith Wilson, who is in the process of researching a doctoral dissertation on Bob Thompson for Yale. She had found or resurrected two articles which I wrote in 1968. I prevailed on her to send them back to me and she kindly did so. I'm stunned, amused, and amazed at what I had to say about Bob Thompson.

I did two versions of Bob Thompson: A straight version for *Arts Magazine,* that has stood up fairly well, and pretty well identified what I felt then and now. In *Avatar* I wrote a gonzo journalism version of Thompson. It was in the fledgling stages of my career as a journalist.

In New York I knew Earle Pilgrim. He had been a good friend who, interestingly enough, shows up as an image in this show of Bill Cardoso. He (Cardoso) is considered to be one of America's premier gonzo journalists, and a former editor of *Boston Globe Sunday Magazine.* Bill told me about Earle as an important and dynamic person in the Boston subculture of the 1960s. He had a loft on South Street in the Financial District of Boston. He built sets. He designed costumes. Earle produced things that we would today identify as performances or happenings. He did a kind of art that would later be called psychedelic art. He made things with blacklight and Day Glo. He was an influence on the thinking of Tim Leary, who was then ingesting psychedelic substances. Leary used to come down and hang out at Earle Pilgrim's studio. His wife, Lily, recalled that they used to refer to Leary as The Professor. You know, "Here comes The Prof." And they would be going about their activities. Earle, by the way, never experimented with psychedelic drugs—I wanted to make that very clear—but Leary felt that Earle was a naturally psychedelic person.

Earle was enormously self-destructive and so, very little of the work has survived. What's left is the collection of his widow in Washington, D.C. They moved a lot.

It was a special pleasure to be able to bring his work to this exhibition because he's an artist that basically nobody knew about, who was really an important presence for that generation of Black artists in Boston.

(In the 1950s Earle had a small jewelry shop in Provincetown. He showed the work of young artists, including Lester Johnson and Alan Kaprow. When Earle gave up the shop it became the space of the formidable Sun Gallery. Earle studied with Henry Hensche whose approach is evident in works from the Provincetown years in the 1950s. In 2024 the paintings were shown, with selections of jewelry and metal work at in Truro Public Library.)

Benny Andrews I met a couple summers ago in Provincetown. We were both houseguests for a weekend at the home of Rhoda and Will Rossmore in Provincetown, and I immediately took a liking to Benny. He's a forthright, amusing and witty, highly opinionated, extremely controversial, pungent artist. He's a very flavorful individual in every sense. I think that his work has a kind of dynamism, power, and intensity. Benny is nationally known and respected as an arts administrator and a former visual arts coordinator for the National Council of the Arts and Humanities.

The sense you're getting here–is a show of Black art, or Afro-American art that is different. There's much less of the presence of the social and political context, and, much more of what I would call personal, visionary, or humanist context. One sees that evidently, particularly in the work of Bob Thompson, who I would describe as a visionary artist, and one of the greatest humanist visionary painters of his generation in American art. I think that he ranks with the very best figurative artists of the late '50s and 1960s.

His work really took two tacks. I'm sure Judith Wilson has some things that she could add to this. There are two main directions in his work. One aspect would be inspired by European painting, and he spent a lot of time in Europe, in museums, looking at Poussin and the Old Masters, and then deriving variations of that. Also, in this exhibition you see another kind of personal, private symbolism. Images coming from Dante's *Inferno* and that kind of thing that are more self-generated and derived. This is really the direction that we see in the work of Emilio Cruz, who has taken this kind of personal symbolism and expanded it. Emilio and Bob Thompson were close friends. The influence between them is direct and evident, and in that sense, it's nice to bring them together in this show. Emilio represents the kind of continuation of that idea, right up into the present time.

EBG I will ask Ms. Wilson if she will agree to come in, perhaps, at a slightly later point.

Let's step backwards a little bit from your description of how this particular group of four artists came to be in this show, and to pose a broader question, which I would like both Dana and Pat to comment on, which I may also comment on. It's one which really seeks to get a fuller sense of the larger context in which Black American artists were shaped. That will apply for this group of artists, as for many other artists, even though the particular experiences vary widely. There are elements of commonality that have to do with roots of Black American experience, and the kinds of manifestations in art that it's taken. So, I would invite a couple of quite broad comments, just a sense of the source of these kinds of works in historical terms.

Dana Chandler You want a historical dissertation on that particular subject from me?

EBG Well, you have actually two things that make you good for this. One is you can speak, to some degree, from your own experience. It's not unrelated, even though it's a slightly later generation of people. But also, you have been very involved with the community of artists nationally over the last decade and a half, and you've distilled from that some salient observations, and we'll hear them now.

DC The catchword, I guess, these days in terms of being active, is being proactive. It's proactive, and one doesn't react to what is going on around them. I would say that much of what has occurred in African American art over the last 25 years has been reactive rather than proactive in terms of those artists who spoke socially about the kinds of things which were happening to African American people in America. Certainly, in my own work, that has been my direction, and still is my direction, largely, to be more reactive to the kinds of oppression that one finds still in the United States and funny little acts of racism which occur every day to African American people.

There are some things which were occurring lately which make me feel really good about what's the result of all of that striving of so many people who have been able, I think is the word—not allowed, but more able—to come to intellectual and, what's the word I'm looking for, skills, maturity, I guess. An example of that was that on my way here I had the occasion to see Don Still, who was standing in front of a new Ruggles Street T extension. And it just amazed me and thrilled me to see so large an example of the works and the creativity of an African American architect. Clearly during the '50s and the '60s one could not expect any of those kinds of things to happen, or for Blacks to take those kinds of positions in development of architecture in the United States.

So, it was also true that one could not expect to see the works of African American artists anywhere in the museums and galleries of American, unless perhaps they were part of a collection, and then only if the works were not necessarily reflective of the Black experience. I mean, you might see them appearing in an exhibition. I'm particularly speaking to a print exhibition that was in the Museum of Fine Arts in the '60s, some years back, with both Calvin Burnett and John Wilson pieces. I'm really not sure how I want to comment on this exhibition, except to say that I'm delighted to see the works of people I don't know. I don't know Earle Pilgrim's work, and I don't know very much about Thompson's work, and so it's exciting for me to see so many examples of their works which I have never seen before. And I certainly don't know any of the recent works of Emilio Cruz. And they're—to me, they're quite astounding. I'm very happy and pleased to see them.

Patricia Hills Well, first of all, Charles is to be commended for actually putting together a very exciting show. When he asked me to be on the panel, he assured me that there wasn't going to be any political art, as if he automatically assumed that I would expect more overtly political art. I think you've done a rather daring thing to, in a sense, not emphasize the overtly political art of many Black artists. I mean, it's almost as if we've sort of gone full circle, and that we went through a phase where—I mean, "we", I mean the art world; I mean the sort of visible art magazine, art world; I don't mean real art world, which consists of a lot of artists, but the sort of art world of the art magazines and the major galleries. We went through a period where you saw no Black artists, and then in the 1960s, with the Civil Rights Movement, artists were making demands of the institutions to be shown. A lot of the art that was expected of Black artists was art that was very angry. And there was a lot of really good angry art.

DC I've seen a lot of really pungent, angry work that he has done. And then there was a period—and I think that the Women's Movement used this phrase: the personal is the political. And I think what you see—at least what I get from these kinds of works—is that maybe that phrase, "the personal is the political," can be applied to what's going on here, that these are, in many ways, personal statements. But I wouldn't say that the political is really removed from them, and I think that the question of what is the relevancy of that phrase, "the personal is the political," in terms of this kind of art, and what is the element of politics in works like this. I maybe, I can certainly think of Benny Andrews where, you have one called *Oppression,* which I think is very obviously making a political statement about the oppression of a man who is wounded, with a chain over there on the side. The figure back there called *Ecstasy,* with the child that's being born, that one might be able to maybe read something into it. There's something rather disturbing as a image of that baby that's being birthed, perhaps, that doesn't have any legs, you know. It's sort of truncated. I mean, one can read a certain amount of symbolism into them. I think that that's the kind of the question.

In Cruz's work, you have images that kind of come out at you, that relate, at least in our minds, to all kinds of early Northwest Indian art, and then also the eagle. Now, the eagle, of course, is an image that is—relates not only to Northwest Indian art, but also one thinks of the bald eagle as sort of America. Again, I think maybe you have to sort of unravel these pictures, and maybe not put too much—I mean, not read too much into them. But there are other qualities. I mean, certainly they share a lot of qualities, but they have a great number of differences.

EBG Now I get to comment before posing the next question. I think that this particular set of works allow us to pose a question that really has to do with existential freedom, which is ultimate personal decision-making. I think that, when we look at artistic production, we're looking at at least three elements that are accounted for in one wise or another, not necessarily in a fixed relationship one to the other. They are the context in which things happen, and it's the context which is the essential forge, as an external pressure on the shaping of American experience, and Black American experience within American experience. I think it's impossible to be born black in America, and to be socialized in America, and be black and not know it. And it is not newly that way; it has been that way for a long time. So, I think the concept of identity, in fundamental racial terms, is virtually a foregone in the context of American experience.

The next consideration becomes what's done with that. What's done with it really has to do with the arena of personal decision-making, with how the individual forms a self in dialogue with the context. And it's that formation of self, and the struggle to form a self in a shifting set of circumstances, that is, in a certain sense, the catalyst for creative activity, not just in the arts but in music and any area that you find yourself directed towards.

I think the third factor is that there are preexisting technologies and traditions in the arts. These men have taken, appropriated to themselves, technologies for making pictures, which already were there before, whether it's canvas and brush, or, in the case of Benny, who has been more inventive, collage techniques, still utilizing approaches to existing materials.

So, I tend to look at the show and to say, what does it tell us about how, three different—four different, men, in slightly different contexts, but with a shared root context, responded to the problem of becoming themselves, where they were. For some people, like Benny, the process of being self is an actively political process, and Benny organizes other artists. Benny challenges things straight ahead. Benny works with themes that are charged themes, with sexism, racism, militarism, with the great isms of our times, and that is a mode of involvement which he has both manifested in his public person and expressed in, in his artistic person.

It seems to me that in the case of Bob Thompson, that he has a closer parallel to what a number of Black writers and musicians have done, which is to, in a certain sense, create an identity that belongs to a smaller concentric circle, to a kind of circle of people of very similar ideas and passions.

And in your discussion of Pilgrim, and we're talking about this world in which Tim Leary came, it's a little bit an ultimate kind of world that's created, in which you can define, on personality, a reality which is within the larger one, but not entirely dictated from the larger one.

So, I think in that context you're looking at very personal resolutions that are expressed, more essentially in the person as artist, than the person as politician. I don't, myself, have a fear of mentioning politics, because I think to be alive is to be political, and we are all involved in promoting one thing or another, if nothing more than ourselves, as a condition of terms of survival. So, we're all involved in prejudice in things, in ways that are affirmative to us. So I think that that kind of issue is also, uh, raised, and in the case of Mr. Pilgrim's work, I really don't know him, and I'm grateful to be introduced to him, because I'm, of course, interested to know everybody who belongs to the story, and not knowing him before, and, in fact, not having encountered in Boston, among the artists whom I know very well, anyone else who has mentioned him, he comes like a vision, that was both there and not there in the same setting at the same time, and that is itself worth a little bit of thought and exploration, because Boston is not a large city and is not a large community of people involved in things.

The work of Emilio's, which I actually knew best, were the works similar to the ones that I presented in 1970, which were less profoundly expressive than these. They were more controlled works. In fact, I think that the works which I showed in '70 were large, hard-edged works, and very precise. They were not this gutsy work. In this work, the two things that stood out to me were, one, that they have an immense vigor in the surface, in the actual working of the medium, in the turn of the material, and the globs of the color, which I take to be part of the kind of passion that he himself has. So, I take it to be a very directly expressive—you might say a mode of expression of internal energy. The iconography, the symbols, are interesting to me, but I have not studied them sufficiently that I would assert what they mean. I have a response to them, on what they present. The response to the eagle, I think, is inescapable. I don't think it's very possible to encounter, such a brave eagle without it, being interpreted to reference to American experience. So, I think that unless Emilio's saying you absolutely got the wrong thing, I would stand by that.

Well, you can't always believe what artists say, anyhow, you know. The first thing you have to learn is to always take what artists say with a grain of salt, because if there's anything that speaking about yourself has built into it, it's a certain personal vision of the best light in which you ought to be seen, which is not always—not the job of the critic. The job of the critic is really to try to see in a larger light, and to be informed by the thought of the artist, but not governed by it. The second work, which has the Pacific Northwest images in it, calls to my mind the rather considerable interest in ritual that has been a large feature for a number of American artists over what is now at least a half decade, both from, performance arts people, who want to recreate rituals, and other people who want to create masks of various sorts. And I think that interest is related to spiritual vacuum, I mean, at a larger level, because I think there is a general feeling in American life that we don't always touch base with the heart of things, and still a certain tendency to think that other people, who are especially non-Western, have done better at it than we have. It remains to be seen if that's true. They certainly haven't made any atomic bombs to get rid of us.

PH As you were describing these four men, what I'm hearing, although you're not using these words, is that somehow you don't consider them, quote, "mainstream," end quote. Maybe it's a word that's not terribly relevant, but on the other hand that's what I'm sort of getting from what you're saying, that Thompson is working in smaller and smaller concentric circles, a sense of personality. What I'm hearing is that you're saying that they're not mainstream, and does that—is that what you're saying?

EBG Well, no, that is not what I'm saying. I'll respond, because it's a nice question. No, it is not what I mean. I, I don't generally refer to mainstream. I don't think that it's a particularly meaningful context. (break in audio) one and the same as the sum of what is creatively vital and important at any particular point. So, I wouldn't, have raised it in terms of the mainstream. I would talk about the works in two ways. One, I think that people do, in fact, belong to communities that ultimately support them, and that are small. So, to belong to a community that is a community of artists, let's say, which is a necessarily small community, does not reduce you or take you out of anything; it merely says that there is a community of substance based around some idea or motivation or set of experiences that people pull together around, and I think that that is a vitalizing factor.

The question of mainstream, I think, does not matter so much, because I can't imagine who would want to think of his work or her work as secondary. The fact of producing the work and putting it forward is the affirmation of the work as having a central value that then may not be stratified. So, I would reject thinking of works in terms of mainstream and not mainstream, and consider those as unfortunate devices that have done lots of damage to the contemporary discussion, not only of work of Black American artists but of the work of any artists who have not found themselves at the top of discussion and dominating the marketplace.

CG I'm interested in the notion you brought up about subcultures, or cultures within cultures, and your whole point about personal decision making, and how that relates to these artists. When you said that you feel that you have kept up on who's who in Boston, in terms of the Black art community, and that—

EBG I said I try to.

CG Or you try to, and then everyone you talk to, everyone has said that they didn't know Earle Pilgrim. That raises an interesting point, because Earle was a celebrity in Boston, an absolute celebrity, but he was in a subculture that was not necessarily the main body of what you would consider the Black community. Bob Thompson and Earle Pilgrim would be examples of Black artists who were really in the kind of subculture we call a hipster jazz literary subculture, in the sense that I think it's very important to realize that Bob Thompson's world was almost fluidly equally a jazz world and an art world; and the jazz world was not talking to the art world; and the art world is not talking to the jazz world. They're two entirely separate entities.

And one of the things that are quite amazing is that there has always been a lot of racial contact, interaction and crossover in the jazz world. I grew up in Boston going to jazz nightclubs, and having integrated experiences in a city that is notorious for its racism, and yet, if you went to Storyville, a diverse audience came to hear the music. My uncle took me to see Duke Ellington when I was 16 years-of-age, and I remember that room in the old Copley Plaza Hotel that was painted in black, brown, and beige, which is the theme of a very famous composition by Ellington. They had black waitresses and white waitresses, black couples and white couples, as well as interracial couples, and that was something that was very striking, and natural if you were involved in the jazz world, as opposed to the art world, which had a huge rift between the white art world and the Black art world, which had not had any confluence or crossover at all.

Bob Thompson was such a celebrity in the jazz world, that when he died, isn't it true that albums were dedicated to him, and, and record jacket covers? By the same token, the artists that were part of his entourage were not capable of making the crossover into his jazz world. It was almost a schizophrenia of working in two worlds. One world was the drug hipster subculture world of musicians. If you see that wonderful painting in the Wadsworth Athenaeum Garden of Music, which has the whole cast of characters in there —John Coltrane and Ornette Coleman, Charlie Haden and, different kinds of people. People in the jazz world weren't looking so much at color of skin. Charlie Haden, (a white bass player) for instance, was in that painting. He was a friend of Bob Thompson's, and an intimate friend of Jackie McLean. They were part of the bebop culture.

A play that encapsulated that feeling for me wonderfully was Jack Gelber's play at the Living Theatre in the 1960s, a play called *The Connection.* It was all about that kind of subculture. So, I'm not surprised that you're not aware of Earle in that sense, because Earle's world was not the world of the Black community or the White community.

Benny Andrews commented to me this summer that he felt that artists like Earle Pilgrim and Bob Thompson, Sam Gilliam, and Ellen Banks, a Black artist here in Boston, that those artists have suffered for the fact that their work was not identifiably Black. Bob Thompson's work was not identifiably Black art during the social protests of the 1960s. And it's very interesting that you did not put Bob Thompson in your MFA show in 1970. (Gaither deaccessioned the one Thompson painting *Nativity* in his museum's collection, as I found out when requesting a loan for *Kind of Blue.*) What we have here is an interesting question of: What is Black art? Is Sam Gilliam (an abstract artist) Black art? Is Bob Thompson Black art? Is Emilio Cruz Black art? is Earle Pilgrim Black art?

EBG That certainly is a question, but I think that you, misframe it a little bit. The comment that you made, vis-a-vis, the difference between the jazz world and the art world. I think that the difference is really very—the structural difference, which is not to say all of the elaborations, but the structural difference, I don't think it's too hard to put a finger on. The structural difference was that in the visual arts world there were not institutions giving a focus to the people who were working. So they were mainly working as individuals where they could find an alliance with a particular supporter, and then they were with that supporter, and they were introduced into that supporter's circle. And people were trying to find a gallery, hit or miss, on various terms, some fair and some quite compromised. But essentially, they were working more as individuals in a sort of linear way.

If you looked at, in Boston, a career like that of, for example, John Wilson's career, which is a career starting in the beginning of the '40s, I think you would tend to see that it goes that way, and the absence of an institutional support to create a forum that would have pulled together groups of people was the central absence. In the case of the jazz world, it is also a commercial world. It's pulled together around the nightspot where the event happens and the money is made, and much of it spent. So, in a certain sense, it is its own patronage, and that's the difference. The difference is a question of patronage—because patronage is fundamental to what things belong to. Jazz is entertainment. Well, that its entertainment is fine, but, it's commercial.

DC You go where you get fed. Okay, now let me explain what I mean by that. If you're a visual artist, and your ego is such that you want what you do to be seen, then there are two determinations that you make: Either you make a world where you get fed, or you go where you get fed. And if you go where you get fed, then very largely what you will do will reflect the world in which you travel. And if the world in which you travel has institutions that will allow your work to be seen, then perhaps you will create things that you think will be acceptable to the world that will allow your things to be seen.

If, however, your ego is such where you do not intend to create works that will reflect the world in which you travel that will allow you to get fed, then maybe you have to work on creating that world. Maybe you have to struggle and strive and push and challenge everything that goes on.

I think that Benny belongs to the category of people who created a world in which he could be fed. And I cannot speak to the other people, because I don't know enough about their works to comment on that, but I do know that an example of what I'm talking about sits presently over in the Museum of Fine Arts, and is called *Boston Collects.* And when you wander through that exhibition, you don't see the works of a large number of African American artists. I think there's one. There's one piece by an African American. I'm trying to remember the man's name now. He recently had a very excellent article in the *Globe.* He usually painted in black and white, does black and white paintings. But that's not the point that I'm trying to get at. What I'm trying to get at is that you don't find Benny Andrews as part of a collection. These are not just Boston painters. These are painters that have been collected nationwide, and you don't find Emilio Cruz's work, and you don't find Bob Thompson's work, and you don't find a number of other people's work, and that may be a reflection of the people who curated the show; it may be a reflection of a lot of things.

But the point that I'm trying to get to is that artists, like most other people, want to be recognized for that which they do. And if you take a particular tack in your work, which talks about reflecting the imagery of a people who have never been, and are not in the near future likely to be, in the economic position where they can create the institutions where the things that speak to their own culture can come about in a large and visible way for the entire community, then you go somewhere else with your thing. And what I'm seeing a lot of what African American artists do is go somewhere else with their thing. I think of people like (Jean Michel) Basquiat and some other folks whose work I don't think reflect the Black American experience, but do reflect a larger experience, and I'm not really sure whether that larger experience is real or contrived, you know, to fit or suit whatever is necessary to get food in one's mouth.

EBG What is your response to artists like Sam Gilliam or Ellen Banks, vis-a-vis the question of—Black artists?

DC I think I took some umbrage at the statement that they suffered because of their choice to not really work in a Black American vernacular. That's what I heard.

EBG Bear in mind that I'm quoting Benny Andrews.

DC Fine, and I still take umbrage. I take umbrage to the statement.

EBG I think—I think that he meant in the sense of whether he was (overlapping dialogue; inaudible)—

DC What I'm saying is that we all suffer, and artists in general in this country suffer because this is not a country that's about art, you know, at least not for anything that I have seen. I think it's a country that uses art for one purpose or another, as decoration, or to make people look good, but I don't see it as being as important as it being an integral part of the cultures out of which it comes, like in Africa and, as a matter of fact, in Europe and places like that. So, I think everybody suffers when they choose visual arts as a field, generally speaking, and I think that some people suffer more than others, and I know, in terms of, of noting artists trying to survive off their own work, I note the Black American artist has suffered more than most. I note that the Black woman artist has suffered more than most women artists, and they're still suffering in terms of the whole idea of finding their work acceptable so that it comes into the purview of the whole American economic thing. I guess what it really boils down to is that, while I can feel great delight at seeing an exhibition of works such as one sees here, one knows that it is an exhibition of the works of Black artists, and one also knows that we cannot expect to see it as part of what the mainstream is, which, of course, is what exactly is over at the Museum of Fine Arts right now. That is the mainstream. And the mainstream, that word really connotes just one thing: acceptable. Okay? And, we have not managed—if we have an interest, which I don't, in becoming acceptable in the larger American context. And that's really what I'm commenting on.

PH I just want to be clear. You're choosing to be outside. That's what you're saying? Outside of a group, mainstream, i.e. the show of contemporary art, at the, MFA. Choosing?

DC No, I'm not choosing to be outside. I just don't see how many of us will get inside without pushing through.

PH Well, what about the word "compromise"? I mean, it's not just. You know, one goes where there's something to eat. You made the comment that you go where you get nourished, that you can get food, you know, where you can get fed, where you make a world, where you can get seen. I mean, isn't there a time when one chooses not to eat in order to make certain statements.

DC I think it's exactly what artists have done, and I'm particularly speaking of artists of color, who have chosen not to eat very often in order to make the kind of statements we thought were pertinent to what was going on around us, because we're artists, so artists are largely affected by what's going on around them, and often react proactively, and interact, as well. Most of the artists I know who work in a social vein don't only just do social things, okay, and have found that whether or not they do social things, of course, or things which fit into the larger American picture, still find themselves in the same position. I don't see how artists who have done things which are socially relevant have done any worse or better than artists who have not. You know, I just haven't seen it yet.

EBG Yeah, you know, vis-a-vis this business of the mainstream, that two really big points I think ought to be made, because it can be a recycling discussion, but it's not really useful. From my point of view, the fundamental obligation of an artist in shaping creative expression is to be personally honest, and to feel what is to be said.

If nothing is felt, there's nothing vital that's going to be said. What is felt is not the function, at least, I don't think should be the function, of a calculation of how to be viable, in one place. I think there has to be some internal strength and reason and community. I think when that's missing; you experience it at missing in the work that is finally entered. So, I think that there's a passion that is fundamental, and that relates to the observation I made at the beginning about existential freedom, because you cannot become your own person, and have your own voice, and put something out that people can respond to as real, unless it, in fact is real, and comes from within. That is a separate issue than the issue of mainstream.

The issue of mainstream belongs to the world of curators and critics and journalists and writers and galleries. It belongs to the world that is about the thing and not the thing itself. It is a world that is orchestrated, that is like any market, an orchestrated item. So, to work with a sense of how to belong to the mainstream, I think from the point of view of where the artist must come from, is a wrong position. I think the obligation falls to those of us who don't necessarily produce art, but are in the business of talking about it and presenting it, to try to put forth the visions of what we believe are the works that are important to be seen, and to try to generate the maximum impact that those can generate, and try to demolish the tendency to close the doors of what things are appropriate at particular points in time, and who is valid and who is invalid. Those are not meaningful notions, and if you accept them as categories, you accept having a great uphill struggle, which is the acceptable, and then having everybody else in some kind of basement. And whoever has made a valid creative statement belongs to this level, no matter whether a critic says so or not, no matter whether a particular institution puts them there or not. They belong there, because they spoke truthfully. They found the right container for the thing contained, which is the job of the artist: to make the picture right to contain what it has to contain. And when we see it, we will have a dialogue with it. The language around the art, which is—I mean, the language is, in a certain sense, almost superfluous.

I remember when I was in graduate school, if I can be tolerated one short story, I had to do a paper on criticism. And I think we got issued an ashtray, a quite simple little glass ashtray, like millions from all over the place. Well, you could write 12 pages about it. All you had to do was posit a starting point, and make it. It's like law: it doesn't have to do with the correctness. You posit a position, and then you extrapolate from the position. And that is detrimental to the meaning of things, but it is, unfortunately, often the case in criticism that you wonder if the person really saw the work, because it's about the language, not about the thing, Charles uses language because he's a journalist.

CG This is a mainstream exhibition, and it was curated by a mainstream critic, a wheeler and dealer, a powerbroker in the art world. I think that's an important point. I'm honored to have Pat here with us today, because she a mainstream powerbroker, heavy-duty wheeler-dealer in the art world today, vis-a-vis the fact that the *New York Times* went through the trouble today to review the Sargent exhibition that she curated for the Whitney Museum of American Art, is bringing 7,000 people a week to—

PH A weekend.

CG A weekend—to the Whitney Museum of American Art. Pat Hills is such a powerbroker in the art world that the *New York Times*, in their review in the *Sunday Times* today, went so far as to take the trouble to completely leave her name out of the review. That's power. (laughter) When they're so afraid of the threat that she represents to their assumptions, that they had to go to all the trouble to disinvite you from the review, then I think that's a comment. I think it's a very important comment that people like Pat and myself, who are part of the White power establishment of the art world, each in our own way, make the commitment to doing exhibitions like this. Consider Pat's involvement this summer with the traveling exhibition of Jacob Lawrence, and contributing a catalog to it. It's efforts like this that make these issues part of the mainstream, and increase the likelihood that these works get into important collections.

This past summer, for instance, it was tremendously important that the Wadsworth Athenaeum included Bob Thompson in its Matrix program, and the work was, reviewed in the *New York Times*, which said, in effect, that he was a very important artist. *Art & Antiques*, in the current issue lists Bob Thompson among 25 most neglected, undervalued artists in America. I think it's a matter of time before the art establishment wakes up to the fact that these are important artists that are existing under their noses, and that they're unaware of them,

EBG I want someone to tell us what the other stream is? I mean, you said the mainstream. What's the other stream? This is like people that say "the third world." What's the other world? This is one world. So, again, I want to hear what the other one is.

DC I would also want to hear, what exactly is meant by "compromise." Compromise with what? With whom? Under what circumstances? To what purpose? Just for some clarity.

PH When I use the word "compromise," compromising in terms of not being so concerned about getting fed—I mean, getting fed. And when you were talking about getting fed, I think you meant getting fed in terms of, you know, getting rent money and getting food to put in your mouth. I mean, there's other ways that one is being fed, and, you know, and maybe you, make when I talk about, compromise. Well, okay, when you talked about "you go where you get fed" or "you make a world where you get fed," are you talking about getting money to feed yourself and your family, or do you mean that kind of spiritual food that sustains you?

DC Well, absolutely because one can't. There are a number of artists who are here presently, who have spent many years making sure that they are physically fed, and have done very well at it. That was not necessarily the reason for them remaining artists, visual artists. It was a spiritual feeding and a social feeding, perhaps a community feeding that we are more interested in. Also, there's a feeding that has to do, in a sense, with ego in its place, and its context with culture. That is to say, when one finally comes to understand that one comes from a culture that values art as part of an integral part of being on the earth, and then comes to a culture which does not value art, there's an integral part of the being of the world. And I don't mean value in the sense that everybody in the culture doesn't value art. I mean the larger culture itself doesn't. It's a very difficult place to be.

But if you are a survivor, then of course you find the things that are necessary to feed you, physically, and if you're also a survivor, then you begin to work on creating the places where you can be fed, in all the other ways that you can be fed. And I'm saying that the struggle is an intense one, it's a long-term one, that sometimes it's a life-lasting one, where you finish up and you haven't gotten that emotional thing happening for you. But then, all of a sudden when you die, which is one of the major American things for all artists is, when we die, your work suddenly achieves some of the importance that it never had when we were living, which can be hilariously funny if you're not the one that died. So, I'm speaking about all of those kinds of things. It's obvious that I have gotten myself fed. You know, I mean, no one can deny (laughter) that, you know, all 1 my life I've been about this size. I was a chubby little boy. I grew up, and I'm still chunky, so that's never been the problem, but there has been an ongoing struggle to make sure not only that I was fed spiritually, but that I was of some resource to other artists to help ease that struggle for them. That doesn't necessarily mean it was always appreciated or seen in the right way, right? That was part of that struggle. That's what I'm talking about. So, I'm curious of what we're talking about in the word "compromise." That's why I asked the question.

PH Maybe I'll get back to this, but I want to raise another issue that has been a kind of a pet peeve of mine, and that is that I see—I've talked to a lot of artists who are involved with political art and social art, art that makes a social statement, and it always strikes me as really strange. And I have one particular artist in mind. I won't mention his name. He's a Boston artist who does these political paintings, year in and year out. (laughs) Not you, Dana, but,...

DC I know, and that leaves one other choice. (Arnold Trachtman.)

PH Year in and year out he does these enormous political paintings, and then he puts a price on them of about $5,000, $6,000, and I'm not saying that they're not worth that much, but the people who have the money are not going to buy those pictures, because they don't like the message. The rest of us, who like those paintings, can't afford them. So, I said to this one particular artist, "Why don't you do silk-screens?" Because he does a kind of art that would translate very well into silk-screens. "Why don't you do silk screens, and then sell them, you know, in an edition of 70 at say $50. Something that maybe somebody can afford?" And he said no. He says what he wants to do, he wants to do in paint; he's not interested at all in the silk screen. So, there's a puzzle. I mean, if you want to reach people with a certain kind of message, or have an audience, then why not do something that people can afford?

DC Adjust to the needs of the audience.

PH Of the audience that you're looking for. So, you find, I mean, this is a kind of problem. There's another artist, a New York artist (Hans Haacke), whose show was canceled at a large museum (Guggenheim) because of the political content. It had to do with New York's real estate (Shapolsky), had to do with political content. So, I suggested to him, "These are nice pictures. What you've done is terrific. Let's set this up outside, you know, on Fifth Avenue and 110th Street. You get a lot of people walking by who might be interested in the way you relate real estate interests and the Rockefellers and the United Baptist Church." He wasn't interested at all. He wants to have his work shown in a museum context; otherwise, he's a political artist. He's been a political artist for many years. So, these two incidents stick in my head as to who do artists think their audience are, and how can they really reach them? And you can't reach them if you're going to make that art inaccessible to them. I mean, that's one of the nice things about a university art gallery, you get a lot of students here.

DC But, you see, most of us, you're saying "artists"—most of the artists that I can think of have exhibited in all the places that you're talking about: On the street, in churches, in Y's, parks, basements, and attics. We've exhibited everywhere that was open for us to exhibit, and when there weren't places open for us to exhibit, we created the places, okay? AAMARP is a creation. (African American Master Artists in Residence Program at Northeastern University) You know, and that says, okay, we're going to create a space for people to exhibit where there was none before, you know, and one does thank God that there were some people who were men—who were amenable to it.

CG Leonard and Ann Marie Lewis are leaving and I want to make a comment before they go. To acknowledge them because they loaned works to this exhibition. I apologize to Dana for interrupting, because I know that they're leaving, and I wanted to catch them before they went. But I think they represent a very important point.

They have over 30 works by Emilio Cruz in their collection. They have a very representative work by Benny Andrews. They loaned five superb Bob Thompson paintings that we see here. They have been deeply committed to figurative expressionist artists over a long period of time. They are committed collectors, and have joined us here today as a part of that mandate. They were among the 90 collections that were seen by the Museum of Fine Arts. The Lewises, who I consider to be among Boston's most unique collectors, in terms of having a very specific point of view and not just picking up art magazines and acquiring what they see. I think it's very important that there be more interaction and networking of people that have mutual interests. That's part of what it's all about if you want to see these artists in the Museum of Fine Arts. If you want to see progress, there has to be more interaction between people like the Lewises that are committed collectors, and more exchange between people like Barry, Dana, Pat and myself, and colleagues, in terms of making more visible and raising these issues, and, and making more of an awareness and presence. It comes down to the question: why is the mainstream—if, in this case, we mean the Museum of Fine Arts—why are they simply not interested in artists of this kind?

DC Let me do a quick—let me do a quick commiseration, because, I mean, I really do understand how you feel, because there was a recent exhibition called *Boston Expressionists* (DeCordova Museum), of which I had been one for more than 20 years, and exhibited all over the country, and I wasn't in it. I'd like to make you an offer, in terms of your (Lewis) collection. When AAMARP opens, we're going to have a total of five galleries, and I want you to go over and just take a look at the gallery spaces, and if you think they're interesting enough, and you want to have an exhibition of the works that you have in your collection, you got it. Check it out.

PH The first thing you think of when you look at these Cruz paintings is not the formalism, but the message, the intensity, and, as you say, the vigor, and the passion. Afterwards, you begin to look at the formal qualities, whereas over there (MFA), there's something very correct. Even in that room, where you've got the Clyfford Still and the Mark Rothko, with the black and white in between, I don't think of those paintings, I think, oh, this is a wall that has black and white in the middle, and sort of yellow-ish paintings on either side, (laughter) you know, and then this wall. You think of it in terms of the wall rather than these individual works.

DC Which is probably how it was hung.

EBG I would like to ask Judith Wilson if she would like to make some comments, vis-a-vis her advanced degree on Bob Thompson, and, her thinking about him.

Judith Wilson One thing I want to throw in, and I'm saying all this, and I would like to make clear very conditionally, I'm in the middle of my research and middle of my writing. I'm sure that this time next year I will look back on many of the things I am saying and, you know, with great distress. I'm struck with this show, in the way that it bridges certain known and unknown, or known and less known, phenomena in recent art. I'm thinking of this in terms of how I think we have generally conceived of the recent history of Afro-American art, as well as the recent history of American art across the boards. I think a show like this is filling in the gaps in both of those histories, and raising questions about our understanding of both of those histories. I think, there's room for revision on every level, and on all sides.

I'm struck by what Charles was saying a while ago about Bob Thompson, and this question of operating in more than one world. And I'm also struck with what Mr. Chandler was saying about this issue of going where you get fed, or making your own place to be fed. I think that's a real valuable distinction between what has happened in Afro-American art in, say, the past 20 years. I also, though, feel like a word needs to be put in edgewise for a kind of historical context in that I would just want to maybe throw in that perhaps before the mid-1960s the conditions weren't there for most Afro-American artists to have quite those options. That before, say, the mid-'60s—before the Civil Rights Movement coming to a certain kind of peak and pressure, you might have wanted to make your own place to be fed, but it would've been a whole lot harder. I think that's something that makes the character of what Black American painters have done since 1965 very different.

And, for me, part of the reason why I chose Bob Thompson was because I wanted somebody who was very close to that critical moment, that what to me is a turning point, in the history of this tradition, and I do see it as a tradition. For me, his career is right before that moment, and yet one of the real excitements for me of my research is that I'm finding out how much earlier things were starting to take off than I had previously realized. Bob Thompson, some of you may or may not realize, was very close to Amiri Baraka, the writer and poet. He was close to Archie Sheep and Ornette Coleman. Some of these literary and musical figures had, by the early '60s, begun to become concerned about issues of Black consciousness that, in the rest of the culture, we think of as not emerging until the late '60s. He was in contact with all of that, and yet, from what I've been able to hear so far, he refused to take a certain kind of position. He refused to take an activist position. He supposedly said that his feeling was that he wanted to be about the painting. That was his activity. He didn't want to be about the politics. At the same time, I feel like there's a real struggle, an attempt, perhaps not fully realized—'cause we're also talking here about an artist who died very young—he died a month away from his 29th birthday. I think that there was a struggle to begin to bring his own ethnic experience into that work, at the same time that he's using traditional Western themes, Old Master compositions, et cetera. That time with the jazz world, that time with some of these younger generation of Black poets, was an attempt to pull something out that was uniquely his own as a Black American artist, and inject that into this other tradition that he had learned in art school in Louisville, et cetera. That's probably my two cents for the moment.

DC Becoming what I became as an artist was directly related to people like Malcolm X, and the whole movement of the Black Islamic movement in the United States, and what was going on at that time; and my inability to really deal with the fact that although I was —had a leaning towards Martin Luther King, and what Martin Luther King was trying to do, there was so much opposition from people who didn't look like me towards that whole idea of not so much integration, as people were calling it at that time, which simply meant the assimilation of Black culture into White culture, so that there's some, some sort of smooth brownness rather than differences. But the whole idea of the integration of cultures, of the joining of cultures which could sit side by side, and exist as themselves, and be seen as being as valid as anything else. And, I mean African American culture, Asian American culture, and so on.

It still reminds me of the of the travesty of an exhibition (*A New World: Masterpieces of American Art, 1760–1910,* 1983, curated by Ted Stebbins) that recently was at the Museum of Fine Arts, that was supposed to be about American painting, in which there were no Asian American artists, and no Indian American artists, because their imagery didn't fit into a European American ideology about what imagery was supposed to be about, and it was as though they didn't exist at all. It was bad enough that there weren't African American artists, but there were no Asian and no Native American. It's just incredible. So that a whole lot of that stuff has not yet ceased, but that—the recognition, of the visualness of the struggle of Black folks being Black folks began very early, you know. It began around 1959 and '60, I mean, in terms of being public within the Black community. And then it became public largely through the efforts of the Nation of Islam, because of Malcolm X. But there were whole bunches of folks who were not connected to the Nation of Islam who were raising their voices and, and making a lot of noises about the validity of the Black experience during that time. So, I can understand why Bob found himself leaning towards that, and a whole lot of artists found themselves leaning towards that.

And I can remember sitting with Sam Gilliam, and have him tell me that he was very insulted because people who were Black didn't think that he was part of the Black experience; it's just that he chose to do with his work something different than what they were doing, and they didn't understand it. And I knew how he was feeling, because I was one of the people who told him I didn't think he was doing anything that was related to the whole Black experience until I came to understand that everything in this country relates to the Black experience, and it's all one experience. You know, it just happens to be all one experience from a different perspective. So, it's all one experience for me, and it's all one experience for Charles, and it's all one experience for everybody that's sitting in here. It just has a different perspective, and we're all part of that oneness, and I'm still waiting, you know. But at the same time, I think it's important and it's valid for us to have our own—be within our own cultural context within this whole sphere, and there's nothing wrong with it, you know, and I think I'll still be waiting when I'm gone, and my children have gone on to their grandchildren. I think I'll still be waiting for that sort of thing to happen, but I have some hope. That's my statement.

CG I'm glad that Judith made the comment about Bob's decision, which was a controversial one when he made it, to concentrate on the art, and to basically not deal with the social and political context of trying to necessarily make a direct statement about being a Black person in America, in the sense that we have discussed Benny Andrews as an example of an artist who is totally socially, politically connected in every breath he takes through the day to everything that he puts on the canvas, every act and statement and movement that he makes as a person and a humanitarian, as opposed to, the artists who are Black that, that pursue a more personal muse. And I think that every artist should have the right with impunity—to pursue their own personal vision, and that's what I think Dana's talking about in terms of Sam Gilliam. What I meant when I said that artists like Sam Gilliam and Bob Thompson suffered because they were not identified with the Black community, with that struggle, in terms of what it meant politically in the 1960s in the Civil Rights era. When Barry mounted an exhibition at the Museum of Fine

Arts in 1970 that was an enormously important political statement. When one saw "Black art" shows in the 1960s, they were primarily emphasizing the political context and the social context, and there was a mood that was very confrontational about those exhibitions.

DC You didn't relate the history correctly. You said that, that Barry mounted an exhibition in 1970, but that exhibition came about because of a document that was delivered by me, that talked about the eradication of institutional racism at the Museum of Fine Arts, Have the historical context correct, and then we can proceed.

EBG You (Charles) said that the exhibitions mainly had to do with political and social themes, and the point I wanted to make was that that reflects the perception of the shows, because if a show was 90 percent nonpolitical work, and 10 percent political work, it was discussed in terms of the 10 percent, as if the 10 percent were the 90 percent.

So, if you look at the discussion, it has no relationship, really, to the balance between these groups of works, so I just wanted to alter your statement to say that it was discussed against that perception, rather than that fact. Because it was not always true that that was the fact.

CG I would fully concede that, but there was a political exigency that, that caused those shows to exist.

EBG Yes, there certainly was.

CG The point that I'm trying to make is, basically, what I would see as a kind of sophistication and growth and change, in the sense that in 1986 it's possible for a White curator to do an exhibition on Black art, and to not do it to raise a social, political comment, so much as to make an important aesthetic comment. My whole purpose of curating this exhibition was that I think that this is first-class art. It deserves to be looked at as art, and to be looked at for its quality, its beauty, its expressiveness. In that sense, what we're talking about is perhaps a modification of how we look at Black art. This is something to consider as we move into the '80s and '90s, in terms of what we've been struggling with today, of coming into the mainstream and having these artists take their place in the museums, its collections and the full history of what has happened in America, not to be pushed off, isolated, and marginalized into, a kind of packaged notion of what Black art is supposed to be and supposed to look like.

PH Well said. I don't have really very much to say as a sort of windup, except that I think what Dana was saying before, that there is a great deal of racism in our society. There is sexism, also, and that's important, but the racism I think is very fundamental. And I think whatever people can do to eliminate that is all for the best. And I think that constant pressure needs to be brought on the Museum of Fine Arts. It was good when we mounted that protest about *The New World* exhibition for not even including Henry Tanner, a major late nineteenth-century American painter. People saw that exhibition, before the insertion of Tanner. Not only did it not have Afro American artists, or American Indian artists, but there weren't any images of these races. There were no Black faces. There were some Indian faces in the bushes.

EBG In the Cole.

PH In the Thomas Cole mountains. A woman who is a librarian in New York said she'd walked through that exhibition and saw no Black faces in a show that was supposed to be called *The New World.* Constant pressure needs to be brought against these big institutions. They probably are never really going to change, but at least let's strive for as many concessions as you can get.

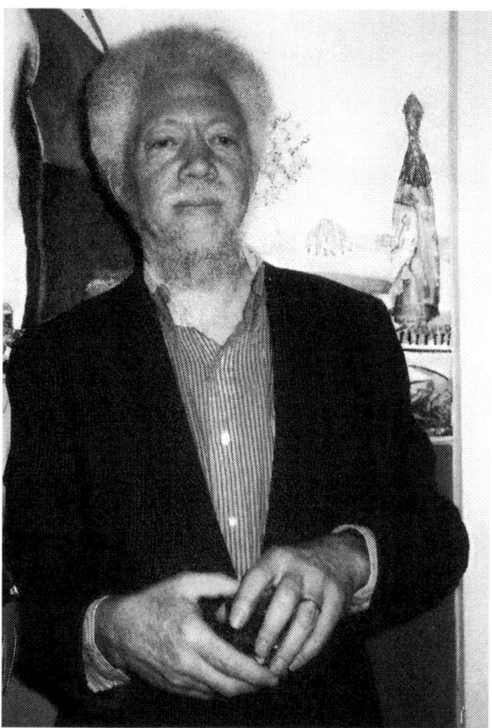

Artist Benny Andrews, Giuliano photo.

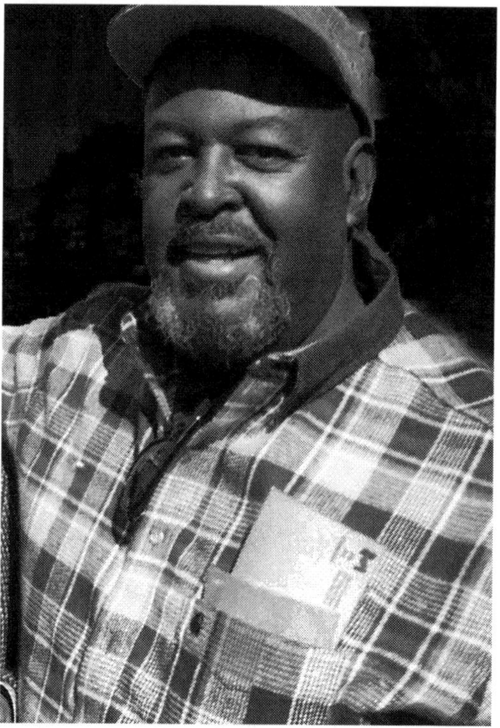

Artist and activist, Dana Chandler, founded AAMARP at Northeastern University, Giuliano photo.

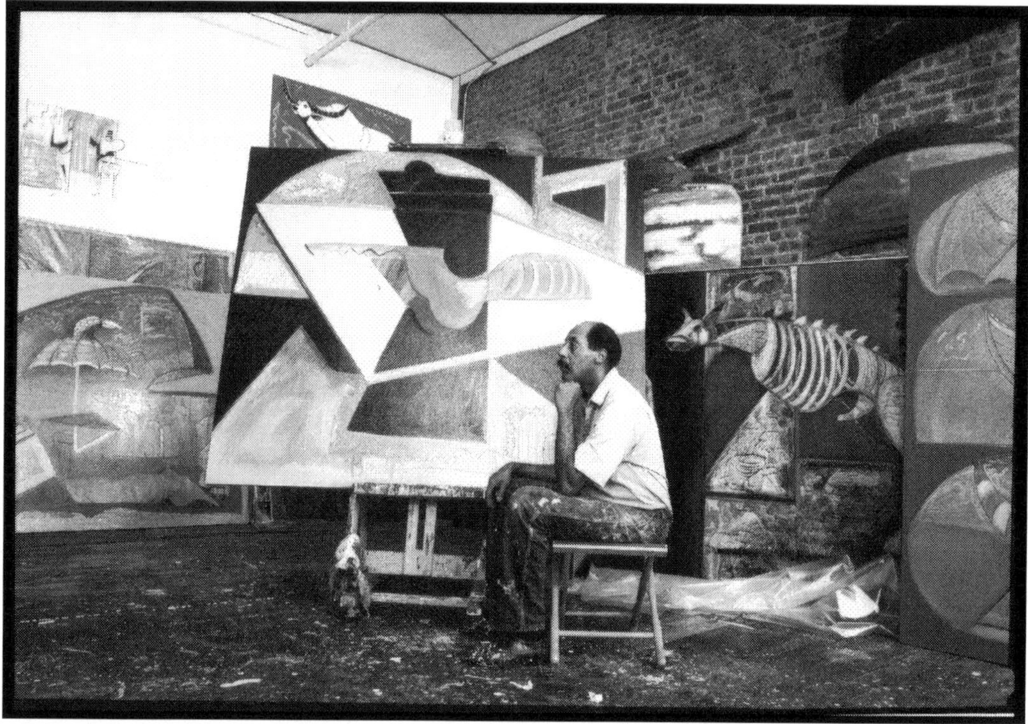

Artist Emelio Cruz, 1990s, photo by A. Barboza, courtesy of Corbett vs. Dempsey Gallery, Chicago.

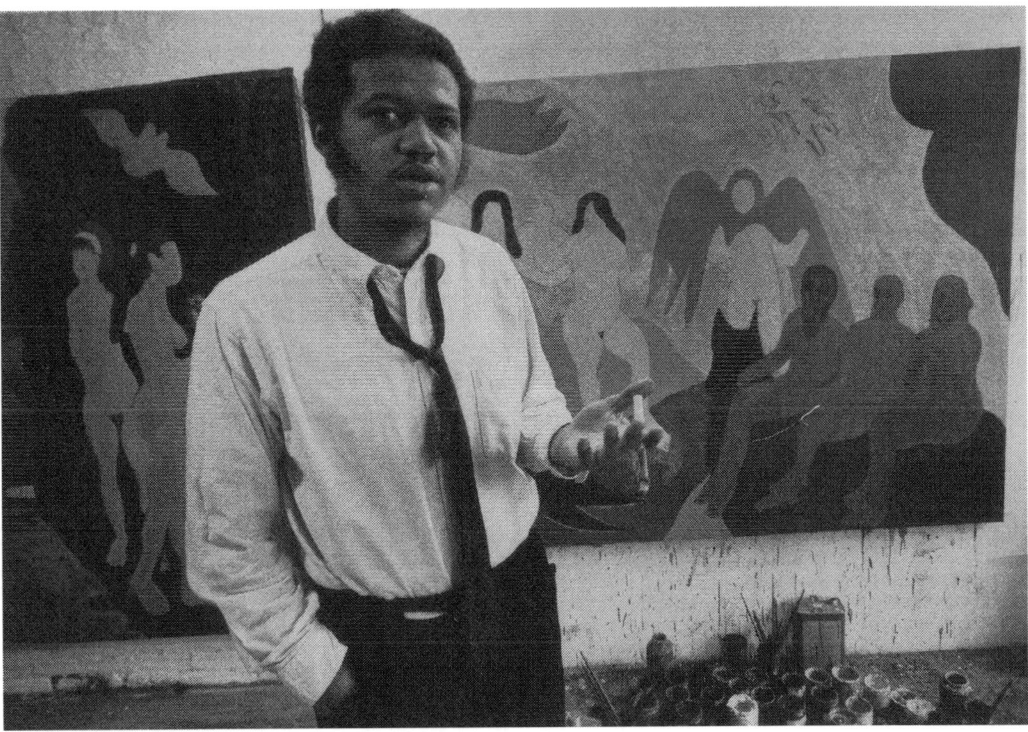

Bob Thompson showed at Sun Gallery. Courtesy of PAAM.

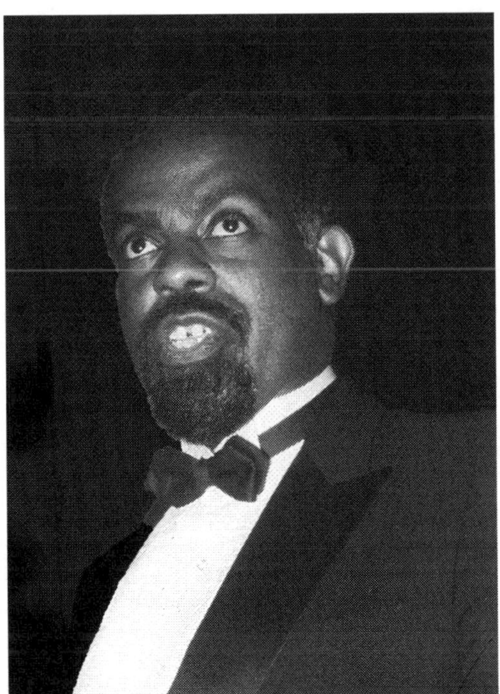

Barry Gaither chaired the Northeastern panel. Giuliano photo.

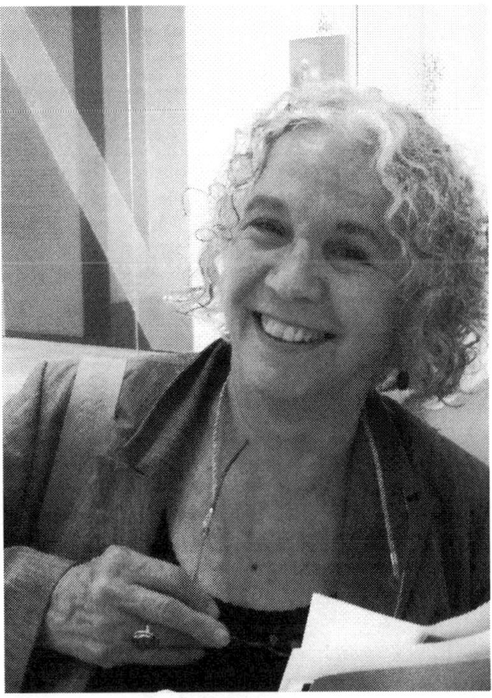

Patricia Hills published a book on Jacob Lawrence. Giuliano photo.

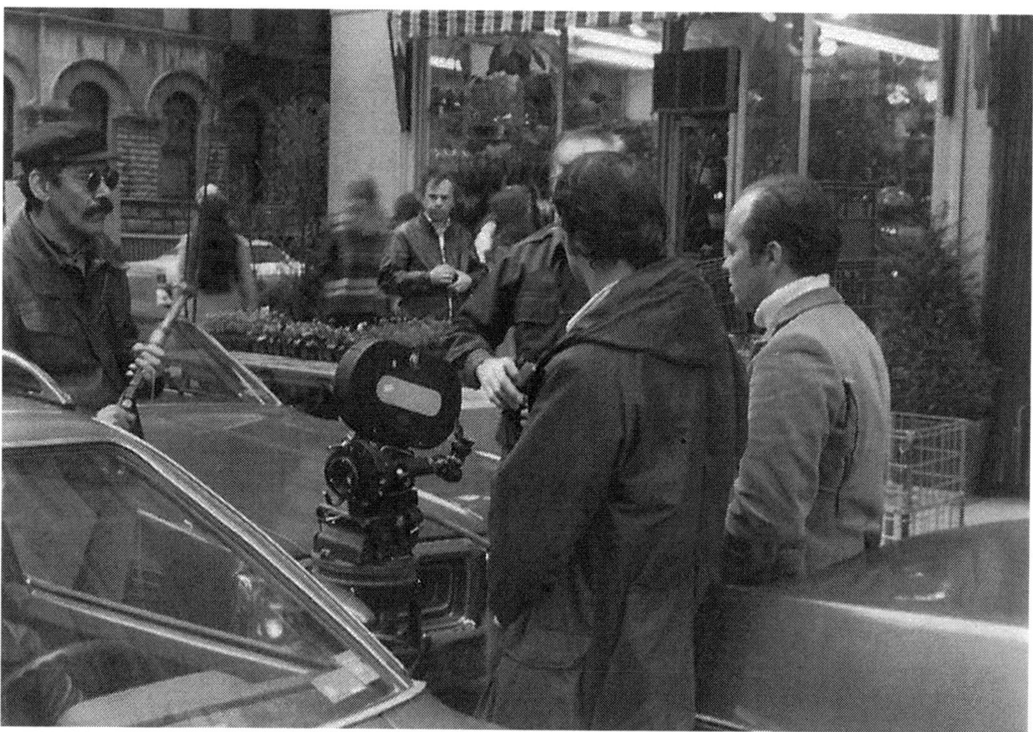

Pilgrim, left, shooting a movie. Courtesy of Pilgrim Foundation.

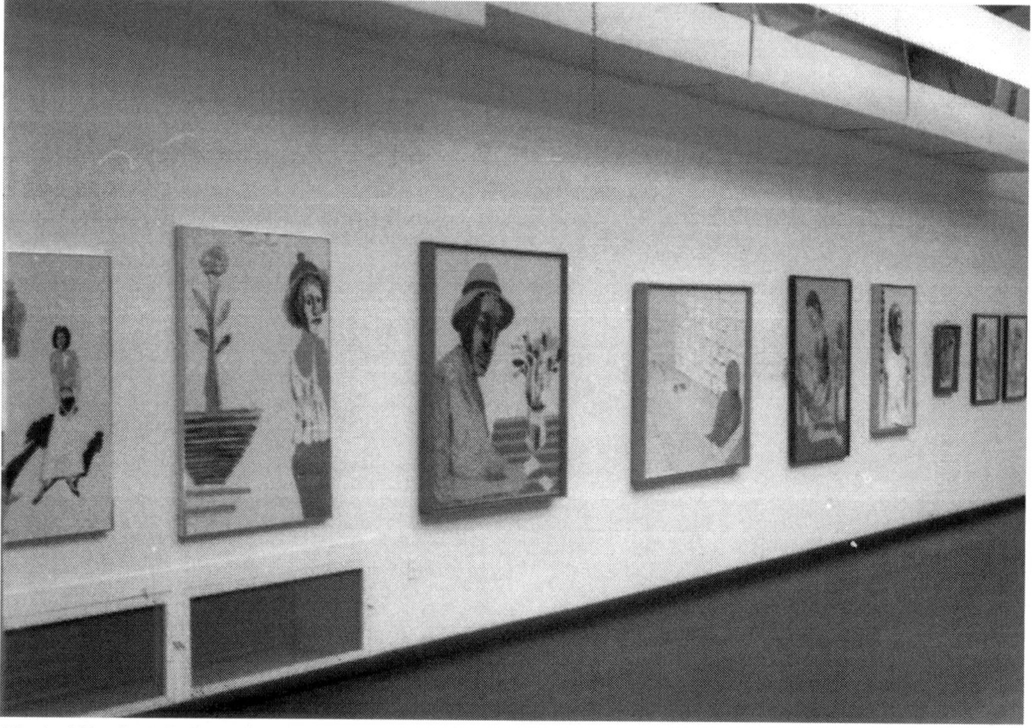

Kind of Blue installation with works by Andrews to the left. Giuliano photo.

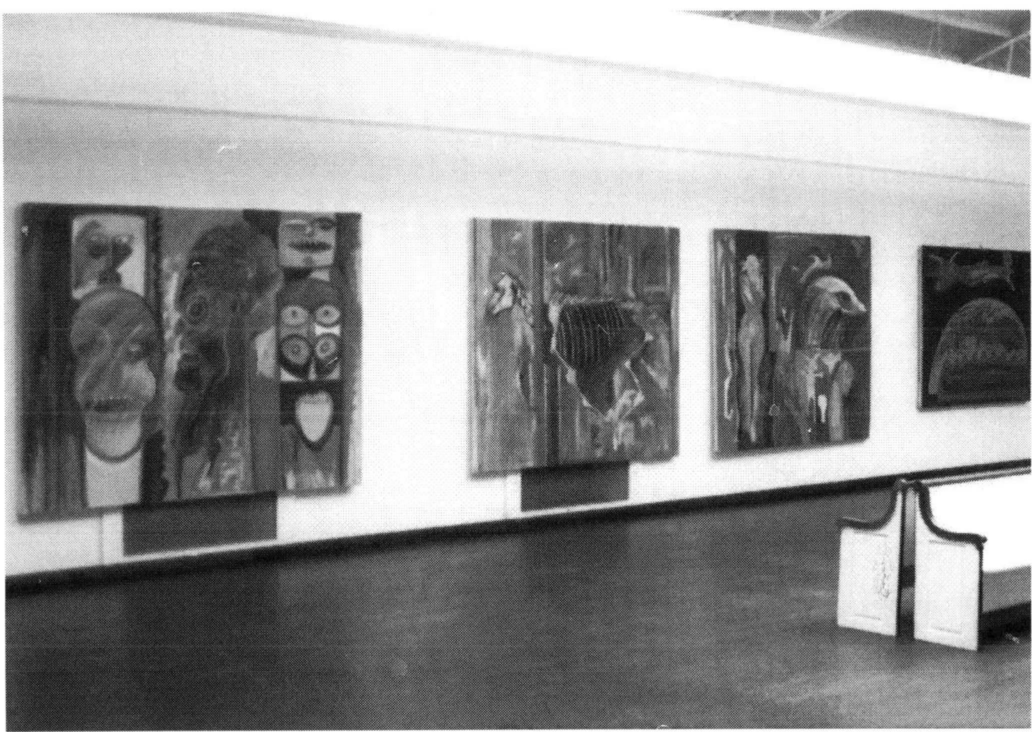

Works by Cruz. Giuliano photo.

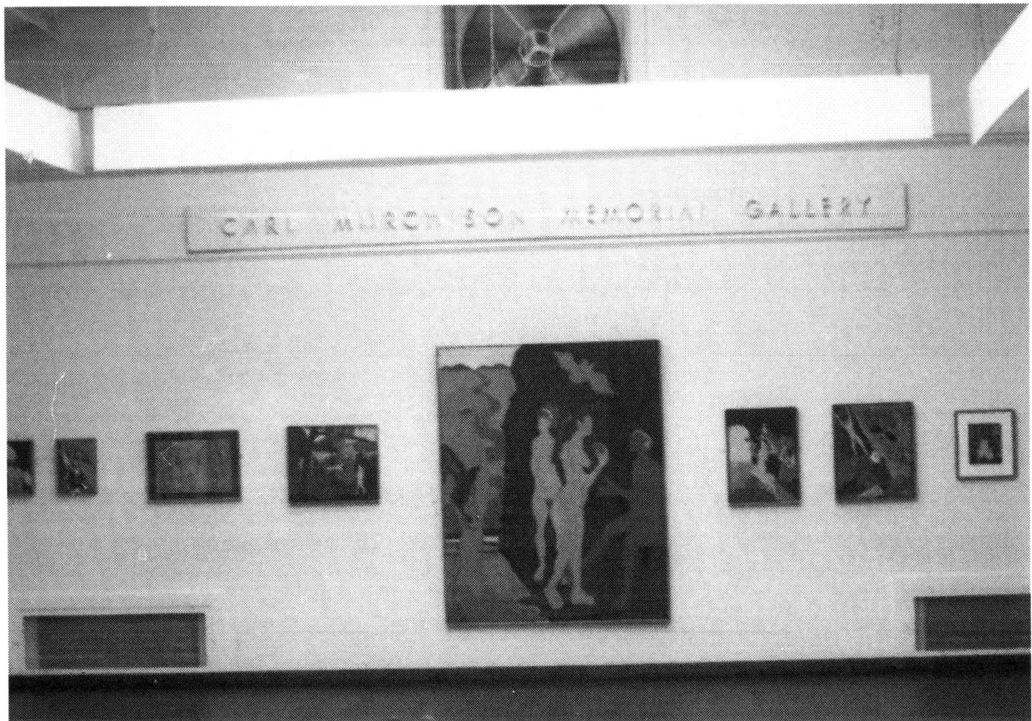

Works by Thompson, Giuliano photo.

The Jewelry Shop of Earle Montrose Pilgrim Became Sun Gallery

From 1951 to 1954 Earle Montrose Pilgrim (1923–1976) and his wife Lily (Touma) Pilgrim ran a jewelry store at 393 Commercial Street in Provincetown. Lily would craft dolls, hooked-rugs, and wrote for *The Advocate,* an early Provincetown newspaper. He taught jewelry-making in adult education programs authorized by the Massachusetts State Board of Education. They also lived in the small space.

Earle, then a student of Henry Hensche, displayed his work as well as that of other artists, including Lester Johnson and Alan Kaprow. In 1954, they moved to Boston with a shop at 80 West Cedar Street on Beacon Hill. The space on Commercial Street was taken over by the artist Yvonne Anderson and poet Dominic Falcone. For several years they ran Sun Gallery with an extensive roster of figurative expressionist artists.

While living in New York in the late 1960s, I got to know the Pilgrims through my friend, the *Boston Globe* journalist William J. Cardoso. He spoke fondly of Earle as an integral part of Boston's hipster element. Earle's acquaintances included tenor sax player Sam Rivers, band leader Herb Pomeroy, drummer Tony Williams, Zen philosopher Alan Watts, as well as Tim Leary and Baba Ram Das, who were experimenting with LSD. Earle did not participate, but Leary observed that Earle was naturally high.

That referred to mental disease that would result in treatment over many years of unstable behavior. "Cause of breakdown unknown; could have been due to physical, mental, and/or any one of the following: 2–3 years of obsessively overworking day and night without proper rest and sustenance, painting, filming, making jewelry, running jewelry and antique shop; difficulty in making money from painting and in starting business without sufficient capital; death of father; accumulation of years of frustration in coping with racial prejudice and finding a place in society, etc.," Lily wrote of his illness.

Tall and slender, Earle was an imposing presence. He had a sartorial flair and renowned flamboyance. The artist Tony Vevers referred to him as "The Earle of Pilgrim." That was largely a thing of the past when I befriended Earle and his attorney wife, Lily.

The Earle that I met in their New York loft, at 275 Church Street above avant-garde musician La Monte Young, was subdued and melancholy, but infused with wit and wisdom. There were years of instability, with Lily as loving care provider. It was a relatively rare night out when I would escort him to Max's Kansas City to hang with other artists. Much of his cutting-edge work had been lost over the years. These included Day Glo paintings and elaborate sets constructed in the Boston loft for performances and films.

In 1986, Ellen O'Donnell, then director, invited me to curate a major exhibition for the Provincetown Art Association and Museum. The curatorial essay for *Kind of Blue: Benny Andrews, Emilio Cruz, Earle Pilgrim and Bob Thompson* was published in the fall, 1986 issue of *Provincetown Arts Magazine*. It presented the work of four African American artists who worked in Provincetown. Thompson was later given a retrospective by the Whitney Museum of American Art.

There was a poignant meeting with Lily, then a widow, in her Washington, D.C. apartment. I was there to choose paintings for the exhibition. Works by Earle covered the walls, but were concealed with fabric covers. As we discussed the work, she explained that it was unbearable for her to look at them. That weekend we intensively engaged in discussion of the artist and his work. I packed the car and drove to Provincetown where I delivered the paintings to the museum.

The show then traveled to Northeastern University, where I organized a panel discussion with the artist Dana Chandler, art historian Patricia Hills, and MFA adjunct curator Edmund Barry Gaither. Judith Wilson, a co-curator of the Thompson's Whitney retrospective, attended the event.

Lily later contacted me as she was setting up a foundation to sustain his work. That continues now with Peter Stebbins as its head. After years of email exchanges, we met in Provincetown in October 2024, while conducting research. He curated *Looking for Earle, Earle Pilgrim Paintings and Jewelry from 1951–54* for the Truro Public Library. It was the first time I had seen the work since the 1980s.

Established in 2016, in the year before her death, The Lily and Earle M. Pilgrim Art

Foundation promotes the visual art of the African Diaspora, an appreciation of artists who lack public recognition, and public access to art through best practices in preservation and placement of culturally important artworks.

Earle was born in Brooklyn and raised at 206 Macon Street by his parents, Leon and Amy (Crane) Pilgrim who emigrated from Barbados. He had a sister, Enid.

He was educated in the public system until the end of sophomore year of high school, when he was expelled for wearing a top hat and coat at a school dance, instead of the required uniform. His father enrolled Earle in an apprenticeship with a printmaker. In 1943, he enlisted in the United States Army, assigned to the 477th Composite Group for the duration of the war, until he was court-martialed for refusing to defer to a white officer.

After service, he settled in Greenwich Village, where he learned jewelry-making through Sam Kramer. He studied at the Art Students League. Allan Malcolm Morrison (1916–1968) quoted Earle Pilgrim in "Twilight for Greenwich Village," published in the *Negro Digest,* Volume VII, Number 3, January 1949, "Bohemians don't fight or crusade," said Earl Pilgrim, a gaunt, bearded youth who haunts the San Remo Cafe and relaxes in Washington Park in the late afternoon. "We go on living our lives as we want to live them. To hell with the sneers of society. We're anti-bourgeois and we're individualists. We don't even like the name 'Bohemian.' It has a bad smell." He explained the only reason why he used the word was because his philosophy has to have a name and 'Bohemian' just happens to be most convenient."

It was absorbing to see a generous selection of the artist's paintings and metal work in Truro. There is scant documentation, so Stebbins selected work on a stylistic basis for when he was in Provincetown from 1951–1954. It comprises primarily portraits, a few landscapes, and still life paintings. In a wall case in another area of the library, small metal pieces and jewelry were displayed. The surprise of this project included two of Lily's small, vertical tapestries which are colorful and richly patterned. One of her dolls is attached to the top of a still life of a doll by Pilgrim.

While African American, via Barbados, race is not a signifier of the oeuvre. The many portraits display their social circle in Provincetown. The artist was committed to learning how best to paint and that did not include social justice themes. His concerns were formal and aesthetic.

The stylistic approach is a painterly naturalism which he learned from Hensche, who continued the tradition of Charles Hawthorne. In that regard, Pilgrim is readily identified as a Provincetown painter. He pushed the limits of naturalism with abstracted areas laid on with palette knife in broad strokes. By pushing the limits, his work is linked to that of other

Provincetown artists like Jan Müller, Jay Milder, Bill Barrell, and Lester Johnson, who are regarded as figurative expressionists. He did not know Bob Thompson. who arrived and showed at Sun Gallery after the Pilgrims had left town.

Pilgrim was Black and an artist, but it is not productive to identify his work as Black art. It is more appropriate to see him as a very talented young painter. There are many flashes of brilliance in these works that make all the more tragic his struggles to establish a successful career. These enticing works provide elements of what might have been. Because of his erratic personal life, the larger, later work has not survived.

After Earle died, in her later years, Lily established resources to create a foundation. Although she was an attorney, Stebbins reported that there were expensive efforts to establish the foundation and its claim to her primary asset, three condo units in Washington, D.C. Her apartment, which houses the work, was sealed by the court until the case was settled.

When access was gained, it was discovered that there had been a leak from above that destroyed a number of works on paper. Lacking resources for archival storage, the work remains in her former apartment. The other two units generate income that covers basic costs of the foundation.

The Truro exhibition was a rare opportunity for the work to be seen. It underscores the need for further study and curatorial support for an important Provincetown-based artist. The *Kind of Blue* exhibition was an early attempt to examine the role of Black artists in a compatible creative community.

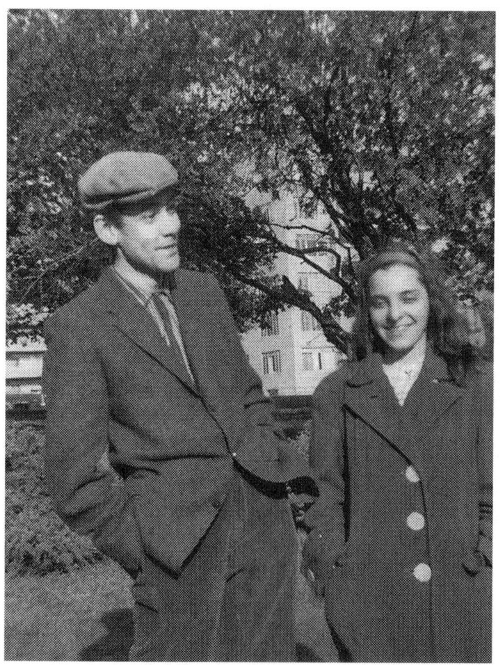

Earle and Lily Pilgrim. Courtesy of Pilgrim Foundation.

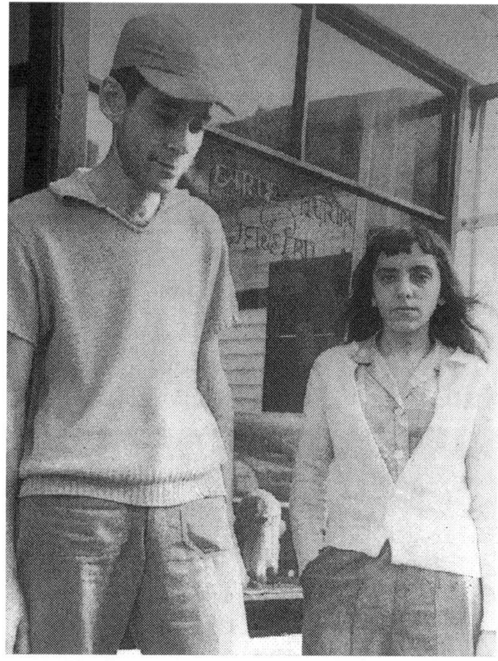

Earle and Lily in front of their Provincetown shop. Courtesy of Pilgrim Foundation.

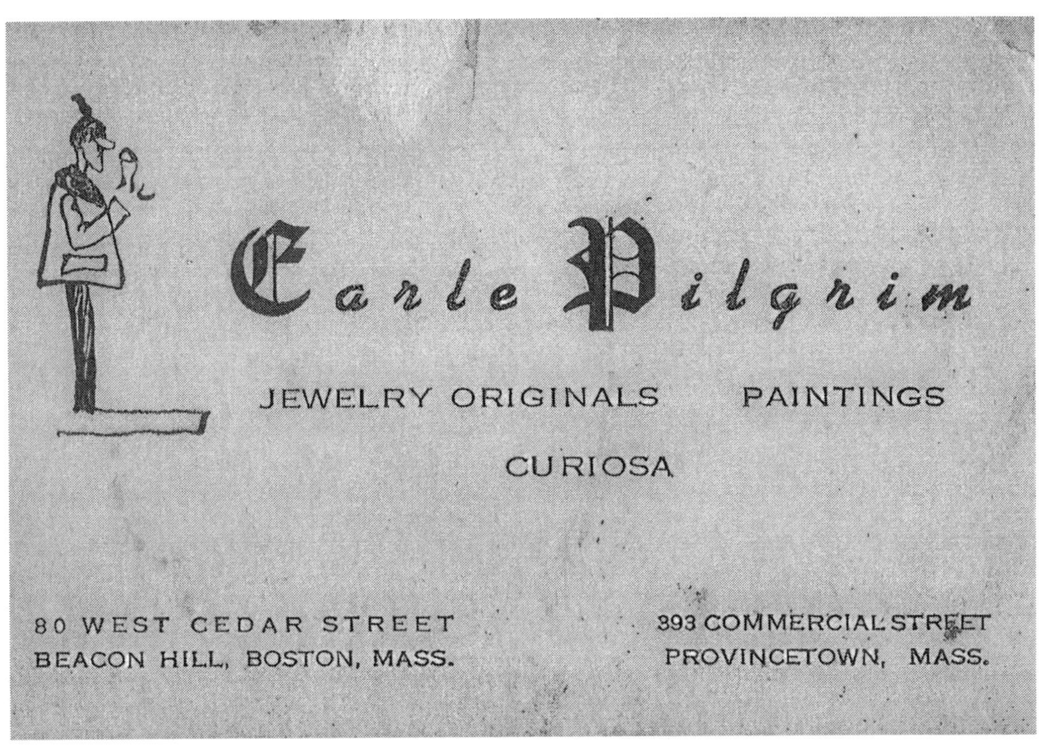

Business card.

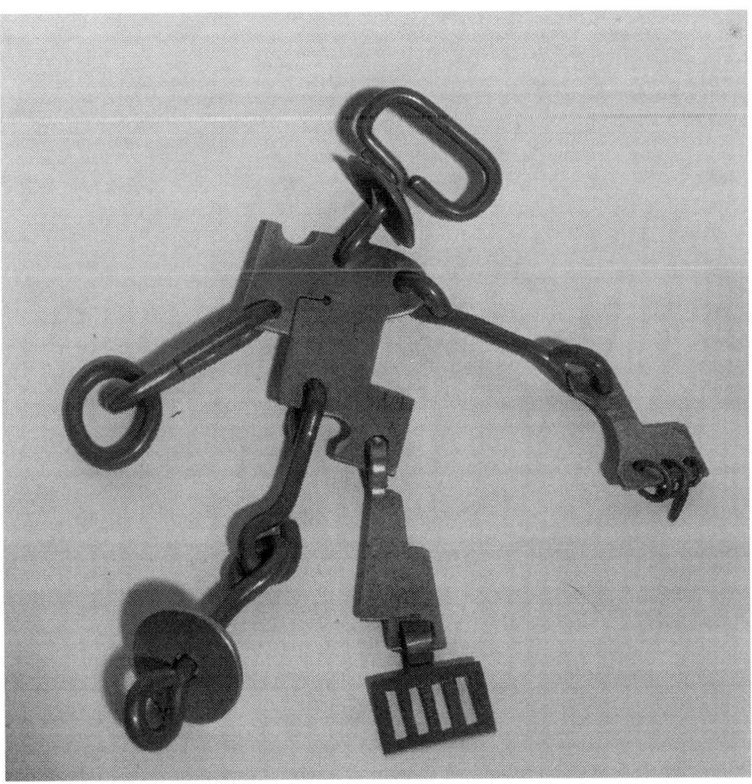

Metal work. Giuliano photo.

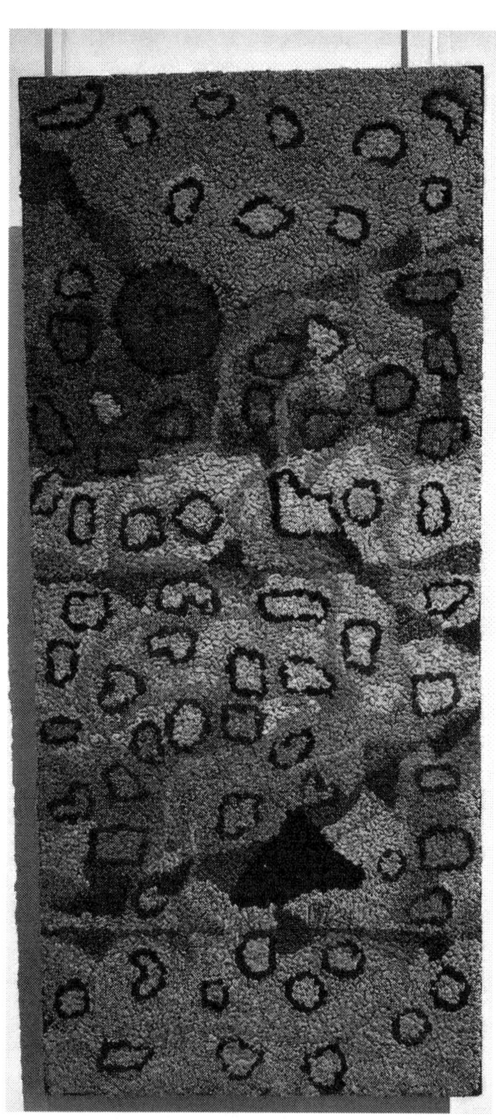

Tapestry by Lily Pilgrim. Giuliano photo.

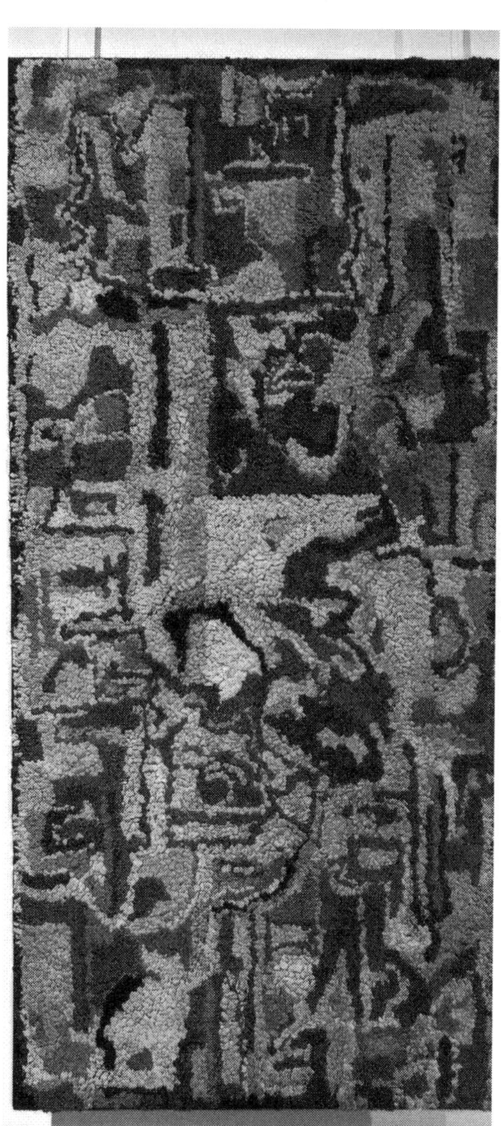

Tapestry by Lily Pilgrim. Giuliano photo.

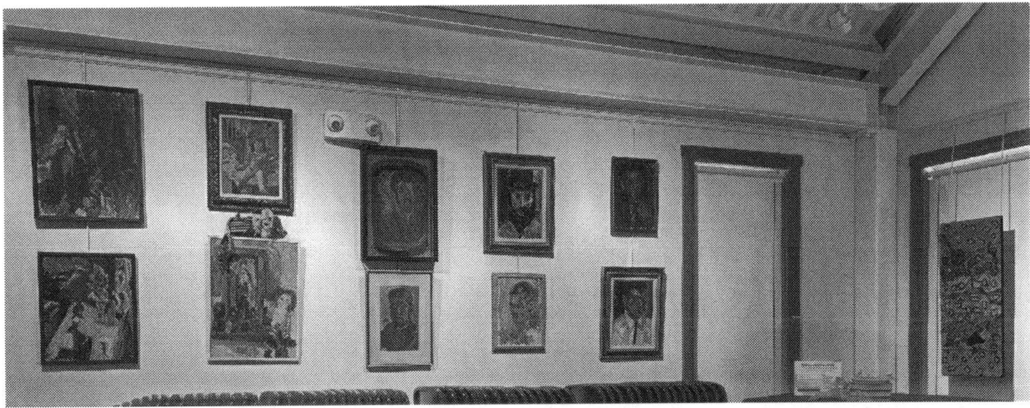

Installation at Truro Library, 2024, Giuliano photo.

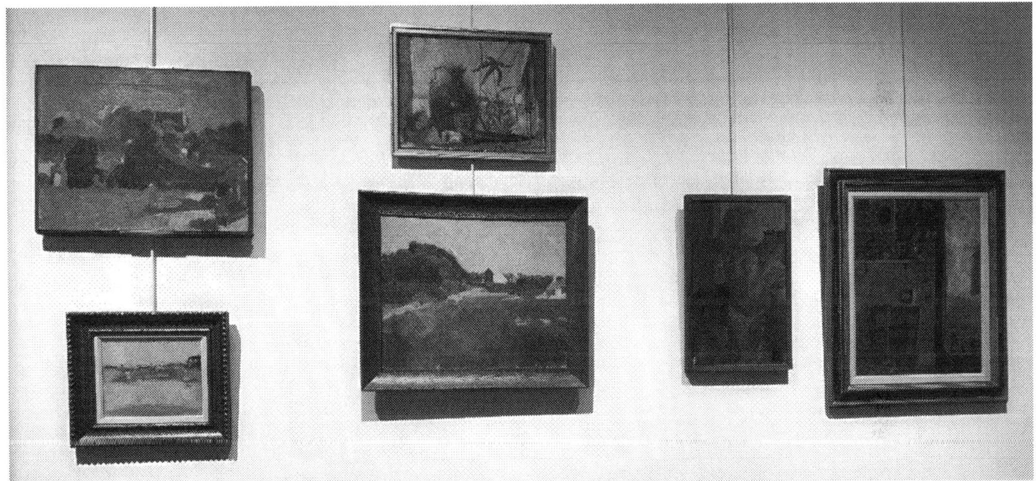

Landscape paintings. Giuliano photo.

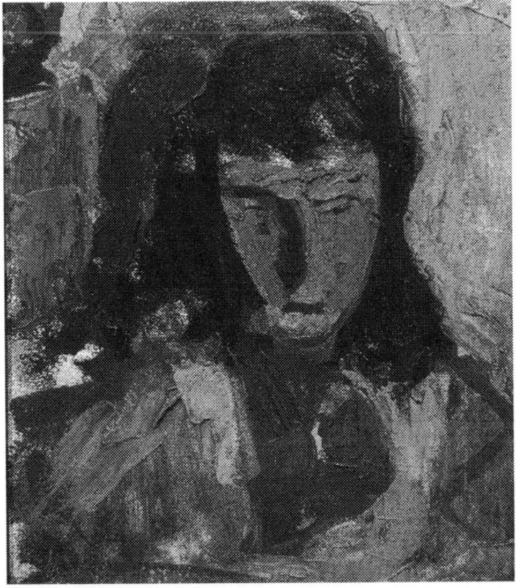

Figurative expressionist portrait of a woman. Giuliano photo.

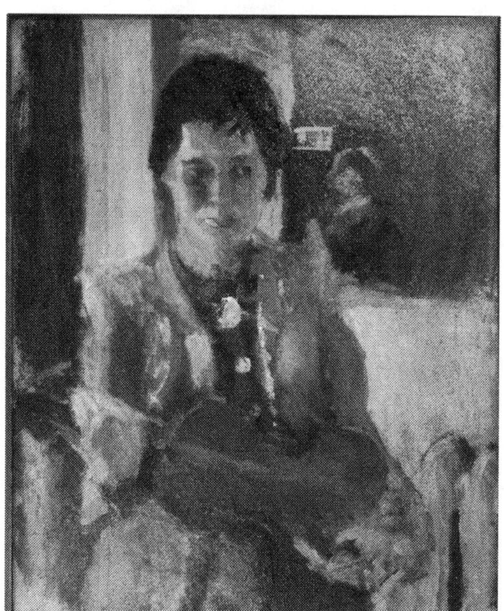

Girl with Violin. Giuliano photo.

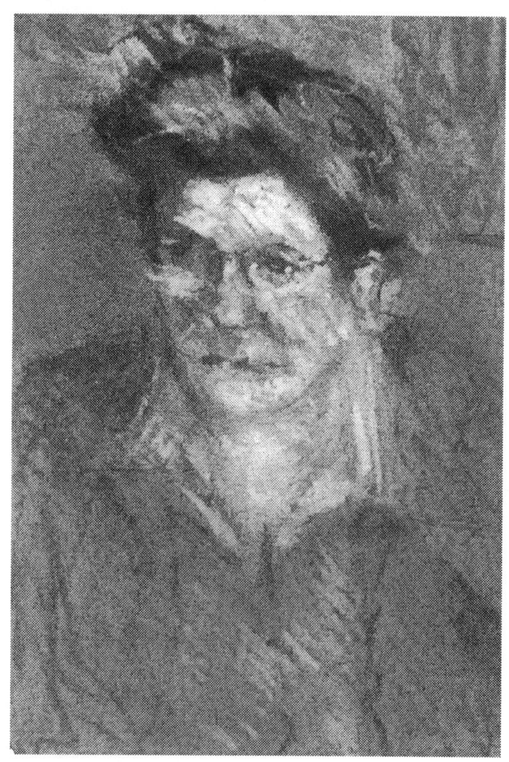

Pastel portrait of journalist *William J. Cardoso.* Giuliano photo.

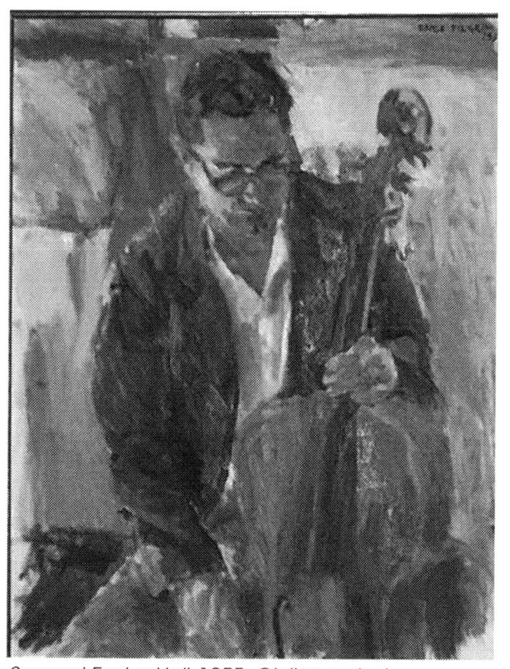

Samuel Foster Hall, 1955, Giuliano photo.

Minimalist Artist Myron Stout

Myron Stout (1908–1987) was an American abstract painter whose geometric paintings and drawings bridged the styles of abstract expressionism and minimalism.

He was born in Denton, Texas. During his senior year at North Texas State University, he decided to become a painter. He worked as a teacher, and spent part of his time painting landscapes. After military service in World War II, he resumed painting, and in 1946 began studies with Hans Hofmann. Stout's works of the period 1947–1952 show the influence of European geometric painting and typically feature multiple intersecting vertical and horizontal bands of color. After about 1950, single forms rather than patterns dominated some of his paintings.

In 1952, Stout relocated to Provincetown. In the autumn of that year his readings of Greek mythology, especially the tragedies of Sophocles and Aeschylus, inspired a new direction in his art. Working in black and white, usually on a small scale, he painted flat monolithic shapes which often resembled forks, shields, or lyres.

Stout worked slowly with no regard for careerism. He had an independent income and was not concerned with selling his work. Critic Hilton Kramer described the work as "a mode of abstraction small in scale, purist in form, and intimate in feeling—an art utterly devoid of expressionist bravura and emotional display."

Although he rarely exhibited, in 1954 he displayed charcoal drawings and paintings at the Stable Gallery in New York. In 1957 he showed at the Hansa Gallery in New York.

He was awarded a Guggenheim Fellowship in 1969.

Stout had a retrospective at the Contemporary Arts Museum in Houston in 1977, and a retrospective at the Whitney Museum of American Art in 1980. Over the years, I rarely encountered the work other than an exhibition at MIT's Hayden Gallery and an exhibition of drawings at the Fine Arts Work Center. Relatively unknown today, he was regarded by peers, curators, and critics as a singular abstract artist of his generation. The work is notable for originality and understated perfection.

Interview with Myron Stout
1984
Provincetown, Massachusetts

Charles Giuliano I doubt that you will remember, but we met in the 1960s. We were dinner guests of the artist Therese Schwartz, who knew you from Provincetown. It would have been 1967 or 1968. I had the impression that you visited New York infrequently.

Myron Stout Over the years I have gone less and less. I used to go quite often.

CG I saw your work at MIT's Hayden Gallery.

MS I thought they did a very nice job. I was there for the opening and can't remember the last time my work was shown in Boston. My ties are more with New York, where my gallery is located.

CG I am researching Karl Knaths and I understand that you were friends.

MS Yes, we were good friends and I can tell you how we met. In 1953, I came here for the winter and didn't know anyone. Of course, in the summer it was a different matter particularly as the New York art world came here. Around March, Kenneth Campbell came to my door and introduced himself. "There are not many of us during the winter," he said. "I am friends with Karl Knaths and we get together." I went with him to see Karl, who liked to do things on a regular basis.

He suggested that we get together on Wednesday afternoons. We probably had already met during the summer, but I can't recall. It was a matter of meeting at his studio, mine, or Kenneth's.

CG This is Day's Lumber Yard, right?

MS No. Kenneth had his studio at 11 Brewster and this is 4 Brewster, though it was built by Day's. The lumber yard was on Pearl Street.

These were built by Day as studios for artists over his lumber yard. Early on, Charles Hawthorne's classes were quite large, but there were no studios. Day knew a number of the artists and created studios for them. He made one set, then another. The Fine Arts Work Center is there now. Then he built this place, which originally had nine studios. The later landlord combined two spaces as his living quarters. Later, I persuaded the landlord to let me combine two spaces. Instead of having my living space and studio all together, I could have a separate studio. So, I have units 4 and 5.

I remodeled it, making it more spacious. We often met here before I did that, as well as after. I've had this space since 1955 and remodeled it 1962–1963. It's an ideal place to live, with plenty of light. Most Provincetown artists, at some point, have lived at Day's Lumber Yard. Karl told me that, at first, he lived in a net shack on Commercial Street.

CG According to legend, Charles Demuth and Eugene O'Neill also lived there at one time.

MS It may be true, but I don't know about that. He got into a New York play group and came here with them. Karl did work with them, I heard him talk about that. It was when O'Neill was here. You know Karl's early history of how he came here from the Midwest. When we met, he was somewhat older than I. Ken and Jim Forsberg were younger. He was translating a book of Einstein's, the art critic, not the scientist; his book on cubism. He was translating it, but didn't feel his German was good enough. His German was what he spoke with his family. It was an important work which had not been translated. He would work on it, then come and read it to us.

CG Didn't Joan (Wye) Forsberg read German?

MS Yes, she did and could contribute to a certain extent. Her German was fresher because she had been born there. Her first years were in Germany but her language wasn't scholarly. None of us had that, including Karl.

CG Where did you fit in?

MS I'm the one who tried to fit it all into English. Karl, when translating, tended to use German syntax. He was educated in Chicago, but still talked with "Dese" and "Dem." I think he liked playing the hick. I used to tease him and say, "Karl you know better than that." When he got excited, the accent was quite genuine.

CG Jim Forsberg said that he liked to play different roles. He would talk one way with colleagues and peers, and another way with the fishermen. Forsberg said that he liked to wear different hats. (In fact, Wye stated that he had some 18 hats for different worker roles.)

MS He had a great interest in people and always wanted to fit in. When he was with a scholar, he discussed philosophy, about which he was well read. I'm sure if he was talking with fishermen he adapted to their way of speaking.

CG Did he discuss theory with you?

MS There was constant talk of theory. He would discuss the Ostwald color system and insist that he was quite free within it. But I didn't agree. I think that color is very intuitive, no matter how much you make gradations and classifications. When it comes to painting, if you have a feeling for it, your own sense tells you what to do rather than having a chart to go by. When it comes to logarithms, you need a chart. But, for me, you don't need one for color.

(The Ostwald color system is a color space that was invented by the Baltic German chemist Wilhelm Ostwald. Associated with *The Color Harmony Manual,* it comprises a set of paint tabs representing the Ostwald color space. There are four different editions of the *Color Harmony Manual.* Each manual is made up of charts, with each chart being a different color space.)

I found it very rigid. I don't know how much of an effect it actually had on his painting because he has his own color sense. He has a strong feeling for the French color sense. Many of his works had a French impressionist or post-impressionist feeling. There is a certain thing about the French use of color.

CG He never went to Europe.

MS But his god was Juan Gris and, of course, Cezanne. He had a copy of Kahnweiler's book on Gris. He loaned it to me and I was delighted to have at it. There was a lot of talk about it because I read it, then one or two others of our circle also read it. Cubism was his basis, and he tried to work out what he learned from the paintings. He had a library of reproductions.

(Daniel-Henry Kahnweiler (1884–1979) was a German-born art collector, and one of the most notable French art dealers of the 20th century. He became prominent as an art gallery owner in Paris beginning in 1907 and was among the first champions of Pablo Picasso, Georges Braque, Juan Gris, and cubism.)

CG Did you visit his home?

MS Yes. He would get out his latest work and ask, "Tell me what you think? Don't be nice, just tell me what you think." He wouldn't hesitate to say what he thought. He would say, "I like this, but you people are younger and have a different point of view."

CG Your work was very different. Was there a basis for mutual respect?

MS We shared a basis in cubism. You couldn't get away from that; it was just too basic. Particularly later in life, he was laying things out with a lot of black lines, which I didn't agree with. I'm not sure whether I told him that.

CG Jim Forsberg did.

MS We probably talked about it and he likely defended himself. For an artist so involved with theories of color, what was the black line doing there? Jim was probably more direct than I was. Those late paintings were very beautiful. He laid out the color before there were any lines. The color planes were laid out in a more or less cubist manner. To me they were beautifully composed and almost quite satisfying paintings. Then he would go back and start working on them. He had a fine sense of composition but representations of reality, whether it was close representation or not, that was somehow very close to him. He would lay out those paintings in a very beautiful manner with color planes. Then he worked his subject into, over, and through them. The best qualities of the structure by this reworking seemed to me to be weakened and diluted.

There were a lot of things we talked about other than painting. There was a time when (our group) was reading Greek drama. There were Jim and Joan, but it seems that there were more than the four of us. Someone else came. I can't remember who that might be.

CG Helen (Knaths's wife) never came.

MS Helen never left the house. When I remodeled this place, I had a big house warming with a hundred people in April 1962. I said, "Karl, bring Helen." She was something of a recluse. They would take drives and visit Washington, D.C. when he was teaching at the Phillips. She came to the party and had a glass of sherry. Karl said, "I don't really drink," then got in a few shots when she wasn't looking because she didn't approve of it. She wasn't interested in that kind of thing. Her interest was music, which she played at home. He maintained an intellectual life apart from their relationship.

CG When you visited, would she be sociable?

MS In her own home, Helen was a charming hostess.

CG Did you ever dine with them?

MS I was never invited and I don't know of anyone they invited. He generally had apprentices. He often took them in with room and board. He had several rental cottages. It was a good piece of land. There was someone to take care of things and clean the house. They would eat with them and I would hear about that. Helen was a stickler about everything and it had to be just so. Karl had his habits—almost the same routine every day. He got up, took his walk, had breakfast. I didn't like to take walks on cold mornings, but he said it was good for you. I tried it once, and didn't know at the time that I was beginning to have arthritis. I came home in terrible shape all that day. I said, "Karl, it may be fine for you but no good for me." It was part of his German background.

CG As a teenager he was apprenticed to an uncle, a baker.

MS I remember Karl saying something about that. He was late to attend art school and was slow about a lot of things. Then he went to New York, where he knew people from both places.

CG This is where Ross Moffett comes in. He also went to the Art Institute of Chicago, where they knew each other, as well as later in New York. It was Moffett who suggested that Karl come to Provincetown.

MS Is that how it was? Yes, he was close to Moffett.

CG Did you know Moffett?

MS Yes, but I wasn't close to him. I knew him best in his last years because he came on staff at Fine Arts Work Center. He was dying then and in bad shape. I knew that they had been close, not then, but in the early years.

CG The same was true with Edwin Dickinson.

MS Oh yes, he had fallen out with practically everyone. All the local artists he felt were old fogies and he told them so before I was around. You know the whole story of the division (modern vs. traditional). Ambrose Webster was one (modernist) and they stuck with Karl. When Charles Demuth was here, he was singular while the rest of them were Hawthorne students and academicians according to Karl.

CG Edwin Dickinson was a Hawthorne student.

MS Yes, a favorite student, and certainly well known.

CG Did you know Dickinson?

MS Yes, I knew him. He was about the same age as Karl.

CG Karl died in 1971 (born October 21, 1891)

MS Helen died just four or five years ago.

CG She lived to be 105.

MS I wasn't surprised. As you know, she never did anything.

CG She was some 18 years older than him.

MS Yes, way older. Her sister Agnes I believe was younger. (Agnes Weinrich 1873–1946 was an artist. Today her work is highly regarded.)

CG Many people comment that they were surprised that he married Helen and not Agnes.

MS I heard him speak of Agnes more often than of Helen. He respected her work, which is based on cubism that she studied in Paris with Albert Gleizes (1881–1953). From friends I got the impression that he was in love with Agnes, but she persuaded him that Helen was the one he should marry. It was peculiar, and I could never decide if it was a real marriage. They got along.

I don't ever think it was a love match. We had great respect for her and treated her well. She had a sense of humor and could laugh about some of his foibles. When he said something, she looked at me and when he left the room she grinned. But it was not an unkind thing, but I never saw it as a sign of affection. I felt there had been an accommodation of some kind. Before she died, he had Agnes in the house as a fellow artist and Helen as his wife. He had Agnes as a colleague and painter. The death of Agnes was a great blow to him, though I did not know him at the time.

CG When did you come to Provincetown?

MS I first came in 1938 but didn't return until 1946.

CG Were you here for *Forum '49*?

MS I was here for part of it. Late in the summer I went to Europe. I remember several of the forums, including one where Karl was a speaker. He was interested in all that was going on because that was the beginning of the avant-garde. That was the summer when *Life Magazine* published an article on Jackson Pollock with big lettering that asked, "Is This Art," or something like that.

CG Do you consider yourself to be an abstract expressionist? Where do you fit in?

MS I was never at all an abstract expressionist. I was an abstract artist. In the beginning I worked both ways. My teaching was very liberal right from the beginning. My teachers were open to everything.

CG Who did you study with?

MS I studied with a man called Chris Martin. I learned by reading Meyer Shapiro, who he had studied with. Martin was at Teachers College of Columbia. It was the most advanced art department in the country from the time when it was started by Arthur (Wesley) Dow.

(Arthur Wesley Dow was born in Ipswich, Massachusetts in 1857 and died in 1922. In 1884, he went to Paris for his early art education, studying at the Académie Julian under the supervision of the academic artists Gustave Boulanger and Jules Joseph Lefebvre. In 1893, Dow was appointed assistant curator of the Japanese collection at the Museum of

Fine Arts, Boston, under Ernest Fenollosa, who introduced him to ukiyo-e, the woodblock prints of Japan, which greatly influenced his later works.

He taught art at Pratt Institute from 1896 to 1903, and the New York Art Students League. In 1900, Dow founded the Ipswich Summer School of Art. From 1904 to 1922, he was a professor of fine arts at Columbia University Teachers College.)

> He was the teacher of Georgia O'Keeffe. He was Charles Martin's professor, who taught me. He taught here in the summer. I hadn't finished the course and he said come and study with me and I will give you the credit if you come and paint some. So, I came and painted with him in 1938. I didn't come back until after the war. Having stayed for the summer, I decided to stay on in the winter.
>
> As time went on, Jim and Joan Forsberg broke up, but I continued to work with Karl some and Angie Meyer, who was helping with the translations. We would get together in the afternoon during the week. I lived then just up the street before I came here. During the 1950s and 1960s, I saw Karl with great regularity. As the 1960s went on, I saw less and less of him. He was ill and eventually died. I didn't know he was ill until he was quite ill. It came as a surprise. as he was always healthy with a big frame and ruddy country cheeks.
>
> **CG** Can we talk about your work and how you came to be a non-objective artist?
>
> **MS** I don't know how best to describe myself. From the beginning I worked both abstractly and from nature. I was a landscapist, which I liked very much, which I painted a great deal. After the war I attended Hofmann's class on the GI Bill. I began to work abstractly and found it very satisfying. No matter how abstractly I worked, I still liked to work with models and landscapes.
>
> **CG** When did you start to work non-objectively and what was Hofmann's role?
>
> **MS** In 1946. It was perfectly natural to me. The abstract mode satisfied me. Hofmann was the most remarkable teacher I have ever known. He was not only himself a fine painter, he also knew how to project his meaning, intentions, and understanding. His classes were remarkable because they included people who were working in all different ways. He took people who worked naturalistically, impressionistically, abstractly, expressionistically, it didn't matter to him. He knew where you were and he had the ability to start from there and show you where it

was possible to go on.

CG Do you recall artists who were fellow students at that time?

MS A lot were the younger abstract expressionists like Mack Goldberg, Richard Stankiewicz, Larry Rivers. There were so many of them who were already different and they went on in their own ways. There was my good friend Jan Müller, who went on to be a figurative expressionist.

CG I notice that you have a small Jan Müller which is stunning. Did you know Bob Thompson, Jay Milder, and the Sun Gallery artists?

MS Yes, they were a bit younger. Bob was a friend of mine. It was John Frank who first brought him. We had a cooperative gallery one summer and John Frank was its director. He was teaching in Louisville and he brought Bob Thompson from there. It was Gallery 256. It went on to different incarnations with different artists. We nearly all withdrew and showed with Nat Halper's HCE gallery.

CG How old were you when you had your first New York show?

MS I had my first one-man show at Stable Gallery in 1954. By then I was older, compared to other artists. I was born in 1908 and graduated from college in 1930. I had a job teaching school which lasted for three years. During my last semester in college, I took a painting course and got hooked. That was at North Texas State University. I graduated with a double major in history and English.

I went back and did a complete undergraduate course in art. From there I went to graduate school. I finished in 1938 and managed to get a good job, but the war ended that. I was painting, but during the war that wasn't possible. I dropped out of painting and didn't get back into it until after the war, when I went to Columbia. My friend said I couldn't stop painting and urged me to come study with Hofmann. Once more I was on my way.

CG Did you sell anything in that 1954 show?

MS Not a thing, but I had the GI Bill for income. I served in the Pacific, but didn't see combat. First, I was in the Army, then the Air Force. I stayed on in New York into the next year, but the Stable Gallery director wasn't doing anything for me. My friends asked me to join Hansa Gallery on Twelfth Street. This is when all the galleries were in Tenth Street. I declined because I thought I had a chance to show uptown. But when nothing happened, I left Stable and joined Hansa. When we closed Hansa, Richard Bellamy started Green Gallery. He has represented me all this time and the gallery is now known as Oil and Steel. There was a time in between when he dealt privately, but he still represented me. I never had but two people that represented me in my entire career.

CG I noticed from labels for your MIT show that the works were dated over a long time. Is this typical of how you work?

MS Yes, that's true. I keep a lot of paintings going.

CG The labels give the impression that you work on a painting for ten years.

MS But you don't work on it for ten years. You work on it over a period of ten years, or twenty. But the painting may be put away for a long time. There are paintings I first laid down in the late 1950s. There were two in the Whitney show that I didn't finish until 1979.

CG How do you decide that a painting is finished?

MS That's part of the business of putting it away. This idea of working on paintings for a long time started when I began to work in black and white and paintings with shapes more than in a geometrical way.

CG The earlier paintings were more patterned and colored like those I saw at MIT.

MS Yes, and for the most part they didn't take that long, just an average amount of time. When I got into black and white, it slows down and took longer to realize what they had to be.

There comes a time when you wear out being concerned with it. So, it is time to put it away and take out something else. Take out something and work on it for months or perhaps just a few weeks. Put that away and take out something else. It doesn't make for being a prolific painter.

CG Can you estimate how much you have produced?

MS No, but probably not as much as most painters. But I was also making drawings, the black and white charcoals. They are like paintings because they are so completely realized. They are not just drawings. I was also working on them all the time as well. There have been many more black and white drawings, but I can't tell you how many.

(I saw a show of the drawings around that time at the gallery of Fine Arts Work Center.)

CG Do you ever destroy work?

MS I do on occasion. I have work that's experimental where I have gone in different directions. I wasn't satisfied and never showed it. I still have work of that kind.

CG You went in your own direction. Was there anyone at the time working in a similar manner?

MS The group American Abstract Artists (AAA) has been together since the 1930s. They worked abstractly and, for lack of a better term, hard edge. That's a terrible term. It may be a clear or clean edge, but I don't like the implication of hard.

CG Do you mean artists like Leon Polk Smith (1906–1996), Ilya Bolotowsky (1907–1981) and Nassos Daphnis (1914–2010)?

MS Bolotowsky was part of the original group, as was Perle Fine (1905–1988, she studied with Hofmann in New York and Provincetown). It was quite a good-sized group.

CG Were you a member?

MS Someone put me up in the 1950s, but they turned me down. Later they invited me, but I wouldn't join.

CG Were you hurt by being rejected?

MS One is never pleased by being turned down. I wasn't that upset because I didn't care for most of the work. I don't think Leon Polk Smith was a member, as he was younger when he came along. I recall meeting and talking with him. We were acquaintances. Nearly all of them stayed close to Mondrian's neo-plastic ideas. I felt that was dogmatism that didn't serve any useful purpose. That's why I was happier to go my own way and find what I needed. I've worked in a very rigorous neo-plastic way, rigorous neo-classical say, so to speak.

CG The earlier works in color?

MS No, not at all, they were all Mondrianesque, but often in the charcoal drawings. Bolotowsky, for example, kept very close to the neo-plastic thing, even with the constructions that he made. I felt they were inadequate. I didn't like the direction that Fritz Glarner (1899–1972) went in. Who was the other artist who painted quite beautifully?

CG Nassos Daphnis?

MS Nassos is an old friend of mine. He came and showed with us at Gallery 256 in 1954. I had many friends among the hard-edge painters. I had great respect for them. For my own work, however, I had to find it for myself.

CG Where does Ellsworth Kelly (1923–2015) fit in?

MS I never even saw his work because he was living in Paris. When he came back, I didn't know him.

CG Jack Youngerman (1926–2020)?

MS I knew his work, and saw Kelly's at the Whitney. I thought it showed great promise. Of course, now I can't see anyone's work because I can't see any longer, in the way that I really need to see it in order for it to register. But Kelly's work in the 1950s and 1960s, he's a remarkable artist, but I felt a lack of personal content. A depth of content, so to speak, that was not satisfying. But I don't like to be critical of artists who are alive and whom I respect as artists.

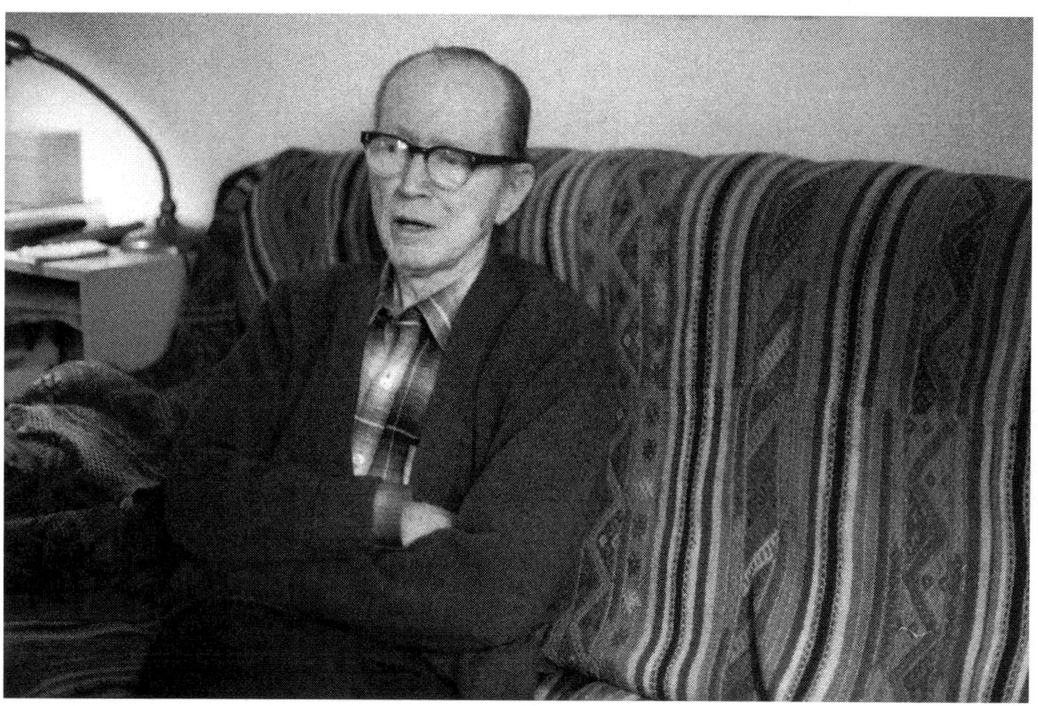

At home with Myron Stout. Giuliano photo.

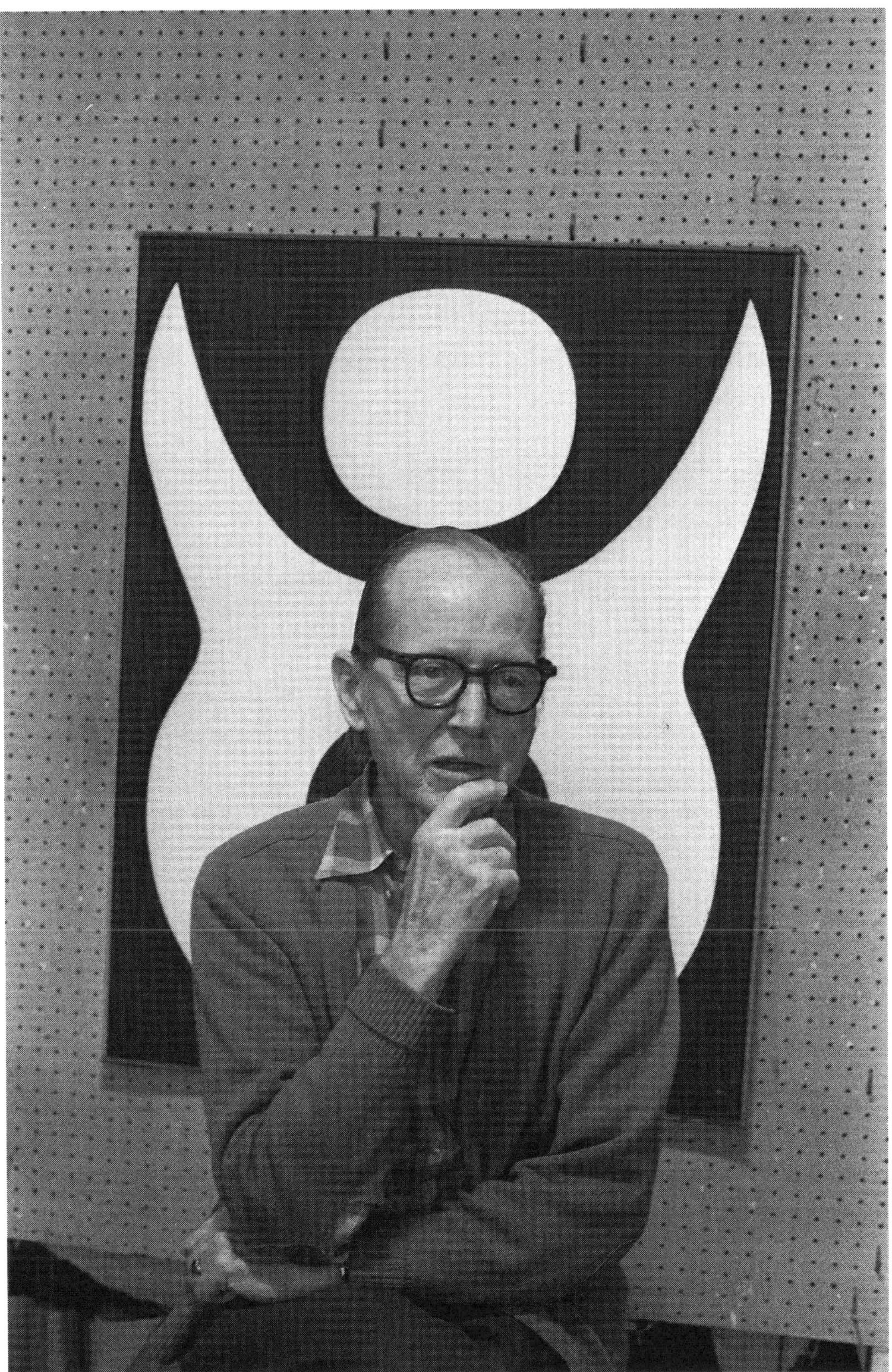

Myron Stout. Photo by Norma Holt. Courtesy of PAAM.

Figurative Expressionist Lester Johnson Showed at Sun Gallery

In Provincetown Lester Johnson had five annual one-man-shows at the legendary Sun Gallery. That was the most for any of its galleries. With Bob Thompson, Jan Müller, and Tony Vevers, also of Sun Gallery, he was a leader of the generally overlooked figurative expressionist movement. What follows was the obituary I published for *Berkshire Fine Arts* June 17, 2010.

Lester Johnson (January 27, 1919 to May 30, 2010) was one of the leading exponents of figurative expressionism. The movement which included artists in New York, Provincetown, Chicago, and San Francisco emerged in response to the non-objective aspects of abstract expressionism. While it flourished during the late 1950s and early 1960s, it coincided with and was overshadowed by pop art.

There are many versions and interpretations of figurative expressionism. The lists appear to expand and contract with little or no consensus among curators and critics. Despite some key artists, the movement is widely viewed as marginal. There has been some cherry picking as individual artists have been researched and shown. But cohesive study, exhibitions, and publications remain unrealized. While there have been isolated exhibitions and catalogs, they tend to further obfuscate a complex history.

In 1986, I was asked to write an essay on Johnson for a traveling exhibition organized by Paul A. Chew, the director of the Westmoreland Museum of Art in Greensburg, Pennsylvania. The project was coordinated by Carl Hecker, the director of the David

Anderson Gallery. There were meetings in the warehouse of the gallery, which was in essence the estate of art dealer Martha Jackson. She had represented Johnson, as well as the African-American artist Bob Thompson (1937–1966). It was Lester who urged Jackson to show Thompson's work.

Over several months I met with Lester in New York and his Connecticut studio. In addition to researching his work, we also discussed the "return of the figure," the debates of the Artists' Club in New York, and the exhibitions of the Sun Gallery in Provincetown.

Lester was frank and insightful in providing a narrative of his own development and relationship to peers. I came to conclude that he, along with Jan Müller (1922–1958) and Thompson, were the leading figurative expressionists of the Provincetown/New York school. My research led to exploring parallel developments in San Francisco focused on David Park (1911–1960), Richard Diebenkorn (1922–1993), Nathan Oliveira (Born 1928), and Joan Brown (1938–1990). There were strong parallels to the early work of Leon Golub (1922–2004) in Chicago.

A major challenge entailed tracking the course of figurative expressionism as a tributary of abstract expressionism. Looking back at that era in the late 1950s and early 1960s, it is important to consider the passion with which movements and their differences were discussed and debated.

Speculation about a return to the figure among avant-garde artists came to a head when Peter Selz organized *New Images of Man* for the Museum of Modern Art in 1959. That seminal exhibition offers few clues to the dialogue among American artists. Selz conflated European and American masters. Of the curators of his generation, Selz had the best shot of defining the artists of the figurative expressionist movement, but mishandled the possibility.

In Provincetown there was lively activity with the legendary Sun Gallery. During the postwar era, artists flocked to the Lower Cape. Many of the artists who showed with Sun Gallery were finding their way back to the figure. These included Tony Vevers (1926–2008), George Segal (1924–2000), Alex Katz (Born 1927), Red Grooms (Born 1937), Johnson and Thompson, Claes Oldenburg (Born 1929), Bob Beauchamp (1923–1995) Lester's brother-in-law, Benny Andrews (1930–2006), Bill Barrell (Born 1932), and Jay Milder (Born 1934).

When the focus of figurative expressionism faltered, the Rhino Horn movement was active from 1967 to 1978. These artists included: Benny Andrews, Luis Cruz Azaceta, Ken Bowman, Emilio Cruz, Peter Dean, Stuart Diamond, Mary Frank, Lionel Gongora, Joseph Kurhajec, Charles Parness, Peter Passuntino, Peter Saul, George Segal, and Nicholas Sperakis.

Of the first generation of Provincetown/New York figurative expressionists, the most important were Johnson, Müller, and Thompson. Jan Müller died at 36 in 1958 and Bob Thompson was dead at 29 in 1966. Arguably, Müller and Thompson were among the most gifted, inventive, and lyrical artists of their generation. One may only speculate the impact had they sustained through longer careers.

While Johnson died at 91, the mantle of leadership rested uneasily on his shoulders. For his exhibition catalog, I endeavored to place him in context. Much of the material that appears above was included in an introduction. Through his daughter, Leslie DeTroy, I was informed that "Lester feels very strongly, however, that the 'introduction' section would be fine for a magazine article on art in general, or a book, but does not belong in a Lester Johnson catalog." (From a letter, November 20, 1986).

Then and now, however, it seems important to place the work into an historical context. Without this connective tissue, the tendency is to view him as an eccentric or maverick. He was neither. In his formative years, Lester was in the thick of the zeitgeist. It's what informs the passion, energy, and enduring power of those early primitive works. There was angst and reckless risk-taking. I feel something demonic in the frenzied execution of the early heads and figures. Taking from the abstract expressionists, he painted from the shoulder in broad, messy, drippy strokes.

From that period is a videotape he gave me of him in the act of painting. It was an all out, intuitive, unthinking train wreck of an attack on the canvas. All of his guts and energy went into the frenzy of the creative act. Those early works are remarkable for their fury and originality.

The Lester I came to know in the mid-1980s was very different from the glimpses of manic agita in that clip of vintage film. By then he was emotionally and financially comfortable, though somewhat guarded and understated. He was an adjunct professor at Yale University. There were interesting ideas of teaching life drawing. The students were asked to draw with both hands or to start with the foot and work their way to the head. He was trying to break up the usual instincts.

The Bowery, where he shared a studio with Larry Rivers early on, had been the source of inspiration and conflict in the work. There were the surging cityscapes, and cavorting *Men in Hats*. The urban environment was a locus for his inspiration. They were invented, rather than observed, figures with an emphasis on mass and volume. The figures were smashed into the space at rakish angles. There were vectors as they deflected humanistic impulses. Lester was striving to find the essence of universal man. The details and specifics failed to engage him. The figure was a metaphor for the turmoil and conflict flowing through him.

The resultant works were among the most potent conundrums of his generation. Even now there is no consensus on what to think about them.

In a 2004 review, Hilton Kramer approached the work as "...some painters have made it a fundamental tenet of their art to resist the templates of their own facility. Rather than aiming for ease of expression, they deliberately cultivate certain obstacles to it, either through distortion in draftsmanship or by creating a facture that eschews suavity in favor of a distressed painterly surface. Figurative painters who came of age in the heyday of abstract expressionist aesthetic were especially likely to play a role in this effort to undermine the effects of facility."

The trajectory from Skid Row and cold-water flats to Greenwich, Connecticut and summers in East Hampton is vividly evident in the work. The generic bowler hats and boxy suits evolved into Yankee's baseball caps. The strongly rendered, angular women became attired in the printed fabrics of designer Emilio Pucci. They intrigued Lester for their color and design. The profiles and soft, flowing hair of the women edged ever more to the classical. If his youth was devoted to Dionysus in later years he succumbed to Apollo. East Hampton inspired him to depict bathers on the beach.

During his student years in Chicago, Johnson was painting small, impressionist landscapes. From 1947 to 1951 this continued in New York. The works were portable enough to take around to galleries. He told me it was an effective strategy, "At least they can't say 'We'll get back to you, just leave the slides.' They either have to look at them (small paintings) or tell you to get them out of there."

He got a response from the dealer Charles Egan, who made a studio visit. Egan told him he didn't have enough work for a show. "I was going to make more paintings for him," Lester recalled. "In the meantime, I got involved with expressionism. When I went back to Egan, I had paintings with wild figures and bright colors, and he responded absolutely negatively. He even got angry and wanted to know what I was trying to pull. He thought I was wild. He liked me and liked my work enough to be angry...When I had a show (1951) at the Artists' Gallery, Charlie Egan came and saw it, but again, he was turned off."

In 1954 Johnson showed with the Marvin Korman Gallery. The following year the stable was merged with the Virginia Zabriski Gallery. In 1962, he was taken on by Martha Jackson Gallery. In more recent years, when Jackson's son, David Anderson, moved out of New York, he returned to Zabriski. For the past few years, Johnson has been with the David Klein Gallery in Birmingham, Michigan. The gallery is in the process of negotiating to represent the estate.

A change in Johnson's work occurred in 1951. Over a two-week period, he was using a mirror to paint a self-portrait. One afternoon he painted out the image. "I was free to start again," he recalled. "I had three colors on my palette and started making diamonds. Two on the top, two on the bottom, and two on the sides, one in the middle." He realized that it was about his family and that "I was the one trapped in the middle." I asked Lester if he still had that painting, but it never surfaced.

In the Kramer piece in the *New York Observer* (October 24, 2004), he quotes a Dore Ashton catalog statement. She wrote that the change to expressionism occurred when Johnson saw a Giacometti exhibition at Pierre Matisse Gallery in 1948. Lester never mentioned that to me. I do not know if any work of that period survives. Kramer compared the paintings of Johnson to the paintings and sculptures of Giacometti. It strikes me as an apples and oranges argument.

Lester elaborated on the importance of the Diamonds painting (my title) from 1951. "I thought that this painting really worked. It really goes across the canvas. It goes up and down. It's natural. But then I said 'no it's not done.' I took a tube of paint and squeezed it right out of the tube painting faces in each of the seven diamonds. I was real happy, but I had no idea what it was all about."

There is a visceral series of heads, mostly in small scale, owned by the Lannan Foundation in West Palm Beach, Florida. J. Patrick Lannan, like Walter Chrysler and Joseph Hirshhorn, was noted for buying the content of an artist's studio at bargain-basement prices. While it exploited cash-strapped artists, this also had the result of preserving key periods in depth.

The Lannan Foundation occupied a former movie theater. There were many curiosities. This included an important series by Johnson. They were almost minimalist monochromes (from the 1960s) in which the features were scratched into the paint. Now that the Foundation has moved, I don't know what has become of these works.

Irving Sandler told me about how he ran the panels and lectures at the Artists' Club. Lester was a rare non-abstract member. "There were always fights up there," he recalled. "It was a mess to get into the place, but once you got in, it was organized. Every Friday night they would have a panel and it was like a Union Hall meeting. There was always a bottle of liquor on the speaker's table. They tried to establish a frontier mentality. Just guys sitting up there drinking and talking. Nobody was going to stick their neck out in that kind of a situation. It was seldom that you got anything really meaty. There were fights between factions. But there were no figurative painters there. I mean, I was a figurative painter. Philip Pearlstein was a member, but he wasn't painting the figure at that time. Alfred Leslie was a member, but he was doing abstract work. It was pretty much an abstract expressionist club. I was on a panel a couple of times and I took my lumps, but got my two cents in. I was asked to give a live presentation of my own work. Years later, I ran into Ray Parker who remembered my talk and asked if I still paint using both my hands."

Although Johnson and Thompson were not included in *New Images of Man,* they were increasingly respected in the community of artists. In addition to the art world Thompson was hanging out with jazz musicians. His masterpiece *Garden of Music* (6-foot by 12-foot, the Wadsworth Athenaeum) depicts an ensemble of avant-garde musicians, including Ornette Coleman and Charlie Haden.

From 1961–62 Johnson accepted a position as artist-in-residence at Ohio State University. As he conveyed to me, it was the wrong time to be out of town. When he returned, everything had changed. At that time, Sam Hunter, the founding director of the Rose Art Museum, acquired some 25 works with about $40,000 from the Mnuchin and Gervirtz families. Hunter hedged his bets with acquisitions of abstract expressionism, color field, and pop art. Significantly, he ignored examples of figurative expressionism. It was the pop selections that are now evaluated in the millions. Prime examples of figurative expressionism from that period are estimated in the low-to-mid six figures.

In 1964, Jack Tworkov, the chair of the department, recommended Johnson for an adjunct position at Yale, which continued until 1989. From 1969–1974, Lester was the Director of Studies for Graduate Painting.

After that frustrating attempt at a self-portrait in 1951, Johnson rarely painted from observation. In 1971, James Joyce surfaced in an ensemble of *Men in Hats.* There is a rare portrait of his son, Tony. By the 1980s the figures and costumes were more decorative and representational. As Kramer correctly observed, he resisted becoming too facile. Arguably, he was picking up details of the world he lived in. From the T-shirts of Tony and his pals, to the colorful dresses of the social circuit in Connecticut and East Hampton.

Of these more colorful and decorative elements, he said, "I don't think that they should be fashion. I really don't. I think they have to be more universal. I used Pucci, the colors, and the design. But I try to make it into a harder content. I mix things up. No one would ever wear that. You just wouldn't put these two together. I think it's important to keep it universal. If it becomes specific fashion, it points to limitations. I don't like specifics in that sense. I don't like paintings that tell stories. I'm not involved with any kind of anecdotal painting."

With Lester, a self-imposed isolation from artists and the mainstream was a personal choice. He seemed to have little interest in the art world, which largely returned the favor. There was an understated resentment about being passed over. He resisted having his work discussed in comparison to other artists.

Commenting on the commercialism of the art world, he told me, "You go back to Titian and Rubens, and I think you wouldn't find that to be true. They had something to say. There was something more for them than just making art. Art was a vehicle for their expression. Once you got into 'Art for art's sake' it's like listening to yourself sing. There is no communication, and there's no priority for expression. Art just becomes something to buy."

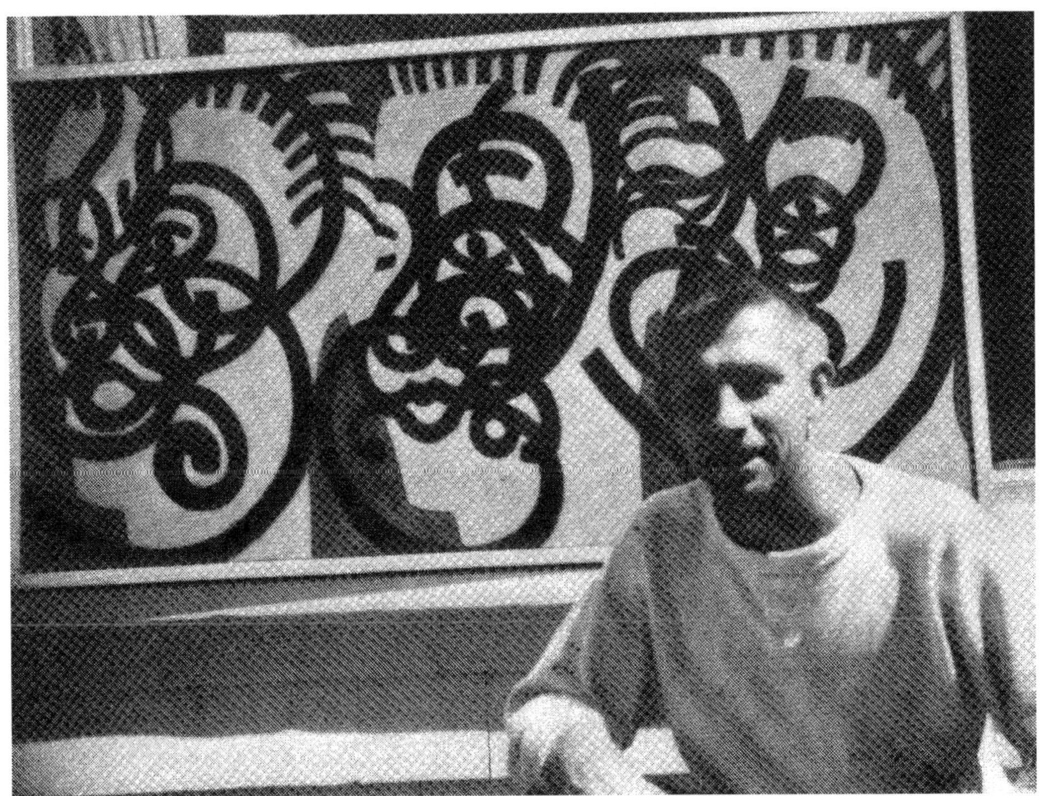

Young Lester showed at Sun Gallery. Courtesy of Yvonne Andersen.

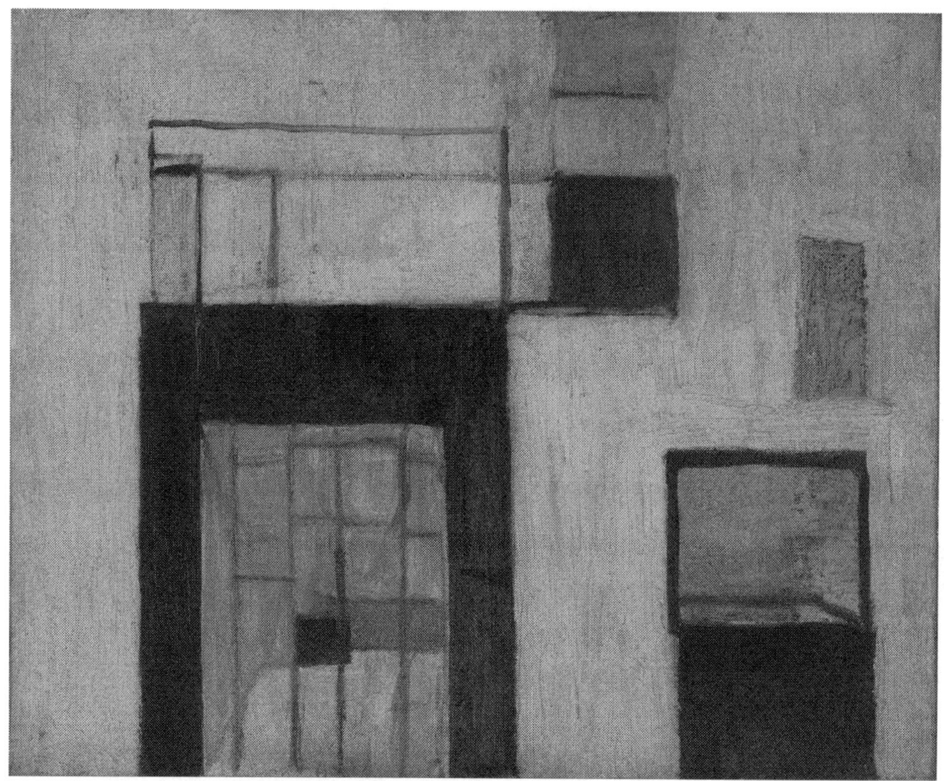

Bowery Door. Courtesy of Acme Gallery.

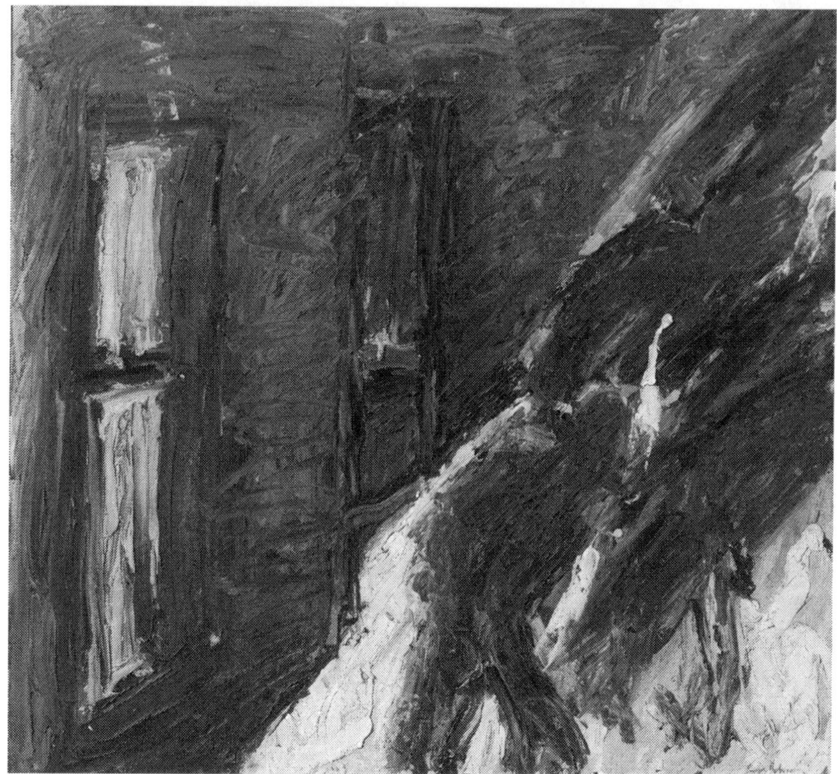

City Street Scene. Courtesy of Acme Gallery.

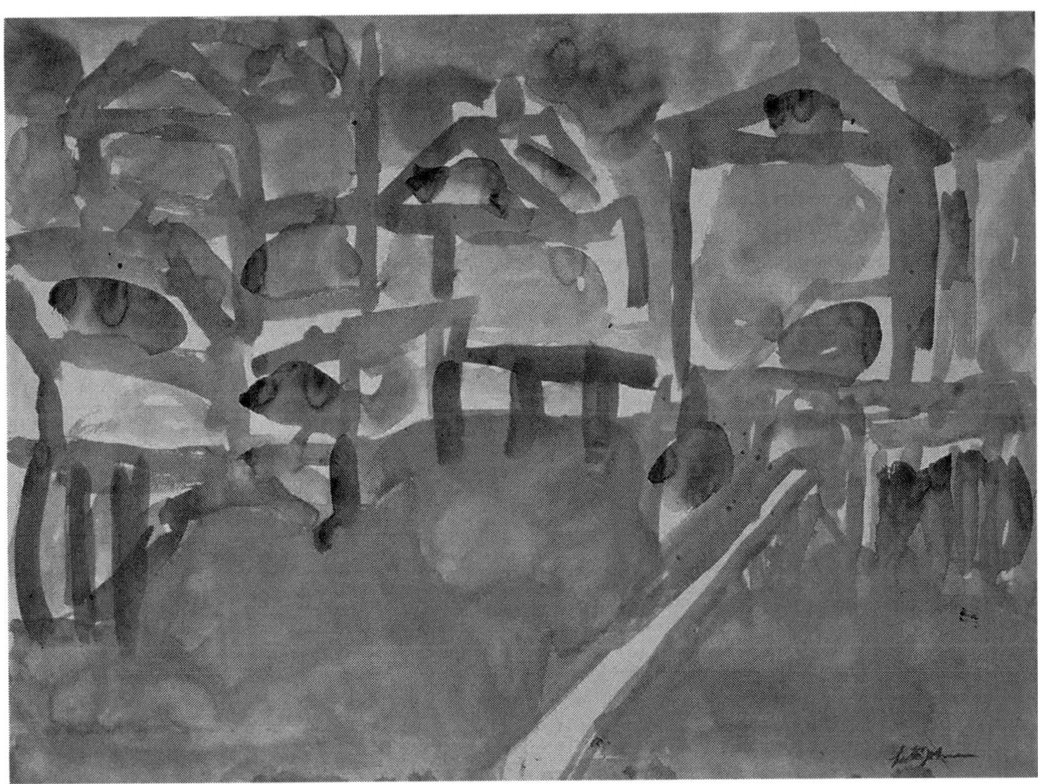

Provincetown Houses. Courtesy of Acme Gallery.

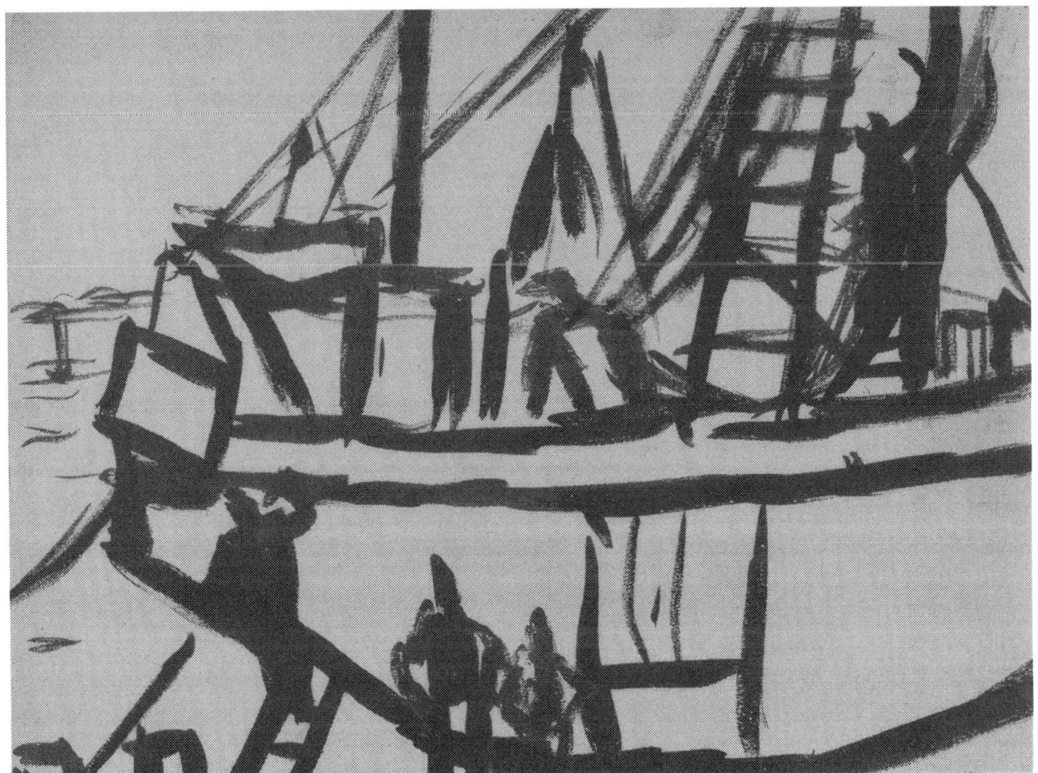

Red Dry Dock. Courtesy of Acme Gallery.

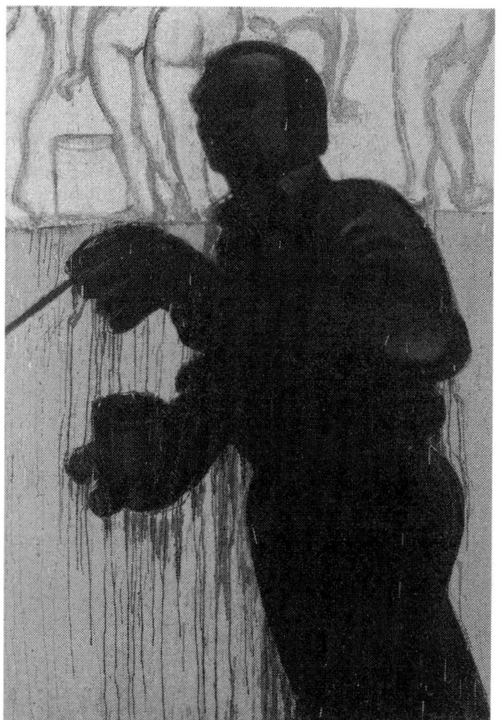

Self Portrait with Five Figures. Courtesy of Acme Gallery.

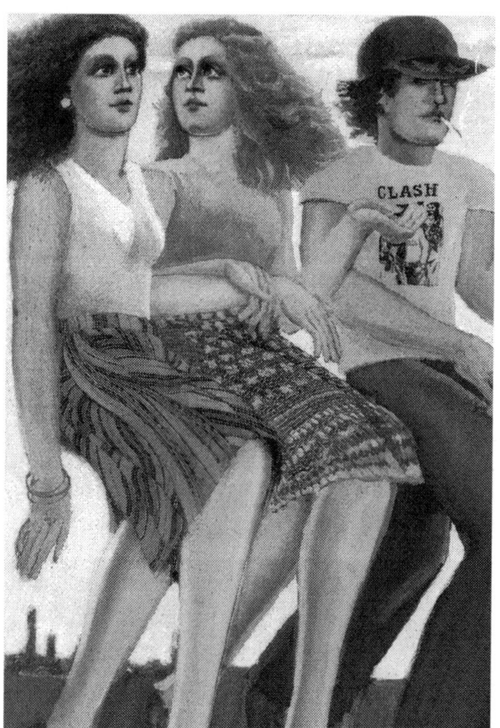

Two Women and A Man. Courtesy of Acme Gallery.

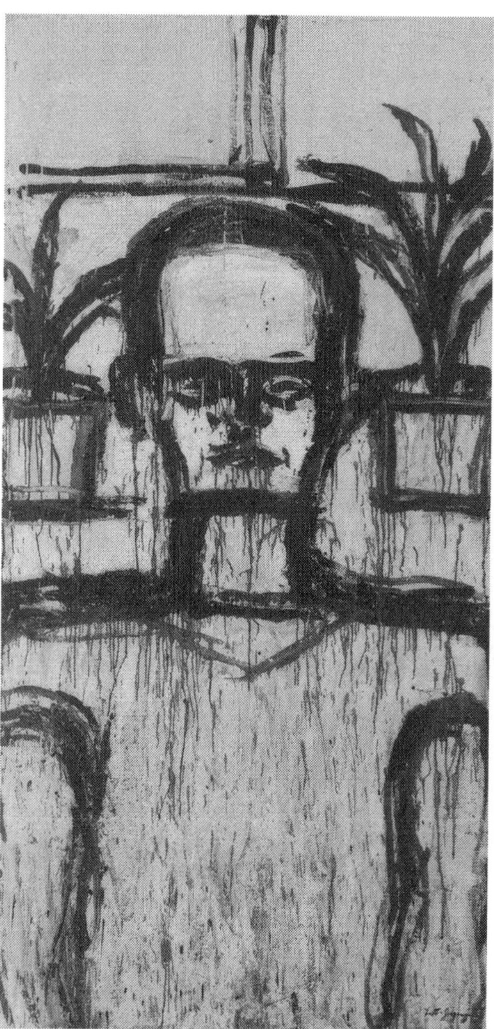

Tall White Figure. Courtesy of Acme Gallery.

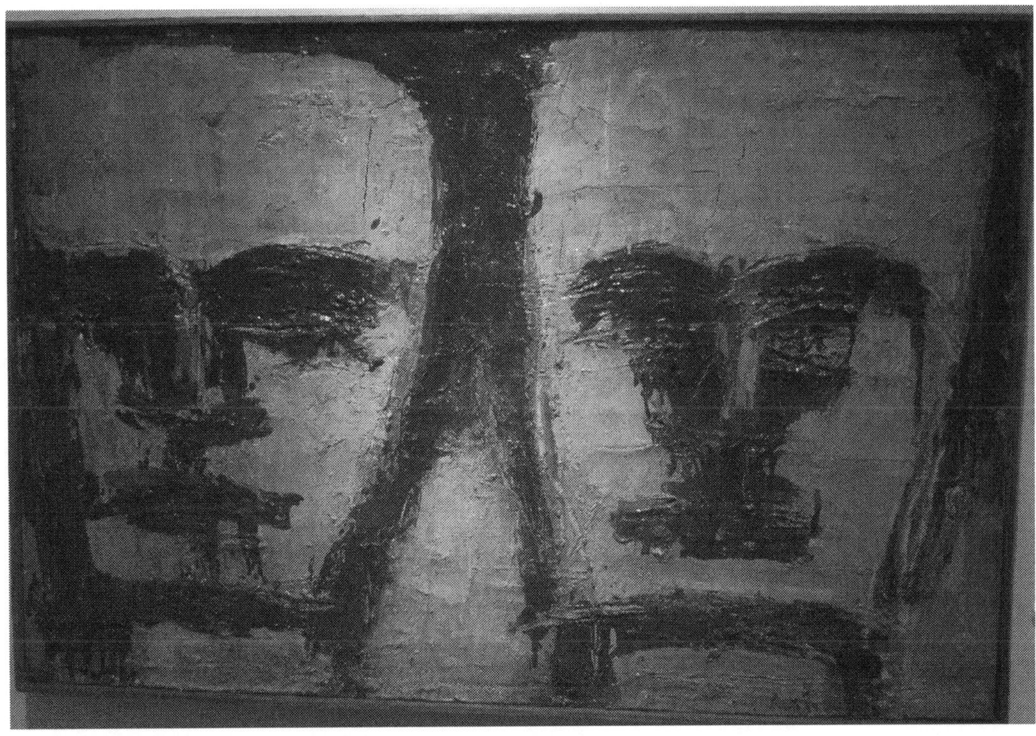

Douible Heads. Courtesy of Acme Gallery.

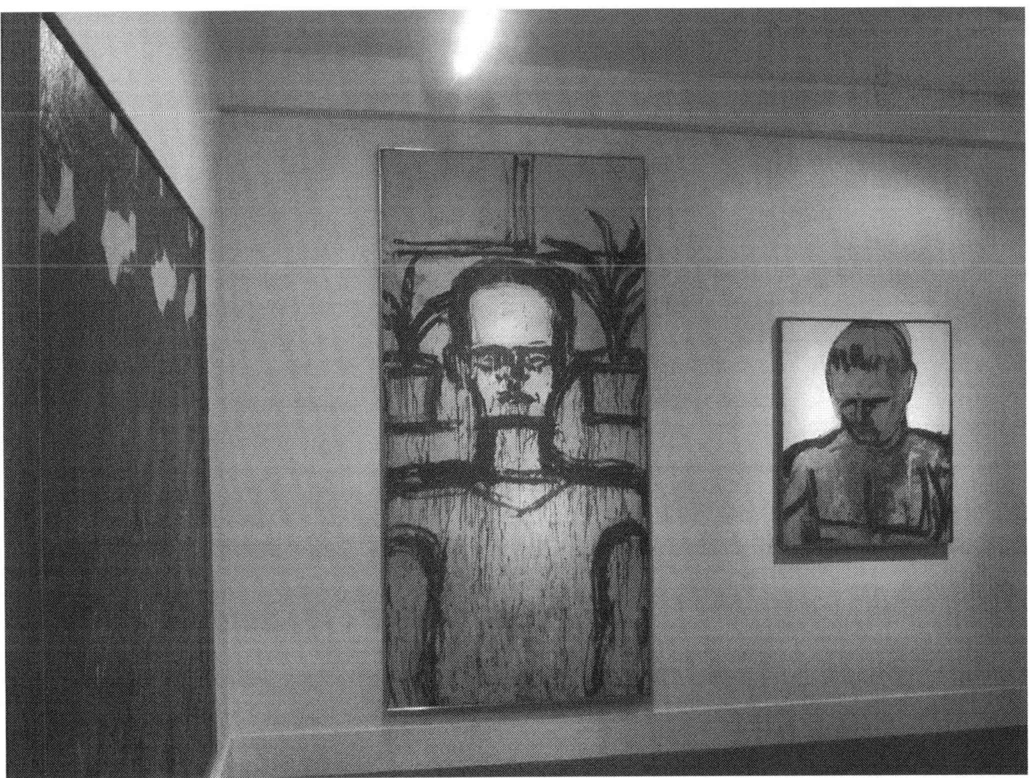

Acme Installation, Giuliano photo.

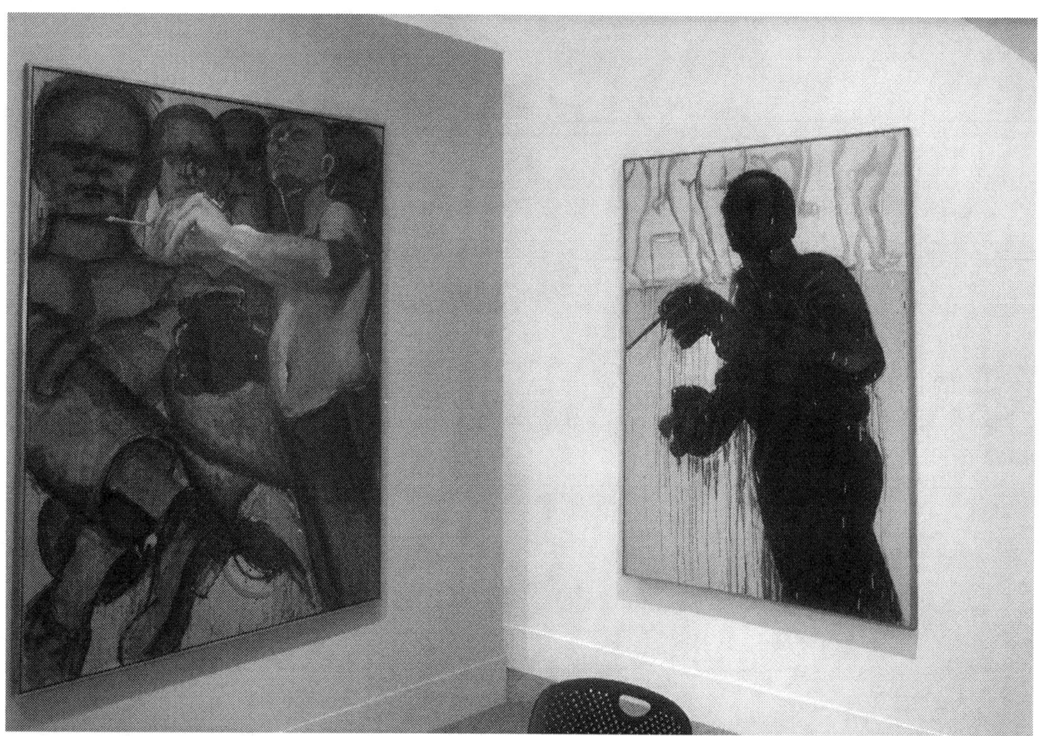
Acme Installation, Giuliano photo.

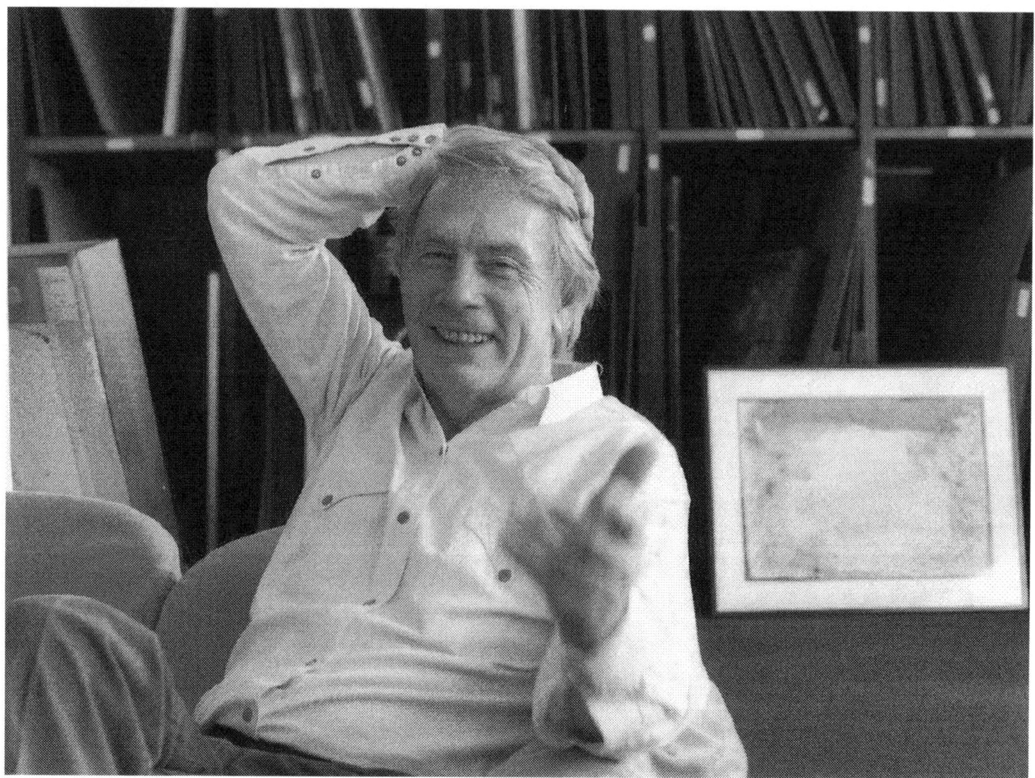
Lester Johnson in his studio. Giuliano photo.

Christine McCarthy Transformed Provincetown Art Association and Museum

When the Institute of Contemporary Art mounted Elvis and Marilyn in 1994, it anticipated a blockbuster. Accordingly, it hired additional staff including the young Christine McCarthy. That show fizzled and the expanded staff was let go. McCarthy stayed and soon proved to be invaluable as assistant to director Milena Kalinovska. When she was ousted, there was a long hiatus and McCarthy ran the museum with a skeletal crew until Jill Medvedow was hired. McCarthy remained as the ICA plotted a transfer from Boylston Street to Fan Pier. When the Provincetown Art Association and Museum courted her, it was a mess. Taking a step back in salary and benefits, she took the job on terms of a commitment for change. Her impact has been formidable.

Interview with Christine McCarthy 2013 Provincetown Art Association and Museum

Charles Giuliano Before Provincetown you were with the Institute of Contemporary Arts in Boston.

Christine McCarthy I was at the ICA from 1994 to 2001. I started with Milena Kalinovska. There was a lapse without a director, then under Jill Medvedow for two years. I was in six or seven different positions and ended as director of administration and planning. My final job was divided between operations and working on the new building. I worked on the lobbying for Fan Pier. That entailed politicians in South Boston and the Mayor's office. I left right when the architects were hired. I was there during the search.

CG What was it that led you into arts administration?

CM I have a BA in Humanities from Providence College. I did my junior year in Florence. All of my classes were in the museums: The Uffizi and the Academia. My first three months were in Siena for intensive Italian language. When I came back from that year, I definitely knew I wanted to do something related to art history and museums. I did an art history program at Syracuse. It was fine but it wasn't doing it for me. Ironically, in my third semester Syracuse started a brand-new museum studies program. Nobody signed up for it. They bribed the art history students and told us that if we took the museum studies courses, we could get two Masters for the price of one; art history and museum studies. That meant staying for another semester. I was intrigued. Syracuse had just built an art gallery which was unbelievable. They had a wonderful print collection.

After Syracuse I did a one-year fellowship at Yale. That was the clincher. I worked in prints, drawings, and photography under Richard Field, who was a genius. He taught me way more than I learned in my program. After that I moved to Boston and got a job at the ICA.

I did tons of internships and had worked in a couple of galleries. But this was my first job using my skills to see how museums work. In 1994 I was hired with the *Elvis and Marilyn* show to be the gallery manager and it ended up being a bust. It was huge in Graceland when they did it there. Boston just didn't love the *Elvis and Marilyn* thing.

When that show closed, they let a lot of people go. They assumed it would be a giant boost for the ICA. It wasn't. I stayed on as the gallery manager but in six months I was upstairs part time in operations. Then I became the assistant to Milena until she left in 1999.

So, I was with her in the director's office for three years, then two years in the office by myself until Jill (Medvedow) was hired. That's when I was moved to administration and planning and started working on the new building.

CG Under Milena, in addition to *Elvis and Marilyn*, it seemed that the ICA was chasing niche audiences. There was the *Malcom X* show which reached out to African Americans. There was a gay-themed show.

CM On the flip side she did *Inside the Visible.* It was probably one of the best shows that the ICA has ever done.

CG That chased a feminist audience.

CM It did. But they came for it. I think Milena has a sixth sense about emerging artists. She would tell you which artists would hit it and she was usually spot on. Kara Walker was one of the first artists we showed there and Carolee Schneemann. The feminist artists who are huge now, Milena was chasing when I was at the ICA.

CG Carol Rama! Claude Cahun (1894–1954) was one of the discoveries of that exhibition. Carol Rama (Italian, born 1918) was hardly an emerging artist. Later Milena gave her a one-woman show. The work was interesting but so-so.

CM True, but she was fabulous. The one who did portraits of all the models who weren't pretty. Oh God, the name is escaping me.

(Rineke Dijkstra who was relatively unknown when the ICA mounted her exhibition. The ICA under Kalinovska also showed Holocaust artist Charlotte Solomon, the British sculptor, Rachel Whiteread, British conceptualist Olivia Parker, and other women artists.)

What was great about the ICA was that there was nobody there to hold your hand. Learn it or leave. Under Milena I got my Contemporary Art 101 and she taught me hook, line, and sinker.

When Milena left, there were nine of us running the ICA. There was no director. There was no director of human resources. There was no development director. There was no director of education. There was no director of operations. It was myself, a curator, gallery staff, an accountant, and maybe one other person. That was it for two years while they did the search.

CG What was the board doing?

CM Freaking out. They were trying to find a good director. It was at least a year and a half before Jill (Medvedow) was hired as director. There were interviews and a lot of different people being considered.

CG When Milena left, I did an exit interview with her. I have tried to contact her in the past couple of years to fill in that gap of the ICA's history. She's at the Hirshhorn. It's an important story which should be told.

(She returned to her native Czechoslovakia where she remains connected to the art world.)

Looking back, David Ross couldn't build a new ICA, Milena couldn't. Jill finally did it.

CM She did it because there was really no other choice. The ICA was either going to close or build a new museum. That's what happened with this place too (Provincetown Art Association and Museum). The same people were on the ICA board for a long time and they got frustrated. Then the opportunity of Fan Pier opened up.

CG Let's step back a bit. Why couldn't David Ross pull it off?

CM He didn't care about a new building. He was interested in exhibitions. Milena was a curator. She wanted to do exhibitions. That wasn't Jill's thing. She was about expansion and growth. She's a good fundraiser and the Fan Pier parcel came up. The ICA was in eleven different locations before where it is now. The other candidates for the parcel didn't fit the bill. It made perfect sense.

Under Mayor Tom Menino, it would be the first new museum built in a hundred years. His administration saw that this would be a good thing for the City of Boston. At the time, the idea was that Fan Pier would all build up at once. It was going to be shops, hotels, and restaurants. Everything was going to happen all at one time. Everything kept falling through. The ICA kept going because they were given a parcel of land at a dollar a year for a hundred years. You're not going to blow that. You're going to figure out how to do it.

CG How did that experience dovetail and carry over to here. What were the similarities and differences in coming to PAAM?

CM Someone sent me the job description for this museum. I had no intention of leaving the ICA and coming here. The job description was eight pages long. There was one other fulltime person and you basically did everything for no money. It was a lot. A typical job description is two pages.

I figured I would apply and if I got an interview I would come to Provincetown for the weekend. I got a call. So, I grabbed my best friends and we jumped on the ferry and came to Provincetown. I came for my interview in June. It was unseasonably hot, probably 90 degrees, and a thousand inside.

The first question they asked me was, "If you got this job where would you find a place to live?" Not, do you have a background in arts, museums, or whatever. One of the trustees was a real estate agent so I said, "You're going to find me a place to live."

She looked at me and said, "I like you." In my head I said "good" because I'm not taking this job anyway. The interview went on for about three hours and it was so hot.

There was a giant hole in the roof over there where the rain used to come in. There were spiders and cobwebs everywhere. The walls had burlap on them. These floors were funky.

Looking around I said, "How committed is this board to doing a renovation?" Half of them were and half of them weren't. I said, "Thanks a lot, but until you are all committed to doing this, it's never going to happen. The only way that I would come and take this job is if you are committed to doing a building renovation."

I stayed over at Ruth Hebert's house and we stayed awake until three or four in the morning. She taught me about Provincetown. Not about gay parties and drag queens. She taught me about the art colony. She told me about living here when artists came to Hofmann's School. Maybe I read about Charles Hawthorne in art history, but I didn't know anything about this art colony. She was the one who clued me in on how potentially exciting this place could be.

Two days later I got the call, "We want you to take the job." I said, why don't I come back for a second interview and have it be more formal. Commitment? Are you going to pay me? Will I have to raise all my own money? Who is committed to doing this, because if you're not committed to doing a renovation, I won't take the job. I'm not going to have bake sales here. I'm done and over with that.

I came back for a second interview and it wasn't as hot, thank God. I still wore a suit though. We went through our whole thing. I got back to Boston and they said, "We want you to start now."

I was 34-years-old. If you are in the museum field your track is that you should finally make it to the point where you are a director. I couldn't come up with a good reason why I shouldn't take it.

This place is about 70 percent second- and third-homeowners with a lot of cross over from Boston. It included a lot of people whom I knew from Boston.

CG It has always felt like Provincetown is a New York summer colony not a Boston one.

CM No, it's quite a Boston summer colony, tons.

CG Is that a change?

CM In probably the last ten or fifteen years it is. It's about a third Boston, a third New York, and about a third Cape Cod. That's my board right now.

CG How many board members are there?

CM Twenty-five.

CG Do they all give?

CM You're damn right they do. They give very generously in many different ways.

The reason why there were so few is because nobody had ever asked those second- and third-homeowners to be a part of this organization; on a governance level, or on a giving level.

I asked people from Boston, "We're getting ready to do a capital campaign." They said, "Nobody has ever asked me before." That's how I raised $8 million to renovate this museum.

CG Over what time frame?

CM I started in 2001. It took a year to figure out who was who. What constituencies were serious about being a part of this museum and tweaking the board. In 2002 we were in a quiet phase. In 2003 we announced the campaign. We broke ground in 2003 and cut the ribbon in 2005. Pledges came in over five to seven years. We increased our membership three times. We increased our budget three times. We increased everything by three times. We doubled the square footage of the space. We didn't have any storage space for art so potential donations were going to other museums.

When you tell people in this town that things that allegedly belong here are going somewhere else, they don't like that. People weren't gifting their collections of Provincetown art. The works were going to other museums. They were going to auctions, because we didn't have the right facility. Now we have one storage unit off-site for really giant sculptures. Some 98 percent of the collection is on site. It's top-of-the-line.

CG Has that had an impact?

CM Oh yeah. Huge. Because people were waiting. When I started, we had 1,000 works now we have 3,000. That's in twelve years with promised gifts, estates, and planned giving. We have superior collections coming here in people's wills and things like that.

CG You made the comment that the Provincetown Art Mafia (Long Point Gallery group) which I mentioned "has died." That being the case, what is the current status of Provincetown as an arts colony?

CM Today there is a handful of galleries still devoted to the historic art colony: Julie Heller, Berta Walker, Schoolhouse. Julie has two locations now. A lot of artists come and open their own galleries to show their work. There's a lot of that. Some of them last and some of them don't.

CG We see a lot of amateur work on your walls. Is Provincetown still a destination for serious artists?

CM It's hard because it's so expensive to live here. If you want to be here, you have to figure out how to do that. You might have to work four jobs during the summer. You can paint all winter and do what you have to do. Yes, I think there is still a committed cadre of artists who come here.

We boast that we are America's oldest art colony and home of American Theater

(The Provincetown Players began when a group of writers and artists who were vacationing in Provincetown, presented their plays July 15, 1915 on the veranda of Hutchins Hapgood and Neith Boyce's rented ocean-view cottage. The two plays were *Constancy* by Neith Boyce and *Suppressed Desires* by husband and wife, George Cram Cook and Susan Glaspell. Boyce had previously had a reading of her play in her home a few weeks prior and this caused Cook and Glaspell to add their play to create a social event for their friends.)

When I came here, this facility was falling down and there was no theater. The library just did a renovation. The Fine Arts Work Center just did a renovation. I think that in the grand scheme of facilities we have all raised the bar. We had to.

CG I like the emphasis on "we had to." Was there a community-wide consensus that something had to happen?

CM I think so. For theater you want to come and see a Eugene O'Neill play or Tennessee Williams. You had to go to the Provincetown Inn because there was no theater. There used to be theater in this building. There wasn't going to be theater anymore in this building, so they had to build a theater. It made sense because there wasn't a viable venue to showcase and represent the legacy of American theater in Provincetown. Which is huge.

The Fine Arts Work Center is bringing fellows from all over the place and the studios are falling down. There is an enormous historical legacy to those studios where Ross Moffett, Edwin Dickinson, and so many others worked. Just for preservation purposes, it needed to be renovated.

We got our acts together and got these facilities renovated and built. We couldn't even get teachers for our program. We had a one-room school house and nobody wanted to teach here. It was too dark and either too hot in summer or too cold in winter. Now we have four studios which have gorgeous light in them. We now have 80 teachers here on a year-round basis.

CG Is anything degree granting?

CM We had an affiliation with Cape Cod Community College where credits transferred. We did it for ten years, but it got dull. It was off-the-shelf Painting 101.

We don't have an accredited program yet. It is something we would like to do. The Fine Arts Work Center has a low residency MFA program. They are affiliated with Mass College of Art. I don't know the status of that. It's been in process for four or five years. We do the thesis show here. Yeah, there are ways. U. Mass Dartmouth, we've had lots of conversations with them of how we can do this; transfer of credits.

Bottom line, if we build it, will they come? Yeah. Will they take classes? Yes. Are they the Peter Busas and Robert Motherwells of that bygone era? I don't think so. Not yet anyway. I don't have the answers. I see people like Bob Henry and Selina Trieff, who not only teach in the school, but also exhibit in these shows. They have been on our board and I see them as the old guard because they studied with Hofmann and continue his traditions. I see people like Peter Watts and people in their 70s and 80s who are the respected artists of their generation, who work and show in Provincetown.

CG What about younger ones?

CM That's part of the issue, how to get younger artists to stay here. The Fine Arts Work Center presents a beautiful cadre of young contemporary artists. The minute they're done with their program, a few of them stay here, but most want to go to New York or Chicago. I can't blame them. They're the ones who want shows at the ICA. When I was there, and we did an Ellen Gallagher show, she had been a Fine Arts Work Center Fellow. There's a huge number of Fine Arts Work Center alumni who have done very well in the contemporary art world. They love Provincetown and want to come and visit. Artists like Paul Bowen don't want to stay here anymore. It's really expensive to live here and it's not the New York scene.

That's different. I don't think we want this to be New York. We love the connections we have to New York. We apply to the foundations in New York and they still support us because Provincetown was important in the careers of so many artists, like Wolf Kahn and Judith Rothschild, Hans Hofmann and his students. There are wonderful foundations which support this institution because of the artist's affiliation with Provincetown.

Provincetown is still a funky, nutty, wacky place, because of the light and geography that still draws people here. There are people who want to paint, photograph, and draw it.

Yeah, I still see that. I do. Are they the best artists I've ever seen in my life? Well, who are the best artists? That changes on a daily basis. I go back and forth when I'm in New York looking at stuff. There are things that I love. There are a handful of things in this show (members) which I could pick out, and out of our collection as well.

I feel very strongly that this is a mission-driven organization. We are a membership-driven organization. People come in here and feel safe. We provide comfort; films, lectures. I still learn something here every day. No matter what we have here, I learn something. This is a place that offers up something different for everybody all the time. It's a community place. It's regional. It's community.

We're not New York. People are given wonderful opportunities to show in a museum. They get picked up by galleries through showing here. They sell their work here. It's a place where we don't discriminate. We accept on all levels, race, faith, you name it. That makes people feel good about being here. That's very important to me as opposed to, is it the best art we've ever seen? Is it the *crème de la crème?* It's all subjective and that's how I feel.

There are shows I've curated that people have loved and shows I've curated that people have hated. I do it because it's work I feel connected to. That's why we have a lot of guest curators. There's not one style of anything here. There are so many people who are actually involved in the process. Curating, hanging and showing, that's what makes this place funky and great.

CG How do you prioritize your programming? One assumes that there is a high season that starts at Memorial Day.

CM Yes, and now it extends through October. We do one giant members' show in July. We do one each summer for the entire membership. That's why from May to October we have Elspeth Halvorsen, she does boxes. Jim Balla, he's been here for 20 years and shows at the Albert Merola Gallery, paintings and abstract prints; Jim Peters has a show of mostly his figures. The *Pioneers of Provincetown,* that's the big group summer show. That's going to be in the Hofmann Gallery, which is our largest space. A lot of the artists were Hofmann students, so we want to have them in the named gallery.

CG I see them more as artists associated with the Sun Gallery.

(Yvonne Anderson, Bill Barrell, Robert Beauchamp, Gandy Brodie, Emilio Cruz, Red Grooms, Mimi Gross, Lester Johnson, Wolf Kahn, George McNeil, Jay

Milder, Jan Müller, Peter Passuntino, George Segal, Tony Vevers)

CM Right. But when I applied to the Hofmann Foundation for funding, I featured Beauchamp and Vevers, artists of the Hofmann ilk.

CG The Sun Gallery was a matrix for the dialogue about the return to the figure. That issue was ubiquitous among artists on the cusp of the apogee of abstract expressionism. It developed into a convergence of parallel streams that spawned the lesser-known movement of figurative expressionism, and the era defining emergence of pop art from the 1950s into the 1960s. The *Pioneers of Provincetown,* as I understand it through dialogues with the curator Adam Zucker, focuses on figurative expressionism. (I wrote an essay for the catalog.)

CM We had a Sun Gallery exhibition of artists that focused on what they did then, and what they do now.

(There was an earlier exhibition July 24–August 30, 1981. In an interview, Red Grooms discussed Hofmann's influence and the Sun Gallery artists, "I loved his (Hofmann's) work. There was always this line about him that he was a better teacher than he was an artist, but I don't think that was true, actually. He really was a great painter. His work has a strong position with Pollock, de Kooning, Kline, and Rothko. He's right in there with them, I would say, at the top level of that great generation. But for some reason, he was a bit put down, I guess, by the success of his teaching. And, of course, he was so influential to a generation that's a little older than mine, but a generation that influenced me, like Larry Rivers.

"The generation that I actually identify with was the generation in Provincetown who ran the Sun Gallery: Yvonne Anderson and Dominic Falcone. They were kind of the anti-Hofmann because their idea was more figurative. They were showing artists like Lester Johnson and Tony Vevers and Alex Katz and Jan Müller. They had this program that I liked and I fit right into, which eventually kind of went in a pop art direction.")

Dominic and Yvonne came and screened some of their films. They ended up gifting some to PAAM. We have films of the exhibitions at Sun Gallery. We have a portfolio of photographs by Jules Aarons that he did of exhibitions at Sun Gallery. So, we have a lot of that stuff in our collection.

CG Will the films and photographs be included in the show?

CM I don't think so. Adam is very specific about what he wants to include, which is primarily the figurative painters.

CG How is PAAM set up for scholars if one wanted to come and do research?

CM We have an archivist on staff. You call for an appointment and he will pull whatever you need.

CG That really didn't exist in the past.

CM We get research requests all the time. We get them almost every day. So, we are set up for that. When Knoedler did Avery/Rothko, we provided most of the archival material for that catalog.

(E.A. Carmean, Jr., 2002, curated for Knoedler & Company the exhibition *Coming to Light: Avery, Gottlieb, Rothko, Provincetown Summers 1957–1961.*)

When the MFA did Blanche Lazzell in 2001, most of the research came from us.

Research is a huge part of PAAM as we are gifted so many papers. My dream would be to get a graduate student here for a year to archive all of that material. Not all of it is digitized. Some is and some isn't. We have so many wonderful, vintage photographs, and I would love to see them accessible online. It's a matter of getting people in here and a grant to do it. We were gifted from The Lillian Orlowsky and William Freed Foundation. They were students of Hofmann. They left a very large endowment to give scholarships to painters who are over 45, do not have gallery affiliations, and are in financial need.

CG That sounds like the Pollock/Krasner Foundation.

CM Kind of. We just started four years ago and are now in the fourth cycle. We have jurors from all over the country who physically come to Provincetown. We give away $40,000, usually four $10,000 grants or two for $20,000, whatever the jurors feel about people who deserve it. Then they have a group show here. I just love that we can give money away instead of always asking for it. This helps quite a bit and it was listed last year as one of the top twenty artists' grants. We have over 400 applicants this year from all over the country.

CG It appears that the permanent collection, which has grown from 1,000 to 3,000 objects on your watch, is all gifted.

CM About 90 percent

CG That means that you have no acquisition fund.

CM We have a small fund.

CG Have you considered growing that fund?

CM Absolutely. It's a part of the Centennial.

CG What's your target?

CM I'm not sure yet. When I started in 2001 there were two full-time people, including myself, with three part-time people. We now have a staff of six full -time and six part-time employees. There are 230 volunteers. We have increased staffing, but need more major positions. I never want to make it seem that a curator is the be all and end of deciding what's on the walls here. I like the community interaction that we have. At the same time, this is a person (curator) who could be out looking at studios. I do that periodically, but I just don't have the time to be looking at what people are doing and discovering that next great Motherwell. That piece is missing, as far as I'm concerned, and we need that position to look at what people are doing on the Cape, because the Cape is large. There are a lot of people living here year-round who are making work we don't know about.

CG What is the status of the Reggie Cabral (1923 to 1996) collection?

(The colorful owner of The A House often accepted works of art to settle bar bills. He was secretive about letting critics and art historians see the collection, which was said to include questionable works. But he also acquired many superb works, including some of the original white line Provincetown print blocks.)

CM I have no idea. Nothing. It could be in a warehouse for all I know.

CG I heard that it went to his daughter, April. Reggie had a major Bob Thompson which we borrowed for the *Kind of Blue* exhibition at PAAM. Thompson was a major Provincetown artist, but is not represented in the PAAM collection.

CM True. We have a major work by Lester Johnson.

CG One can think of many major Provincetown artists not represented in the collection. What is sadly true is that the longer museums wait, the more expensive the works become, to the point where it becomes impossible to fill gaps. That's the dilemma of the MFA, which stuck its head in the sand for too long. The ICA has only decided to collect in the past few years. Between those two major institutions, with the exception of Harvard and Brandeis, Boston is a major city with mediocre modern and contemporary museum collections. The collectors are aging. You talked about the great collection of Ruth Hebert, who you stayed with when you first came for an interview.

CM That's an example of a collection that we got.

CG What is the possibility of filling the gaps with the acquisition of works by major Provincetown artists? Have you compiled a punch list?

CM We definitely have. Edward Hopper was one of those people. Even though there is the Hopper dilemma. (His antipathy as a Truro resident to any involvement with PAAM and Provincetown.) We had a Jo Hopper but not an Edward Hopper.

I lecture a lot about this place and its position in art history. I was doing a lecture and I said that one of the things we don't have in our collection is an Edward Hopper. Everyone wants to see our Hopper and I tell them it's not here yet. I jokingly said if anyone has one, let me know. I got a call from Herman Merrill's son. He said that "My mother has a Hopper that he (Herman) traded with him for a nude figure, and our foundation wants to give it to PAAM."

It's a beautiful, beautiful drawing and Herman Merrill inscribed it on the back as a gift to his wife.

So yes, we are compiling a hit list and our Centennial strategy is a hundred acquisitions of significance to fill in gaps in our collection. Our collections committee is in the process of putting that together.

We have a number of collections that are being left as in-kind gifts here. I am trying to see if those gifts can be accelerated. Can we get those pieces now so we have them for the Centennial? Even though they might want to have them on extended loan for awhile so we can get them in the building. I think actually we will do quite well in that realm.

We have a big, beautiful (Jack) Tworkov from the show that we did a couple of years ago. That's on extended loan as an intended gift.

("The collection's painting is typical of Tworkov's work in the 1950s: a colored expanse against which fiercely brushed linear strokes hide or cast a veil across the surface. Jack told me once how he yearned to paint a landscape directly in nature, and I've always seen these pictures of his as evocations of Cape marsh grass or reeds. But in point of fact, this work is a preview of what was to become the magisterial painting of the last years before his death in 1982." Tony Vevers)

CG Perhaps I don't understand the tax code, but I understood that the loophole had been closed for donations of works of art, that the donors don't get the full value of the work as a deduction.

CM If an artist donates, they don't, but if a collector does, they do.

With the Hopper, for example, we had an appraisal done and the donor is going to get a write-off of the full value of the work.

If an artist donates, they get to write off the value of the materials. That stinks and needs to be changed. That's an issue that goes back and forth.

CG So there is an incentive to donate.

CM No question about it. Also, knowing that it is going to a facility that is now capable of taking care of it and will exhibit it.

CG That also seems to equate with a mandate in programming to function more as a museum. If you do ambitious shows and publications, you get major loans, which leads to important acquisitions. It's all a part of the quid pro quo. Also having a collection provides leverage in working with other museums.

CM That's true. We now get more loan requests than ever before. The fact that we've been accredited and now have a good history of borrowing has really worked in our favor.

One of the great stories comes from when we did the (Edwin) Dickinson show here and we borrowed from a private collector *The McMillan Pier in Wintertime*. It had been on extended loan to the Philadelphia Museum for fifteen years. When the donor came and saw the piece here, he said this has to stay here. This is where it belongs. I said, "Will you tell that to the Philadelphia Museum?"

For me, having that exhibition with a major publication and getting that piece is why we need to be doing this kind of work. It brings things back which were created here.

CG It's interesting that you mention Dickinson because beyond our immediate circle people don't know who he is.

CM Nobody does. The Albright Knox did a major traveling show of Dickinson. But people don't know who the hell he is.

CG For the Dickinson show we posted several articles by various contributors to *Berkshire Fine Arts*. We now have an enormous archive and we get a lot of Google searches for that material. On a consistent monthly basis, we get significant traffic for the Dickinson articles. So, people are indeed interested in the artist.

CM How about Blanche Lazzell? Nobody knew who the hell she was until the MFA did that show. Nobody knew who she was. I know you did. But the average person didn't know her work.

CG She's in the famous photo of *Forum '49*. There's Blanche sitting on the bench along with Karl Knaths, Weldon Kees, and the other artists.

CM With her cardigan sweater on. We have two white-line Blanche Lazzell prints gifted here. A donor said, "I have two and I want to gift them to you. Do you want to know where I got them? In a flea market hanging on the back of a van. Marked down 'second day.' She bought them for $20. They have been appraised at $80,000. That's crazy.

We did a small show in 2001, which was before the renovation. The MFA had done the show and we had a few Lazzell's up. We borrowed a few from the restauranteur Napi. We had a couple in the collection. After we did that, we got the two, colored prints and a whole portfolio of studies and sketches for the blocks.

So that happens a lot when people know what you don't have. They help you fill in the blanks.

CG This past winter I have been reading the history of jazz, blues, and rock. I came across a reference to Weldon Kees (1914–1955). It just popped up out of the blue. Of course, I knew him as the artist who organized the seminal, summer-long project *Forum '49*. But here I was encountering him in an entirely other context as a part of music history and theory.

CM We have a great archive for *Forum '49.*

CG It all comes full circle. At that time, it seemed like Provincetown was the summer home of Tenth Street. The artists came and argued. Some of the topics, by today's standards, were off the wall, like the role of psychoanalysis in art.

Walking down Commercial Street to PAAM today, we passed a building which I remember from when I first came here as a student in the 1960s. I recall that as the Kootz Gallery. That became HCE, which Nat Halper ran. I recall seeing a Bruce Conner relief sculpture in a summer space run by Ivan Karp. There were a number of important galleries and dealers at that time. There was a serious presence.

The artists came here, hung out, talked, looked at each other's work.

CM Knaths, Avery, Merrill. They all went to each other's studios. They sat and talked to each other all day long. They went to the East End to a place now called The Patrician, which was a soda fountain. They would sit there and talk and talk and talk.

CG Is that dialogue happening now?

CM We have a lecture series which is pretty well attended. We get a hundred people for every lecture.

CG Do they fight and argue?

CM When John Grillo (Born 1917) did his lecture he was in his 90s. When he started talking about the reason he had so many affairs was because of his big penis That certainly caused controversy because he was 95-years-old. That kind of thing still happens occasionally. It's not fighting and screaming. I would say it's more intellectual conversations which are stimulated.

We do a series of art films and there is always a good argument after. It's a winter thing we do that's really well attended.

CG We are on the cusp from the past hundred years to the future. When we think of the past, we envision a place where artists could come and get a cheap rental for a shack, dig clams on the beach, and make their work. Now when you drive around, the prevailing sense is that everything is quaint and cute. All of the homes have been renovated. Those simple cottages and waterfront condos are just prohibitively expensive. We go from funky to cute to what?

CM When Provincetown is fun and funky is February. We go clamming in February then have a fantastic dinner party that goes until three in the morning—talking about all kinds of stuff. There are now less than 4,000 people here year-round. I don't want to hang out with the 60,000 people who are here in August. I'm so glad that they come into this museum and support it. But are these the people I sit around and have clams with? No, because they blow in and blow out. People who really live here and appreciate Provincetown, like my friend Jimmy, who just got back from a dune shack where he painted for a week. We just had some clams and talked about the dune shack. He lives here year-round. He starts his restaurant job next week and will work his ass off until September. Then he'll get back into it again.

It's so expensive and hard to live here. There are like just a few jobs with benefits. It's hard to live here. People get discouraged and they move somewhere that they don't have to work four jobs just to pay their rent, or live in a place with off-season rent for five months and then have to move out.

CG How has that worked for you?

CM When I came here the first year, I had a summer rental which cost as much as I paid for my Boston apartment for the year. I had a kick-ass apartment in the North End (of Boston). I loved it. I lived on Garden Court Street and I thought I would be buried there. I couldn't believe that I was paying four times what I paid for my beautiful North End apartment for a dump. It was a dump. It was like the size of this bench. But where else was I going to live?

That fall I moved, which is the bipolar nature of Provincetown in many ways, to a winter rental on the water, from October to May, and it was the most beautiful house I ever lived in. It was cheap as a winter rental, but then I had to be out again.

I don't like moving, so I found a condo on the other side of Route 6, away from the riffraff, and I've owned it now for eleven years. I couldn't do the back-and-forth stuff. The opportunity to live in that house on the water for the winter was magical.

CG One would think that the board provides lodging for the director.

CM Yes. The Fine Arts Work Center provides its director with a house. When I moved here the board members were giving $40 a year and they thought that was all they should be giving.

CG I take it that it's more than that now.

CM I have a much more sophisticated board now.

(President, Judyth Katz, Vice President, James Bakker, Treasurer, Joy McNulty, Secretary, Marian Roth; Lennie Alickman, Ellen Burbank, Arthur Cohen, Paul Dart, Doug Dolezal, Charleton Dukess, Sharon Fay, Joe Fiorello, Stephen Fletcher, Ruth Gilbert, Terence Keane, Brian Koll, Lise Motherwell, Jane Paradise, Anne Peretz, William Rawn, Irma Ruckstuhl, Stewart Tabakin, Carol Swarshawsky, Gail Williams)

When I was hired here my salary was 50 percent of what I was making at the ICA. So, I spent my savings to move here.

CG Why did you do that?

CM Because I got to be the director of a museum. Look what I built. It was the biggest risk I ever took in my life. My board has done well by me. I took a huge risk.

CG Did it pay off?

CM Huge. I'm so proud of this. The space, the programming, and the many people who participate.

CG Will you be buried in P'town?

CM I was raised Catholic, but I don't practice. I went to Ciro's funeral at Saint Peter's. (Ciro was co-owner of Ciro and Sal's.) I'm going to tell you it was the most beautiful funeral. Sal got up and sang an Italian song. This lady got up who had been a childhood friend of Ciro's kids. She talked about what it had been to be a kid wandering in and out of Ciro's life. There was a fire at St. Peter's, so they've renovated it. There's stained glass windows. The altar is a giant rock. It's a huge rock. It's the Catholic church up on Prince Street near the Monument.

As I was listening to this I thought, Oh My God, I definitely want to be cremated, but I want to have my service here at St. Peter's Church. I want part of my ashes spread here and part of my ashes spread in Old Saybrook, Connecticut, where I grew up. I grew up on the shore and have an affinity for the shore, which is where I have spent the best times of my life.

As far as this place, I could never have gotten this far in my career unless I was handed something and told to figure it out and do it. The ICA helped me to do that. It was in such turmoil and transition for so long that you had to be proactive in figuring out who is going to help you. How are you going to get to them? What can you do for them? That's very much how I operate.

I still keep in touch with many, many people in Boston. I teach at BU in the arts administration program. I have been there for eleven years. One of the best collectors in Boston comes to my class each year. She still does this for me.

I went to the 75th anniversary celebration for the ICA last year. I was sitting there and they had a slideshow going. You were looking at images of when the ICA was on Soldier's Field Road. Then they did the years when I was there. I was looking at the exhibitions and thinking, "I'm so proud of this."

I'm very proud of my career track. I've been working in the arts now for 25 years. I don't know anything else. This is what I know and this is what I love. I love that we can do so much for so many people here.

Whether you're an artist or a kid who is being bullied at school. Kids can come here and be safe. People can say what they want to about the programming and content of what goes on here, but I know what it takes to go from a building that was falling down to a major competitor in the field of small American museums.

If you compare us with our sister museums–Bennington, The Farnsworth, Newport, New Britain–we're right up there. We all collaborate. We lend to each other and talk to each other. We were accredited because we run a "best practice" and that's what I'm very proud of.

CG What is your endowment?

CM In the bank we have about $3 million. In the pipeline there is about $8 million. We would like to endow my position and that of a curator. We would like to build an acquisitions fund, and support education, like the programming for kids. We're not going to get NEA funding forever or Mass Cultural funding forever. So, we want to build up reserves for the education programming because I could never get rid of them. I want to make sure we have the youth programs here.

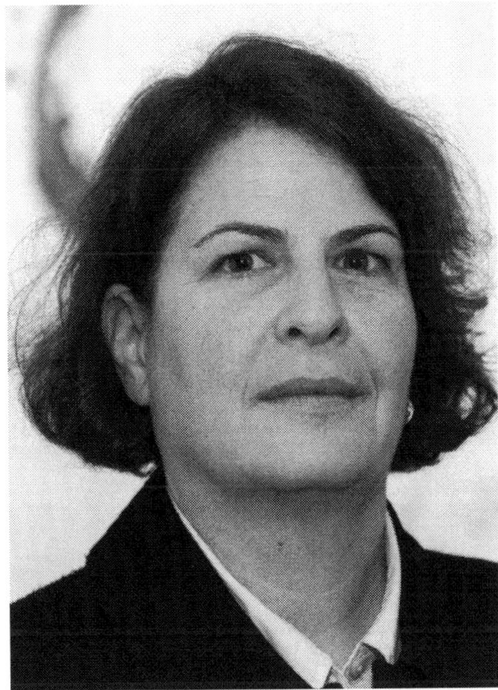

Christine McCarthy has transformed PAAM. Photo courtesy of PAAM.

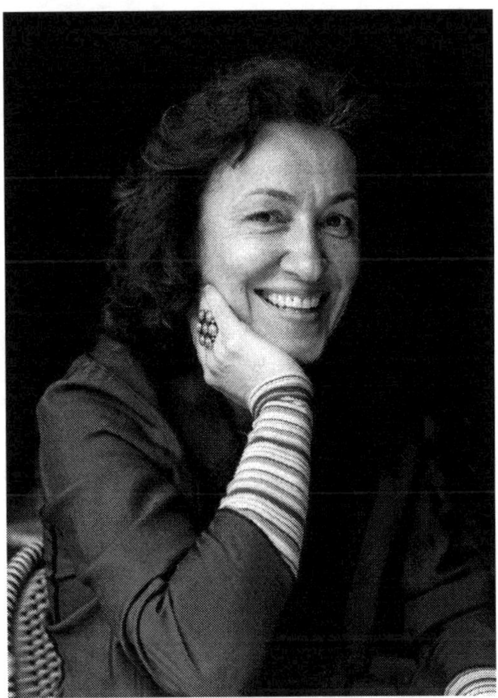

Milena Kalinovska hired McCarthy for the ICA, then left it in her hands while there was a long search for a new director. Giuliano photo.

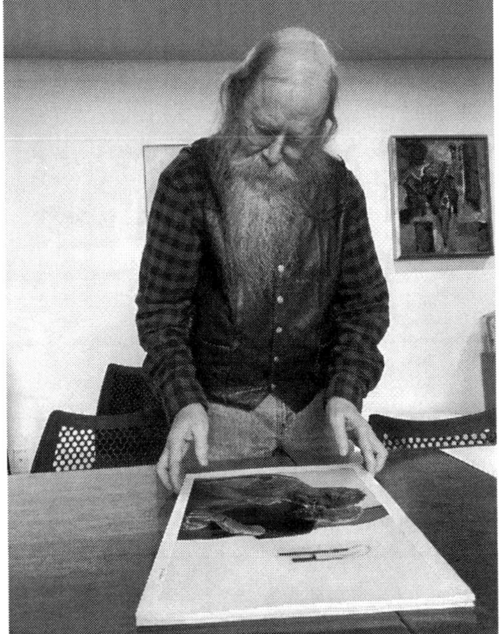

PAAM archivist Jim Zimmerman helped in obtaining vintage images for this book. Giuliano 2024 photo.

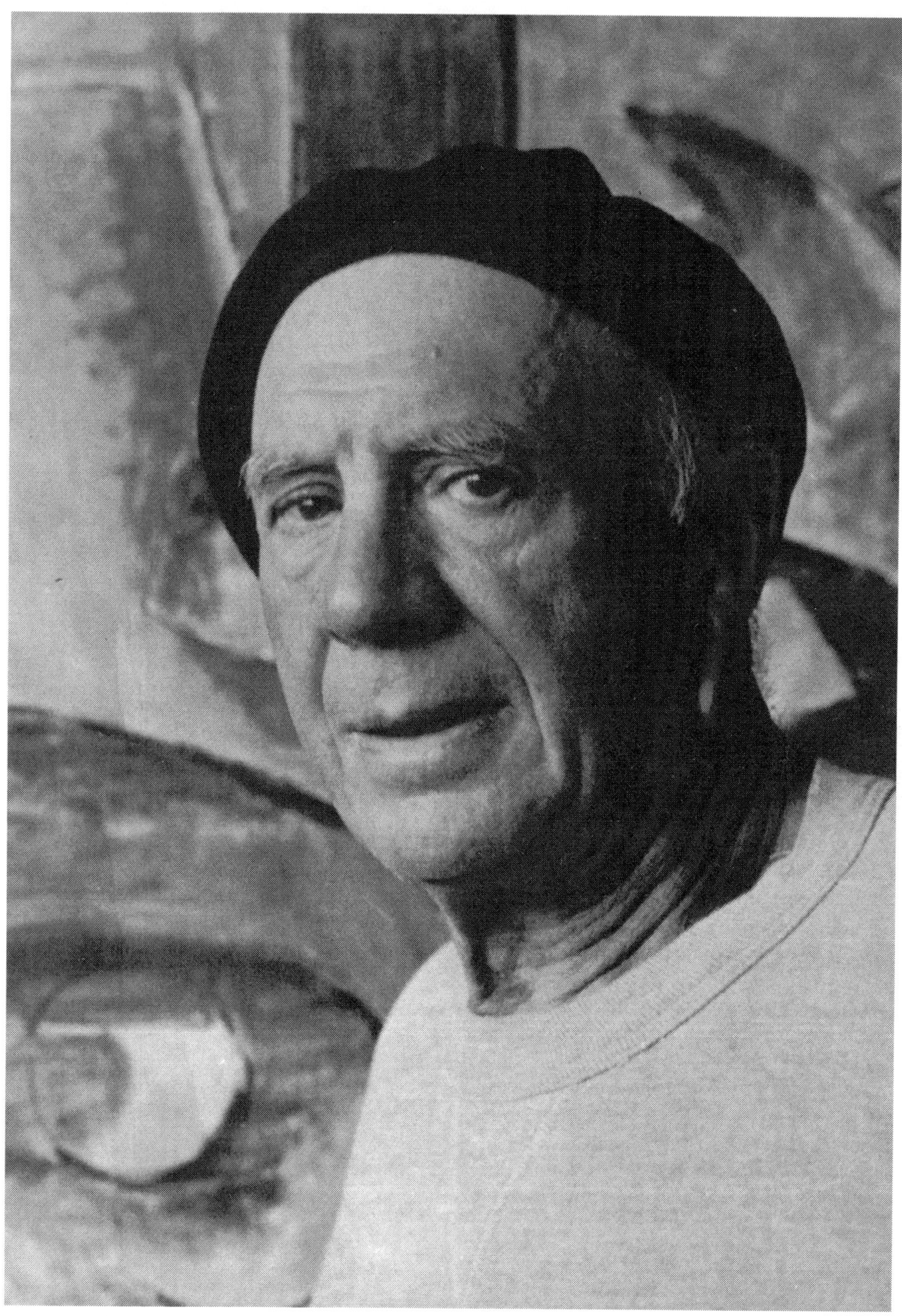

Karl Knaths is represented in the permanent collection. Photo by Bernard Gotfryd. Courtesy of PAAM.

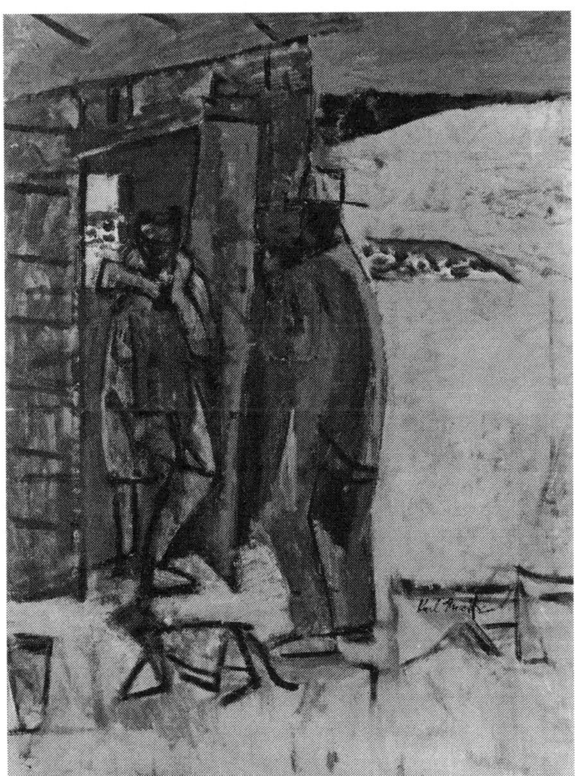

Knaths. *Clam Diggers,* 1949. Courtesy of PAAM.

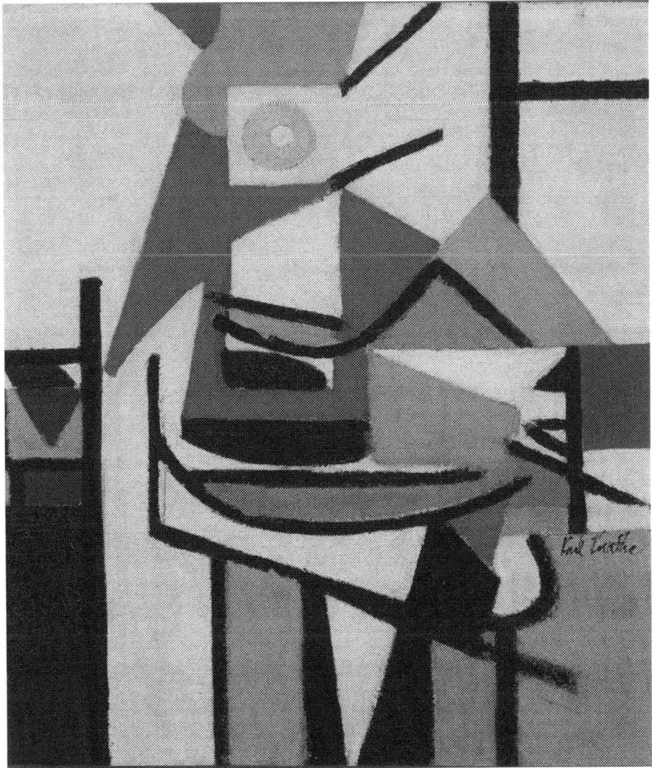

Knaths. *Cock d'or.* Courtesy of PAAM.

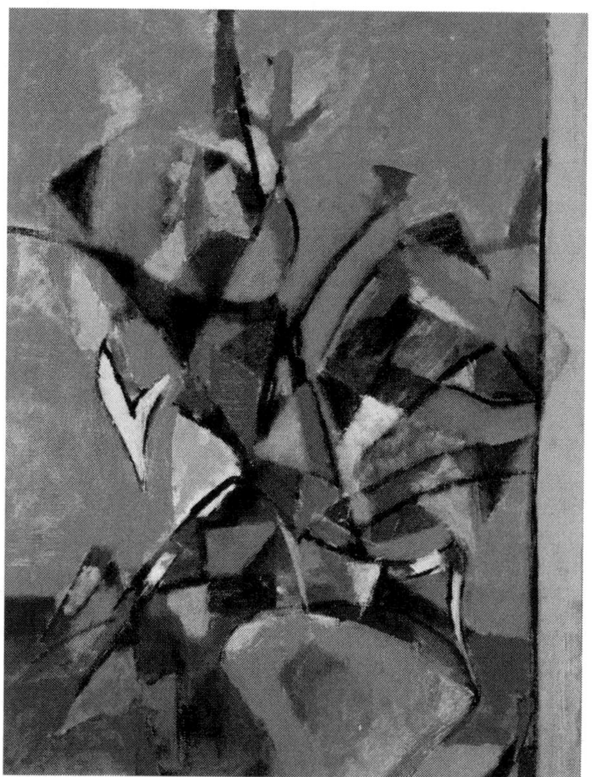

Knaths, *Flowers in Vase*. Courtesy of PAAM.

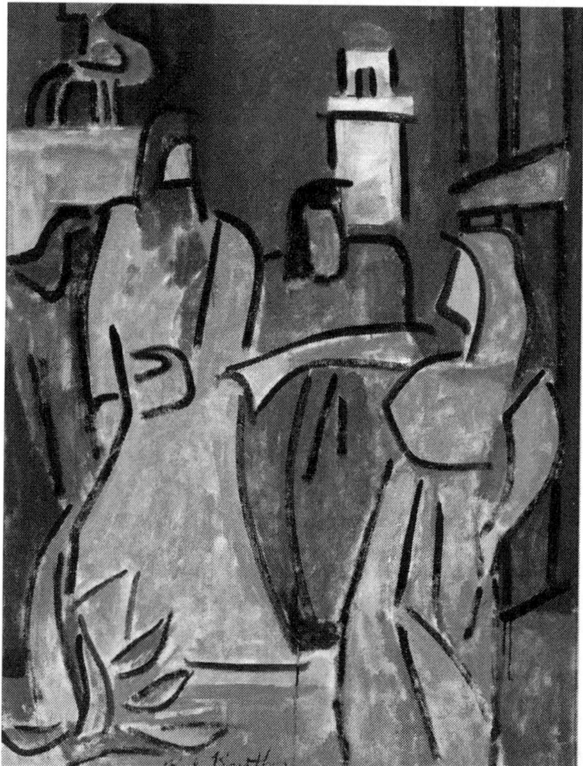

Knaths, *Peter*. Courtesy of PAAM.

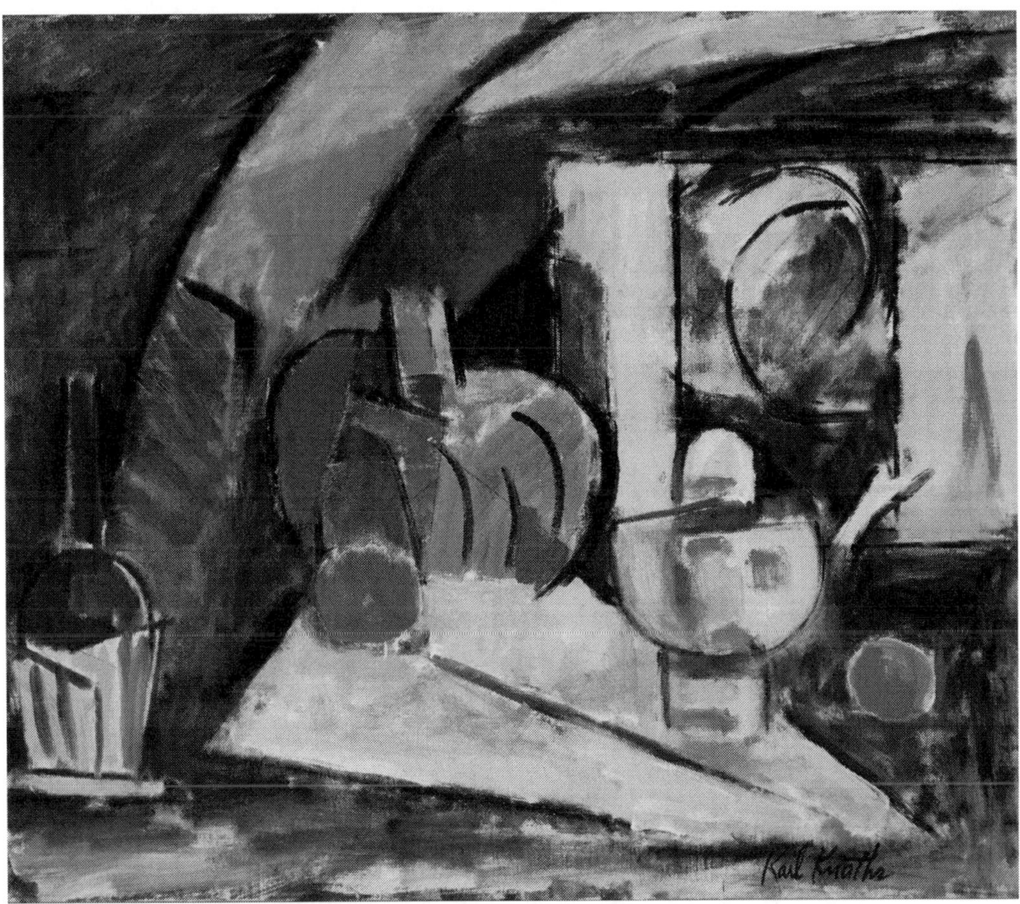

Knaths, *Pumpkin*. Courtesy of PAAM.

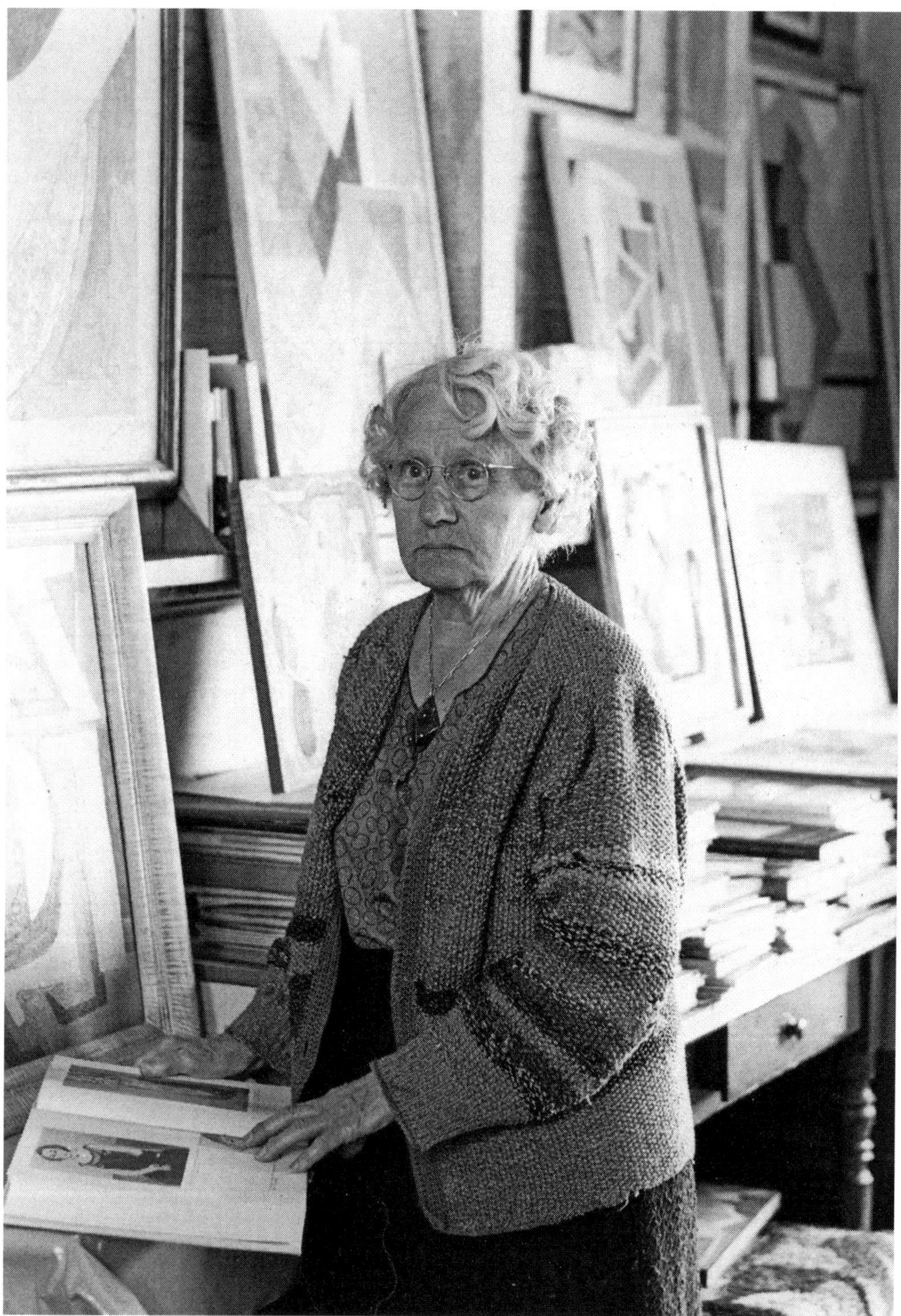

Blanche Lazzell is well represented in the collection. Photo by George Yater. Courtesy of PAAM.

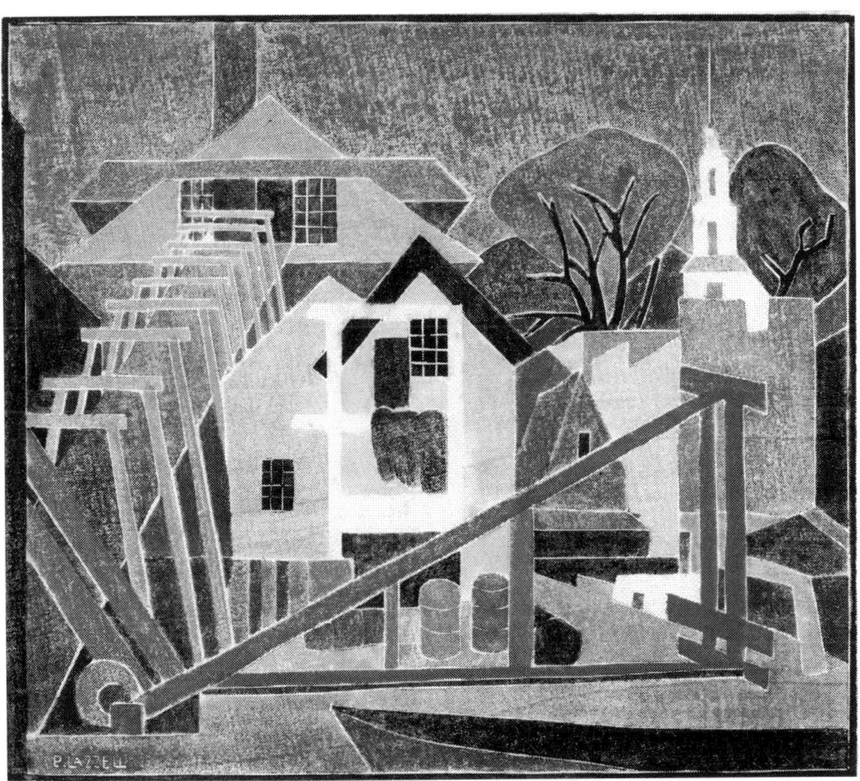

Lazzell, *The Pile Driver,* 1945, white line print. Courtesy of PAAM.

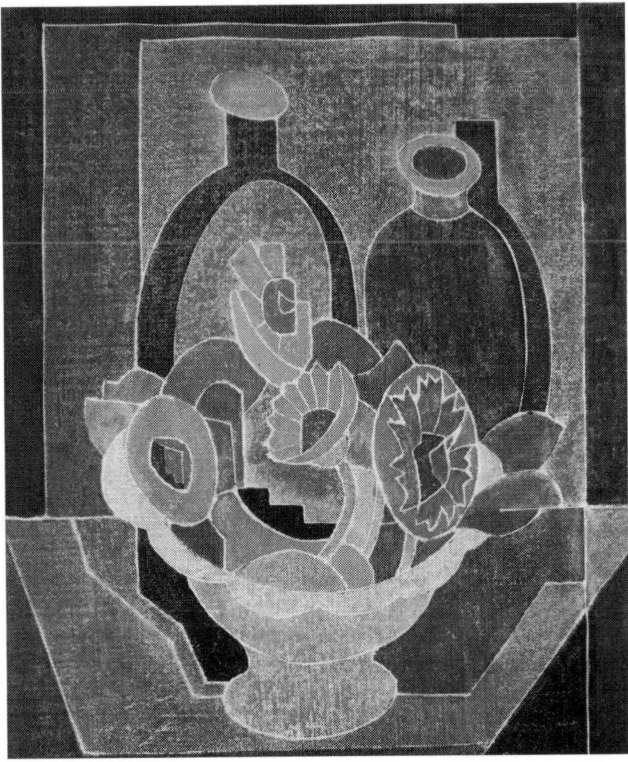

Lazzell, *Marigolds,* oil on canvas. Courtesy of PAAM.

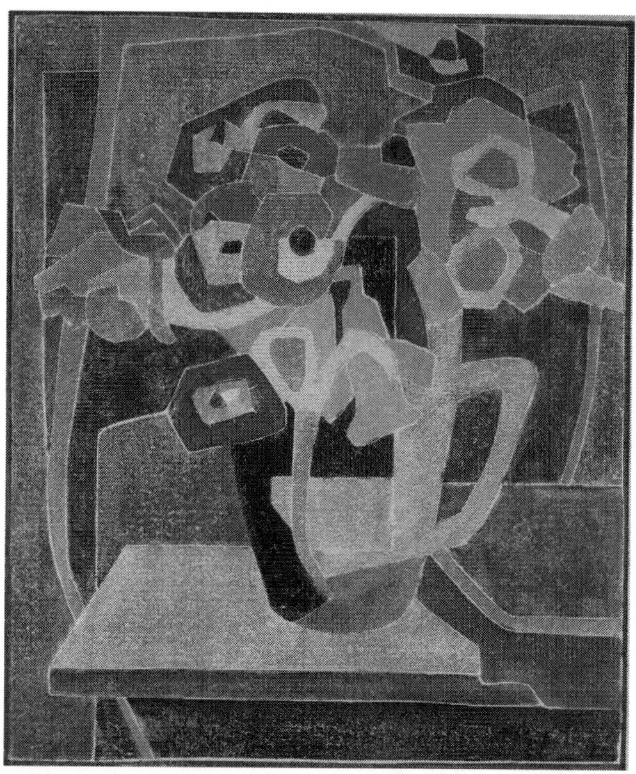

Lazzell, *Anemones,* 1937, oil on canvas. Courtesy of PAAM.

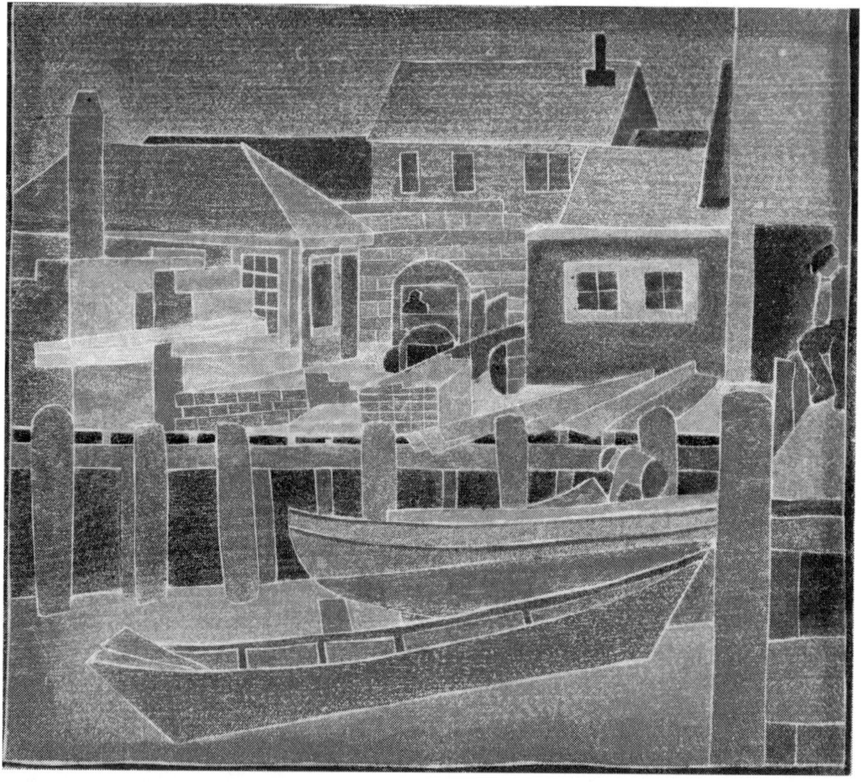

Lazzell, *The Lumber Wharf,* 1929, white line print. Courtesy of PAAM.

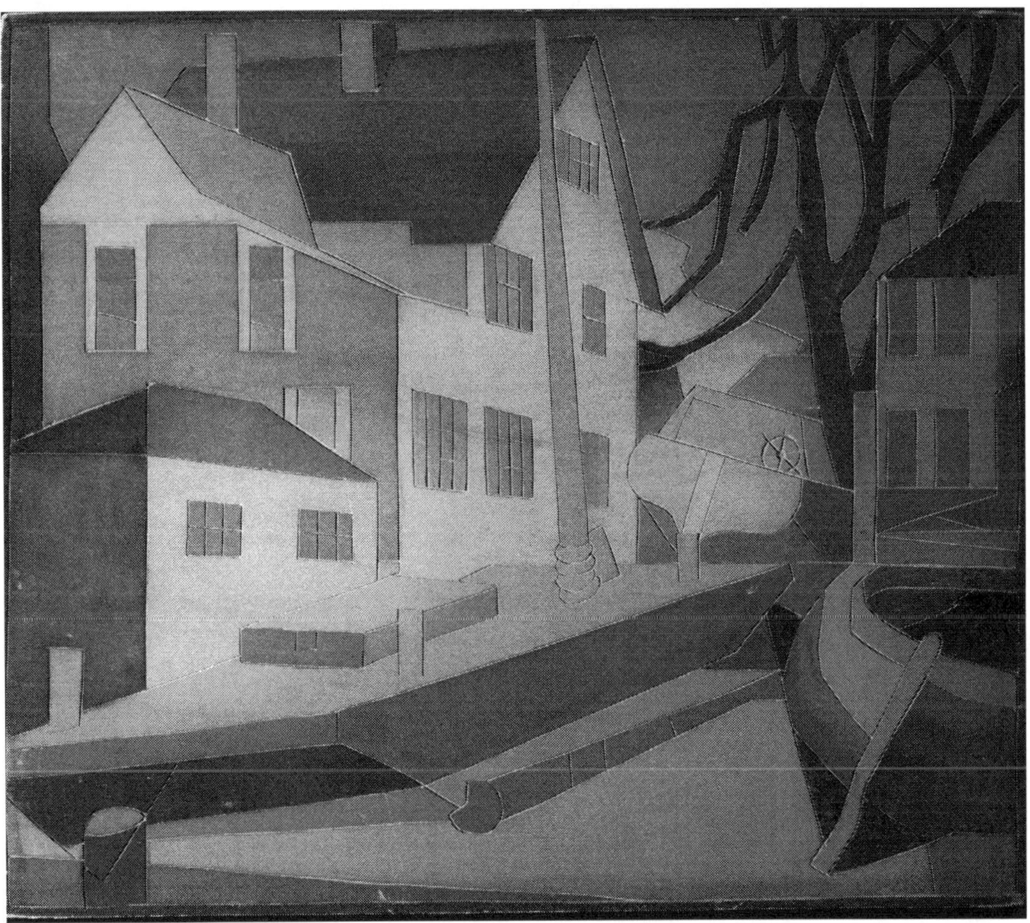

Lazzell, *The Red Scow*, 1934, wood block. Courtesy of PAAM.

Conceptual Artist Jay Critchley Raised More Than $7 Million for Charity

In October 2024, Astrid and I spent a week of research in Provincetown. My artist friend, Jay Critchley insisted, "I don't fit in. This is a town of painters. That's not what I do."

At Fairfield University, a small Jesuit school, he majored in English with minors in religion and philosophy. Nothing prepared him for a remarkable career in social justice advocacy.

The long way around, he "came out" as an artist by default. In 1981 he created a piece *Just Visiting for the Weekend, Sand Car Series #1.* A sister abandoned a Dodge which he encrusted with sand. Properly registered and insured, it was parked at Macmillan Pier in the heart of Provincetown.

There was a competition to create a sign for Route 6 promoting Provincetown. He submitted the idea of a sand car parked by the highway. That notion was summarily dismissed. Jay does not take rejection lightly. Ignoring City Hall he parked the sand-encrusted car, one of three, that remained on view through the summer.

He reasoned that no permit is required to park a car in a public space. Nor are there restrictions on how long it may remain as long as the fee is kept up to date. With a natural audience of tourists, it attracted considerable attention. So much so that the police deemed it a public nuisance and tried to have it removed. Fearing a loss of its license, the tow company refused to remove a parked and paid-for vehicle.

With no prior art education or practice, inadvertently, Critchley had created an example of conceptual art. There was no other way to look at it. People and media began to refer him as an "artist." That was difficult for him to accept. Having struggled to come out as a gay man, he now was tasked with coming out as an artist. Both entailed complex identity issues and dramatic lifestyle changes.

The Critchleys were named 1958 Connecticut Catholic Family of the Year. His father was a patent law secretary for GM. He also raised and trapped minks which were skinned and processed in the basement. It was partly a hobby, as well as a source of income. Jay helped to set traps but now cringes at the thought, though forms of taxidermy figure in the work. There were pieces entailing fish skins retrieved from processing plants.

"We were a family of Irish Catholics with not one an alcoholic," he recalls. "There were no child beatings that we know of. No abuse. No extramarital affairs."

It was a large and remarkably functional, loving, and devoutly Catholic family. His sister Betsy was the victim of a serial killer. Other siblings include Eileen, Anne, Irish Twin Geri, Ceecee, Donny, Mark, and Kathleen.

The brood was routinely kicked out of the crowded house. Jay liked to play marbles but wasn't keen on sports. By default, he played four years of soccer, which he wasn't particularly keen on.

Early on, he loved to perform, with leads in high-school musicals. He was the male voice in a family sextet which appeared on the popular *Ted Mack Amateur Hour*. They won the first week, but were voted off the following one. Jay won a national essay-writing contest.

"Dressed in uniforms, officials visited my homeroom to award me a prize," he recalled.

Our combined families summered at Uncle Cliff's home on a small island off the coast of Connecticut. The ramshackle house needed constant repair. Jay helped and acquired skills with hand tools. That proved to be invaluable in later years. "I learned to work with my hands," he recalled.

In such a loving and supportive environment, he strove to do the right thing. "At Fairfield I got a terrific liberal arts education," he said. "That doesn't happen anymore with a shift to preparing for professions and careers." That background in critical thinking would provide a foundation for his work as a social justice activist. It was more useful and pragmatic than art school. It's also part of why his work is difficult to define and appreciate. What it's not is a compelling aspect of its wit and originality.

Often, when discussing his absurdist projects, there is a self-deprecating wink and nod, a bit of chortle to confirm whether we are buying into the con. Like Christo and Hans Haacke, it's the complex process, legal and otherwise, that is integral to the work. Jay routinely takes on the establishment, like battling for a patent for his product *Old Glory Condoms.* Created during the height of the AIDS epidemic, he conflated the American flag and safe sex. Old Glory was never displayed at half mast. After an epic battle, he secured a patent and the product reached global markets.

After college he was a Vista volunteer. When he returned home in 1971, he cohabitated with Alva Russell, who he married in 1974. Their son, Russell, was born in Provincetown in 1974. The marriage ended in divorce not long after. Custody and visitation schedules were issues that went on for years. "They never spoke of me and told him that I was dead," Jay said.

They later connected, and Russell has three children by different women. Communication continues to be difficult.

When first visiting Provincetown, Jay knew that something wasn't right. It took time and years of therapy to find his sexuality and identity. That process was extended to include confronting the pollution and corruption of major corporations with legal tactics and by subversion from within. For his projects and products, he has created a number of corporations and is one himself.

Much of his coming out and identity struggles are laid out in vivid detail, in Peter Manso's controversial book, *Provincetown: Art, Sex and Money on the Outer Cape* (2002). Knowing that I would talk about it with Jay, I read the book the week before we visited. It's a scandalous page-turner, and I was surprised that Jay threaded through the book.

Describing Manso as a friend that he spent a lot of time with, Jay said, "Peter liked to pick fights and stir up trouble." That was the case when Norman Mailer, a friend, turned on Manso when his biography, *Mailer: His Life and Times,* was published. He also published a major biography about Marlon Brando. The son of Long Point artist Leo Manso, Peter died at 80 in 2021.

"Peter grew up here, then went away to Berkeley for a decade," Jay said. Upon his return, Provincetown had changed, and according to Manso, not for the better. "He was a little guy who identified with macho men like Mailer and Brando." Manso documented how Provincetown had been gentrified and "taken over" by gays, both in real estate development as well as politically.

There was such outrage in response to the book that "People were mad at me for even talking to Peter." Manso moved from Provincetown to the woods not far away.

I asked Jay how he felt about intimate details of his private life appearing in the book. "If you are an artist, your life is part of the work," he told me. "So how can I object to that?"

Over the decades that I have known him, it's always interesting to hear about his latest projects. He has shown and performed globally. On this visit, he updated progress on a project in Ireland.

"I went there first, years ago," he said. "More recently I have been there four times. I went with family, reconnecting with relatives. I have a large project. Friends procured for me a large tractor that I am covering with peat moss." All these years later it sounds like an update of the *Sand Car.*

"When I got home, I met for two hours with my son and his family," he said. Clearly hurt he said, "I wasn't asked a single question about Ireland." He speculated about what that implied in what is a difficult relationship.

In 1975, having taken up residency in Provincetown, Jay joined the Drop-In Center, a free health clinic, as program coordinator for its social services programs. The town had, since 1919, been under the care of the eccentric and incompetent Dr. Daniel Hiebert, about whom Manso relates disturbing, but hilarious, anecdotes. With an influx of hippies in the 1970s, there was a lapse in providing affordable health care. When Dr. Hiebert died, Patti, the second wife of artist and restaurateur Ciro Cozzi, founded the Center, which was housed in a variety of inadequate venues. After several years, it was precarious. As Manso reported, "Jay Critchley scrambled like crazy, along with various board members, to raise $75,000 to $100,000. Then the need for the Center itself wasn't as pressing as it had been in the past. Times had changed. There weren't as many runaways. The kids weren't coming in crazy on quaaludes like they had before."

After an epic struggle, the Center was no longer sustainable. The experience, however, created a foundation for administrative and fund-raising experience for the social justice programs Critchley later initiated.

While at the Center, he struggled to survive on a salary of $6,500. He formed a relationship with a staff member, Dr. Doug Kibler. They bought a house in a densely populated working-class neighborhood for $38,000. "Smartest thing I ever did. I could never be in town now if I hadn't done it," he said. "We might have been lovers for maybe a year. I was still not happy about being gay and I was not enjoying it." As a lapsed Catholic, with emphasis, he told me that "What I was doing was sinful."

There was an amicable separation when Doug left during the summer of 1980 for graduate study at UCLA, Irvine. In the late 1980s, Doug died of AIDS. With help from his family, Jay bought Doug's share of the property from Kilber's estate. It entails a rental unit that, with years as a waiter, paid the bills. Today he has an income from Provincetown Community Compact, a nonprofit he established in 1993. Primarily through the annual Swim for Life, PCC has raised some $7 million.

Astrid and I were invited to visit for afternoon tea in his Provincetown Theme Park. The cluttered home is surrounded by twelve-foot hedges. The backyard and its many artifacts remain much as we recalled from prior visits.

Deftly, he guided us through the points of interest. A salvaged double-seated outhouse is now a gallery. There were recycled Christmas trees, a grotto, the slowly deteriorating sand car with some its original veneer. The highlight is a repurposed former cesspool. It has been modified as rental property.

"Has anyone stayed there?" I asked. "Yes," Jay said, "I have." It has also served as a venue for underground theater and musical performances. "The audience stood over there," he said, pointing to an area which is now a garden. He paused to harvest a late-season cherry tomato offering me one.

In the office gallery he showed us the vintage legendary *Miss Tampon Liberty.* He had recently unpacked it and taken it to Ireland. In 1985 he established Tampon Applicator Creative Klubs International (TACKI). When walking the beach the plastic tampon applicator was the most common item he encountered. Some 3,000 of them were fashioned into a gown that he wears for performances and protest demonstrations.

He was barred from wearing it during a committee appearance at the Massachusetts State Legislature. *No with the Flow* was a protest attempting reform of the Boston Sewage Outfall Pipe which dumped waste into the harbor. It has since been modified. The plastic applicator is a product of Big Oil, which has lobbied against developing a biodegradable version.

When we visited, he had recently overseen the 37th annual Provincetown Swim for Life & Paddler Flotilla! It was inspired when Jay and some friends were challenged to swim from Long Point to the Boatslip Resort. The event has grown to include global swimmers and sponsors.

Because of the ever-increasing danger of sharks, the swim is sited next to the shore as well as in a large pond. "Seals are now protected and have proliferated on the ocean side," he said. "Sharks, including Great Whites, have swarmed to feed on the seals. Beaches aren't safe, and surfing is risky."

Post holiday, January 7, 2025, marks the 42nd annual Re-Rooters Day Ceremony. It's another Critchley event that has been modified. The initial concept was to stick Christmas tree stumps back into the ground. He tried to encourage families to use potted trees that could be recycled, but that never proved to be viable.

The event has evolved into a ritual Valhalla burial for a single recycled tree. Jay fashions a rustic boat which, with a communal participation, is dragged to the beach. In ritual garb, Jay leads onlookers in chants. The boat and its cargo are pulled into the water and set ablaze.

"Every year is different, depending on the weather," he said. "We have endured blizzards as well as enjoyed unseasonably balmy weather. It's a wonderful bookend to the holiday season." He noted that the Cape has ever more mild winters due to global warming.

There is a time to be born and a time to die. A time to plant and a time to uproot.

Passages and their rituals are an integral part of Critchley's remarkable life and work. We spoke of legacy and what will come after. It's obvious that artifacts like *Miss Tampon Liberty* and the *Sand Car* belong in major museum collections. But what of the ephemera cluttering his home and backyard Theme Park?

He hopes to keep it largely intact, and has a plan. Now 77, he wants to develop the backyard into upscale condos. That would fund a foundation in his name to preserve the home and its content as a work of art. For the ever-whimsical and inventive artist, the end of life is potentially another and final conceptual art piece.

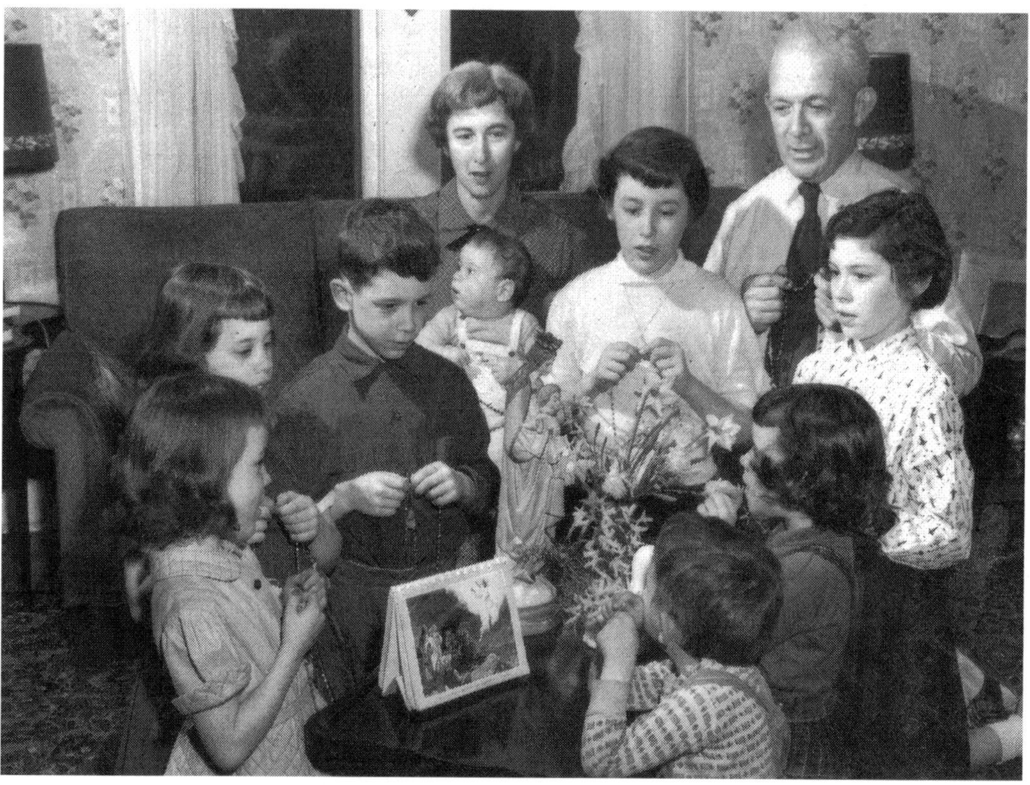

The devout Critchley family saying the Rosary. Critchley Archive.

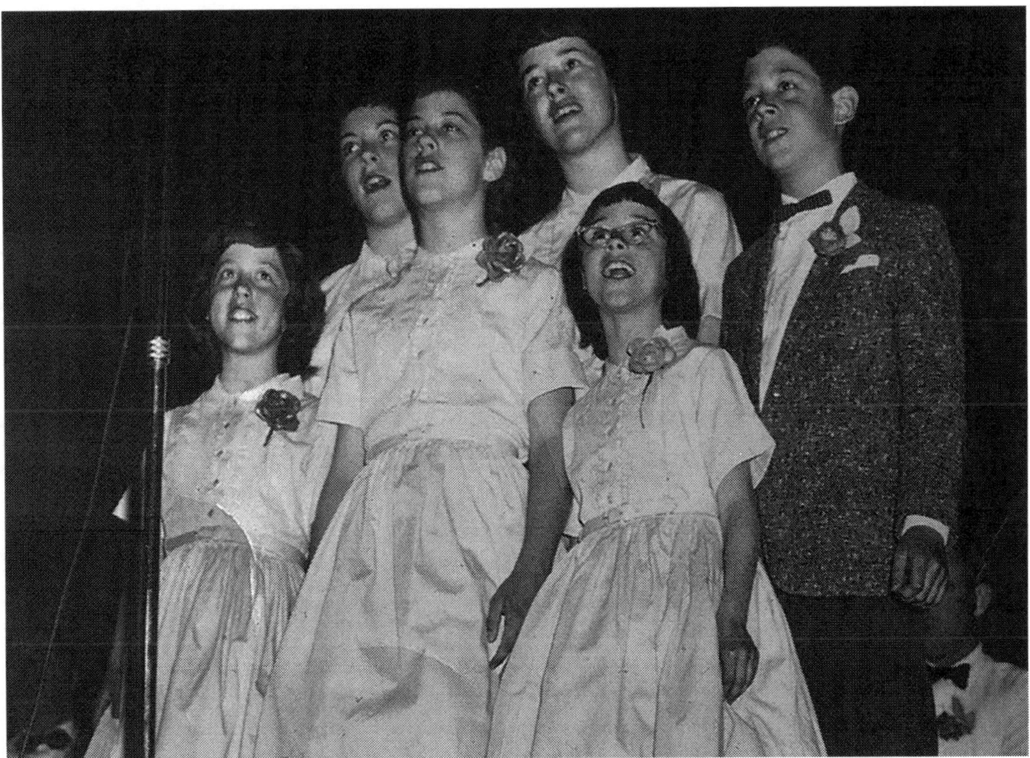

The Critchley Quintet performing on the *Ted Mack Amateur Hour.* Critchley Archive.

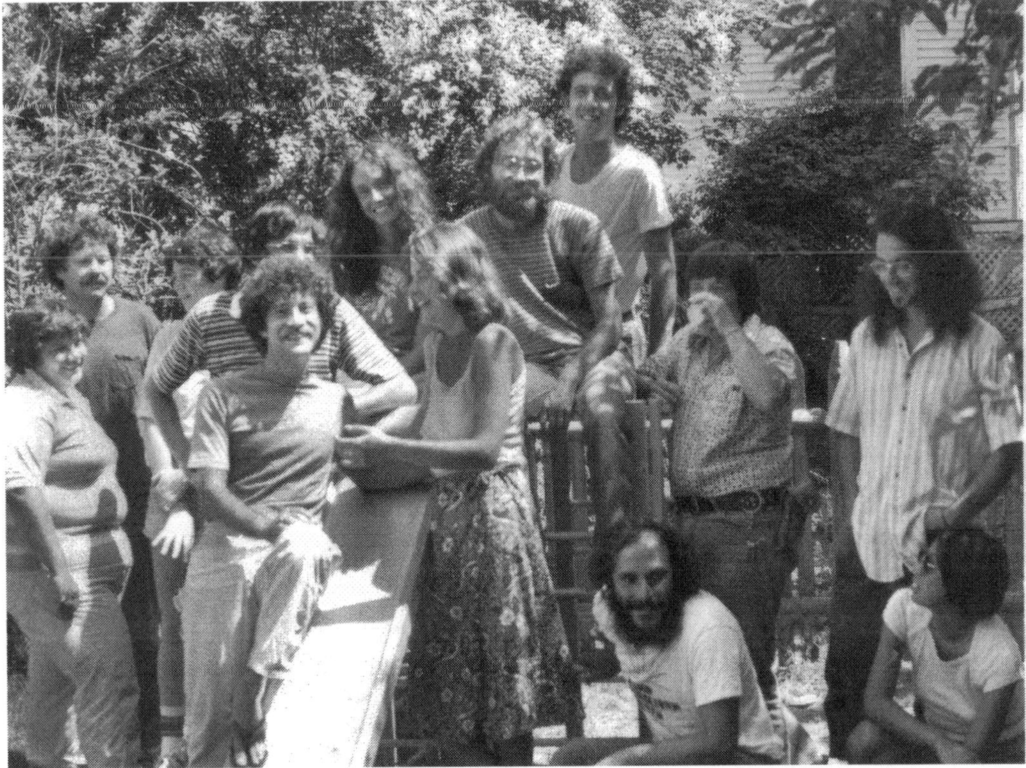

Critchley, top row, worked for the Drop-in Center, a free health clinic. Critchley Archive.

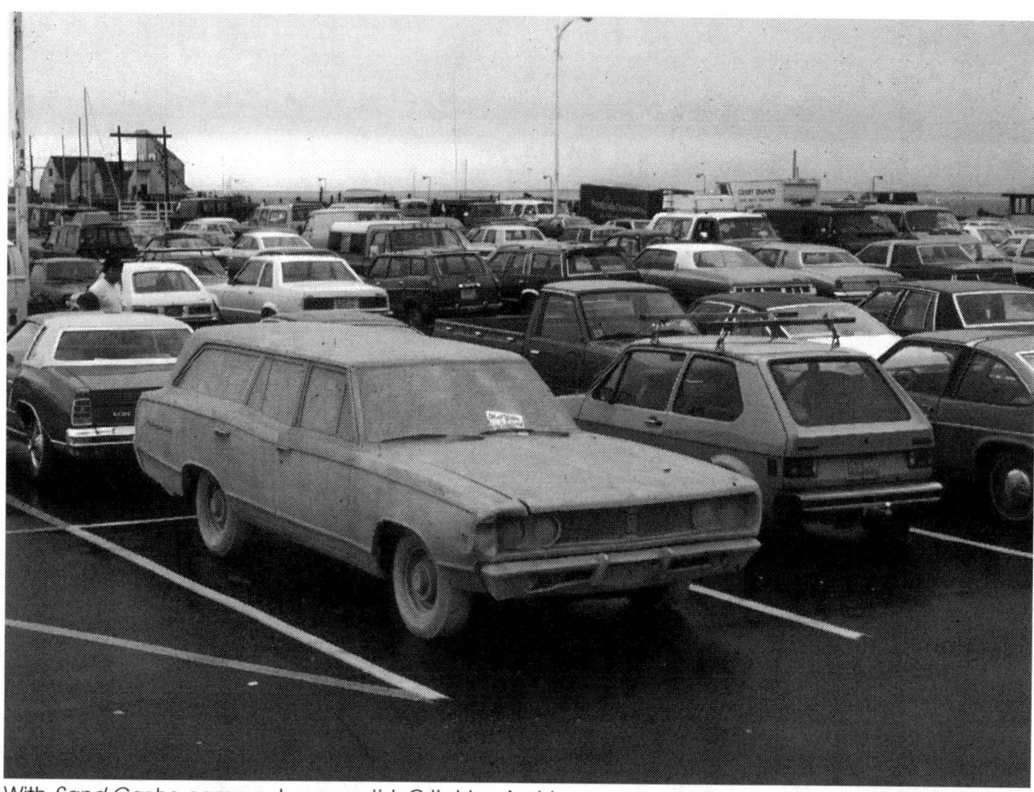

With *Sand Car,* he came out as an artist. Critchley Archive.

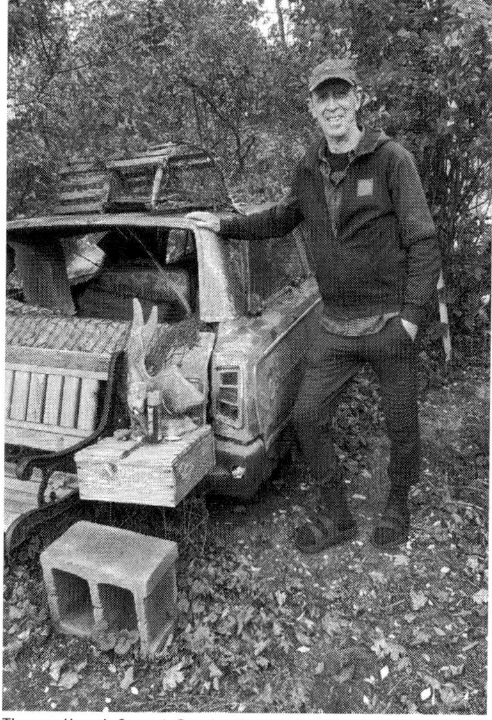

The retired *Sand Car* in the artist's cluttered backyard. Giuliano photo.

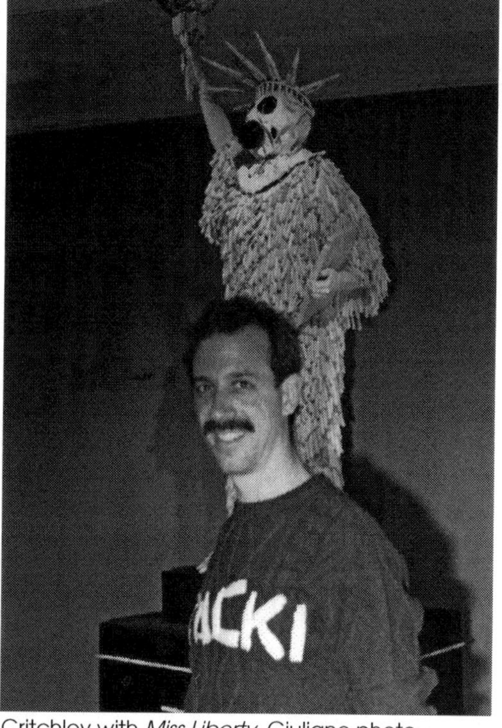

Critchley with *Miss Liberty*. Giuliano photo.

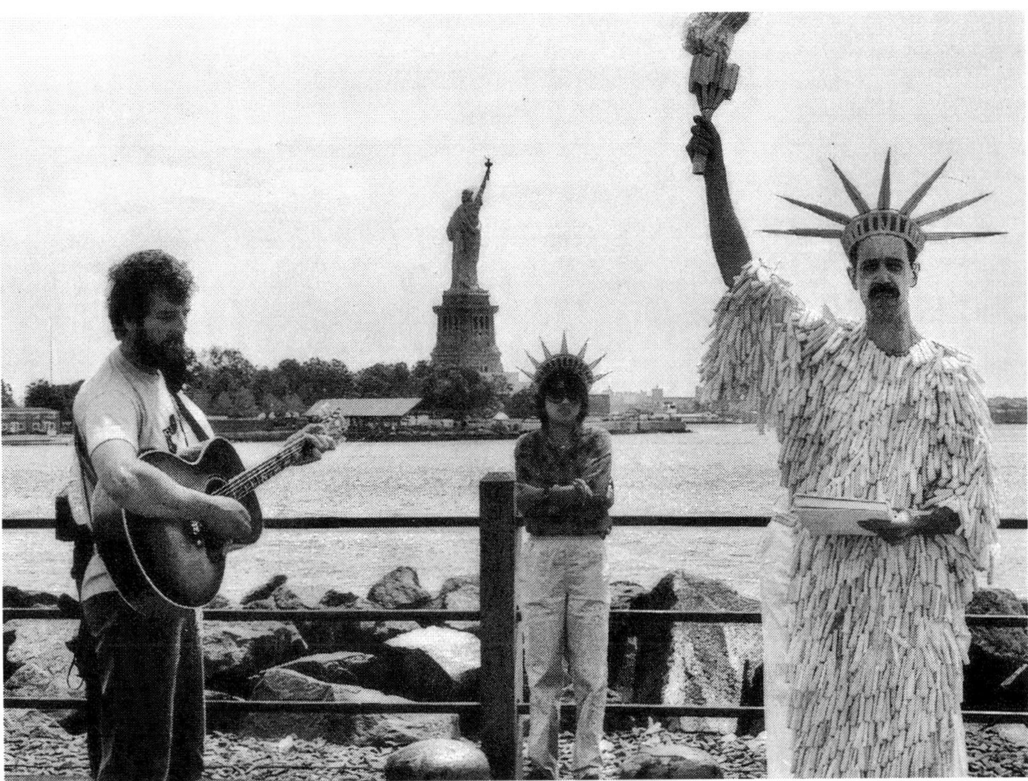

Miss Liberty with *Statue of Liberty* in background. Critchley Archive.

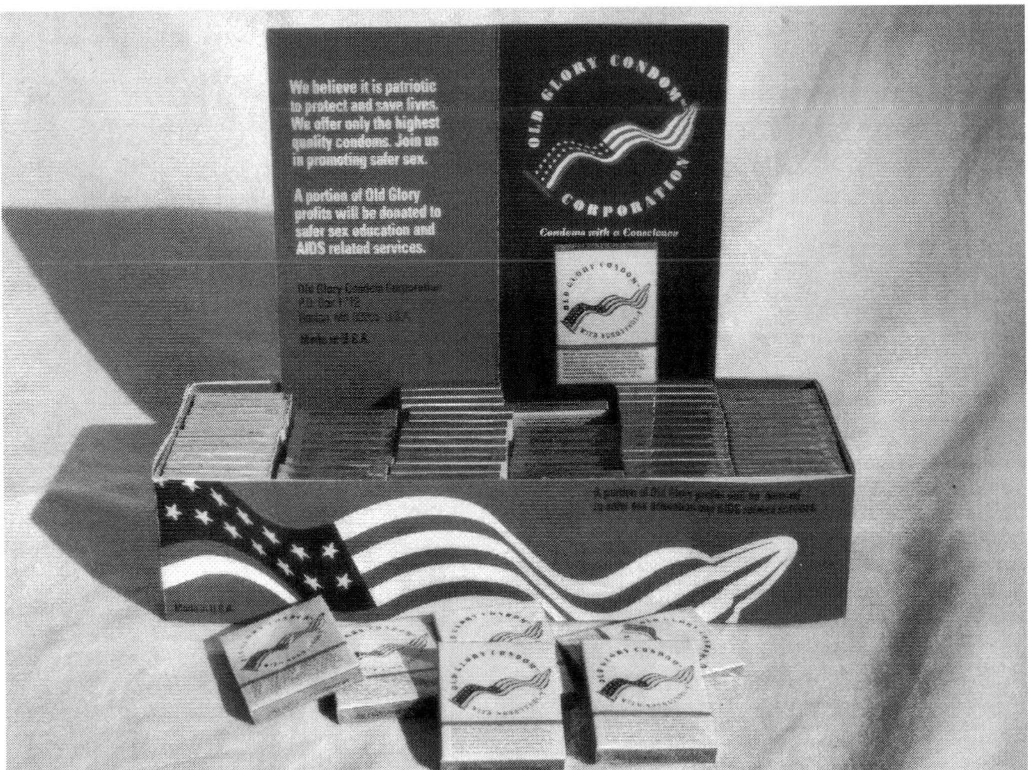

Old Glory condoms never hang at half-mast. Critchley Archive.

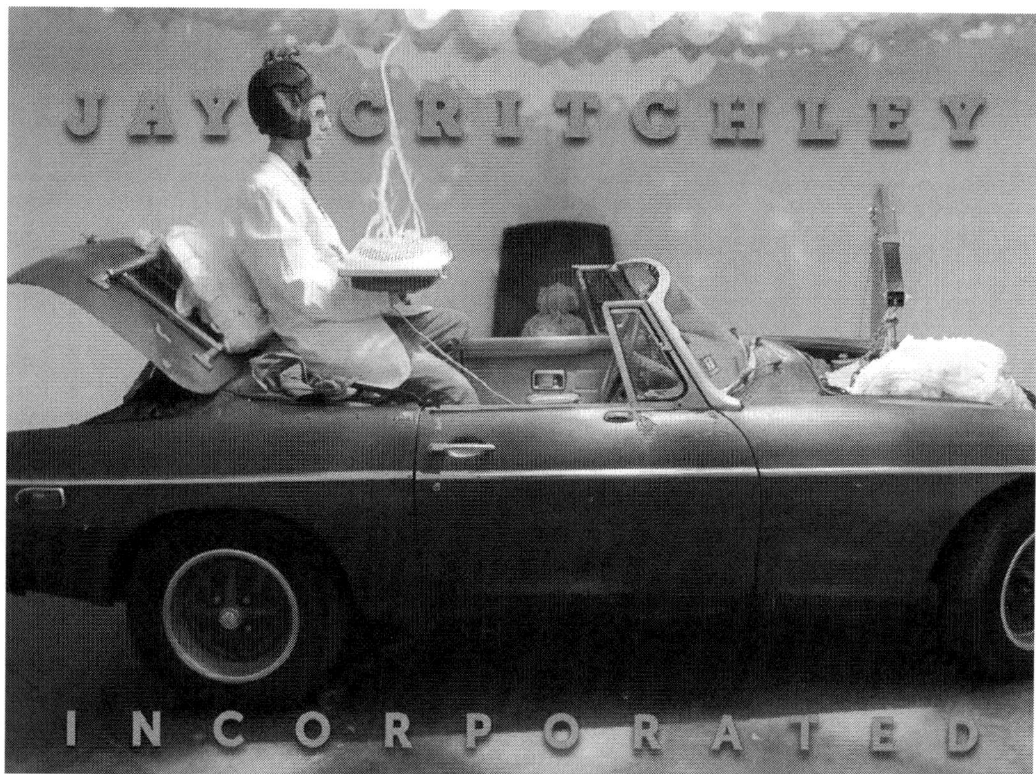

Jay Critchley Inc. Critchley Archive.

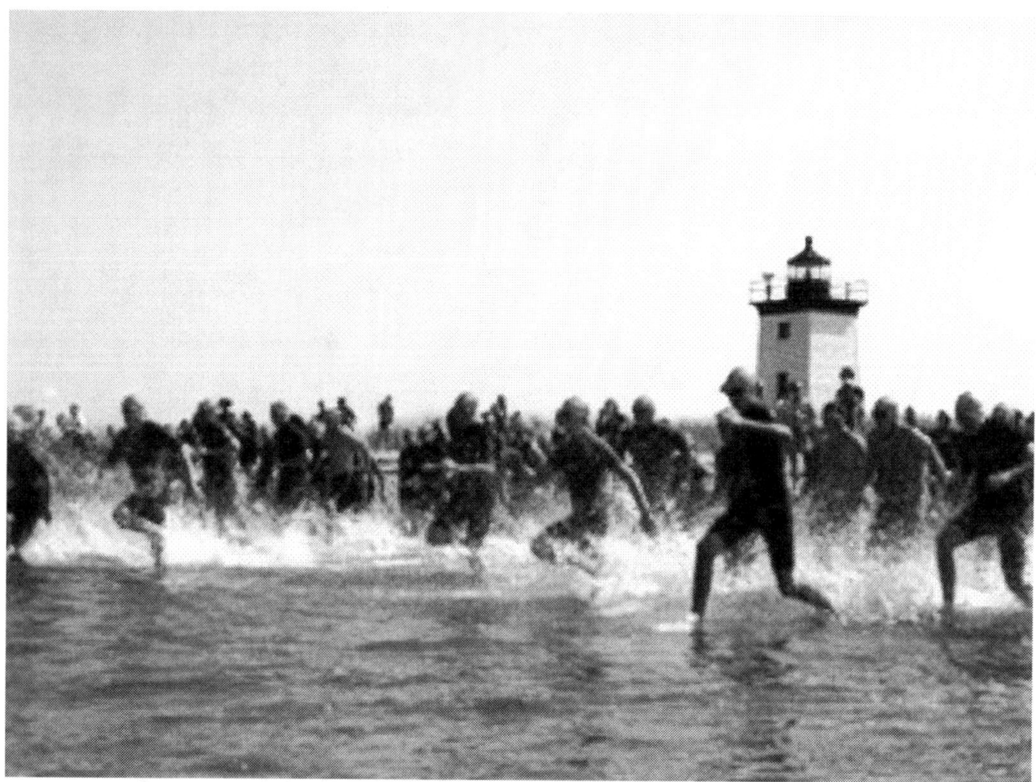

Swim for Life has raised millions for charity. Critchley Archive.

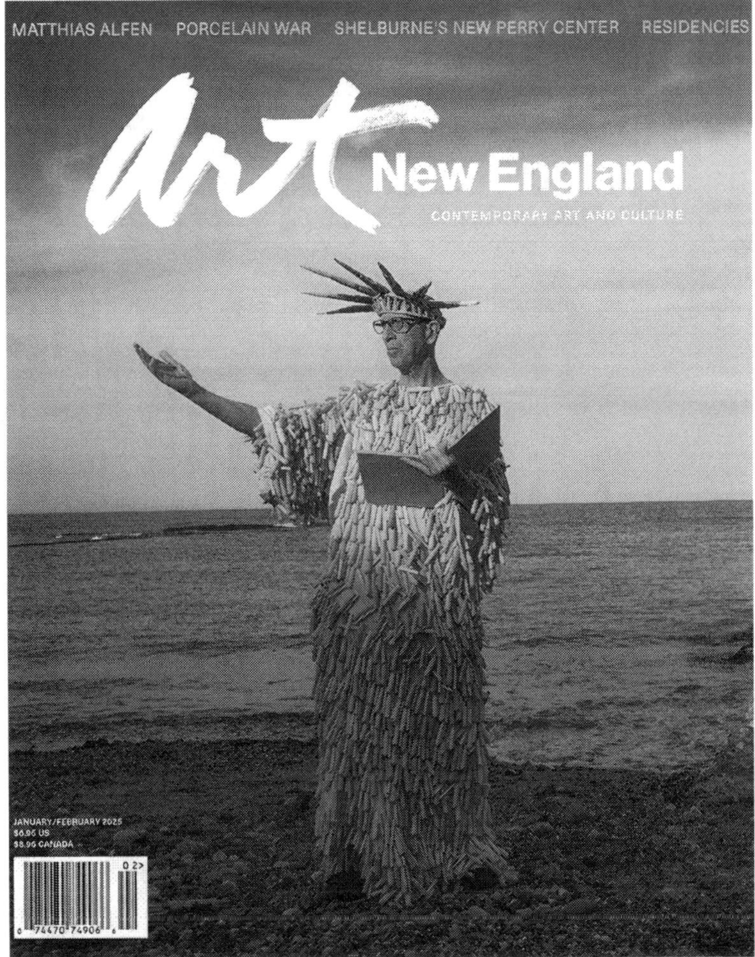

Miss Liberty on the cover of *Art New England*. Critchley Archive.

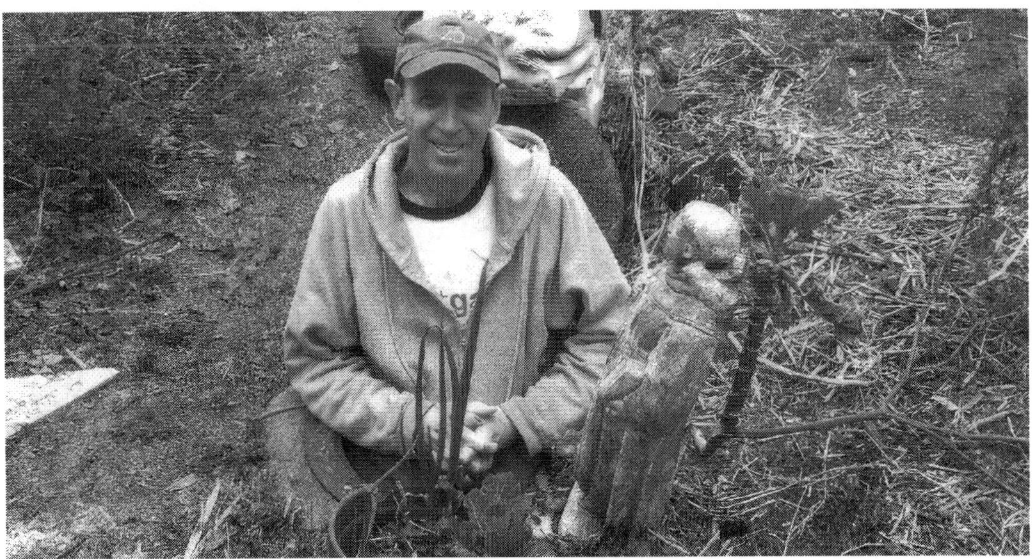
Underground artist in his septic tank bunker. Giuliano photo.

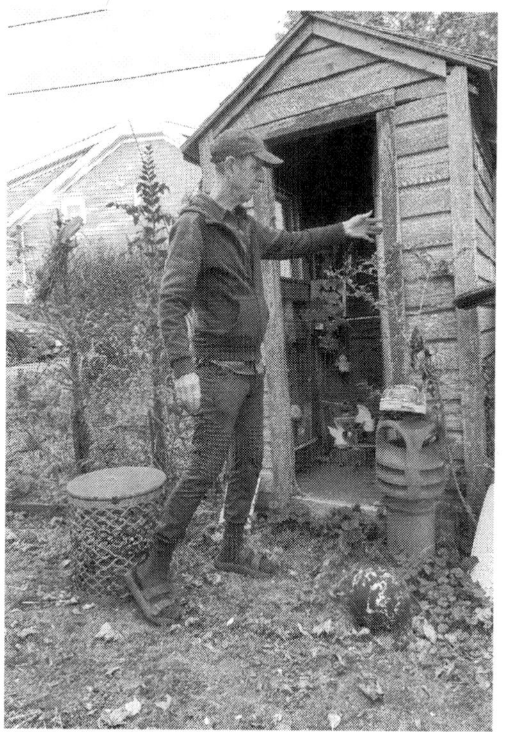
The Outhouse Gallery. Giuliano photo.

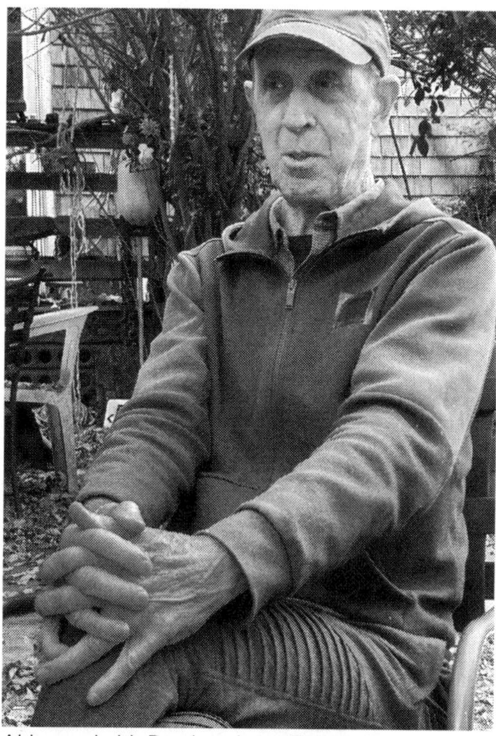
At home in his Provincetown Theme Park. Giuliano photo.

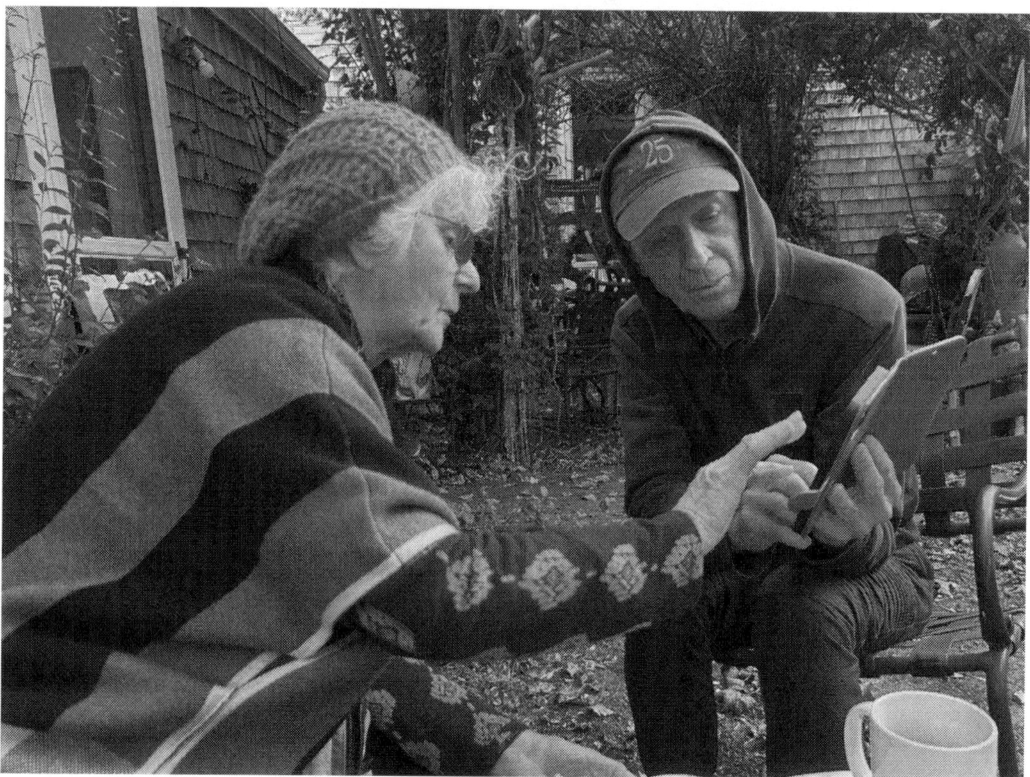
Jay discussing his work with Astrid Hiemer. Giuliano photo.

Chris Busa Was Publisher/Editor of *Provincetown Arts Magazine*

Chris Busa (1946–2020) was the eldest son of the artist Peter Busa who, after a career in New York, settled in Provincetown where he taught out of his studio. Chris described himself as "bilingual," having two lives, growing up in New York with summers in Provincetown. He was also bilingual, having interest in both fine arts and literature. He pursued, but did not complete, a dissertation on D.H. Lawrence.

With Ray Elman, who dropped out several years later, he founded *Provincetown Arts Magazine*, an annual. We shared mutual interests and he published several of my articles. Most importantly, was an essay for the exhibition *Kind of Blue: Benny Andrews, Emilio Cruz, Earle Pilgrim and Bob Thompson,* which I curated for Provincetown Art Association and Museum. At the time PAAM had no funds for publications.

He was passionate about the arts, but also volatile. An obituary in *The Provincetown Independent* stated in part that "Chris could be adversarial and had a temper, which led to him being banished from the Provincetown Tennis Club, something he unsuccessfully fought for years… Last year, Chris went through a bitter confrontation with the board of *Provincetown Arts Press,* and the board resigned. It was replaced and is now headed by Livia Tenzer."

Chris Busa
Interview at his home
2015

Charles Giuliano How old is *Provincetown Arts Magazine?*

Chris Busa This summer (2015) is the 30th annual issue. You were there at the beginning, when we launched it.

CG You cover the fine arts as well as literature. It started as a newspaper and evolved into a magazine.

CB Initially, we put out three separate issues during the summer. Then we switched to the idea of an annual magazine. We were running around like crazy with three different printing bills. We decided that we could consolidate.

When I started there was a guy, Tony Kahn, who was Terry Kahn's brother. He was the editor of *The Banner.* He said, "You'll never survive as an annual." I said to Tony, "Christmas comes once a year and we don't forget about it. The summer season comes once a year and we don't forget about it."

It's a built-in seasonal activity and it has worked as an annual. I couldn't do it in the winter. There's no point to that. First of all, it's like a book. I write six or seven articles for every issue. We average 170 pages and sometimes more. A page contains 1,500 words.

It's quite an undertaking. I do an awful lot of reading and have a staff.

CG Is that manuscripts?

CB Mostly books which I have to read for articles.

John Yau, who is on our cover, has published 50 books. I've read 20 of them before I started this year's work. I read his two books on Jasper Johns and his Warhol book. I read a collection of essays, *Passionate Spectator.*

Each year it's like earning a master's thesis to write a six- to eight-thousand-word cover article. It entails a lot of work, effort, and growth. It means taking on new challenges. This time in particular, I was interested in Yau because he's in the tradition of Frank O'Hara. He's been coming here for years. He did the first article on the Fine Arts Work Center when they had a show at Graham Modern when Berta Walker was the director.

He wrote about people like Paul Bowen and Jim Peters. They were my colleagues at the time. He helped me to get my article on Bowen published in *Arts Magazine*. I had met him downtown in New York hanging out with Jeannie Motherwell. They had gone to college together at Bard.

I have known him for many years. He was married to Frank Stella's daughter. But that didn't work out.

CG Art historian Barbara Rose was his mother-in-law.

CB Yes, for a period of time. He studied with John Ashberry at Brooklyn College for his MFA. Ashberry encouraged him to write about art. Ashberry wrote about art for the *International Herald Tribune* when he was in Paris for a decade.

CG Let's talk a bit wider.

Around WWI Provincetown became the foremost artists' colony in America when many artists and creators left Paris and settled here. They founded the Provincetown Art Association in 1914. Let's fast forward. Is Provincetown still a significant artists' colony?

CB Absolutely. For the publication people like my father (Peter Busa) dominated the cover in the beginning. Now it's all the people I grew up with, like Paul Bowen and John Yau, who is my age. He developed as a poet writing about painting. That's very different than an art critic or an art historian. He finds a parallel insight into the working process and motivation of an artist.

CG In what sense is Provincetown still an art colony?

CB Look at the people who are in our milieu. If you want to know where the art colony is don't go to the bars. Read a copy of *Provincetown Arts*. It's all between the covers. Last year I wrote about the Art Association and cut it down by 6,000 words from 15,000 words. It says a lot of the things you were just talking about.

CG Aren't there concerns. Paul Bowen, for example, now lives in Vermont.

CB He still shows at Art Strand.

CG Jim Peters is now our neighbor in North Adams.

CB There are new artists coming in every minute.

CG How can they afford it?

CB The Work Center brings in a lot. Each year they bring in ten artists and ten writers of the highest standards. They bring in guest artists and writers one after the other, really stellar, new, talented individuals. They're chosen by the fellows. These are really hot-to-trot young people. Every week at the Work Center there is a lecture, slide show, or exhibition. There is a mingling between the fellows and invited guests.

CG The Art Association has grown enormously, as I wrote in my article about Chris McCarthy.

CB I used your article (interview) quite a bit.

CG Did you quote from it?

CB I paraphrased from it.

CG I hope I got a little credit.

CB In my 15,000-word piece I'm sure I did because I used it a lot. I interviewed her myself and covered a lot of the same material with detail. I also included the ICA (Institute of Contemporary Art) and all of that stuff. Moving from Boylston Street to Fan Pier, which she had a part in, had a parallel in her having to raise $8 million to add a new wing to our museum.

The local trustees were freaking out. They were just used to paying the light bill. How she pulled that off is a miracle. She got a lot of important donors like Robert Duffy to pony up. He donated a hundred paintings including by Myron Stout and my father, Motherwell. It was a gift of a hundred paintings for the Centennial. There is a wing named for him. There's been an influx of money here.

The Work Center offers winter stipends. They stay here and through networking find all kinds of possibilities. The capitalist economy takes money out of circulation. The art economy, however, is a gift economy. There's bartering.

In the poetry world you don't make any money by publishing, but you get good jobs through the resultant prestige. There are grants and prizes.

Provincetown teaches artists how to live as artists. The Work Center teaches them how to spend the entire day, with no job to distract them, and focus entirely on their work. Before that experience many of them had to squeeze in some time in the morning or evening. That's an important experience for people to learn to think and function as an artist.

There's a big two-week celebration of Robert Motherwell at the Work Center. I'm giving a lecture as a part of that on the theme of ekphrasis.

(One particular kind of visual description is also the oldest type of writing about art in the West. Called ekphrasis, it was created by the Greeks. The goal of this literary form is to make the reader envision the thing described as if it were physically present. In many cases, however, the subject never actually existed, making the ekphrastic description a demonstration of both the creative imagination and the skill of the writer. For most readers of famous Greek and Latin texts, it did not matter whether the subject was actual or imagined. The texts were studied to form habits of thinking and writing, not as art historical evidence.)

It's about how poetry speaks differently from visual art. This is what I have explored from the beginning of the magazine. As Matisse said, "Every artist should have his tongue cut out."

I absorbed the ethos of Motherwell, who was my neighbor for many years. I grew up with his daughters. My father was his colleague. Motherwell started *The Documents of Modern Art* through translations of European artists' writings. Then he started a magazine called *Possibilities* with Harold Rosenberg. It dealt with what happened in New York in 1949 for that entire year. That became the basis for my doing an annual. He did it for one year and I've done the magazine for 30 years.

CG Did that connect with *Forum '49* that summer in Provincetown?

CB It was the same time period and Motherwell participated in *Forum '49*. He was always very involved in discussions with artists and symposia.

CG I read his Dada book. It's a wonderful anthology. Talk about growing up here.

CB I was born in New York City and grew up here during summers.

CG When did your father buy a house? (There is a dispute about that house among the heirs. Chris purchased his home when Provincetown real estate was still relatively affordable.)

CB My father bought his house in 1952, but he was in New York from 1932 to 1952. He taught at Cooper Union. He stopped teaching because he had major patrons like Walter Chrysler. They bought his entire annual output for decades. He had taught at Cooper Union, the Art Students League, Brooklyn College, and NYU.

CG Talk to me about summers in Provincetown.

CB Sometimes I would stay here with my father until October or November before we went back to New York. I started school here.

CG Were you an only child?

CB I'm the oldest of five.

I became bilingual in terms of the local world, as well as the one in New York. When summer came, my entire set of friends would shift. There were the winter people I walked to school with and played basketball with. The summer people in the neighborhood were painters or psychiatrists. At the tennis club I became involved with a whole other ethos. I gave lessons to Mark Strand, Stanley Kunitz, Erica Jong, all kinds of interesting people. I swapped lessons for art or rare books, as a part of what I call the gift economy. I bartered a lot for dinners at Ciro's. He took lessons and there was no cash. There was a lot of that back and forth.

When I was thinking of starting the magazine, a client asked me if I had done a marketing study? I thought about it, and for 14 years I had run my own business giving tennis lessons. So right from the beginning of the magazine, we were in the black. Ads have always paid our bills.

CG Was Ray Elman your partner? (He is on the magazine's board and does commissioned portraits.)

CB He was my partner in the very beginning. He dropped out four years later. It started in 1985, and he dropped out in '90 or so. After that, I changed the legal structure to a 501c3. That's when we started to get grants. The reason I changed it to nonprofit is that we were doing the Kunitz issue in 1992 and I needed fifteen grand to pay the printing bill.

I didn't know what to do. I sent a letter to a hundred people and twenty-five grand came in within a month. I figured if they would do that for a profit, they would do that for a nonprofit. Now that it's 30-years-old, we have expanded our board. Terry Kahn is the new president. He's Jack Kahn's son, the *New Yorker* writer. Margaret Murphy, the director of the Work Center, is now on the board. We've got savvy people and are getting NEA grants.

CG In addition to the magazine, how many books have you published?

CB We've published 22 books. The latest is the Jay Critchley catalog for his show at the Provincetown Museum.

CG The magazine seems to have crosscurrents between fine arts and literature. The other night we saw the Clifford Odets play *Waiting for Lefty,* directed by Bragan Thomas at Provincetown Theater and attended the reading of his play based on Caligula. It's great to see theater again in Provincetown, which of course has a great tradition.

In New Orleans recently, we attended parts of the Tennessee Williams Festival and met David Kaplan who directed *The Hotel Plays*. He runs the O'Neill Festival in Provincetown, which we will attend in September. There is a real diversity of the arts reflected in what the magazine covers. There seems to be no end of material from the historical to present.

We heard John Lahr speak about Williams in NOLA. Since then, both Astrid and I have read his 600-page book. So that is great background for attending the festivals. In New Orleans we saw a production of *Suddenly Last Summer*, in addition to readings and panel discussions.

You pursued graduate level research on D.H. Lawrence.

CB I wrote a dissertation on Lawrence, which I could revise, but I am an ABD (all but dissertation). When my father was teaching, there were always fights between the art history professors and studio artists.

CG That's usually the case.

CB As the critic, Stanley Fish put it having professors running MFA programs is like having animals run the zoo.

CG You are trained in literature, but growing up as the son of an artist, you have an understanding of the fine arts. How does that work its way into the magazine?

CB To me it's all connected. *Provincetown Arts* focuses on art and writing, but theater, architecture, and film are also topics we cover every year. Art and writing are solitary activities. Theater is a sociological art form. We do all aspects of the arts, including the politics; which is why I did an interview with Governor Deval Patrick. Karen Finley got the idea to become a performance artist by attending the Democratic National Convention in Chicago. She was inspired by politics as spectacle.

The ten years I spent at Rutgers University teaching and working on my doctorate was highly sophisticated. Some of the top people were my professors.

CG Didn't you publish a book on Lawrence?

CB It was an anthology, which I wrote a long introduction to. It's a big fat book called *The Erotic Works of D.H. Lawrence*. Crown Publishers published it and it sold out. That gave me a sense of completion for that work. I taught until a couple of years ago at Wilkes University near Scranton. I got the job through Mike Lennon, who is the biographer of Norman Mailer.

We do the best we can with a staff of just five people. Susanna Ralli, our editor, was with Houghton Mifflin for many years. The graphic designer is Irene Lipton. Heather Bruce is in advertising, and Ingrid Aue handles marketing and advertising. It's a small staff of really good people. Irene did many books while in New York and worked for Random House. They are all pretty savvy. We do a lot with very little.

We're getting more and more grants and are surviving. We pay salaries every month. Each year we get a grant from the Mass Cultural Council. They used to give us $10,000, but now with cutbacks, that's about half. We've gotten three NEA grants. We've been funded by Dedalus, which is the Motherwell Foundation. We got a major grant from the Judith Rothschild Foundation. We also have individuals who give us money.

The annual budget is only $175,000. It should be at least $200,000. We're working on fund raising with the new board. We're trying to digitize all of our back articles. You can get onto scholarly indexes and sell articles for a fee.

We will end up doing an anthology, *Best of Provincetown Arts*. I have two books of memoirs which I am close to being done with. One is personal and the other is about the magazine. It's a collection of all of my published pieces and is about 800 pages. It's called *Provincetown Arts: An Editor's Memoir*.

I needed a long piece on Motherwell. I have only done short ones. But I am doing this lecture at the Work Center about his works illustrating James Joyce, Stéphane Mallarmé, Baudelaire, and T. S. Eliot. He did a series of artists' books that are very high quality. He worked with Tatania Grossman and some of the top printers. They are very elegant books.

One was for Octavio Paz another for Lorca called *At Five in the Afternoon* about the bullfight with the refrain of "At Five in the Afternoon." That amused me because it's when the bullfighter was killed but also cocktail hour.

Like the magazine, I feel thirty years old. A lot of problems have surpassed me. My mother died recently. I won a major lawsuit about her house. My brother unfairly influenced her and had her change the will to favor him. There was a big trial in Plymouth and we won that flat out. My brother was convicted of fraud and has to pay the legal bills.

CG I started coming to Provincetown during my college years. There was a lively gallery scene that was beginning to change. This was the mid-sixties, and before that there were a number of serious galleries.

CB Yes, in the '50s.

CG Now there is a proliferation of galleries that are geared to tourists.

CB Except for Merola, Berta Walker, Schoolhouse, and Art Strand. There are still good galleries.

CG But there was a time when there were serious galleries like Sun Gallery, Sam Kootz, and Nat Halper's HCE.

CB Ivan Karp, Martha Jackson, Gallery 256, Sun Gallery. I was talking to Jeannie Motherwell, who lives near my girlfriend Ingrid. She saw Yvonne Andersen (Sun

Gallery) just last week. I just wrote a piece about Mimi Gross, who showed at Sun Gallery. That's how she met and married Red Grooms.

As kids, Mimi and I were close and we have started to spend time together. The Chaim Gross Foundation in New York has been sponsoring poets and artists in collaborations. Charles Bernstein, a language poet, got us together. It's all part of a network.

CG When I came here in the 1980s, as a graduate student, it was still kind of funky. You could stay with Frank Schaefer at his White Horse Inn which was affordable and friendly. There was always a way to shoehorn your way in. Now and then I got put up by Mervin Jules or Rhoda Rossmore. I loved the diner on Shank Painter Road for a bowl of Portuguese soup. The town has become ever more expensive and precious.

I recall lively interactions with Reggie Cabral, a collector and hustler. He never let critics and art historian examine his collection, which was notorious for works of questionable attribution. At one time I tried to work with him on a possible exhibition. He blew me off saying he knew the work better than I did because the artists drank at his bar. (The A House). Some of them settled bills with paintings. The collection went to his daughter April, who has her own problems in addition to seeing after the works.

There was still a lot of richness when I was researching. There is not much left of the historical connections, although you say that new artists arrive all the time. This new generation will have to make their own histories.

CB There's no question that you're right. There has been a slow evolution. If you put a frog in cold water and bring it to a boil, the frog adjusts to the changing temperature until it dies.

I bought this house in 1978 for $32,000. My father's house is 600 Commercial Street. That's the house we had a lawsuit about. That's a sizable house with two lots and three buildings on it.

CG Where did you get the money to buy your house?

CB I was teaching tennis and would make over $30,000 in a summer of giving lessons. I had forty grand in the bank when I bought my house. I put $20,000 down and the mortgage was $180 a month. It was cheaper than rent. Then I didn't come here for about four years. I rented it to friends.

You probably saw the documentary by Deborah Forman which talked about real estate prices driving out artists. They're trying to do affordable housing here now. The town is well aware of that need. The Work Center has bought a lot of property and a motel to house visiting artists. There is a network of supporters particularly among people involved with the Work Center. It's a big operation and quite famous. Fellows have won Pulitzer Prizes and National Book Awards.

The artists have been less successful than the writers. The artists Jack Pierson and Ellen Gallagher were fellows. Dennis Johnson, a poet and Sam Messer, an artist, started collaborating when they were fellows in the same way that I describe poets writing about painters. There is an osmosis of the working conditions that they can parlay into an understanding with evocative ways to describe the work.

Today I subscribe to the art magazines mostly to look at the pictures and ads.

CG I let my subscriptions lapse because there is essentially no critical content in the mainstream art magazines. It is all about sustaining the inflated art market. As a veteran writer told me, and I have experienced myself, the writing is handled by too many people. Publishers have influence over editors.

CB There was a time when there was at least a pretense of separation between advertising and editorial.

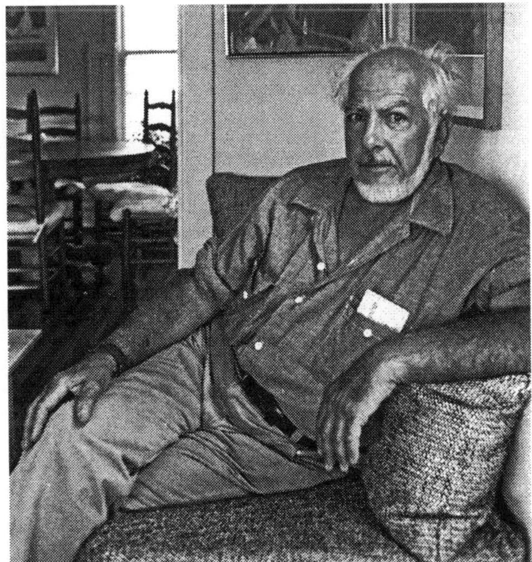

Artist Peter Busa, father of Chris Busa, photo by Phil Malicoat, courtesy of Chris Busa.

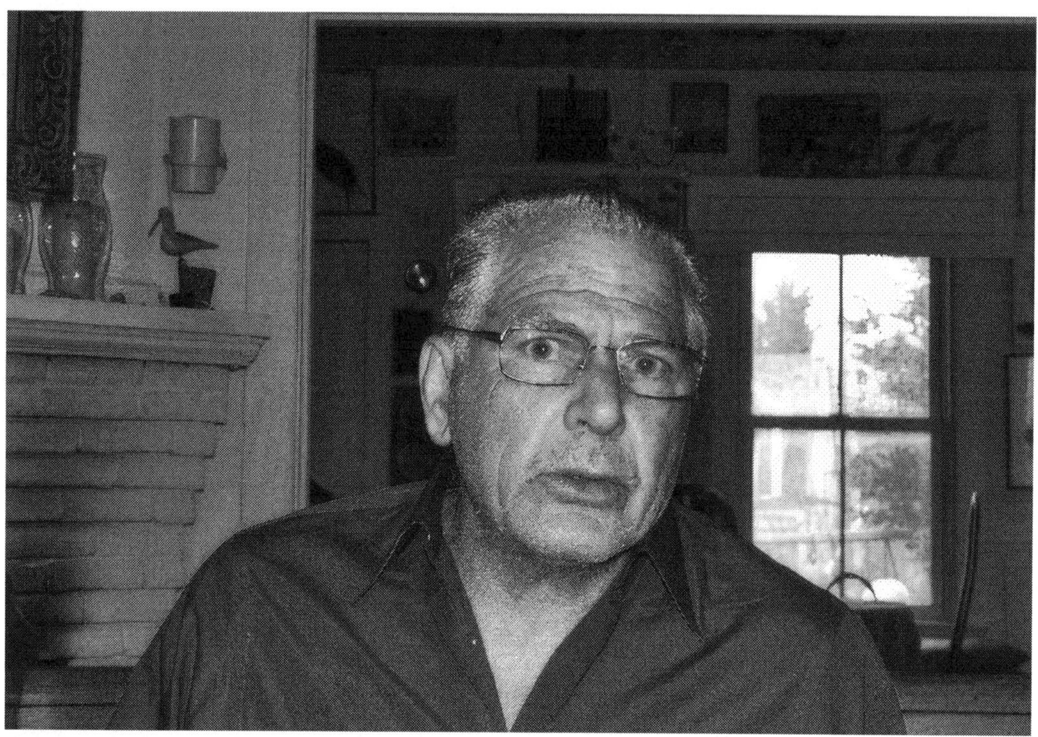

Chris Busa was the son of artist Peter Busa. Giuliano images.

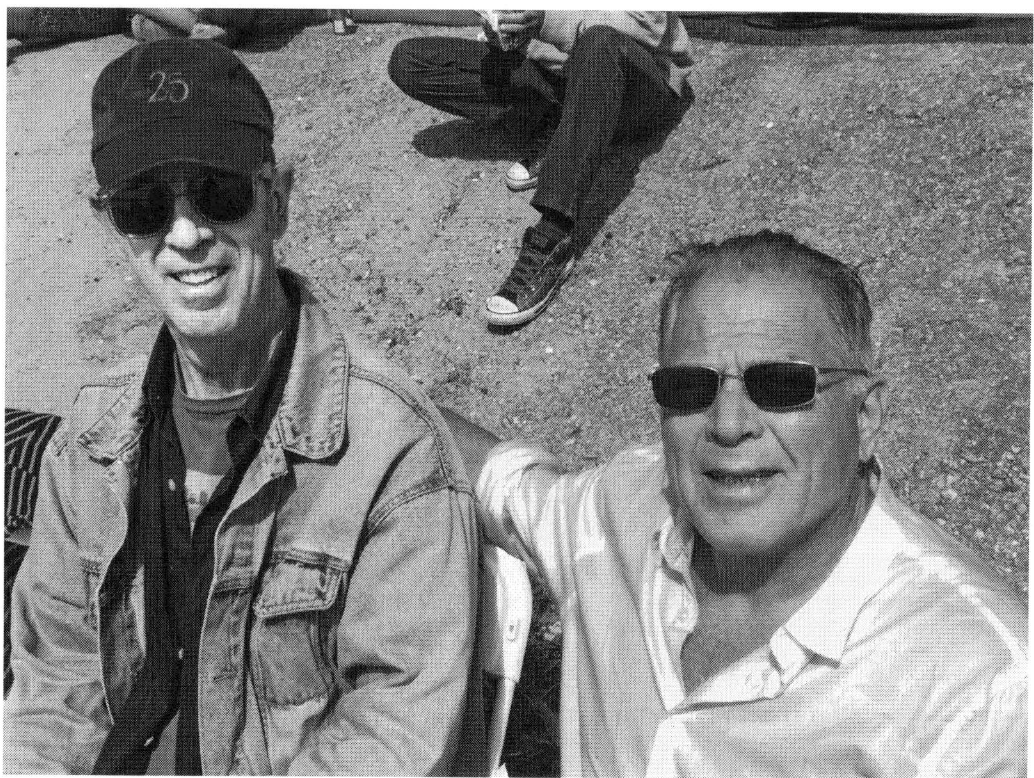

On the beach with artist Jay Critchley.

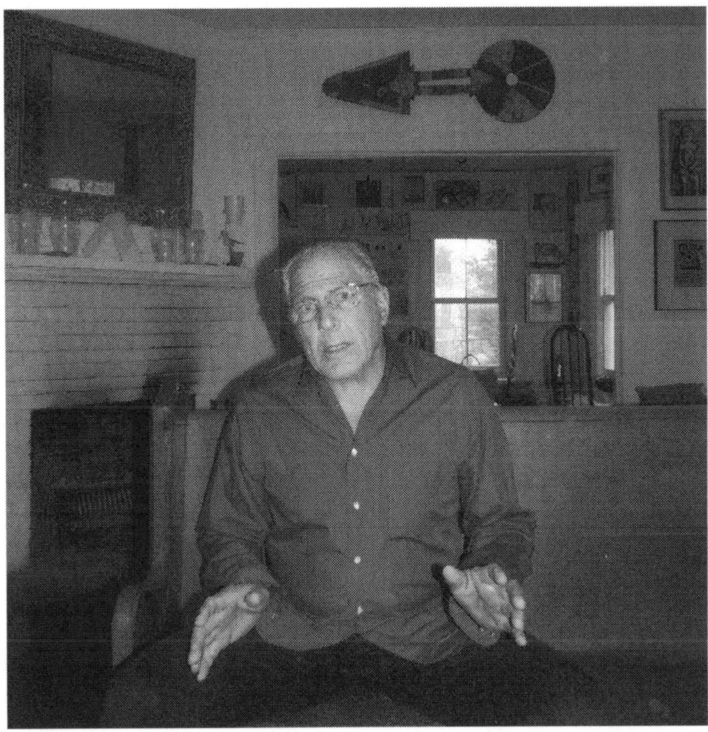

He was scholarly but contentious.

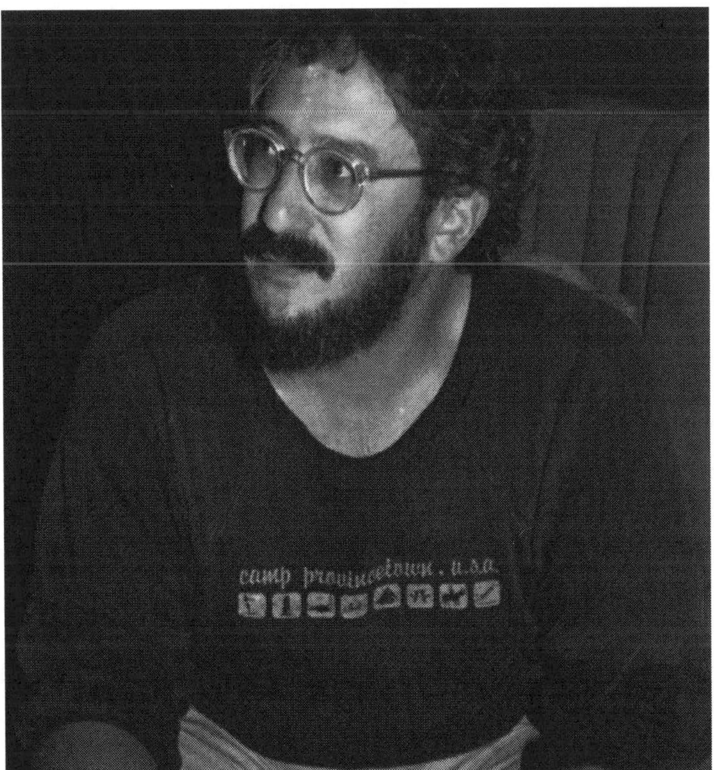

He co-founded Provincetown Arts Magazine with Ray Elman, who later dropped out.

Berta Walker Gallery, Then and Now

The grandparents of Berta Walker arrived in Provincetown in 1915. Her parents, Hudson and Ione (an artist), ran a New York gallery which closed in 1940. They represented Marsden Hartley, among others, and acquired numerous works from Georgia O'Keeffe. They had three daughters of which Berta is a twin, with an older sister.

Early on, when property was still affordable, Berta acquired the building which houses her gallery. In October, 2024, we met there and discussed her remarkable legacy.

Charles Giuliano So this is the 35th year of Berta Walker Gallery.

Berta Walker (laughing) So, I'm being interviewed! How many years has it been? I knew you before we opened the gallery. That's how far back we go. You're old enough to know the saying "I got my job through the *New York Times.*" I got my job through the Fine Arts Work Center. I was chairman of the board for years and did all kinds of fundraising. I was behind the annual special event in New York, where I was working for the Whitney Museum and other places. I was familiar with the Center for years. I came up one year and said maybe I should do some R&D (research and development). I was founding director of New York's Graham Modern. Bob Graham brought me in to bring Graham Gallery into the contemporary phase.

I came here as a two-year-old and have been here every summer since then. That's why I know all the people you have been interviewing.

(The Fine Arts Work Center [FAWC] was founded in 1968 by a group of artists, writers, and patrons, including Stanley Kunitz, Robert Motherwell, Fritz and Jeanne Bultman, Josephine and Salvatore Del Deo, Alan Dugan, Jim Forsberg, Phil and Barbara Malicoat, Myron Stout, Jack Tworkov, Hudson and Ione Walker. The founders envisioned a place in Provincetown, the country's most enduring artists' community, where artists and writers could live and work together in the early stages of their creative development. They believed that the freedom to pursue creative work within a community of peers is the best catalyst for artistic growth.)

One summer there was an emergency at FAWC and they had to let the director go. The board president said, "You know the Work Center, so why don't you become the acting director?" and I did. It must have been 1989 because at the end of that year was when I opened the gallery. There was a space available downtown and a friend said, "You have to open a gallery." I said, "No way," but the response was, "Of course you can." It was 1990, and I opened across the street from the Post Office.

I rented that space for two years but she kept increasing the rent. You can't do that to a gallery and have it survive. In those days I could buy a building for less than the rent in town. So, I bought this building.

CG What did you pay?

BW I can't remember.

CG Was it under $100,000?

BW Yes. It was a complex and behind it is an apartment that I now regret not having purchased. At the time I didn't have the extra $50,000. It's just fortunate that this property came on the market and could be renovated as a gallery space.

(She greets Stephanie Vevers and discusses her mother, the artist Elspeth Halvorsen.)

You think of Elspeth as such a gutsy woman instead of being an ignored woman in a field which is dominated by men. When Long Point started, instead of kicking and screaming about not being included, Elspeth started her own gallery, Rising Tide, in the same building. She was the founder of that cooperative. Her husband,

Tony Vevers, was part of Long Point Gallery. When they started Long Point, I was in New York working at the Whitney. Budd Hopkins called me and said, "We're starting a co-op gallery and you should come and run it for us." I had a full-time job and couldn't leave it for Provincetown. All these years later, I got to meet his daughter, Grace, who is director of this gallery. Today there is no Berta Walker Gallery without Grace Hopkins.

CG When did you step back?

BW I didn't step back, though I am not in the gallery as much as previously. I do all the advertising and PR. I do the plotting and planning.

CG I wrongly assumed that you took over the Hudson Walker Gallery. (As Hudson Walker told Dorothy Seckler, "I went back to Minneapolis and the family's lumber and real estate business until '36, when I was married, and my wife and I opened a gallery in New York at 38 East 57th Street, which we continued until 1940.")

BW There is the Hudson Walker Gallery at the Fine Arts Work Center. My mom, Ione, and dad ran the New York gallery. Mom was an artist, and there is a small piece in the current show that a lot of people like. She said, "I can't be in the studio and raising twins, etc., etc." There are three of us. I have a twin sister in California, so we anchor America coast to coast. We have a sister who is 22 months older.

They had the New York gallery from 1938 to 1940. The war started, and he closed it and never again had a gallery. He was very much an anchor as an administrator of the arts. He was involved with MoMA and was the founding president of Artists Equity. It was the only time it had a non-artist as its head. It was started by the artists of the WPA in New York.

CG What was his source of income?

BW He was a jeweler. What I now understand is that colors and the chakras are very important. In this show I looked up the metaphysical description of the color blue. This show is meant to show the strength of Kamala (Harris).

Why Dad ended up as a jeweler was because he liked color. That's what I do. Red anchors you, while blue is the void. Green represents love and moving on. That may sound foreign, but I learned about chakras. He loved gems, so it is a parallel intuition.

He was the silent mayor of the arts here in Provincetown and in New York. I first went to work as a runner for him. It meant that I was taking diamonds from the shop to the diamond district on 42nd street. I remember when a dealer dropped his diamonds down on a grid in the street. There was chaos as they recovered them. (laughing) That was my introduction to being a runner. They step outside to look at the diamonds in the sun and he dropped it. I'll never forget it.

Dad was very involved with the arts and I think he was on the board at MoMA for awhile. I will have to look it up, but I didn't know that today we would be going to memoryville.

My parents came here because my mother's parents came here in 1915. My grandmother was a writer who had the pen name of Avery Ball because she was a woman. My parents came from Pittsburgh. My grandfather was a musician, and traveled all around the world. He performed negro spirituals which was the term used at that time. He performed them in Russia. They came in 1915, which I feel connects me back to the early days of the art colony.

My grandmother was a close friend of Mary Heaton Vorse. She was very important and her house has been refurbished. She was a writer and went overseas as a correspondent during WWI. It was in her boathouse that the first plays of the Provincetown Theater (Provincetown Players) were launched. (Mary Heaton Vorse [October 11, 1874–June 14, 1966] was an American journalist and novelist. She established her reputation reporting the labor protests of a largely female and immigrant workforce in the east-coast textile industry. Her later fiction drew on this material profiling the social and domestic struggles of working women. Unwilling to be a disinterested observer, she participated in labor and civil protests, and was for a period the subject of regular U.S. Justice Department surveillance.

In 1915, Vorse helped stage the first performance of a repertoire that included Ida Rauh, Susan Glaspell, George Cram Cook, John Reed, Hutchins Hapgood, and Eugene O'Neill. Once established, the Provincetown Players moved to Greenwich Village in November 1918, opening their own Provincetown Playhouse with O'Neill's one-act play *Where the Cross Is Made.*)

CG When your father closed the gallery in 1940, he helped to place the artists he represented with other galleries. Can you discuss that?

BW It was so long ago that I can't remember. I can't remember who he placed where, but I can tell you a story about my father and Marsden Hartley. He was with Stieglitz at the time, and Dad loved his work. Hartley and Stieglitz were not getting along, so he joined my father's gallery. I will always remember that he couldn't sell the work. Artists don't get supported. Today, with the auction world and all that, it's getting worse.

CG Did he collect?

BW Yes. When O'Keeffe (the wife and heir of Stieglitz) was selling from the estate, Dad offered to buy all of the Hartleys for $5,000. He got a call from a man I can't remember and he told my father, "I have talked to O'Keeffe and she will sell me her Hartley's for $5,000. What do you think?" Dad said, "I just put a check in the mail for the work." Dad said, "I'm not going to let that bitch make us compete. Why don't we just take our money ($5,000) and split the work?" There were two stacks of paintings which they took turns for.

CG What did he end up with?

BW That I don't know, but a lot. More than a hundred, most of which are now in the museum of the University of Minnesota. He was the founding curator when he was there. His grandfather was T.B. Walker, who founded the Walker Art Center.

(In 1879, lumber baron T. B. Walker invited the public into his downtown Minneapolis home to view his art collection. In 1916, Walker bought land in Lowry Hill that he offered to the city of Minneapolis as space for a public library and art museum. After five years of futile negotiation, Walker resolved to build his own museum. Construction began in 1925, and the Walker Art Gallery opened in 1927. After 1935, Walker's grandchildren, Hudson Walker and Louise Walker McCannel, ran the gallery until the Minnesota Arts Council took charge in 1939.)

As a young man Thomas Barlow Walker was in the lumber world. He and a friend took a wagon of supplies to sell to loggers in California. One day the wagon disappeared. Whoever his partner was, took it and disappeared. There he was abandoned, but he didn't indulge in "poor me" as so many do. When you get knocked out you stay down or get back up. So, he said, guess I'll learn to cut trees. One thing led to another and he did very well. He invested in timber. He collected a lot of art and opened his home to the public in Minneapolis. It was the same year that the Met was founded.

CG That would have been 1870.

BW See, he knows these things. That's what happened. The Walker Art Center was T.B. Walker's collection.

CG What was the collection?

BW A very mixed bag. Dad left most of his art estate to the University. They own the largest single collection of works by Hartley.

CG Did you inherit any of the work?

BW The first work I owned was at birth. Marsden Hartley gave my older sister a big print when she was born. When I was born, we were twins and he gave us a painting.

(Disruption to greet and converse with visiting artists Paul Bowen and Bert Yarborough.)

CG Can you give me a few more minutes. Please discuss the historical collection of the gallery.

BW I like to pair past and present. A Grace Hopkins work with one by Hans Hofmann, for example. The community is so vibrant today, and even though I didn't know the early artists, my grandparents did. They came when artists arrived in Provincetown after war broke out in Europe. Many of them, like Oliver Chaffee (1881–1944), who is somewhere on the walls. He was an early master who came to Provincetown then connected and studied with Charles W. Hawthorne (1872–1930). So, there is that whole group that came. A lot of them were women, like Ethel Mars (1876–1959) and Agnes Weinrich (1873–1946).

CG What does a print by Blanche Lazzell (1878–1956) sell for now?

BW A good white-line print goes for $50,000 to $70,000. What I'm showing is modest in the $5,000 to $7,000 range.

CG Weinrichs?

BW In that range as well. ($5,000 to $7,000) It's a matter of the individual piece.

There's a catch-22 because these works come up at auctions which sell for less. That's a whole other conversation. Ultimately, auctions can destroy art. For me, a passion is for what happens when an artist goes public and starts selling their work. Artists grow, expand, and try all kinds of wonderful things. Sometimes things happen and at other times they don't, but an artist needs faith to be shown just to get out of their own way. So, they need a gallery. I'm not hustling my gallery, but I've witnessed it. The walls have given the artists the chance to expand. There are now not a lot of galleries, and we are losing more each year. Artists need those walls to show their work.

CG Do you represent estates?

BW I do on occasion. (Varujan Boghosian, Gilbert Franklin, Sue Fuller, Elspeth Halvorsen, Budd Hopkins, John Kearney, Anne MacAdam, Marjorie Strider, Selina Trieff, Ione Gaul Walker, Peter Watts, Nancy Whorf.) If there was a Weinrich estate, I would say I represent it, but there really isn't one. I've had many over the past 35 years, but they've come and gone.

CG Is she valued more than Karl Knaths, her brother-in-law?

BW That's a delicate question. Again, it depends on the particular Knaths. I don't think she is more valued. I did a show called *Creative Couples.* It was an interesting project. Sometimes it took forever to find the name of the wife of an artist. In many instances they made art but stopped working. They got married and raised children. So, it was really challenging to find them. Then there were gay couples. We did a whole summer on that theme in two galleries. It was so much fun.

Knaths was a great artist but he does not command the kind of prices of the New York School artists. None of the Provincetown artists do (there are exceptions), and I don't talk money very well. Today, money is strange and I don't understand what goes on any more. I've shown a lot and sold a lot over the years and I knew Knaths. But I can't give you financials because they change a lot and art is very personal. Covid is a good example because it isolated us. People were not going out. I did window shows. I changed the shows and had window openings. If you buy a work and take it home you look at it very differently. Emotionally and energetically the work becomes so different. When people fall in love with a work of art it's such a turn-on because they have just made a soul connection. It's a personal connection to that secret part of us that's called the spirit.

CG Over its 35 years has the gallery been self-sustaining?

(Currently she represents Donald Beal, Tom Boland, Paul Bowen, Polly Burnell, Mike Carroll, Lucy Clark, Ted Chapin, Joe Diggs, Rob DuToit, Robert Henry, Grace Hopkins, Brenda Horowitz, Penelope Jencks, David Kaplan, Judyth Katz, Danielle Mailer, Deb Mell, Rosalind Pace, Erna Partoll, Sky Power, Blair Resika, Paul Resika, Laura Shabott, Bert Yarborough, Murray Zimiles.)

So, it's a viable business and not a hobby.

BW For me, it's my life. The artists are my family. A lot of people refer to me as Berta B. Luckily, I'm still in business and can afford to pay staff. In the past 35 years, I have had two galleries, one way down in the West End for ten years, and one in Wellfleet for ten years. It closed just before Covid.

CG You're the longest running gallery.

BW At this point, Julie Heller (opened 1980) might be. I think she was here before me. I don't quite know, but the gallery is not quite as active.

CG What about Cherry Stone?

BW They were here before me. (50-plus years) When the gals (Sally Nerber and Lizzie Upham) were active they showed a lot of great artists.

CG How many Weinrichs do you have?

BW About ten. I acquire them from individuals.

CG Do you acquire them at auctions?

BW Not that much. At auctions they are what they are. You don't get to choose or determine quality. I don't buy at auction that much. I don't have that much flow to be buying art so much as supporting it. That's the reality. We sell to walk-in traffic. We do a lot of advertising and some computer selling. We do a lot of mailing, like the show that is up now. We do a lot of different things, and the shows are knock-outs. I started putting up shows in New York years ago, but after 35 years I know how to put up a show (*Celebrating Blue*). Grace (Hopkins) and I work on hanging a show and it's quite a creative process. It's also true that when you go home, you don't walk, you crawl. You have so much energy. I learned that from Andre Masson (1896–1987, surrealist) when I did a show with him with Marisa del Re Gallery, which Hartley was with. I was in music and administration at the Whitney. I met Marisa because she thought she would like to do a show at FAWC. I went to see her gallery and thought we might do a benefit. Four months later, I got a call from her and she said, "I have a new gallery on the fourth floor of the Fuller building." It was a huge space, which I helped her to renovate, and we opened with a benefit for the Fine Arts Work Center. I ended up hanging the show for her. I did the press release, and told her she couldn't print the catalog as it was written, as she was now a major gallery in the Fuller Building. She asked if I could fix it. I'm not a good writer, but we fixed it and she said,"Why don't you come and work for me?" So, I got my job through Fine Arts Work Center. It's part of the synergy of the art world, the way things flow.

CG Did you have any interaction with Walter Chrysler (1875–1940) when he was here?

BW I met him when he was here.

CG Did your father have any interaction with him?

BW He was on the board of the Chrysler Museum, until he noticed that a number of the pictures were questionable. Chrysler had a lot of fakes, and Dad resigned. They knew each other and I knew both of them. He was active in the community and I remember him bringing in Warhol. I was pretty young then.

CG How about Joseph Hirshhorn (1899–1981)?

BW My boss at the Whitney went to work for him as an administrator at the Hirshhorn Museum. I didn't know Hirshhorn, but I knew his wife.

CG What about your grandparents in Provincetown? Did Tabitha Vevers' grandmother know your grandmother? Did she first visit at her invitation?

BW My grandparents came in 1915. My grandmother hung around with Mary Heaton Vorse, as I said. She was a very important anchor of Provincetown. My parents came here, then Dad was in OSS during WWII. We subsequently learned it was the Monuments Men. He was in Rome for two years. He never talked about it. The people who did the research were all friends of Dad who went with him to college. They were all names I knew from my father. Dad couldn't be drafted as he had rheumatic fever and was deaf in one ear. So, I knew he wasn't a soldier. He never talked about it, but mother bought our little house while he was away. So, she bought our little house in Provincetown.

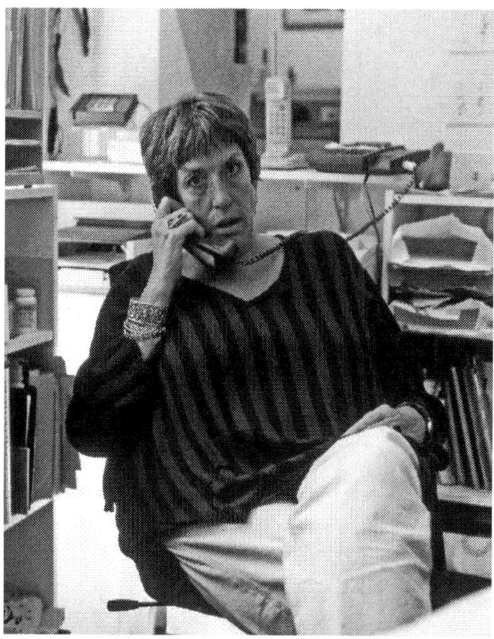

Berta on the phone, 1998. Giuliano photo.

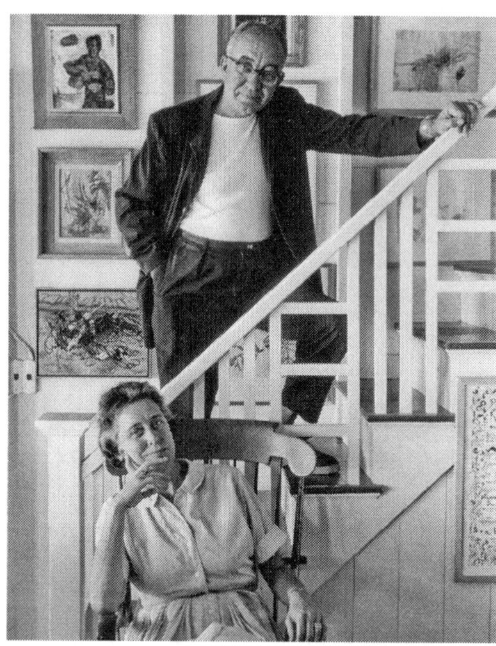

Berta's Parents Hudson and Ione Walker. Courtesy of Walker.

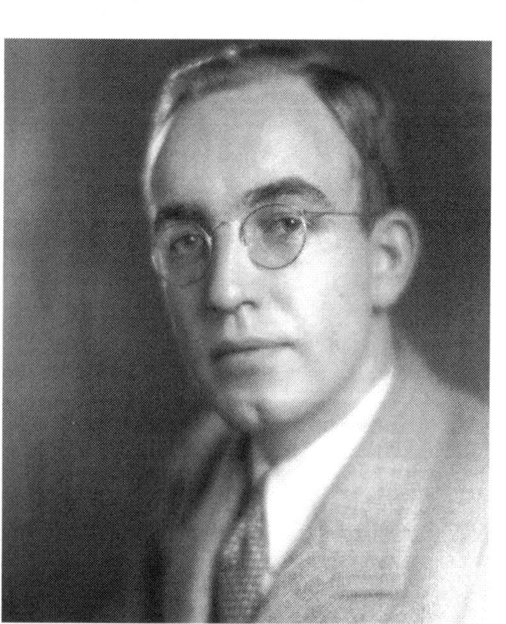

Hudson Walker was a gallerist and philanthropist. Courtesy of Walker.

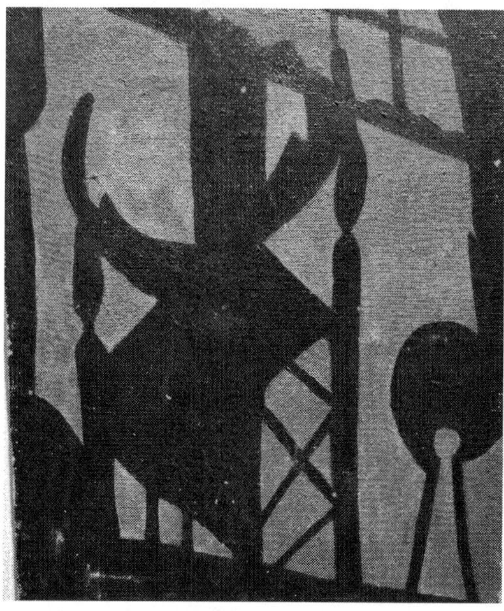

Painting by Berta's mother, Ione, courtesy of Walker Gallery.

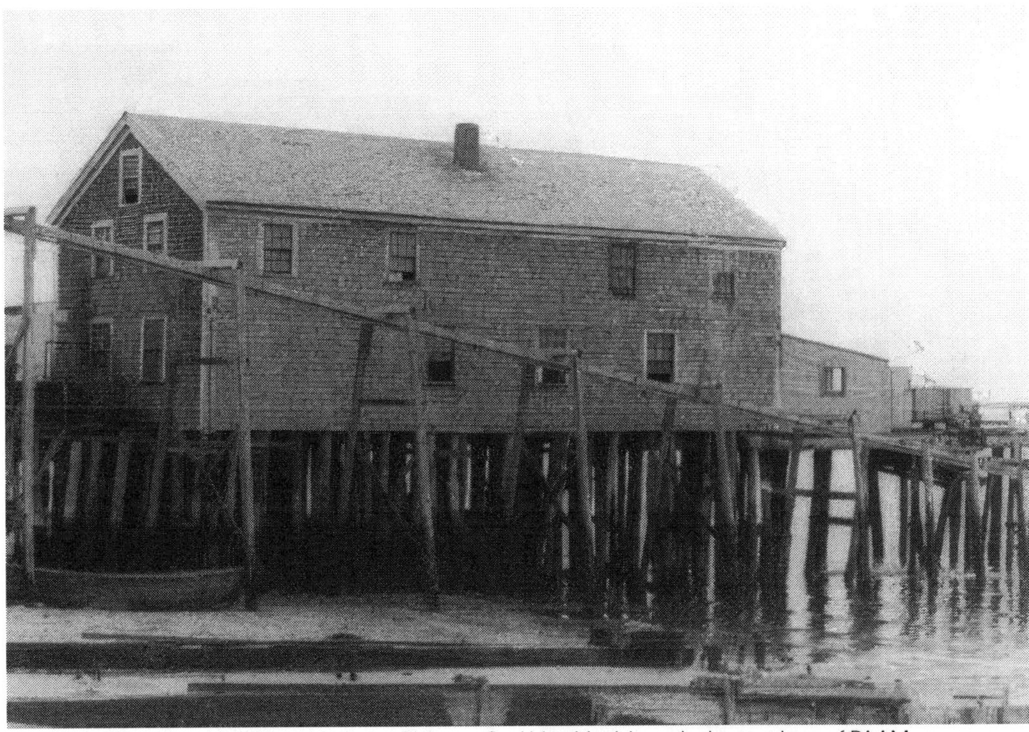

The original home of the Provincetown Players, Carl Van Vechten photo courtesy of PAAM.

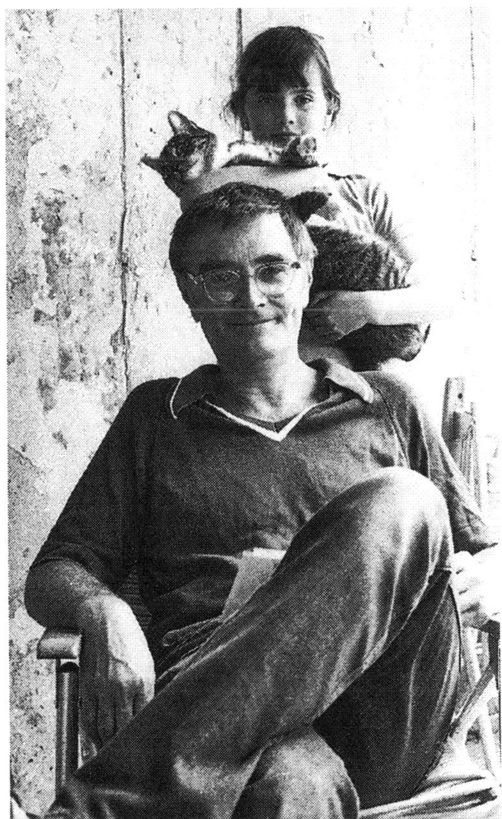

Grace Hopkins and cat with her artist father, Budd Hopkins, Giuliano photo.

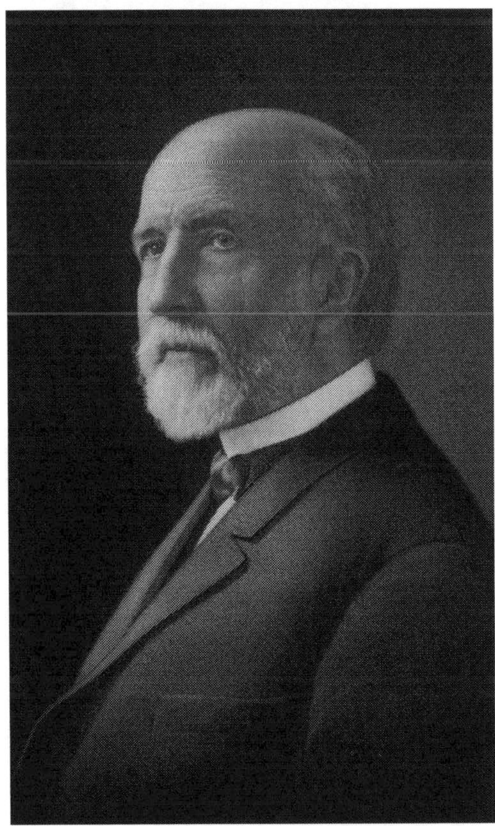

Berta's grandfather, Thomas Barlow Walker, founded the Walker Art Center in Minneapolis. Courtesy of Walker.

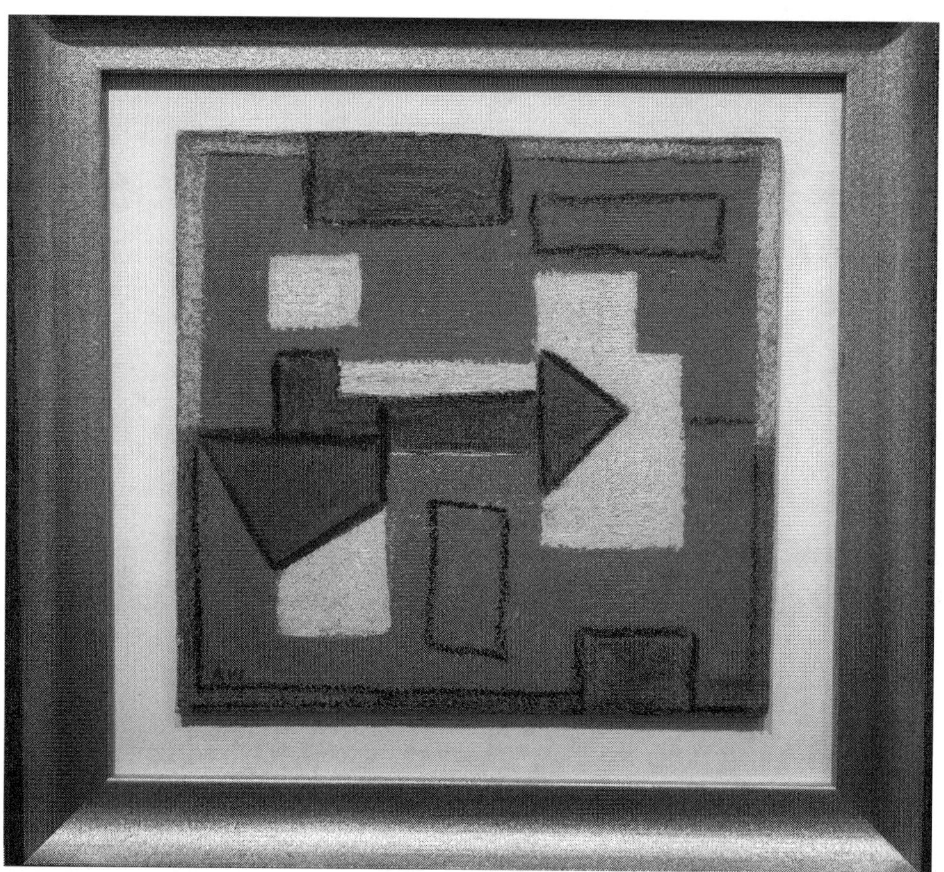

Weinrich painting courtesy of Walker Gallery.

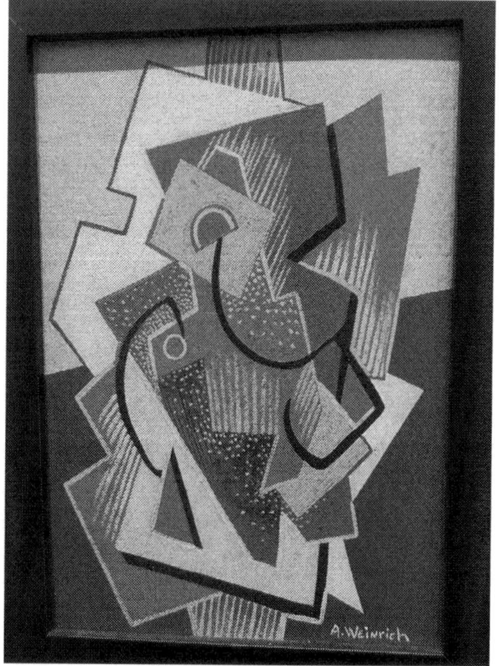

Agnes Weinrich painting courtesy of Walker Gallery.

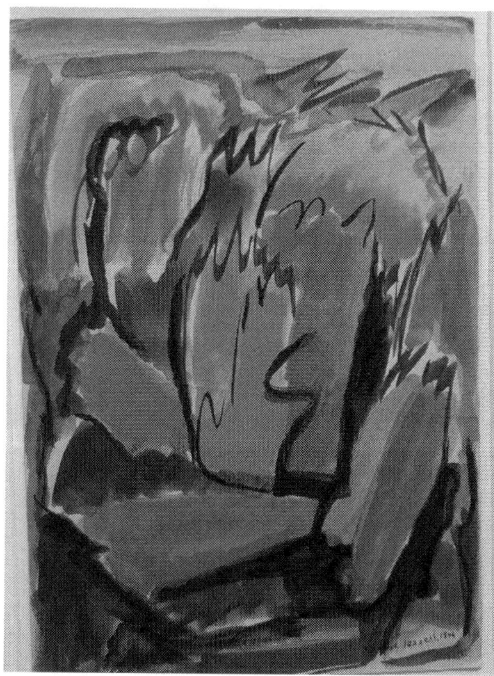

Blanche Lazzell painting, 1946, courtesy of Walker Gallery.

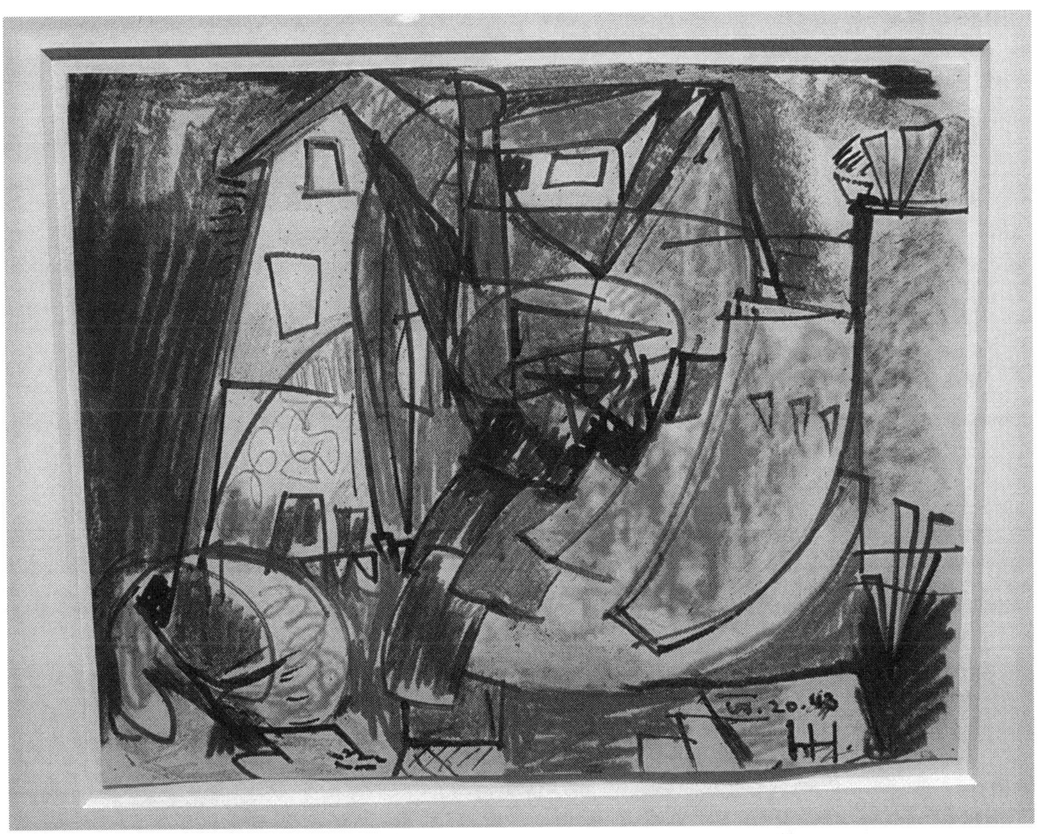

Hans Hofmann painting courtesy of Walker Gallery.

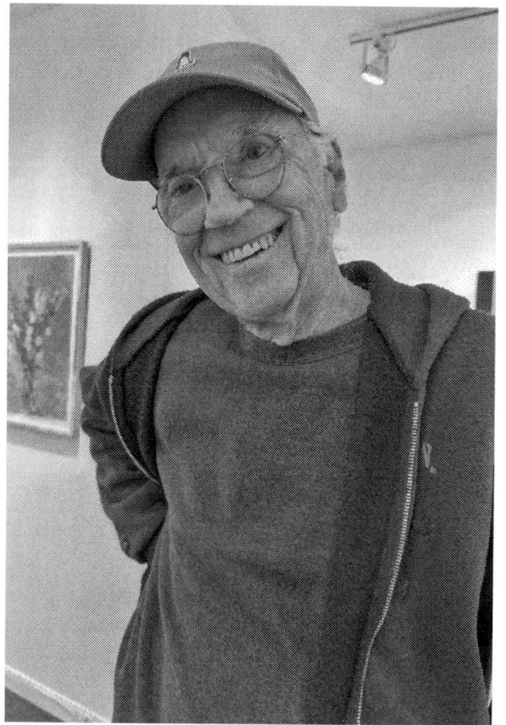

Artist Bert Yarborough. Giuliano photo.

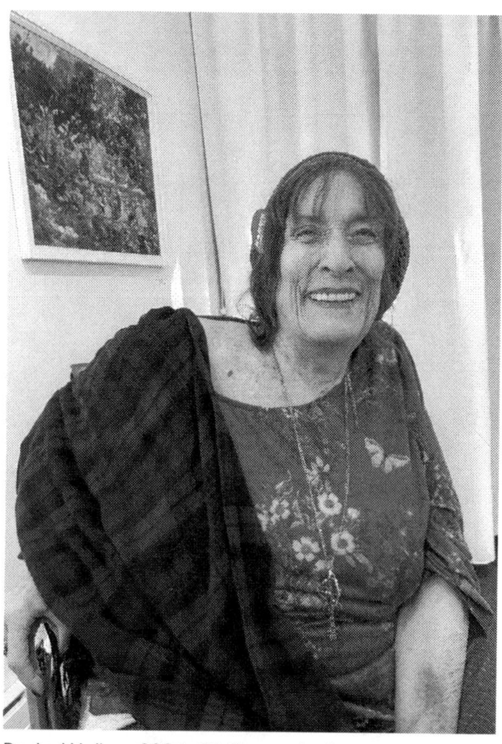

Berta Walker, 2024, Giuliano photo.

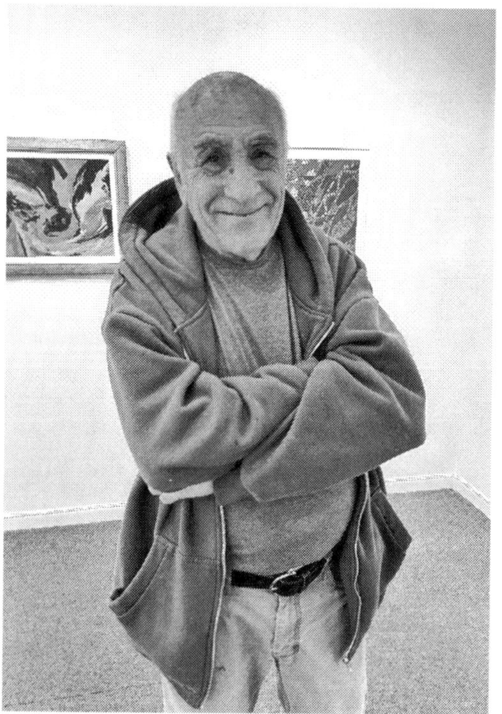

Artist Paul Bowen moved to Vermont some years ago. Giuliano photo.

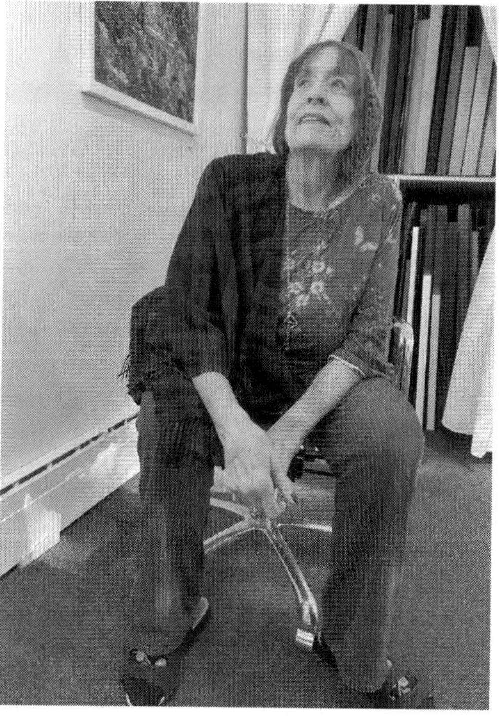

Sharing memories, Giuliano photo.

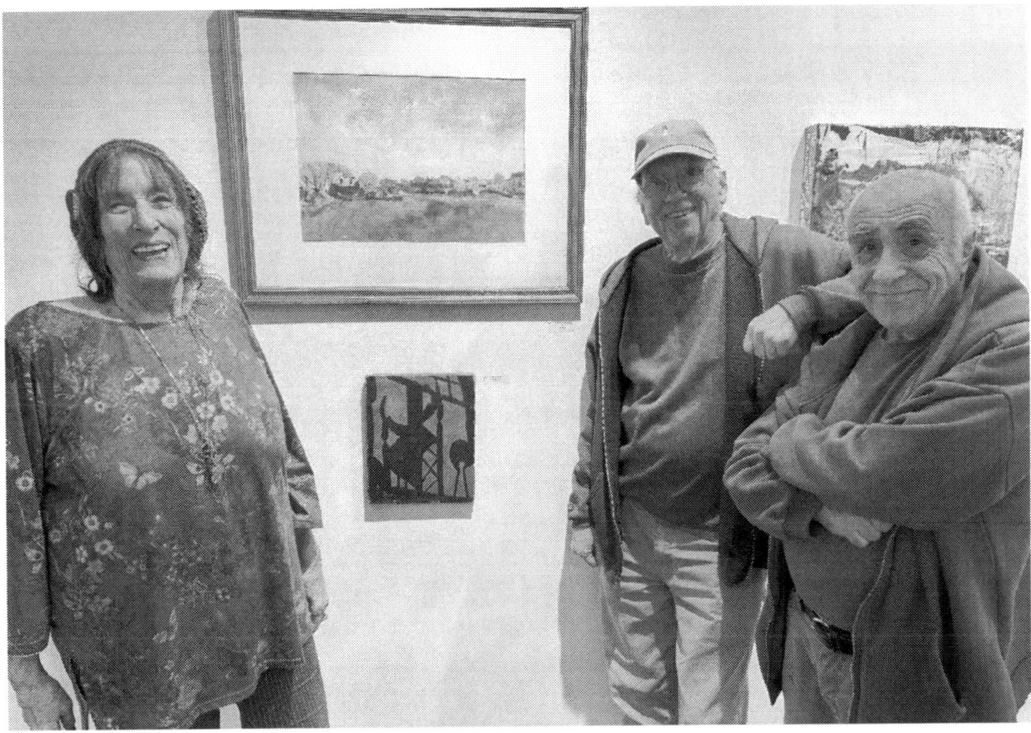

Berta with artists Bert Yarborough and Paul Bowen. Giuliano photo.

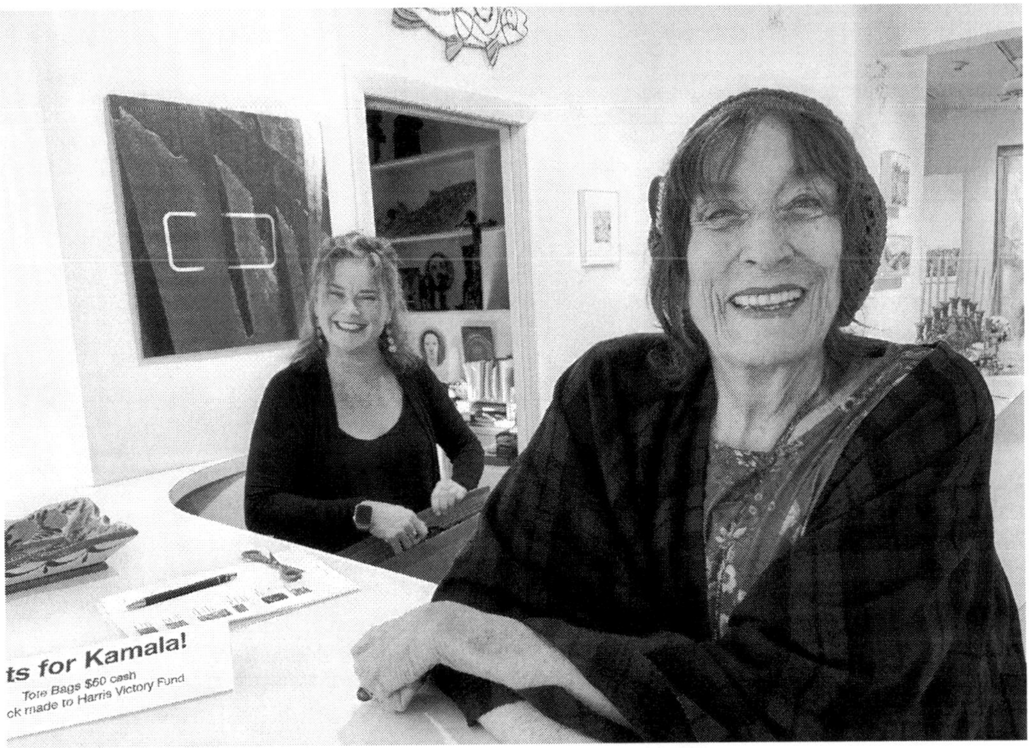

Berta at the front desk with gallery dirrector Grace Hopkins. Giuliano photo.

Acknowledgments

The team for this ninth book has been consistent. Astrid Hiemer has been the first reader with comments and edits. Leanne Jewett has been a meticulous editor. Design has been executed by Amanda Hill, this time with substantial support from Heather Rose. My sister, Pippy Giuliano, has provided moral and financial support.

Boston University professor Peggy Smith initially encouraged the project to research Karl Knaths. When she left for Wake Forest University, she was replaced by Patricia Hills, who supervised my project. As director of the Boston University Art Gallery, she provided me the opportunity to curate an exhibition of works by Karl Knaths.

In Provincetown, Ellen O'Donnell Rankin, then director of the Provincetown Art Association and Museum, helped to launch my research by introducing me to Nat Halper and Mervin Jules, who shared their vast knowledge and opened doors to other artists, including Tony Vevers and artists of Long Point Gallery.

Through an ongoing relationship with O'Donnell Rankin, I curated the exhibition *Kind of Blue: Benny Andrews, Emilio Cruz, Earle Pilgrim and Bob Thompson.* That allowed for ground-breaking study of African American Artists in Provincetown. I was then working with Lester Johnson on his traveling exhibition. Karl Hecker of David Anderson Gallery supported that research and helped to secure major works for the exhibition.

Research on Johnson evoked the larger topic of figurative expressionists in Provincetown. Many of them showed with the legendary Sun Gallery whose founding co-director, Yvonne Andersen, helped in this research.

During repeated visits, insights and advice were provided by Chris Busa, of *Provincetown Arts Magazine*, who published my essays. Grace Consoli, director of Group Gallery, and artist Jay Critchley, kept me up to speed with the arts in Provincetown.

The initial effort widened into networking that went on for decades. That culminated in extensive archival research at Provincetown Art Association and Museum (PAAM) with enthusiastic support from Jim Zimmerman, who provided me with many images for the book.

I would like to thank all of the artists and individuals who provided interviews for this book. They made me feel welcome in their homes and studios.

Made in the USA
Middletown, DE
08 May 2025